Self and Deception

Self and Deception

A Cross-Cultural Philosophical Enquiry

edited by
Roger T. Ames and Wimal Dissanayake

State University of New York Press

Cover: *A Shinto deity from a shrine in the Izumo region of Japan made of hinoki wood and dating from the 12th century. This deity is Priest Hoshi (Ch. P'ao-chih, 425–514 A.D.), an early Chinese Buddhist priest, a favorite of artists because he was a person of many visages, constantly altering his face by tearing it apart with his hands. It is a gift of Robert Allerton in the permanent collection of the Honolulu Academy of Arts and is printed with their permission.*

Published by
State University of New York Press, Albany

© 1996 State University of New York

All rights reserved

Printed in the United States of America

No part of this book may be used or reproduced in any manner whatsoever without written permission. No part of this book may be stored in a retrieval system or transmitted in any form or by any means including electronic, electrostatic, magnetic tape, mechanical, photocopying, recording, or otherwise without the prior permission in writing of the publisher.

For information, address State University of New York Press, State University Plaza, Albany, NY 12246

Production by Dana Foote
Marketing by Nancy Farrell

Library of Congress Cataloging-in-Publication Data
Self and deception : a cross-cultural philosophical enquiry / edited by Roger T. Ames and Wimal Dissanayake.
p. cm.
Includes bibliographical references and index.
ISBN 0-7914-3031-6 (alk. paper). — ISBN 0-7914-3032-4 (pbk. : alk. paper)
1. Self-deception. I. Ames, Roger T., 1947–
II. Dissanayake, Wimal.
BD439.S45 1996
128'.3—dc20
96-1329
CIP

10 9 8 7 6 5 4 3 2 1

CONTENTS

Introduction
   Roger T. Ames and Wimal Dissanayake   1

ONE
On the Very Possibility of Self-Deception
   Brian P. McLaughlin   31

TWO
The Vital but Dangerous Art of Ignoring:
   Selective Attention and Self-Deception
   Annette C. Baier   53

THREE
User-Friendly Self-Deception: A Traveler's Manual
   Amélie Oksenberg Rorty   73

FOUR
Self, Deception, and Self-Deception in Philosophy
   Robert C. Solomon   91

FIVE
Bad Faith and Kitsch as Models for Self-Deception
   Kathleen Marie Higgins   123

SIX
Unloading the Self-Refutation Charge
   Barbara Herrnstein Smith   143

Self and Deception

SEVEN
Falsity, Psychic Indefiniteness, and Self-Knowledge
   Joel J. Kupperman   *161*

EIGHT
A Confucian Perspective on Self-Deception
   A. S. Cua   *177*

NINE
A Confucian Construction of a Self-Deceivable Self
   Robert Cummings Neville   *201*

TEN
The Classical Chinese Self and Hypocrisy
   Roger T. Ames   *219*

ELEVEN
Our Names Are Legion for We Are Many:
   On the Academics of Deception
   David L. Hall   *241*

TWELVE
A Half-Dressed Emperor: Societal Self-Deception
   and Recent "Japanokritik" in America
   William R. LaFleur   *263*

THIRTEEN
Facing the Self with Masks: Perspectives on
   the Personal from Nietzsche and the Japanese
   Graham Parkes   *287*

FOURTEEN
Self-Deception: A Comparative Study
   Eliot Deutsch   *315*

FIFTEEN
Self-Deception and Cultural Contextualization:
    Reflections on Two Indian Novels
    Wimal Dissanayake *327*

SIXTEEN
Ritual, Self-Deception, and Make-Believe:
    A Classical Buddhist Perspective
    Richard P. Hayes *349*

Contributors *365*

Index *369*

INTRODUCTION

Raphael Demos, in his seminal article "On Lying to Oneself," describes self-deception in the following way: "Self-deception exists, I will say, when a person lies to himself, that is to say, persuades himself to believe what he knows is not so. In short, self-deception entails that B believes both P and not-P at the same time."[1] It is clear that Demos is here confining himself to one significant dimension—for philosophers of his bent, possibly the most significant dimension, of self-deception. Although many subsequent commentators (including Brian McLaughlin in this volume) have joined the discussion, assuming that this paradox encapsulates the general notion of self-deception, it is feared by others that this description might not capture the full complexity of the phenomenon and its ramifications. It also entails certain presuppositions about human agency that are not commonly subscribed to in all cultures, or even by all philosophers within our own tradition—that is, it entails a unitary conception of self as both subject and object of "self-deception." In fact, it is to underscore the contingent status of "the self" as a superordinated agent that this volume has been entitled *Self and Deception* rather than *Self-Deception*.

Disagreements about the phenomenon of self-deception are many and varied. They spill over into the diverse areas of concern expressed by our authors: the nature of consciousness, conditions of intentionality, rationality, gradations of rationality and irrationality, the importance of cognition in psychological processes, cognitive relativism, categories of belief, epistemic foundations of self-deception, incontinence, wish fulfillment, authenticity, hypocrisy, character modification, the nature of intentional explanation, the social construction of self and self-deception, rhetorics underlying self-deception, the positive function of irony, and so on. These domains of inquiry, most of which have already received considerable scholarly attention, attest to the breadth and the complexity of the issues surrounding self-deception.

The paradoxical nature of self-deception as a starting point is an issue that has generated a great deal of discussion and continues to do so. For example, Mary Haight argues that self-deception is literally a paradox, and hence it cannot occur.[2] Her argument, familiar in the more analytic literature, is that deception requires a split between deceiver and deceived and hence it cannot take place in relation to one and the same person. While she focuses on what she thinks is the paradoxicality of self-deception, other exegetes such as Herbert Fingarette have attempted to provide a nonparadoxical and morally unforgiving reading of self-deception.[3]

The psychological and moral dimensions of self-deception have generated much interesting discussion. Jean-Paul Sartre's concept of 'bad faith' (*mauvaise foi*) served to bring the diverse issues surrounding self-deception to a much wider audience. The epistemic implications of being self-deceived have also attracted their share of scholarly attention.

There is also a cross-cultural dimension to this problem of self-deception, brought into focus in the opening pages of Eliot Deutsch's essay. Is it the case that the same phenomenon of self-deception is conceptualized and valued differently in different cultures, or is it—self-deception—fundamentally a different phenomenon? Is self-deception a cross-cultural issue, or is it (like alienation or *amaeru*) a culturally specific phenomenon? If it is present in some form and with some value in alternative cultures, what does it entail? To what extent do culturally specific conceptions of 'self' enter into the discussion? For example, if the peculiarly Western "mind-body" problem is entailed in the discussion of self-deception through assumptions about self, thereby "psychologizing" self-deception, what are the non-Western alternatives? Does it make sense to think of a somatic aspect of self-deception? This, we would hope, would enable us to wrestle with two questions: How can self-deception take place? And how does self-deception take place in an enlarged discursive setting?

The concept of 'self-deception,' impinging as it does on such important areas of exploration as the nature of belief, rationality, and cognition, underlines the importance of drawing on, if only for purposes of heuristics, rapidly developing fields such as cognitive science, cultural anthropology, theoretical biology, sociology of knowledge, and decision science. The interplay of the dynamics of cognition and cultural constructions of belief might well open up newer and more fruitful avenues of inquiry into cognitive relativism and motivated irrationality.

Questions of rationality and belief are at the center of current discussions of self-deception. This, of course, means that questions of bounded rationality, pseudorationality and irrationality, unbelief, and desire are pivotal in these discussions. On the one hand, there are those who argue that self-deception represents the power of irrationality in human affairs. On the other hand, some maintain that deception of self does not constitute a form of irrationality based on incoherence of belief, but rather an incongruity between a person's self-conception and one's praxis. Fingarette advocates the latter view. Jon Elster would argue against the assumption that the function of rationality is to tell the agent what to do, so that if one behaves in a way that is contradictory, one is irrational. Instead, he would assert that rationality can do no more than exclude certain alternatives, while providing no guide to one's choice among those that remain.

The concept of 'self,' understandably enough, is central to any sustained inquiry into self-deception, the pertinent question being what sort of self is victim (or beneficiary?) of self-deception? Basing their thinking on the model of "other-deception," some would bring in notions of 'double selves,' 'multiple selves,' and 'subsystems of the self,' to address this troubling problem. Others would argue that other-deception is not an adequate or a reliable model to guide our thinking on this issue.

Similarly, the concept of 'emotionality' is important. What is the relationship between desire and belief, between emotion and self-deception? Does self-deception, in the domain of emotions, imply an agent who is misled by his or her emotions, or are there alternate ways of formulating these relationships? What then is the nature of the relationship between desire and belief?

It is now increasingly remarked upon that our investigations into the phenomenon of self-deception are excessively intrapersonal and that issues pertaining to the social dimensions of self-deception—namely, rules of human interaction and social conventions—are receiving inadequate attention. The whole question of the relationship of intersubjectivity to acts of self-deception needs to be explored afresh. Since the complex and intriguing ways in which people make sense of their behavior, construct systems of meaning, and develop strategies of interpretation are all grounded in their sociality, this interpersonal aspect requires deeper study if we are to uncover the social bases of self-deception. The fundamentally relational definition of person in the East Asian cultures might be a source of direction and encouragement in this respect.

Let us, for example, consider the concept of 'rationality.' In view of the fact that rationality is subject to public scrutiny, it has the effect of bringing into social purview the various processes that go to form rationality. Here again, the social basis of rationality as formulated and manifested in Asian cultures has the potential to promote profitable discussion.

We normally regard self-deception as a moral failure and valorize it negatively. Sartre, for instance, thought of it as the unparalleled vice. But there are others who wish to invest it with positive value, seeing it as a potential strategy of coping which serves to enhance self-respect and strengthen community bonds. Taking a cross-cultural perspective on this issue will enable us to locate this problematic in a wider discursive field.

What kind of person is capable of self-deception? This question takes on a further layer of complexity when we introduce Asian traditions of thought. For example, the Hindus, most notably the Advaita Vedāntins, believe that the true Self (*ātman*) is pure, undifferentiated, self-luminous consciousness. It transcends normal consciousness, being aware of only the Oneness of being. The individual human being is regarded as representing an admixture of reality and appearance. According to early Buddhism, the self is unreal and impermanent. As everything is in a state of flux, there cannot be an unchanging self. The Buddha conceived of the self as a cluster of aggregates or *skandhas*. Confucianism conceptualizes the self as an open system which is vitally connected to the family, community, state, and cosmos. It is irreducibly interpersonal. The ideas of relationality and context are central to a robust understanding of the Confucian notion of 'self.'

These three culturally specific formulations of self are developed in the pages that follow as a necessary foundation for examining the phenomenon of self-deception. When discussing the concept of 'self,' the distinction between the private self and the public self is indeed important in some cultures. In Japanese society, for example, this binarism has deep implications in terms of action and behavior. Japanese modes of communication are closely linked to this distinction. When examining the antecedents, dynamics, consequences, and rationalizations of self-deception in Japan, one must pay careful attention to divisions such as the private and the public selves. In the Chinese tradition, by contrast, any severe distinction between public and private selves is entirely suspect.

One reason why the whole phenomenon of self-deception and the attempts to deconstruct it becomes so intriguing is because in Western philosophical discourse, the paradigms for the explication of belief and action are largely based on rational behavior. Consequently, when a seemingly irrational form of behavior such as self-deception becomes the focus of discussion, the immediate tendency is to seek to accommodate it within existing paradigms of explication—that is, to explain it rationally. Even to describe it as "irrational" organizes it in some degree. How have the less rationalistic Asian traditions grappled with this same issue, and in what ways can these efforts illuminate Western thinking?

In Eastern intellectual traditions there are a number of concepts that are centrally related to the idea of deception: 'ignorance' (*avidyā*), 'illusion' (*māyā*), 'delusion' (*moha*), 'obscuration' (*pi* 蔽), 'acting unnaturally' (*you-wei* 有爲), and so on. These are closely linked to questions of knowledge, action, behavior, and emancipation. An examination of these issues opens up lines of inquiry that can both complement and challenge the work carried out by Western thinkers.

In classical Greek philosophy, the idea of *akrasia* or weakness of will is closely associated with the phenomenon of self-deception. The opposite of *akrasia* is *enkrateia,* or self-control. If *akrasia* is manifested in behavior that contradicts one's better judgment, *enkrateia* is manifested in behavior that is in accordance with one's better judgement. Self-control is indeed a virtue that is highly prized in Eastern traditions of thought, whether it be Hinduism, Buddhism, or Confucianism. What light do the functional equivalents of *akrasia* and *enkrateia* as found in these traditions—darkness and clarity of heart and mind in Confucianism, for example—throw on our understanding of self-deception?

The semiotics of self-deception is another area that can be of great value in promoting profitable discussion. The ways in which the concept of 'self-deception' is articulated in everyday language, and the diverse locutions characteristic of different cultures, enable us to approach this concept from alternate vantage points. Some believe that although the locutions *self-deception* and *self-instruction* display a semiotic kinship, they are in point of fact so different phenomenologically that they should not be placed in the same category. This is the situation encountered within the context of the English language. What are some of the semiotic problems found in Chinese or Japanese languages, and what do they tell us about the conceptualization of self-deception? What is the cluster of locutions which needs to be scrutinized and reconstructed in order to pursue the discussion within these cultures?

Clearly, some very exciting work has been done in the understanding of self-deception in Western philosophy. The work of Mary Haight, Herbert Fingarette, Donald Davidson, David Pears, Amélie Rorty, and Jon Elster, as well as that of Jean-Paul Sartre, to name but a few, has opened up promising avenues of inquiry. Several of the papers in this volume take their lead from the published work of these scholars and provide us with a framework from which we can extend the discussion to the non-Western traditions. In so doing, we can expose ourselves to different styles of reasoning and different conceptual schemes characteristic of different cultures and provide a basis for Western and Eastern traditions to interrogate each other.

Brian P. McLaughlin presents an important introduction to the analytic discussion of self-deception by laying out the terrain of the current debate. The volume begins with his reflections, since he belongs to a conversation that has held important sway in Western literature on self-deception. He initiates a dialog between the "nonskeptic" who asserts that self-deception is not only possible, but pervasive (a position joined by almost all of the

Self and Deception

contributors to this volume), and the "skeptic" who asserts that there are "excluders" of its possibility (where the term *excluders* is defined as conditions required for self-deception that cannot obtain).

There are two commonly cited excluders of self-deception, the first being *the contradictory belief condition:* the condition of X believing P and not-P at the same time. One common strategy for nonskeptics who would claim that this is only an apparent excluder is to introduce some notion of 'separation' or 'dissociation': not-P might be repressed in some way while one entertains P. Another response for the nonskeptic is to deny that self-deception entails believing P and not believing P at the same time—self-deception can be otherwise understood.

The second commonly encountered excluder is *the knowing dupe condition:* the condition of being duped by a stratagem executed on oneself, by oneself. This situation requires that both the self-deceiver and the self-deceived know that it is a stratagem, and yet the self-deceived is still duped by it.

The nonskeptic again has two avenues of response. Most nonskeptics, according to McLaughlin, do not attempt to argue that one can be taken in by a stratagem one regards as such: that is, that one can be misled by information that one knows to be misleading. Rather, they choose to argue that self-deception does not require this knowing-dupe condition at all.

McLaughlin then turns to the attempts on the part of the nonskeptics to argue that these two excluders—the contradictory-belief and the knowing-dupe conditions—are only *apparent* rather than *genuine* excluders. The nonskeptic is able to provide an example of a person with normal memory loss deceiving herself into missing an appointment she does not want to attend by misscheduling it. Both skeptic and nonskeptic can agree that this "appointment" case requires neither of these excluder conditions, and also that self-induced deception is possible. The skeptic, however, allowing that self-induced deception is necessary for self-deception, will not allow that it suffices for self-deception. The argument here is that both skeptics and nonskeptics can generally agree self-deception that P entails at some level the recognition that the weight of evidence is against P. No such requirement is necessary for self-induced deception. The woman in the appointment case never recognized at some level that the weight of evidence was against her having an appointment.

The tension between skeptic and nonskeptic lies in the following. The skeptic will insist that in a genuine case of self-deception that P, recognition at some level that the weight of evidence is against P, will give rise to the belief that not-P. Nonskeptics generally, while not conceding this claim, will allow that the self-deceiver that P might harbor some anxiety that not-*P*. The nonskeptic will argue that the self-deceiver that *P* is able to maintain this situation by either repressing evidence of not-*P* or dissociating oneself from such evidence in some way. The problem with homuncular models of self-deception—models that depend on relatively autonomous subsystems—is that in explaining self-deception, they explain it away. Dissociation makes the phenomenon disappear. A distinction is introduced that separates deceiver from deceived that dissolves the possibility of self-deception. These homuncular models reduce to exotic cases of other-deception: something like multiple personality disorders.

In considering how separate mental divisions must be for the degree of dissociation or repression necessary to generate self-deception, McLaughlin introduces the possibility of "inaccessible" belief. Someone can believe that *P* and that not-*P*, as long as one of them is inaccessible. Beliefs, according to McLaughlin, can slip back and forth between accessibility and inaccessibility.

In explaining how the self-deceptive belief that *P* might be acquired and sustained, nonskeptics frequently appeal to rationalization, evasion, and overcompensation as activities in which self-deceivers unintentionally mislead themselves. The skeptic replies by insisting that for self-deception, one must be a deceiver, and since an unintentional misleader is not a deceiver—that is, need not perform an act of deception—there is no self-deception. Stated more simply, there is no such thing as unintentional deception. Thus the fact that unintentional misleading is possible does not make self-deception possible.

According to McLaughlin, this is the current geography of the debate. The following represents the kinds of questions which remain: Are the conditions placed on self-deception by the skeptic not simply over-rationalizing what are really only cases of unintentional misleading? This would give the nonskeptic at least a partial vindication of the notion of 'self-deception' while allowing the skeptic the claim that *literal* self-deception is impossible. The nonskeptic would reply that the unintentional misleader can be a deceiver in whatever sense a self-deceiver is a deceiver, and thus unintentional misleading suffices for self-deception.

Whatever the case, McLaughlin sees the real payoff for better understanding the architecture of our minds to lie in discovering how desire affects belief-fixing mechanisms. And this question can best be investigated by trying to determine if the kind of self-deception the skeptic has in mind is possible—that is, the toughest case of self-deception. It is only of secondary importance if there are kinds of self-deception which do not require the contradictory-belief or knowing-dupe conditions.

Annette C. Baier chooses to focus on self-deception as a kind of selective attention, a situation in which ignoring, like attending, is something one must work at. Our ability to foreground and background is, far from ignorance, an important cognitive capacity that allows us a degree of impartibility in making moral judgments. Baier's essay concentrates on the line between the positive achievement of a functional and efficacious selective concentration and the negative eliding of purposely ignoring with purposeful ignorance. By understanding self-deception in terms of a motivated unwillingness or inability to recall what we have chosen to ignore, we escape the paradox that more cognitively focused accounts abjure.

Self-deception as selective ignoring is a normal aspect of the human experience, for persons, for groups, and even for nations. It can be a kind of denial, dissociation, and rationalization necessary to preserve one's self-conception intact, and as such, can be literally a life-preserving skill. Baier's interpretation of judicious self-deception as a global psychological and intellectual capacity for would-be rational human beings to deal with the fact that they are only imperfectly equipped to understand their worlds resonates comfortably with the positive turn on self-deception developed both by Amélie Rorty and by Robert C. Solomon in this same volume.

To further explore this phenomenon of self-deception, Baier goes back to Descartes in the *Meditations* where he begins by the deliberate pretence of regarding all of his previously held beliefs to be false, fortifies this pretence by introducing the possibility of the evil genius who makes the mediator the victim of deception, and then combines deliberate pretence and deception into a kind of self-deception by having the meditating *I* conspire with the evil genius to prolong the deception indefinitely. Ironically, the meditating *I* never seems to awake from what began as a deliberate strategy to avoid self-deceiving beliefs. The analysis is complex, and the real difficulty seems to lie in the failure of Descartes to stipulate explicitly when the mediator moves from pretended denials to real denials.

Baier rehearses this well-known tract to demonstrate the positive and the negative implications of self-deception. The problem of self-deceit arises when the mediator ignores the fact that what was announced as a deliberate strategy—the suspension of preconceived beliefs—is never itself suspended.

A distinctive feature of self-deceit is its tendency to confuse itself with plain deceit and to prefer the role of deceiver to deceived. It is the temporality of the *Meditations* that enables Baier to resist the importance of those analyses which resolve the paradox of self-deception by appealing to contemporaneous subsystems deceiving each other. It is the complexity of the temporal shifts in the *Meditations* between the deliberate and the inadvertent, between the deceiver and the deceived, between self-deception and deceit, that make it a worthy presentation of this phenomenon. An interesting aspect of the entire discussion of the *Meditations* that Baier reflects upon is its seeming asocial nature. Given that there are only the relationships between mediator, demon, and God, the focus of notions like 'trust' and 'deceit' is open to speculation: Are we talking about present self in relationship to past self, partial self in relationship to another part, or the relationships that obtain among various powers within the same psyche?

It is only with the *Objections* that the meditating *I* in the *Meditations* at last has the benefit of friendly (and less friendly) counsel to demonstrate that rationally motivated self-deception in the company of our fellows is indeed difficult to sustain.

Baier concludes by observing that the more contemporary attempts to deceive ourselves philosophically by denying the phenomenon of self-deception as a way of saving our favorite rational theories contrasts rather starkly with Descartes. For Descartes takes self-deception both as his method and as his main theme and illustrates rather too clearly what self-deception is, what we risk when we engage in it, and probably most important, the price we would have to pay to give it up.

Amélie Rorty allows that self-deception can be pernicious. But the narrow understanding of Enlightenment rationality that makes self-deception the epistemological equivalent of original sin overshadows the necessary and indeed positive function of a range of self-induced illusions that sustain us in the everyday. Rorty observes that as a complex phenomenon, the negative or positive valorization of self-deception is often a matter of subjective interpretation where the same situation can be read in even contradictory ways at the pleasure of the observer. Nonetheless, there are interpretive constraints which can be invoked to bring at least some focus to a rather nebulous area in human experience. On the one hand, if we proceed from the perspective of theory construction in attempting to deal with the possibility of knowledge itself, self-deception and like concerns stay marginal to the inquiry, if they are considered at all. On the other hand, if we proceed from the perspective of everyday lived experience, leaving abstract systemic demands aside, these same theoretically marginalized concerns can be seen to be pervasive in all areas of human activity. And the dialectical nature of our philosophical tradition guarantees that generationally the discussion moves back and forth between these extremes.

Rorty underscores the social and political complexity of deception and self-deception as entailing subtle strategies of persuasion, making it exceedingly difficult to draw any sure demarcations in what is fundamentally an interactive process. Having said that, one way of moving closer to an adequate understanding of self-deception is to establish what it is *not* by clearing away popular misconceptions of it. First, self-deception is a pattern of behavioral dispositions and habits of the mind rather than isolatable incidents.

Second, such dispositions are socially interactive, being reinforced by encouragement frequently elicited by the self-deceiver. Third, self-deception need not involve false belief. One can deceive oneself by concentrating on true yet marginal information at the expense of considering immediately relevant data—this too is a mechanism of denial. An established disposition to ignore what is pertinent information is at once an act of self-deception and a strategy for self-deception. Further, the performance of ritually and habitually constituted patterns of behavior might entail mistaken beliefs about oneself rather self-deception.

Fourth, self-deception is as likely to be formed in the ordinary events of daily life as it is to characterize important undertakings. Fifth, self-deception has a very real social aspect, where although it is always *by* the self, even its initiation can be fostered collaboratively in one's association with others. The social and even the physical environments can encourage self-engrandizement.

Sixth, self-deception can function as a psychological habit or a disposition acquired by repetition or imitation that is really lacking in any specific desire or motivation. Finally, Rorty observes that while it is natural to confront the manipulations of deceivers and self-deceivers with some suspicion, the motivations and the consequences of such deceptions can be at least benign, and even beneficial, for those involved.

Having attempted to set aside popular and most often simplistic assumptions about self-deception, Rorty then moves to explore what are genuinely complex strategies for effecting deceptions: distraction from what we do not want to see; the use of vagueness to compel ourselves into serious action; the creative reconstruel of descriptions to throw good light on a bad situation; the appeal to positive generalization to lift us out of the tedium of wearing details; or contrarily, the selective abstraction and attention upon a few positive details as respite from an overwhelmingly onerous chore; and so on. There are also second-order policies which aid and abet self-deception by allowing us to rationalize our manipulations. Compartmentalization allows us to entertain conflicting projects. The assignment of high social value to certain customary ways of acting allows us to get away with questionable personal habits. The construction of general theories of human nature and identity provide a screen for certain activities that shield them from closer scrutiny. We ignore the contingency that qualifies all of our intentions and activities and are happy to focus our attention on the anticipated "normal" outcome. We invent personal dispositions which we do not initially have in the hope that such constructions will serve our goals. There are often real traces of the self-deceiving self when self-deception is employed as a strategy for self-transformation, and yet practically speaking, it is usually easier to affirm the socially sanctioned self we are trying to perform than it would be to justify the self we would leave behind.

There is a global kind of self-deception that enables us to overcome the uncertainty and doubts which attend a thoughtful understanding of our life in the world: what Hume would regard as a natural inclination to believe and to trust beyond the evidence that we should. This kind of self-deception is the standard filler in the psychological operation of believing and imagining, and we couldn't get along without it.

Our personal and particular self-deceptions are beneficial to us in enabling us to get on in our relationships and occupations by making them more tolerable than they really are. At a social level, self-deception is so essential to maintaining communal harmony and equilibrium that it is impossible to conceive of a society which would not actively encourage it.

Rorty wants to move away from seeing the individual as either primary agent or beneficiary of self-deception or belief. Self-deception and belief sometimes occur at a superpersonic level in identifying with a group or community, and sometimes, at least if we accept the analyses of some kinds of psychological theorists, at the level of relatively independent subsystems that make up our complex psychological organization.

One very real danger in appreciating the collusive nature of self-deception and of subscripting agents and beneficiaries, deceivers and deceived, is the problem of assigning appropriate responsibility. For Rorty, this concern about self-deception is of a piece with many other, at least superficially, rational activities, which in fact themselves rely on shadier intellectual and psychological activities to function at all. And our only safeguard is Socratic inquiry—"the permanent possibility of asking critically evaluative questions." Given the social context and complicity that attends self-deception, another practical tactic we can employ in protecting ourselves against the more pernicious forms of self-deception is being careful about the company we keep. Finally, we must rely upon our other established psychological and intellectual habits—a distaste for hypocrisy, for example—as well as luck, to keep us from being victims of our selves.

For Robert C. Solomon, it is not clearly or obviously the case that deception is always wrong. And it is neither clear nor obvious that what is "true" is self-evidently so. Given the historical failure in coming to terms with the very contingencies of truth, Solomon wonders why over the centuries it has retained its value as a grounding moral virtue. Ironically, the most persistent deceivers and self-deceivers are those who take their noble vocation to be the unrelenting pursuit and defense of truth itself: the philosophers.

To begin his discussion of deception as a philosophical issue, Solomon chooses to distance himself from analytic discussions of self-deception—the

Self and Deception

paradox of asserting contradictory propositions—as being a rather profitless foray into a complex psychological and cultural landscape. To the extent that the self is an embedded social self, differing significantly in different cultures, "self" deception goes well beyond deceptions directed *at* the self. In surveying the record of truth in the Western philosophical tradition, Solomon arrives at what many philosophers (perhaps themselves self-deceivers) would regard as a rather perverse conclusion: the actual practical value of truth has been grossly overrated, and deception is a much undervalued mainstay of social solidarity. Moving from the Western experience, where many good minds have recognized the often negative value of accepting the very notion of 'truth,' Solomon observes that there are indeed alternative cultural sites where social harmony is a value that far outweighs the importance of simple truth-telling.

Solomon rehearses the three most familiar arguments against lying: the deontological moral law that proscribes lying under any circumstances; the utilitarian position that calculates the relative good or bad consequences of lying; and the virtue-based argument that honesty is the expression of a cultivated character. What makes this third position more interesting is the possible assumption that lying and (self-) deception can have a corrupting affect on intersubjective and communal relationships. Solomon wants to redirect attention from individualistic concerns with principles, consequences, and character, to deception as a social phenomenon that possibly undermines particular interpersonal commitments. Virtue ethicists tend generally to assume a personal autonomy and persistency that marginize the ongoing negotiation of interpersonal relationships in favor of tricky situations. The problem with lying as Solomon sees it is that it can betray trust in concrete, personal relations. However, when we consider deception at the level of specific personal interaction instead of at some more rarified theoretical level, we realize immediately that deceptions of one kind or another are so important in maintaining working relationships that blanket condemnation of interpersonal dishonesty is morally naive.

In relocating both deception and self-deception as often mutually entailing aspects of a socially embedded self-consciousness that informs all of our interpersonal relationships, Solomon is anxious that the complexity of the pattern of feelings and the tenuousness of the lines that demarcate them be fully appreciated. As such, nuanced sympathy and understanding are often more appropriate responses to deception than raw blame. Taken a step further, the entire fabric of our cultures is spun from inherited rituals and myths. This cultural mythology is our resource for communal meaning, and to "debunk" it would impoverish our lives utterly.

Introduction

Turning to a philosophical interrogation of the phenomenon of deception, Solomon recommends a holistic approach that focuses attention not only on the victim of the deception, but also on the probably self-deception of the person who would deceive. Again, deception is a radial phenomenon, the repercussions of which spread from a single act to incite public cynicism and mistrust. Each of the traditional approaches to the phenomenon of deception give us a partial understanding: the Kantian deontological analysis provides some insight into the nature of lying; the utilitarian analysis looks to its consequences; and the virtue-based approach focuses on the character of the deceiver. An adequate philosophical understanding cannot be constructed by combining partial perspectives, but must begin from an appreciation of the interpenetrating and interdependent nature of all aspects of the phenomenon. It is the complexity of deception and its implications that makes it difficult to sustain a lie, and that gives self-deception an important supporting role. It is this same complexity that makes deception and self-deception omnipresent colorations in the myths and metaphors by which we live. While deception can at times be morally reprehensible, there are just too many instances where it is a factor in the underdeterminacy and productive vagueness of our interpersonal transactions to allow for any globalizing characterization.

Finally, how "universalizable" is any culturally specific understanding of deception, and particularly, self-deception, when notions of 'human agency' differ so markedly in different cultural locations? While Solomon would allow for radically different social constructions in other cultures (as posited by Ames among others in this same volume), he would argue with some enthusiasm that the current caricature of the Western liberal individualist self is a most unfortunate and simplistic misconstruel of a tradition that left Descartes far behind in its development of social sensibilities. We "Westerners" are much more socially constructed in our practices than our theories (and often our adumbration of our theories) would allow.

Solomon concludes by reiterating his distinction between the *internalist* and the *externalist* models of self-deception, based upon internalist and externalist conceptions of 'self.' The former is fundamentally an epistemological problem—knowing and yet seeming not to know—that describes a relationship between a persona and a set of beliefs. The resolution of the paradox is to suggest various alternative models of the architecture of the self that would explain away this contradiction.

The externalist self by contrast is embedded in a fluid set of roles and relationships, and externalist self-deception is an always-social performance which attempts to manipulate such roles and relations to given effect. Solomon's point is that regardless of what many of our philosophers might

Self and Deception

want us to believe, our own working models of self and self-deception are probably considerably closer to the contextually based externalist conception than they are to the more abstracted internalist conception. This being the case, our greatest and most insidious self-deception is to believe and to act upon our myth of the autonomous individual.

Kathleen Marie Higgins joins Allen Wood in his critique of Jean-Paul Sartre's several models of "bath faith" as self-deception. The interrogation of Sartre's position is important because he is so often referenced in discussion of self-deception. Higgins points out that Sartre's typical case of bad faith depends upon a severe subject/object dualism. To begin with, given that bad faith is largely a condition of self-awareness, third-person reports such as Sartre's have marginal reliability. Again, the dependence of Sartre's models on conflicting propositional content makes self-deception into something much simpler than it seems to be, leaving out as it does a whole range of propositionally unspecificable feelings and attitudes. Rather than contradictory propositions, we more likely have open-ended circumstances that are in a constant process of complex renegotiation and compromise. This is particularly true when so many of Sartre's examples depend upon human sexuality, a rather multivalent aspect of the human condition that few would claim to understand, even with respect to their own feelings. The case of wives denying inescapably factual sexual pleasure by distracting themselves in the act of intercourse with their unfaithful husbands is at best a contrived and unconvincing third-person (indeed male) attempt to anticipate the self-awareness of another person.

Higgins moves on from Sartre to reassess both the nature and the moral culpability of self-deception. Consistent with Amélie Rorty and Allen Wood, Higgins chooses to define self-deception as part of an integrative process where selective inattention saves us from circumstances we would rather not confront. To explore the positive content of consciousness experienced by the self-deceiver, a concern unnoticed in Sartre's reflections on self-deception, Higgins introduces "kitsch": not only bad art, but bad art that often generates self-deception. Higgins uses Karsten Harries and Milan Kundera to define the term *kitsch* as ironically charged objects which, irrespective of aesthetic merit, have the power to elicit deep, often socially generic, emotions in the observer. Kitsch is not an object, but the function of an object as a shared human image to establish intersubjective emotional relations.

Kitsch differs from Sartrean self-deception in that disclosure of a particular positive atmosphere is more focused than what is concealed. It is emotional stimulation that can serve many ends—nationalism, propaganda, and so on—by filtering out all that is incompatible with the overwhelming and totalizing feeling. It would appear that most of the concern expressed in Sartre's "bad faith" was directed at his own specific situation in which political apathy was an acceptable alternative to political responsibility. Higgins suggests that even with this concern, the kitsch explanation is more compelling than Sartre's assumption that particular propositional content is being denied in bad faith. At least the sometimes enjoyment of kitsch cannot be condemned with the same moral fervor that Sartre directs against bad faith. Higgins, then, arrives at a conclusion not altogether unlike that of William LaFleur in this same volume. The hunt for hypocrisy, to the extent that it entails an unquestioned and global interpretive scheme, can easily become a far more dangerous undertaking than the occasional, often therapeutic lapse into self-deception.

Barbara Herrnstein Smith, in "Unloading the Self-Refutation Charge," sets the problem: it is a common ploy of defenders of philosophical orthodoxy to accuse "the deniers, rejecters, and abandoners" of such views, of incoherence, exposing in the course of the debate how the positions of these relativists, skeptics, perspectivists, constructivists, postmodernists, and so on are self-refuting. Further, given the social goods that philosophical orthodoxy sustains and the evils that it denies, it is also characteristic of our theoretical conservatists, even prior to the demonstration of self-refutation, to demonize the theoretical innovators as morally suspect and intellectually capricious. The charge of self-refutation, while clear enough to the audience of sympathizers to whom it is directed, is often empty and irrelevant to the positions of those so exposed, signaling nonengagement and even incommensurability. Herrnstein Smith's stated purpose is not to defend any specific unorthodox views against the orthodoxy, but rather to examine the often questionable ways in which the charge itself is deployed in an effort to make it just a bit less automatic.

The discussion begins from the classic accusation of self-refutation in the *Theaetetus* where the "relativist" Protagoras is taken to task, setting the model for the exposé of our more recent subversives. The structure of the self-refutation is simple, and the dubious paraphrasing and inferences are obvious to most classical scholars. Even so, these same scholars are willing and able to redeem it by a sympathetic appeal to the nonnegotiable vocabulary of logical argument that saves the condemnation of Protagorean relativism. An important point that Herrnstein Smith makes here (and in several other recent publications) is to challenge the egalitarian fallacy supposed by many of the critics of Protagoras' position, namely that Protagoras and all such relativists in rejecting the absolutist and objectivist claims to validity are asserting that any opinion is as good as any other. This is a fallacy because, in Herrnstein Smith's own words, "if someone rejects the notion of validity in the classic sense, what follows is not that she thinks *all* theories (etc.) are *equally* valid but that she thinks *no* theory (etc.) is valid *in the classic sense.*" Theories can be evaluated on standards such as "applicability, connectibility, stability," and so on that depend on locating specific conditions of perspective, interpretation, judgment, and so on rather than on objectivist standards. The "anything goes" accusation is simply a restatement of "any opinion is as good as any other" and is properly dislodged by the countercharge of question begging that leads to impasse.

The heart of the matter, then, is that many philosophers of the more orthodox turn believe and further claim that there are given constraints—"prior, autonomous, transcendentally, presupposed, and (properly) universal"—characteristic of our cognitive activities and their conceptual and discursive products. Herrnstein Smith would assert (and many of the perspectives taken from other traditions represented in this same volume would confirm) that what are being posited as "inescapable presuppositions" and "truth absolute" are the effects of participation in a specific conceptual tradition and its idiom. Bringing this kind of universalism into a comparison with the Chinese tradition, as one example, would expose it as a peculiarly and sometimes pernicious Western ethnocentrism.

The theater of instruction and the players that we discover in the *Theaetetus* are mirrored in the modern academy: the bright student enthralled by dubious doctrines is, after undergoing a thorough cleansing often through public trial and humiliation, led to the light and confirmed in the community of the orthodox.

In the remainder of her essay, Herrnstein Smith offers an explanation for what she takes to be the "intriguing phenomenon" of "the orthodox believer's conviction that he believes what he does because it is true, while skeptics and heretics believe what they do because there is something wrong with them." While this kind of "cognitive conservation" provides us with "intellectual stability, consistency, reliability, and predictability," when taken to an extreme it leads to the dangerous assumption that one's convictions are undeniable, and no adequate alternative formulations are possible or even coherent.

The alternative to the "cognitive conservatist," honed in rationalist philosophy to a fine and ambitious art, is the modesty of the postmodern skeptic who, allows that the conceptual systems of classical epistemology operate well enough for some, but not for all, and that alternative schemes can be advanced and defended on the basis of other, always contingent criteria. This skeptic is not embarrassed or disturbed by the contingency that attends her and everyone else's favorite theories. Unfortunately, as she would allow the classical epistemologist a place among competing doctrines, all that the traditionalist can hear is her self-refutation on the basis of his presuppositions.

All is not lost. This play has had an enormously long run—a persistence that suggests an inherent instability that prevents real deadlock and incommensurability.

Joel Kupperman begins by rehearsing several of the possible models of self-deception and some of the accounts available in recent philosophical literature (such as Stephen White's new turn on homuncular subsystems), acknowledging that many of these solutions depend upon the application of an over-determined, and hence less than nuanced, psychological vocabulary that brings their adequacy into question. An important aspect of "desire" that Kupperman underscores is the generally acknowledged extent to which context influences behavior. What compounds the "situational" aspect of desire is the indefiniteness of most people's sense of self. This fluidity both of self and of situation leads Kupperman in the direction of Mark Johnston's understanding of self-deception as "subintentional tropisms" rather than deceitfulness among those homuncular subsystems that are ultimately constitutive of a self. Moving down this path, the major question that emerges (a question posed in the *Tao Te Ching* passage which is discussed at the beginning of this chapter) is that given this fluidity, is there any knowledge which can be contrasted with self-deception? In the *Tao Te Ching* passage, self-deception only becomes a possibility when better and worse behaviors are acknowledged and persons as a consequence begin "representing" (and "misrepresenting") themselves among these choices.

A further complication in the analysis of self-deception is the distinction between a rehearsed inner self-image and one's more external presentations. This distinction often serves a positive function, for a self-deceptive and exaggerated inner presentation can be an encouragement to do better in one's external presentation. Another dimension of the fluidity of desire comes with the Sartrean recognition that "I am what I am" (good faith which can also be bad faith if it is resignation) which stands in some tension with "I am what I choose to be" (good faith).

But what are the limits on what one chooses to be? What are one's live options? Whatever they are, it seems in Sartrean terms they would be deliberate adjustments in one's decisive yet unchosen original project. Having said this, Kupperman would hold out (with Confucius) that morality is more than following the right rules. What then is moral goodness? First, it is more than doing the "normal" thing. It is (*pace* Confucius) a kind of self-knowledge of a processional, and thus provisional self who knows who he genuinely is, and yet who is open to further articulation through self-reflection.

Self and Deception

In part 1 of his essay, A. S. Cua uses a careful and nuanced analysis of the *Ta-hsüeh* 大學 (the Great Learning), one of the canonical *Four Books* defining classical Confucian philosophy, to reconstruct a vocabulary both of personal cultivation and of self-deception. Cua avails himself both of classical texts and of medieval commentaries to flesh out the cluster of terms necessary to bring the Confucian project of self-realization into focus and to identify the specifically Confucian species of self-deception. In attempting to allow the text to speak for itself, Cua wants to find an internal perspective that foregrounds the cultural significance of the classical Confucian conception of 'human agency' without overwriting it with more familiar Western models.

In part 2, Cua explores self-deception as an interpretative diagnostic concept for one's failure to achieve sincerity in one's thought (*ch'eng yi* 誠意). In Hsün Tzu, self-deception is a failure to take the entire picture into account. It is a kind of obscuration (*pi* 蔽)—a kind of darkening of the heart and mind—brought on by preoccupation with one aspect of a situation without a balanced assessement of the consequences. Obscuration is invariably motivated by desire of one kind or another and can only be rectified by wise and informed deliberation through which one clarifies the heart and mind.

In attempting to articulate a Confucian conception of 'self,' Cua begins from Stephen Toulmin's observation that entifications of self generally emerge by hypostatizing "self" as it occurs in everyday reflexive idioms: for example, *self-reproach* and *oneself*. In examining the reflexive binomials that occur in the classical Confucian texts, Cua discovers that almost without exception they have a diagnostic and interpretive function in the process of self-examination (*tzu-hsing* 自省) that necessarily attends the project of self-cultivation (*tzu-hsiu* 自修).

Attempting to bring the Confucian conception of 'self' into sharper focus, Cua borrows Hsün Tzu's distinction between generic terms (*kung ming* 共名) and specific terms (*pieh ming* 別名) to distinguish a free-floating abstraction from a concrete, reflexive usage of self that emerges in the context of practical discourse. Through a critical examination of the interpretive commentaries of other contemporary scholars—Herbert Fingarette, Tu Wei-ming and Roger T. Ames—Cua affirms the relational and inspirational character of this polymorphous "self" while at the same time insisting upon the crucial role reflexive *tzu* 自-locutions play in moving from generic to specific discussions of self.

Robert Cummings Neville begins from a comparative reflection on self as "self-reference" in representative thinkers of the Western tradition (Paul, Augustine, Hegel, Kierkgaard), and the curious absence of this same notion of objectified and superordinated 'self' in the Confucian tradition. The engine that has driven a Western philosophical interest in self is the observed tension between self-contradiction and self-consistency. Neville singles out the cultivation of normatively efficacious responsiveness to one's particular world as the signature of the Confucian self, where this responsiveness operates on many different levels of discourse through physical, cognitive, and emotional habituation. Excellence in the complex of sign-structured behaviors is authenticity in its broadest sense: a "sincerity" that precludes sustained contradictions.

Turning to self-deception, the West owns three dominant species: inner psychological self-deception directed by the unconscious (Freud), ideological self-deception which emerges when one allows one's authentic self to be overwhelmed by membership in and identity with a particular class or group (Marx), and the self-deception that arises from ignorance of the world in which we live combined with ignorance of our own limitations (tragic self-deception). Likewise, Confucian self-deception can be organized under three major headings. In rather sharp contradiction to the popular Western notion of 'unitary, autonomous self,' the dominant model of self-deception in the Confucian tradition is precisely the selfishness entailed in the identification of and service to an isolated self. A mechanism designed to thwart the rationalization of selfishness is the deep commitment to seriousness and self-criticism.

The second Confucian model of self-deception arises from the inadequate performance of formal, ritually structured habits, a concern that is signaled in the tradition by an emphasis on self-awareness, caution, and self-criticism. The problem stems from a semiotic dysfunction where one's social vocabulary is insufficient to effectively communicate the desired relationship—one thinks one is performing signs of friendship but in fact is miscommunicating.

A third kind of self-deception is a consequence of ritual expression (*li* 禮) outstripping a cultivated humanity (*jen* 仁). Under such circumstances, form (*wen* 文) overshadows substance (*chih* 質), a situation unacceptable to basic Confucian sensibilities. It is in this sense that *jen* is more fundamental than *li*—a touchstone whereby to evaluate all personal, social, and political structures. When one's heart is not invested in the relationship, no amount of formal correctness is sufficient to secure the bond, where increasing reliance on ritual behavior only leads to pompousness.

Roger T. Ames begins by suggesting that self-deception as it is generally understood is a decidedly Western philosophical problem that has its origins in the "one-many" structure of classical metaphysics. The assumption of a "unitary self" necessary to make the problem coherent is an analog to the familiar "one-behind-the-many" chain-of-being model that grounds much of classical Western thinking, making it both metaphysical and dualistic. As such, this superordinated self has little relevance to Chinese philosophy. In fact, given that person is irreducibly social and multivalent in Confucian philosophy, the kind of duplicity that has been a central concern in this tradition is a decidedly social phenomenon.

Ames introduces a "focal-field" notion of 'self' to establish a contrast with the one-many model and follows the Platonic attempt to define a viable conception of 'person' by appealing to the analogy of a viable state. While Plato's is an abstract theoretical structure with ambitious claims about the universal nature of humanity, Ames insists that the Chinese equivalent, in the absence of metaphysical assumptions, must be a specific, concrete political regime which is historically and culturally contingent. Using the dynamics of the formation of the Han dynasty as a model for the way in which a person in Confucian society comes to be constituted, Ames suggests that the radial structure of the political and intellectual character of the dynasty is shaped by and reflected in the overlapping radial structures of those persons who collectively constitute it.

Ames then moves from the specific historical example of the formation of the Han dynasty to suggest that this radial or focal sense of order is pervasive in the tradition, identifiable in the way in which Chinese culture has come to organize its world, its history, its canonical literature, and knowledge itself. Perhaps the most obvious illustration of this radial order is the ritual constituted family, and by extension, community. Each "self" is an abstraction from a constantly shifting matrix of hierarchical roles and relationships which make life within family and community meaningful by providing a social syntax that establishes both one's place and one's status.

In this focus-field alternative to the one-many model, there is no superordinated, unitary self. Ames uses his engagement with Herbert Fingarette in the published literature to clarify the point that "self" can only be a reflexive impulse within a repertory of socially embedded experiences, desires, and beliefs that are articulated through multiple levels of communal discourse. Self is a specific, open, and provisional pattern of social discourse. As such, it is always positively and productively underdetermined in the sense that the constitutive patterns of each person are responsive to changing environments, being renegotiated in each and every particular circumstance. The alternative to a teleologically driven model of self is a notion of 'self-sufficiency': a self which achieves personal harmony by maximizing its possibilities in each situation.

Coming to the Confucian equivalent of self-deception, then, Ames insists that it is "selves"-deception in the sense that Confucian self-consciousness is an awareness of oneself as a locus of relationships within community. As such, deception is a two-way street: a duplicitous matrix of relationships, inspired at one extreme by deliberate hypocrisy, and at the other extreme by deliberate obsequiousness and flattery. It is "the counterfeiting of interpersonal transactions" by breaches both in personal integrity and in social integrity.

David L. Hall, having noted the ambiguity and vagueness that makes any definition of the Western notion of 'self' problematic, focuses his reflection on "deception" itself. He takes this approach because the plethora of meanings of self and the conflicting vocabularies through which we attempt to communicate this idea render self so ambiguated that questions about the very subject of self-deception must necessarily arise.

Hall attempts to narrow his discussion to the academic world, claiming that intellectual culture generates the greatest degrees of self-articulation, and also the greatest degree of self-ambiguation. In order to appreciate the many conflicting models of self which have emerged in the Western philosophic tradition, Hall rehearses a brief historical narrative which begins in classical Greece where self is relatively unfocused and manifold. This complex narrative has given rise both to a *modern* conception of 'unitary self' made pluralistic by rival claims to the actual unifying element, and to the again manifold *post-modern* self, distinguishable from its Greek ancestor by its hyper-self-consciousness.

In an attempt to organize the various theoretical models available in the tradition, Hall appeals to the taxonomical methods of the systematic pluralists who seek to account for the variety of models by relying upon their mutual incompatibility and irreducibility. A true pluralism is guaranteed by the relative adequacy of each closed system, combined with the irrelevance of competing systems. The menu of alternative materialist, idealist, naturalist, and volitionist conceptions of 'self' are each self-contained, providing us with a troubling array of self-describing vocabularies, none of which are open to intertheoretical considerations.

Hall appeals to Richard Rorty's pragmatic turn on metaphilosophy and his distinction between *philosophical* and *real* theories to make communication possible among competing theoretical visions. By subordinating rarified philosophical posturing to "getting along" with the practical concerns of everyday life, Rorty is able to lead the theoretical pluralists beyond the worst kind of relativism that their mutually exclusive programs entail, and back into conversation. By inverting the relationship between practices and principles, Rorty makes practices themselves determinative and principles only "reminders" that some practices are worth remembering.

Self and Deception

Rorty's inversion of theory and practice has immediate consequences for the philosophical conversation. Clarity, the erstwhile goal of theoretical models, is rejected as exclusionary, and a "fruitful vagueness" that allows for multiple interpretations of our real circumstances becomes the recommended alternative. Semantic vagueness is the ability to entertain competing and even conflicting meanings without succumbing to literal claims; pragmatic vagueness is the ability to entertain a variety of narratives in explanation of any particular event without surrendering to the need for a univocal account.

These reflections, brought back to the subject of self, require that we acquiesce in and even defend semantic and pragmatic vagueness, eschewing formal definitions in favor of interpretable models and instances. The alternatives—ever increasing stipulation and clarification—leads rapidly in the direction of ideolects and even solipsism, what Hall calls "Cartesianism gone bad."

The role of the intellectuals in social deceptions lies first in their knowledge that we are always saying more than we mean. Our communications one with another are freighted with richly vague semantic clusters, and our actions one to another are laden with a richly intepretive range of significance. This being the case, the selves that accommodate and appreciate this vagueness are hopelessly ambiguated. And if one allows that one is seriously ambiguated in communications with others, how does one draw a line between truth and deception? When this problem is carried into the academy, the academician is led both into self-deception and into other-deception by having to pretend to be theoretically and conceptually clear while at the same time knowing full well that we are anything but unitary in our understandings.

William R. LaFleur traces American perceptions of the Japanese national psyche through a marked shift in the postwar years. The great deception of Pearl Harbor together with the seeming inability of the Japanese public to comprehend the absolute futility of their war goals in the latter part of World War II generated in American eyes the perception that the Japanese as a culture are both purveyors of deceit and susceptible to self-deception. With the emergence of Japan as a modern Asian state in the late 1950s and 1960s, "coverging" with the developed nations of the West in her development, the image of Japan as a nation of the deceiving and the deceived gave way among some scholars to a more positive anticipation of a growing liberal society. However, the issue of deception and self-deception has persisted in some quarters to the present day. The neo-Marxist *Ideologiekritik* is a warrant that has entitled its adherents to locate Japanese consciousness in a self-perpetuating predicament, and to provide themselves with a basis for a kind of epistemological condescension. On their reading, the inability of the Japanese psyche to escape anachronistic reversions to its latent mythologies locks it in a kind of irrationality: a contradiction between mythologically grounded "Asian" institutions of the past, and rationally grounded "modern" and "Western" institutions of the present and future. The specifically Japanese version of *Ideologiekritik*—what LaFleur calls "American neo-Marxist *Japanokritiek*"—interprets the contemporary claims of Japanese culture to have easy access into a *post*modern discourse as being a self-deceiving affirmation of this society's own *pre*modern agenda. The interpretation has moved from E. H. Norman's heavy-handed Marxist indictment of a recalcitrant Japanese feudalism to the more subtle neo-Marxist analyses of today, but the bottom-line ideological assumptions of the critics remain intact. And the living symbol that *Japanokritiek* appeals to as clear evidence of Japan's continuing feudal commitment is the emperor system.

LaFleur, like Wimal Dissanayake in this anthology, uses a literary narrative to explore what for *Japanokritiek* is being construed as an instance of national self-deception. In his case, the medium is a recent film, Kazuo Hara's *The Emperor's Naked Army Marches On* (*Yukiyuki to shingun*), in which a conscience-stricken veteran of the Pacific war, Kenzo Okuzaki, travels around Japan forcing other aging veterans to face up to their crime. After the surrender, a group of officers without provocation had killed some of their younger subordinates with the intention of cannabalizing them. The fervor of the crusading Okuzaki to serve the truth is such that he increasingly resorts to physical force as his means of exposing both the deception and the self-deception of these officers. Finally, he goes to the extreme of deliberately shooting and killing the innocent young son of one of the officers.

Beyond the more obvious ironies of the film, LaFleur uses the narrative to explore the narrow obsession of theorists with exposing "truth," while at the same time ignoring the obvious real social costs that the success of their own programs would entail. In fact Okuzaki's obsession with exposing a truth that ruthlessly fragments society into "good" and "evil" persons, leaving a series of wrecked families in its wake, brings the priority of truth over cruelty into serious question.

LaFleur sees in *The Emperor's Naked Army Marches On* broad political implications, where the self-deception of the military officers is a synecdoche for the entire nation and its war guilt, and in particular, the concealed guilt of the imperial household itself. It is in respect to Hirohito himself, still alive at the making of this film, that the veiled reference to "the emperor's new clothes" has obvious and immediate reference. With the gradual slide of Okuzaki into the ranks of those accused, the situation shifts from the simple value of "truth" accusing "falsity," to the ethical complexity of social solidarity as it gets on with its story.

LaFleur's dissatisfaction with the sometimes strident and always effete soldiers of *Japanokritiek* is clear in the parallel he draws between their project and Okuzaki's ironical crusade. He cannot countenance the blindness of intellectualist concerns to the horrendous social and political cruelties perpetrated by recent political regimes in implementing doctrines which these critics uncritically assume. Like David Hall in this same volume, LaFleur appeals to Richard Rorty in his impatience with the incommensurabilities of dueling theories which fail to factor into discussion the way the world actually is, and the way in which different cultures work out their real lives. Those who would rail against Japanese imperialism would make a stronger argument if they were able to appreciate the ironies of their own position, and if, as a consequence, they were to base their argument on the real cost in human suffering of the institutions they decry.

Where irony everywhere devalues stock in truth, it also makes deception, self-deception, and hypocrisy somehow less pernicious. And, in fact, the cruelty that often attends the exposé of hypocrisy and deception becomes the greater irony.

In "Facing the Self with Masks: Perspectives on the Personal from Nietzsche and Japan," Graham Parkes begins by suggesting a range of senses in which the duplexity of the mask—the function of revealing while concealing—can be understood. It is a complex, always bidirectional metaphor. By comparing the function of masks in classical Greek drama and the very stylized Noh drama of Japan, Parkes generates a thematic and a vocabulary for interpreting the role of masking in Nietzsche and its reinterpretation in modern Japanese philosophy upon which Nietzsche's ideas have exerted considerable influence. Reflexively, the contrastive function of the mask itself is appropriated as an interpretive strategy. In Western languages, the word *mask* takes us back to Greek drama, where it would serve both to identify one and to conceal one's facial expressions and further, as a sounding board amplifying one's voice, thereby focusing attention on one's oratory. In the Noh tradition, the mask functions to draw attention to the subtle, stylized movements of the actor's body.

Turning to Nietzsche, in *Birth of Tragedy* there is reference to "a mysterious primordial One" which serves as a basis for distinguishing the epic poet who generates images separate from himself, from the lyric poet, who is one with his images, and as such, has access to the primordial One. The lyric genius, composed of images of an ever-deeper self, is at once "poet, actor, and spectator." For Nietzsche, one is only a dramatist if "one feels the drive to transform oneself and to speak out of other bodies and souls." In

Greek and in Noh drama, the focus is on the mask, which, on the part of the audience, induces a Dionysian inspired collective projection of the visionary character, and on the part of the actor, allows the image of his role to play itself out through him. This same masking phenomenon occurs in the larger human drama.

The Nietzschean image of the dramatist being a conduit through which some primordial One projects itself as images is the underlying structure of Mishima's *Confessions of a Mask*. Mishima's youthful reveries are a series of impulses to change into the powerful characters he encounters, recognizing that the discovery of his natural self was to be found in this masquerade.

Parkes then returns to Nietzsche and moves from the literal to the metaphorical masking that is part of the human experience. On the one hand, Nietzsche deplores the inauthenticity that our layers of masks represent; on the other hand, he appreciates the power of the mask to "give style to one's character." In fact, the projection of images is not fantasy at all—it is the construction of life itself.

It is this life as masquerade that draws Parkes back to Mishima, where his adolescent subject is beginning to lose his grip on any firm line between his masks and his true self. If *Confessions of a Mask* is a psychoanalytic attempt to get behind the masks created in childhood, the narrative ends with masks still firmly in place.

Again, Nietzsche wants to draw a clear line between the inauthentic and self-deceptive act of masking a world in order to simplify and stabilize it, and the self-conscious, authentic masking where, by participating fully in the working of archaic fantasy, one is able as poet (rather than as mere spectator or actor) to create a higher life. Nietzsche sees the process of mask making as our natural condition, and in *Beyond Good and Evil* leaves us with the possibility that we are in fact masks all the way down.

The contemporary Japanese philosopher Nishitani Keiji begins from *Beyond Good and Evil* to affirm that behind the *phenomenon* of person, there is nothing at all, absolute nothingness. For Nietzsche the answer to the question, Who speaks? could be "the primordial One," or later in Nietzsche's career it could also be a psychical multiplicity of personal drives, and ultimately, polycentric will to power. Although Nishitani would insist that his ultimate "field of emptiness" is distinguishable from the Nietzschean abyss—self and world as will to power—the language used to describe absolute nothingness is indeed reminiscent of will to power as well. The reflections of the contemporary Japanese philosopher Sakabe Megumi are instructive here. Both in Noh drama and in the postmetaphysics of presence the voice that speaks is indeterminate and diffuse. The chorus in Noh drama sings for any one of the masked performers. The impersonal "arche-person" that comes through the various masks seems comparable to the Nietzschean primordial One and Nishitani's absolute nothingness—an affirmation that the true identity is one's masquerade.

In attempting to articulate an Indian perspective on self and deception, Eliot Deutsch begins by addressing the fundamental cultural question: Is the same phenomenon of self-deception conceptualized and valued differently in different cultures, or is it a fundamentally different phenomenon? In taking a comparative approach, Deutsch here (and in all of his work) is more concerned to generate creative new ways to think through philosophical problems than he is to compare traditions. In order to contextualize his discussion of self-deception in the Indian tradition, Deutsch first rehearses several familiar positions that are mainstream in Western philosophy: the psychoanalytic, the epistemological-analytic, the social psychological, and so on. His own developed position on self-deception is summarized as emerging from a situation in which one desires to be precisely what one is, and yet one recognizes that one's own values are in such conflict with prevailing social values that one must believingly claim to be what one is not in order to gain social affirmation. By locating at least this species of self-deception within the domain of desire rather than knowledge, Deutsch avoids the more obvious self-contradiction entailed by denying that one knows what in fact one knows to be the case and must tolerate the more intuitively acceptable paradox both of wanting and of not wanting something to be the case.

Deutsch then turns to an exploration of what he takes to be the "root" form of self-deception: the refusal of someone to allow the spontaneity of the self to be a creative force in shaping one's life. This is the basic concern of the Advaita Vedāntic tradition as espoused by its leading exponent, Śaṃkara (ca. 830). This form of self-deception arises from superimposing attributes of subject and object upon each other. We confuse our real self (which is Reality itself) with our empirical, physical self, and in so doing, are subject to ignorance (*avidyā*). When this metaphysical (rather than psychological or epistemological) affliction is resolved and one becomes aware of one's essential spiritual identity with nondifferentiated reality, one achieves a quality of self-understanding and freedom (*mokṣa*) that eliminates self-deception utterly. The metaphors which are repeatedly used to express the split between "selves" necessary to make self-deception coherent is the dreaming self and the waking self, delineated philosophically in ascending levels of consciousness. The Vedāntic tradition understands *karman*—what we purposely make of ourselves—as the principal source of one's duty (*dharma*) both to oneself and to other human beings. As such, self-deception can arise from confusion over the kind of self one has made of oneself, and also over the degree of responsibility one must take for one's self-making. In relative terms, self-deception is a failure to recognize, accept, and fulfill one's karmic-based duty. In absolute terms, it is to confuse one's empirical karmic self with one's true self.

Turning to the creative aspect of the comparative exercise, Deutsch identifies three areas in which the Western discussion of self-deception can be advanced by taking under consideration the Indian experience: (1) the ontological dimension of self-deception, (2) its social grounding, and (3) the responsibility one bears for one's deception. On the first count, the Indian tradition is an encouragement for us to re-evaluate the basic problem of self-deception, extending it from a rather minor and specific condition of a few hapless souls to a basic malaise that afflicts almost the entire self-deluding human race: a race of isolating individuals who fail to recognize their ontological continuity with their social, natural, and spiritual environments. Second, an appreciation of self-deception in the Indian tradition as a social phenomenon, reflecting a fundamental failure of imagination in the performance of social roles and relationships, would preclude us from trivializing it as a rather silly game we play with each other. Finally, by appreciating both the ontological and the social implications of self-deception, not only do we have to take responsibility for our self-deceptive situation, but further, we must recognize the effort and discipline necessary to overcome it.

Wimal Dissanayake uses two recent Indian novels, Raja Rao's *The Serpent and the Rope* and R. K. Narayan's *The English Teacher,* to explore two components of the self-deception discourse: self and rationality. Dissanayake's argument is that these two concepts are cultural constructions and if we move to interpret the protagonists of these novels on the basis of exogenous criteria—concepts of 'self' and 'rationality' that are foreign to the literature—we are bound to arrive at questionable conclusions.

For example, Ramaswamy, protagonist in *The Serpent and the Rope,* is a Brahmin. When we understand the premises of this cultural commitment, the storyline is transformed from a kind of self-deceptive escapism precipitated by a failed marriage and a temporary affair into an honest quest for the higher Brahmanic truth. Using the language provided by Eliot Deutsch's essay, Ramaswamy is bent on *overcoming* that ontological self-deception that is a condition of superimposing our empirical selves on our higher self, our identity with nondifferentiated Reality. *The Serpent and the Rope* is a metaphysical novel in the sense that it presents the cure for a metaphysical affliction. It narrates the Vedāntic path from empirical self as subject to the nondual reality in which the knowing subject is identical with what is known.

Madeline and Savithri—Ramaswamy's wife and lover respectively—are illusion and Reality. His identification with Savithri enables him to overcome dualistic thinking and to begin on the path to Absolute Truth.

At another level, the novel works through the thematics of self-deception, where Ramaswamy, the Westernized academic and connoisseur of French culture, must overcome this intellectual imaginary self to rediscover his culturally rooted Indian and Brahmanic self—his metaphysical self. As a postscript to his discussion of this novel, Dissanayake observes that for its author, the "narrativization" of the pursuit of transcendental truth has ironically the opposite effect, miring him deeper and deeper in the phenomenal world and leading further into self-deception.

Turning to the second novel, *The English Teacher,* Dissanayake again moves to contextualize it, recognizing a fundamental tension between Krishna the Westernized college teacher of classical English literature and Krishna the brooding believer in supernatural powers. Here too, coming out of the author's own autobiographical commentary, is the passage from the imaginary empirical self to the metaphysical realm. Ironically, what appears to be a blatant act of self-deception from one cultural vantage point—the attempt to overcome the trauma of a lost spouse by inventing her in one's mind—appears to be precisely the opposite: the movement from a self-deluding life as a purveyor of some alien culture back to the metaphysical roots of one's own tradition. It is, after all, the supernatural, the transmigration of souls, and the spiritual worlds beyond which are most fully real.

In his analyses of these two novels, Dissanayake's main concern is that the relationship between self and culture be fully respected in the interpretative exercise. Self is an ever-present cultural variable which, when taken into account, demands a radically different understanding of how self-deception is to be understood.

The final portion of this essay is given over to a more abstract discussion of three topics: self and culture, rationality and culture, and the nature of meaning production. Appealing to recent literature—Hallowell, Geertz, Elster, Winch, Rorty—Dissanayake underscores the need to locate our discussion of self-deception within specific cultural spaces and to give full play to those endogenous factors which shape and are shaped by very different cultural narratives. In fact, he restates theoretically what the earlier narrative portions have so clearly demonstrated.

Beginning from the observation that most of us, save those who are *really* good at it, have some knowledge of self-deception, Richard Hayes explores the phenomenon of self-deception as it is relevant to a Buddhist modular conception of 'personal identity.' There are several perhaps unfamiliar conditions of Buddhist identity. First, there is no defining characteristic which remains constant and unchanging across the career of the complex organism. Again the organism is "many" aggregates as opposed to one individual thing, and hence can be referred to as a "party" of attributes in order to respect this basic plurality. Physicality, consciousness, memory, and character are all modular, and having been shaped from a variety of independent sources are naturally and hopelessly divided and conflicted. In fact, the human "party" lives in a world which shares the same absence of unifying purpose that is characteristic of oneself, and as such, one's only retreat from chaos is to recognize and accept both oneself and one's world for what they really are. The Buddhist expression for the condition of having no fixed nature and of being ever susceptible to change is *emptiness*. And it is through an understanding of emptiness that one is able to confront and to overcome the anxiety that one experiences as a fragmented and inherently unstable existent. Although self-deception is not a theme in the Buddhist literature, the Buddhist notion of 'modular self,' to the extent that it has persuasive force, can be exploited to give an account of this phenomenon.

As mentioned above, because the human party emerges out of a range of influences, it arrives at maturity with a conflicting set of desires, aspirations, attitudes, and beliefs. Some of these attitudes are competent: they conduce to a feeling of well-being: Others are incompetent: they are a source of agitation. Since one cannot entertain both competent and incompetent attitudes at the same time, there is a psychological contest between one's various momentary selves. When and if the incompetent attitudes overwhelm the competent attitudes, one is living in self-deception. In this theory, agent and patient are relatively independent subsystems.

According to Hayes's construction of a Buddhist theory of self-deception, an important factor in one's progress toward competence is the company of salutary friends. It is such company that enables one to abandon the belief that aggregated phenomena are real (that is, the belief in personal identity) and to overcome the addiction to devotional ritual, a frequently associated pair of attitudes that are mutually reinforcing and which together foster self-deception. The addiction to devotional ritual has a negative consequence by generating a clear distinction between those who participate in ritual performance and those who do not. This partisanship, evidenced in bondings such as patriotism, racism, monasticism, theism, and so on is just one more form of personal identity constituted by believing that collections are real.

At this point and in conclusion, Hayes introduces a qualification to save the rather ritualistic life of the Buddhist from self-contradiction. Specific rituals that have the effect of reinforcing competent mental habits, such as serenity and generosity, are healthy rituals and can be distinguished from those which are conducive to self-deception.

Self and Deception

Having thus surveyed the many faces of self and deception presented by our authors and represented by our cover, the editors would like to acknowledge that two of the essays included in this volume appeared, following the August 1992 East-West Center conference on "Self and Deception: An Interdisciplinary and Intercultural Exploration," as journal articles. Barbara Herrnstein Smith's contribution, "Unloading the Self-Refutation Charge," has appeared in *Common Knowledge* 2:2 (Fall 1993):81–95. Amélie Oksenberg Rorty's article, "User-Friendly Self-Deception: A Traveler's Manual," has appeared in *Philosophy* (April, 1994), published by Cambridge University Press. We would also like to thank Daniel Cole, Coordinator at the Center for Chinese Studies at the University of Hawaii, for his expert assistance in compiling the Index.

Roger T. Ames
Wimal Dissanayake

NOTES

1. Raphael Demos, "Lying to Oneself," *Journal of Philosophy* 57 (1960):588–95.
2. Mary R. Haight, *A Study of Self-Deception* (Sussex: Harvester Press, 1980).
3. Herbert Fingarette, *Self-Deception* (London: Routledge and Kegan Paul, 1969).

ONE

ON THE VERY POSSIBILITY OF SELF-DECEPTION

Brian P. McLaughlin

Much of the literature on self-deception focuses on its very possibility. Skeptics argue that self-deception is impossible. Nonskeptics try to explain *how* self-deception is possible. Why, one might well wonder, is the possibility of self-deception an issue? Self-deception seems not only possible, but fairly common. Allen Wood goes so far as to say that "self-deception is so undeniable a fact of human life that if anyone tried to deny its existence, the proper response would be to accuse the person of it."[1] Unintimidated, the skeptic claims that while self-deception may seem possible, one can, upon reflection, see that there are *excluders* of its possibility: conditions that are required for self-deception and that cannot obtain.[2] Once one sees this, the skeptic claims, one will see that neither she nor anyone else is ever really self-deceived. The nonskeptic responds that the conditions in question (to be presented below) are, at best, *merely apparent* excluders of the possibility of self-deception, conditions that may *seem* both required for self-deception and impossible, but which can, upon reflection, be seen to be either unnecessary for it or possible after all. The apparent excluders of self-deception, the nonskeptic claims, are not as they seem, for they are not genuine excluders of it. Whomever is right, the possibility of self-deception is an issue because, on the one hand, it seems that self-deception is possible (indeed, fairly common), while, on the other hand, it can, upon reflection, come to seem that there are conditions that both are required for self-deception and are impossible. Something is amiss: not everything is as it seems. Either self-deception is impossible, despite appearances to the contrary, or the apparent excluders of self-deception are merely that—*apparent* excluders—not genuine excluders of it.

So, then, the skeptic argues that there are excluders of self-deception. The nonskeptic argues that the conditions in question are, at best, *merely* apparent excluders of it. One thing is certain: self-deception is possible if and only if there are no genuine excluders of it. Are there, then, genuine excluders of self-deception?

I do not plan to answer that question; I will not say whether self-deception is possible. My aim here is modest. I will first chart the logical geography of the key issues that arise in attempting to answer the question.

Then I will say why one apparent excluder of self-deception is more formidable than nonskeptics have recognized. Finally, I will say why I think that an investigation of the possibility of self-deception is of theoretical interest.

The skeptic claims that someone who is self-deceived about P is both deceived and a deceiver.[3] Someone who is self-deceived about P is deceived in believing that P and has deceived himself into believing or continuing to believe that P. (A deceiver can, of course, either deceive his victim into believing something or into continuing to believe something.) As deceiver, he believes that not-P; as deceived, he believes that P.[4] As deceiver, he executes a belief-inducing or sustaining stratagem; as deceived, he is taken in by the stratagem. The skeptic appeals to such considerations, among others (to be discussed shortly), to argue that self-deception requires conditions that cannot obtain, and is thus impossible.

There are two frequently cited apparent excluders of self-deception; I will discuss each in turn. The following is, by far, the most frequently cited: *The Contradictory Belief Condition:* the condition of believing that P and believing that not-P (disbelieving that P) at the same time. Two questions arise concerning this apparent excluder: Is it required for self-deception? Can it obtain? If the answer to the first question is no or the answer to the second is yes, then the condition is not a genuine excluder of self-deception, but only an apparent excluder of it. Let us focus briefly on each question before turning to the second apparent excluder of self-deception.

Skeptics maintain that self-deception requires the contradictory belief condition. Many nonskeptics maintain this as well. Why might a skeptic hold that the contradictory belief condition cannot obtain? The skeptic answers that the contradictory belief condition implies a *self-contradictory* condition: the condition of believing that P at some time t and not believing that P at t. If the contradictory belief condition indeed has this implication, then of course it cannot obtain.

However, the contradictory belief condition implies the self-contradictory condition only if believing that not-P at t implies *not* believing that P at t. And the nonskeptics who wish to defend the possibility of the contradictory belief condition will deny that believing that not-P has this implication.

To justify this denial, such a nonskeptic will have to explain how one could believe that P and believe that not-P at the same time. Indeed, the nonskeptic faces the perhaps more formidable task of explaining how one could believe that P and believe that not-P at the same time in circumstances typically involved in self-deception. Suppose one believed that P and believed that not-P at the same time. Then, were one to think of whether P, would one think that P, or think that not-P, or would one simply not know what to think?[5] Of course, the thought of whether P might not come to mind. But there would still be the problem of saying how it is that one could have acquired both the belief that P and the belief that not-P. To put it mildly, it is hard to see how one could have acquired both beliefs at the same time. And if one first believed that (say) not-P, how is it that one could have acquired the belief that P without losing the belief that not-P? Moreover, the issue of whether P typically *will* come to mind in cases in which someone is self-deceived in believing that P. It is characteristic of a self-deceiver to rationalize the belief that P and overcompensate by springing to the defense of P. But if one believed that P and believed that not-P at the same time, then were the thought that P to come to mind, would not one of the beliefs overturn the other or both beliefs be lost? In response to such considerations, a common strategy nonskeptics employ is to try to explain how the beliefs can be "separated" in a way that keeps them from "clashing" when P comes to mind. It is claimed that the belief that not-P may be repressed or that the subject may be dissociated from it when the thought of whether P is true comes to mind.

Of course, another response available to the nonskeptic is to deny that self-deception requires the contradictory belief condition. If this denial is right, then it makes no difference to whether self-deception is possible whether the contradictory belief condition can obtain. To justify this denial, the nonskeptic must explain how self-deception can occur in the absence of the contradictory belief condition. Nonskeptics who deny that self-deception requires the condition attempt to do precisely that. But of the contradictory belief condition, more later.

The second fundamental apparent excluder of self-deception is *the Knowing-Dupe Condition:* the condition of being taken in by a stratagem (deceitful plan) one regards as such.[6] The skeptic claims that as deceiver, the self-deceiver will execute what he regards as a stratagem; as dupe, he will be taken in by that stratagem. So, the self-deceiver will be taken in by a stratagem he regards as such. But that is impossible; thus, self-deception is impossible, or so the skeptic argues. As before, two questions arise: Is the knowing-dupe condition required for self-deception? Can it obtain?

Why can't the knowing-dupe condition obtain? What self-contradictory condition is implied by it? The skeptic claims that the knowing-dupe condition implies the self-contradictory condition of being taken in by a stratagem and not being taken in by it at the same time. Now the knowing-dupe condition indeed implies that the person in question is taken in by a stratagem. The condition also implies that when the person is taken in by the stratagem, the person regards it as a stratagem. But why does the knowing-dupe condition imply that the person is *not* taken in by the stratagem? The skeptic responds that one cannot be taken in by a stratagem one regards as a stratagem. If this is right, then the knowing-dupe condition indeed implies the self-contradictory condition of being taken in by a stratagem and not being taken in by it at the same time.

As before, there are two avenues of response open to the nonskeptic. The nonskeptic can either argue that self-deception does not require the knowing-dupe condition or argue that the knowing-dupe condition can obtain. One avenue of response, then, is to explain how one can be self-deceived without ever having been taken in by a stratagem one regards as such. The other avenue is to explain how one can be taken in by a stratagem one regards as such. That avenue requires explaining how one's regarding a stratagem as such could fail to forestall one's being taken in by it. That is no easy task. Consider lying. Lying involves intentionally misrepresenting at least one of one's beliefs to the intended victim of the lie. But how could one successfully intentionally misrepresent one's beliefs to oneself?[7] Of course, one can deceive by means other than lying. For example, one can deceive by concealing relevant evidence or by presenting misleading evidence, and these stratagems need not involve lying. But how could one successfully conceal relevant evidence from oneself? How could one be taken in by what one regards as misleading evidence?

It is generally recognized that the second avenue of response mentioned above—showing how the knowing-dupe condition can obtain—faces enormous difficulties. Most nonskeptics are happy to concede that the knowing-dupe condition cannot obtain, but insist that it is not required for self-deception. That is, most nonskeptics take the first avenue of response: they deny that a self-deceiver must have been taken in by a stratagem she regarded as such.[8] However, this first avenue is not the easy road many nonskeptics think it is. There is something to be said for the claim that self-deception requires the knowing-dupe condition. The skeptic may be making mistakes in thinking that self-deception requires it, but even if this is so, her mistakes are fewer and more interesting than has generally been recognized. But of that, more later.

Now that we have noted these two apparent excluders of self-deception, let us turn to some attempts to show that neither apparent excluder is genuine since neither is required for self-deception. If any of these attempts succeed, then it makes no difference to the possibility of self-deception whether the contradictory belief and the knowing-dupe conditions can obtain.

Some nonskeptics argue that self-deception requires neither the contradictory belief condition nor the knowing-dupe condition since one can deceive oneself into falsely believing something without either of these conditions obtaining.[9] Here is a straightforward case of someone's so deceiving herself in which neither condition obtains:

> In order to miss an unpleasant meeting three months ahead, Mary deliberately writes the wrong date for the meeting in her appointment book, a date later than the actual date of the meeting. She does this so that three months later when she consults the book, she will come mistakenly to believe the meeting is on that date and, as a result, miss the meeting. Mary knows that she has a poor memory and a very busy schedule. And she justifiably counts on the fact that when she consults the book around the date in question, she will have forgotten the actual date of the meeting and that she wrote the wrong date. Sure enough, three months later, having forgotten the actual date of the meeting and the deceitful deed, she innocently acquires the intended mistaken belief by consulting her appointment book. Her stratagem succeeds. Mary thus deceives herself into believing that the appointment is on a certain date. Moreover, she is deceived in believing that it is.[10]

I call this "the appointment case."[11] The situation depicted could surely occur. Moreover, neither the contradictory belief condition nor the knowing-dupe condition is satisfied in this case. Thus, neither is required for being deceived in believing something one has deceived oneself into believing.[12] The appointment example utilizes the familiar fact that a deceiver need not know her stratagem at the time the victim is taken in by it. When Mary acts to implement the stratagem, she regards it as a stratagem. However, once she writes the wrong date in her appointment book, she proceeds to put the stratagem out of her mind. As a result of memory loss by usual means, Mary no longer possesses any knowledge of the stratagem when she is taken in by it. The appointment case also utilizes the familiar fact that to deceive someone into believing that P, the deceiver need not believe that not-P at the time the victim comes to believe that P. When Mary writes the incorrect date in her appointment book, she believes that not-P. But when she later comes to believe that P, she no longer believes that not-P; for she has simply forgotten that not-P. Thus, the possibility of such a case is explained by the familiar fact of the possibility of memory loss.

The skeptic will, of course, deny that the appointment case is one of self-deception. To be sure, Mary is deceived in believing something which she has deceived herself into believing. However, the skeptic will claim that while that is required for self-deception, it fails to suffice for self-deception. But it will not do for the skeptic to claim this on the grounds that deceiving oneself does not require the contradictory belief or the knowing-dupe condition, and that self-deception does. That would be question begging in the present context. For a nonskeptic might take cases like the appointment case to show that self-deception requires neither condition.

So as not to beg the question ourselves, let us introduce a technical term by stipulation. Let us stipulate that one is in a state of *self-induced deception* in believing that P if (1) one is deceived in believing that P and (2) one deceived oneself into believing or continuing to believe that P.[13] The appointment case is one of self-induced deception. As the case shows, self-induced deception requires neither the contradictory belief condition nor the knowing-dupe condition. Moreover, the case shows that self-induced deception is straightforwardly possible. However, the question that must not be begged is whether self-induced deception is self-deception.

The skeptic claims that it is not. Self-deception, the skeptic claims, requires self-induced deception, but the latter does not suffice for the former. To be sure, the skeptic owes us a nonquestion-begging reason for claiming that self-induced deception does not suffice for self-deception. But, as we will see shortly, the skeptic can provide such a reason. For the moment, however, let us simply note that the appointment case, while a case of self-induced deception, is very different from paradigm cases of self-deception. And it is not the kind of case that skeptics and nonskeptics have been arguing about. No one in this debate ever really doubted that a case like the appointment case is possible. Whether self-induced deception is possible, then, is not what has been at issue.

Indeed, this last point is acknowledged even by some nonskeptics who hold that cases of self-induced deception such as the appointment case are ones of self-deception. Thus, Mark Johnston, for instance, remarks that

> not all self-deception takes a form in which stages of the self-deceiver's history are successively stages of deceiving, forgetting, and being the victim of deceit. One can simultaneously develop as deceiver and deceived. A case of progressive and self-deceptive alcoholism might be of this sort. As the alcoholic's case worsens and more evidence accumulates, his self-deceptive denials develop concurrently.[14]

One of Johnston's points here is that while certain cases of self-deception can be explained by the familiar possibility of memory loss, nevertheless, there are cases of self-deception whose possibility cannot be explained in that way.

However, the skeptic will deny that any cases of self-deception can be explained by appeal to memory loss. Johnston believes some can because he believes that self-induced deception suffices for self-deception. It is worthwhile noting, however, that Johnston also holds a view about self-deception that commits him to denying that self-induced deception suffices for self-deception. "A self-deceiver," Johnston tells us, "is properly charged with wishful thinking." "Self-deception," he says, "is a *species* of wishful thought."[15] Suppose it is. Then, self-induced deception does not suffice for self-deception.[16] For self-induced deception is not a species of wishful thinking. Believing that P is wishful thinking only if the believer wants P to be true. But one can be in a state of self-induced deception in believing that P, yet not want P to be true. Mary, for instance, does not want the appointment to be on the date she reads in her appointment book; she wishes (as she did when she wrote in that date three months earlier) that she did not have the appointment at all. If self-deception is a species of wishful thinking, then self-induced deception does not suffice for self-deception; for self-induced deception does not suffice for wishful thinking. Thus, Johnston cannot consistently hold that self-induced deception suffices for self-deception and that self-deception is a species of wishful thinking.

Johnston is mistaken in claiming that self-deception is a species of wishful thinking, however. One can be self-deceived in believing that P even when believing that P is not wishful thinking on one's part. In wishful thinking one believes that P, in part, because one desires that P. But one can be self-deceived in believing that P without desiring that P.[17] Self-deception often involves our believing something we want to be true, but it can involve, instead, our believing something we want to be false. We can torment ourselves by our self-deceptions. Motives for beliefs can be infused with self-hatred.[18] A mind can be divided against itself. Self-deception often involves wishful thinking, but it does not require wishful thinking.[19]

But does wishful thinking suffice for self-deception? It seems that it does not.[20] In response to the question of what differentiates the species self-deception from the genus wishful thinking, Johnston plausibly says: "The self-deceiver is to be distinguished from the mere wishful thinker by his perversely adopting the wishful belief *despite* his recognition at some level that the evidence is to the contrary". Suppose Johnston is right. Then, wishful thinking does not suffice for self-deception since one can wishfully believe that P without recognizing, at any level, that the evidence points against P. If believing that P is wishful thinking on one's part, then the desire that P biases one's assessment of evidence that bears on P.[21] But there need not be recognition, at any level, that the evidence points to the contrary of the wishful belief. Indeed, in cases of wishful thinking, the weight of the evidence need not even point to the contrary. The wishful thinker believes on less than adequate evidence, but need not believe against the evidence. The claim that self-deception differs from wishful thinking in the way in question is, of course, independent of the claim that self-deception is a species of wishful thinking. And the former claim, unlike the latter claim, is quite plausible.

(How, in wishful thinking, does the desire that P bias one's assessment of the evidence? The desire that P leads one to come or to continue to believe that P, without adequate support by the evidence.[22] This typically happens in cases of mere wishful thinking as a result of the affect of desire on interest. For interest affects attention. We are all familiar with such effects. Hearing one's name across a noisy room immediately catches one's attention; the boring conversation taking place before one's eyes cannot hold it. In wishful thinking, one's interests are such that evidence for P captures one's attention, while evidence against P deflects it. The wishful thinker that P enjoys thinking about reasons for P, but is uncomfortable and stressed when thinking about reasons against P. As a result, the wishful thinker may dwell on evidence for P, and not properly attend to evidence against P. When the question of P arises, the wishful thinker may immediately think of a reason for P, and then, whether or not it is good reason, drop the issue.[23] Moreover, the desire that P may make evidence for P capture the wishful thinker's imagination. When the question of P arises, the wishful thinker might commence to imagine all the wonderful consequences of P, rather than coolly assessing whether P.)[24]

Self-deception that P seems to differ from mere wishful belief that P in that self-deception that P does, and mere wishful belief that P does not, require recognizing at some level that the evidence is against P. Many nonskeptics hold this.[25] The skeptic insists on it. The skeptic can readily concede that wishful thinking is possible, indeed that it is quite common. But the skeptic will insist that that is no reason to think that self-deception is possible.

It is worthwhile noting that if Johnston is right that self-deception that P requires recognition, at some level, that the evidence is against P, then he is, for that very reason, mistaken in taking self-induced deception that P to suffice for self-deception that P. For one can be in a state of self-induced deception in believing that P at t and not recognize at t, at any level, that the evidence points against P. Moreover, one can be in a state of self-induced deception in believing that P, even when the weight of the available evidence is not against P. Mary, for instance, does not come to believe that the appointment is on the date in question in the face of counter-evidence. Indeed, she may possess no evidence that the appointment is not on that date. The most effective way to deceive someone into believing something is to conceal counter-evidence (if necessary) and present the person with only misleading positive evidence. If then, as seems plausible, self-deception that P requires recognizing at some level that the evidence is against P, self-induced deception does not suffice for self-deception; for self-induced deception requires no such recognition; nor does it require that the available evidence be against P.[26]

We noted earlier that the skeptic will claim that self-induced deception fails to suffice for self-deception. We now see how the skeptic can justify that claim by appeal to an assumption the skeptic shares with most nonskeptics, namely the assumption that when one is self-deceived in believing that P, one recognizes at some level that the weight of the evidence is against P. There is no such requirement for one's being in a state of self-induced deception in believing that P. So, self-induced deception does not suffice for self-deception. The skeptic will claim, for this reason, that cases like the appointment example, rather than being unproblematic cases of self-deception, are not cases of self-deception at all. The skeptic will further claim that while self-induced deception is (as the appointment case illustrates) straightforwardly possible, that is no reason to think that self-deception is possible.

Let us pause and take stock. We have thus far failed to see how *any* case of self-deception is possible. Wishful thinking and self-induced deception are both straightforwardly possible; but neither seems to suffice for self-deception. Moreover, we have found some interesting common ground between the skeptic and the nonskeptic (or at least many nonskeptics): when one is self-deceived in believing that P, one recognizes, at some level, that the weight of the evidence points to not-P.

Now the skeptic will claim that in a genuine case of self-deception, recognition of the evidence for not-P will engender or sustain the belief that not-P. Some nonskeptics will deny that that has to happen in a case of self-deception. However, it is fairly common for nonskeptics to concede that when, as often happens, the self-deceiver desires that P, the recognition of the evidence against P will engender the fear or anxiety that not-P. But, arguably, one cannot fear that not-P or be anxious that not-P unless one at least believes that P may well be true. Moreover, as the self-deceiver moves from such emotions to regret or disappointment that not-P, the self-deceiver will believe that not-P. For one cannot regret or be disappointed that not-P unless one believes that not-P is true. And it seems that someone self-deceived in believing that P at least sometimes regrets or is disappointed that not-P.

Be that as it may, how is it that the belief that P persists in the face of mounting evidence that not-P and growing fear and/or anxiety that not-P? Johnston notes that

> it is hard not to see how anxiety could be reduced by wishful belief if the wishful belief is copresent in consciousness with the

recognition that the evidence is strongly against it. Indeed it is hard to see how the wishful belief could persist in consciousness under these conditions. Some play must be given to the concept of *repression* in discussing self-deception. If anxiety that not-p produced by recognition of telling evidence for not-p is to be reduced, not only must the wishful belief that p arise, but the recognition of the evidence as more or less establishing the contrary must also be repressed, i.e., the subject must cease consciously acknowledging it.[27]

Now it is far from certain that the concept of repression must be invoked here. Another possibility is that the self-deceiver becomes *dissociated* from his recognition of the telling evidence for not-P and, thereby, from his anxiety that not-P, at least when the issue of whether P explicitly arises. But, whatever the mechanism, the self-deceiver's belief that P must be "separated" from his anxiety that not-P and from the recognition of the telling evidence against P in such a way that the self-deceiver does not lose the belief that P. The subject's mind, so to speak, must be in some way divided.

However, if the dissociation is too wide or the repression too deep, we seem to lose the phenomena of self-deception. So-called homuncular theories of self-deception run into trouble for this reason. These theories postulate subsystems within the self-deceiver which are capable of rational agency. They credit the self-deceiver with subsystems that can function as relatively autonomous agents capable of belief, desire, and intentional action. Stephen White endorses a homuncular model of self-deception. He tells us,

> On the basis of such a model we can describe the process of self-deception without conceptual strain. Subsystems S1 and S2 originally both believe that p. S1 causes S2 (either directly or indirectly) to lose the belief that p (and possibly to believe its negation), while itself continuing to believe that p. S1 also tries to prevent S2's coming by any evidence that would reveal S1's activity.[28]

S1 and S2 are subsystems of a system that constitutes a human being, and S1 deceives S2. The deceived subsystem, S2, is held to be the one who is in control of the speech center and gross motor skills.[29] In White's scenario, S1 believes that P, while S2 believes that not-P (or at least does not believe that P).[30] S1 executes stratagems; S2 is taken in by them. But neither S1 nor S2 satisfies the contradictory belief or knowing-dupe condition. The person (the human being) may appear to an observer to satisfy the conditions; but that is only because the observer fails to appreciate that there are two intentional agents operating within the person (the human being).

Homuncular approaches face a host of problems.[31] I will mention only the most pressing ones. Why does the fact that S1 is a deceiver make the person of whom S1 is a subsystem a deceiver? Similarly, why does the fact that S2 is deceived make the person of whom S2 is a subsystem deceived? Subsystem S1 is a deceiver, but not deceived. Subsystem S2 is deceived, but not a deceiver. If the person is S1, then the person is not deceived, for S1 is not deceived. If the person is S2, then the person is deceived. But, then, the person is not a deceiver, for S2 is not a deceiver. Either way, the person is not both a deceiver and deceived. The person cannot, of course, be both S1 and S2, for S1 is not S2, and identity is transitive. Granting that the person is not identical with S1, could S1's continuing to believe that P count as the person's continuing to believe that P? And could S2's ceasing to believe that P count as the person's ceasing to believe that P? I don't see how. For how could it be that the person both continues to believe that P and ceases to believe that P? If the person continues to believe that P, then the person did not cease to believe that P. Could S1's performing an act of deception count as the person's performing an act of deception? In a word, no. The notion of intentional agency transmitting from one agent to another is incoherent.[32]

I will stop, for homuncular approaches to self-deception seem to me to be nonstarters. Either states and acts of the subsystems count as states and acts of the person the subsystems constitute or they do not. If they count as states and acts of the person, then the puzzles of self-deception are reintroduced. If the states and acts of the subsystems do not count as states and acts of the person they constitute, then the person is not in a state of self-induced deception and so is not self-deceived.

The homuncular approach appears to treat self-deception as an exotic kind of other-deception, a kind that might occur in multiple personality disorder.[33] The skeptic need not deny that such exotic cases of other-deception are possible. Perhaps, on occasion, Eve Black deceived Eve White. But the skeptic will deny that such exotic cases of other-deception are cases of self-deception, for in such cases, there is no one who is both deceiver and deceived. Self-deception may well involve dissociation, but not dissociation as wide as the dissociation characteristic of multiple personality disorder. So much, then, for the homuncular approach.

Still, some mental division seems required for self-deception. The relevant mental divisions of a self-deceiver must be wide enough (in the case of dissociation) or deep enough (in the case of repression) to keep the self-deceiver's belief that P from being overturned by his recognition of the telling evidence against P. How wide must the dissociation be? Or how deep the repression? The mental divide must be at least wide enough or deep enough to ensure that when the self-deceiver thinks of whether P, then the self-deceiver does not think that not-P.

I have argued elsewhere that someone self-deceived in believing that P can believe that not-P, provided that his belief that not-P is not such that when he thinks of whether P, he thinks that not-P.[34] I call a belief that not-P "inaccessible" if and only if when the believer thinks of whether P, the belief is not manifested in conscious thought by the believer's thinking that not-P. Thinking that not-P is the characteristic manifestation of the belief that not-P in conscious thought (just as saying that not-P is the characteristic manifestation of the belief that not-P in speech); a belief that not-P will be inaccessible if and only if it lacks this characteristic manifestation.[35] But an inaccessible belief that not-P may be manifested in others ways both in thought and in behavior.[36] And postulating inaccessible beliefs does not require postulating autonomous subagents in a person. That there are mental divisions does not imply that there are subagents. Someone can believe that P and also believe that not-P, provided the belief that not-P is inaccessible. If self-deception is impossible, that is not because it requires the contradictory belief condition. For that condition can obtain. The condition can obtain if one of the beliefs is inaccessible.[37]

Suppose, then, if only for the sake of argument, that someone self-deceived in believing that P could have an inaccessible belief that not-P, and that the person's recognition of telling evidence against P could consist of inaccessible beliefs. The question remains as to how the belief that P is acquired or sustained and how the other beliefs are rendered inaccessible. Johnston has spoken of the role of what he calls "mental tropisms" in bolstering wishful beliefs and keeping recognition of telling evidence against them from overturning them. I think that there may very well be mental tropisms involved in self-deception. It is likely that beliefs are typically rendered inaccessible by dissociation, and processes of dissociation may well be tropistic. However, be all that as it may, the skeptic will insist that in a case of self-deception that P, the belief that P must be one the self-deceiver deceived himself into holding or into continuing to hold. And the skeptic will ask how that can happen.

Nonskeptics describe activities by which the self-deceptive belief that P might be acquired and sustained. Johnston mentions the activities most frequently cited by nonskeptics:

> One may selectively reappraise and explain away the evidence (rationalization). One may simply avoid thinking about the touchy subject (evasion). One may focus one's attention on

invented reasons for p and spring to the advocacy of p whenever opportunity presents itself (overcompensation).[38]

However, the skeptic will claim that unless a person's acts of rationalization, evasion, and overcompensation count as acts of deception, we will not have been told *how* the self-deceiver deceives himself. Well, then, cannot the nonskeptic respond by saying that the self-deceiver deceives himself by rationalizing, evading, and overcompensating? Nonskeptics sometimes respond in that way. However, the skeptic counters that to engage in rationalization, evasion, or overcompensation *in order to* deceive oneself, and to succeed, thereby, in deceiving oneself, one would have to satisfy the knowing-dupe condition. And that condition, the skeptic insists, cannot obtain.

In response to just such considerations, Johnston claims that the skeptic is grossly over-rationalizing self-deception, for self-deception does not require *intentional* deception. He says: "To be deceived is sometimes just to be *misled* without being *intentionally* misled or lied to. The self-deceiver is a self-misleader. As a result of his own activity he gets into a state in which he is misled, at least at the level of conscious belief."[39]

The activities of rationalization, evasion, and overcompensation are, he holds, *not* activities by which the self-deceiver *intentionally* misleads himself; they are, rather, activities by which the self-deceiver *unintentionally* misleads himself. The knowing-dupe condition need not obtain in a case of self-deception since the self-deceiver need have no stratagem when he engages in these activities. The self-deceiver is just a self-misleader: he unintentionally misleads himself into believing and/or continuing to believe that *P*. The activities by which the self-deceiver so misleads himself serve the purpose of reducing anxiety that not-*P* by sustaining the belief that *P*. But the self-deceiver does not engage in the activities *for* that purpose. Johnston takes the skeptic's assumption that such activities are intentional as an instance of a widespread tendency to "over-rationalize mental processes that are purposive but not intentional."[40]

Now the skeptic can allow that there are mental activities and processes that are purposive but not intentional. Further, the skeptic can even allow that some such processes are characteristically involved in self-deception. Moreover, the skeptic can readily agree with Johnson that "to be deceived is sometimes just to be *misled* without being *intentionally* misled or lied to. The self-deceiver is a self-misleader. As a result of his own activity he gets into a state in which he is misled, at least at the level of conscious belief."[41]

Self and Deception

Finally, the skeptic can readily concede that self-misleading is possible. The wishful thinker is typically a self-misleader; and wishful thinking is possible. However, the skeptic will claim that being a self-misleader does not suffice for being a self-deceiver. For a self-deceiver must not only be deceived, she must also be a deceiver. And a misleader need not be a deceiver. An intentional misleader is a deceiver. One can be a misleader by unintentionally misleading someone. And an unintentional misleader is not a deceiver, for a deceiver must perform an act of deception, and an unintentional misleader need not. To be sure, an unintentional misleader must do something that is misleading. But while intentional acts of misleading are acts of deception, unintentional acts of misleading are not. There is a distinction between intentionally and unintentionally misleading acts. But, the skeptic will claim, there is no distinction between intentional and unintentional acts of deception, for there is no such thing as unintentional deception.

As Donald Davidson notes, "some verbs describe actions that cannot be anything but intentional: asserting, cheating, taking a square root, and lying are examples."[42] One of these examples, lying, is a paradigmatic way of trying to deceiving someone. It is indeed the case, the nonskeptic will concede, that lying cannot be unintentional. But the nonskeptic will point out that one can deceive someone without lying. The skeptic will respond that while one can indeed deceive without lying, nevertheless, all deceiving, as opposed to misleading, is like lying in that it must be intentional. The point, the skeptic will claim, is this: no act is an act of deception unless it was performed with the intent to deceive.

The skeptic will further claim that for a self-misleader to be a self-deceiver, the self-misleader must have deceived himself, and so must have *intentionally* misled himself. A self-misleader can fail to be a deceiver, but a self-deceiver cannot. A self-deceiver is a deceiver; self-deception requires self-induced deception. If the subject's acts of rationalization, evasion, or overcompensation are not intentionally misleading, then the subject is not a deceiver by virtue of performing them. However, if these acts are intentionally misleading, then the skeptic will ask how it is that they result in the subject's being deceived. How could the subject be taken in?

I have argued elsewhere, following William Ruddick, that one must be careful in drawing analogies between other-deception and self-deception.[43] Perhaps when one plays the role of deceiver with respect to oneself in cases of self-deception, one does not, so to speak, play all the parts of the role. When one is self-taught, one is one's own teacher. But while in such cases one plays some parts of the role of teacher, one does not play all the parts. When one is self-taught, one has done some of the things teachers characteristically do, though certainly not all of the things teachers characteristically do. For example, one does not impart knowledge to oneself. Perhaps the self-deceiver plays some parts of the role of deceiver by misleading himself, but the self-deceiver is not literally a deceiver since the misleading is unintentional, and thus the self-deceiver does not perform acts of deception. But this word of caution does not settle the issue. The skeptic insists that the self-deceiver is *literally* a deceiver, that that requires that the self-deceiver have performed some act of deception, and that acts of deception must be done with the intent to deceive.

Most nonskeptics would concede that self-deception requires self-induced deception. If the skeptic is right that a self-deceiver is *literally* a deceiver and that requires having performing some relevant intentional act of deception, then a self-misleader can indeed fail to be a self-deceiver. For, then, an unintentionally misleading act is not an act of deception. The fact that unintentional self-misleading is possible, then, arguably does not show that self-deception is possible. The skeptic has yet to be fully answered.

I will not attempt here to determine whether the skeptic can be fully answered.[44] As I noted at the outset, I will not attempt here to determine whether self-deception is possible. My aim has been to chart the logical geography of the issues and to note some territory that remains in dispute. Suffice it to note for present purposes that even if the skeptic is wrong in claiming that self-deception is impossible, it remains to be seen exactly why the skeptic is wrong.

Now one might wonder why it matters whether the skeptic is wrong. Given that self-misleading is possible, does it really matter much if self-deception is impossible? Maybe our notion of self-deception cannot be vindicated, or at least not fully vindicated. Perhaps, for instance, when we make attributions of self-deception we are, on the best of occasions, simply grossly over-rationalizing what are really just cases of unintentional self-misleading. If that is so, one might say, then so be it. Perhaps the possibility of self-misleading is at least a partial vindication of the notion of self-deception. And it may not be of great moment whether our notion of self-deception can be fully vindicated. The notion of self-deception plays nothing like the central role in our understanding of ourselves played by the notions of, for example, perception, memory, reasoning, or decision making. Folk psychology could surely weather the result that *literal* self-deception is impossible.

Moreover, no doubt some will find that their ears go tin on whether there is such a thing as unintentional deception. And they will insist that the possibility of self-deception is fully vindicated once we see how certain kinds of unintentional misleading are possible. An unintentional misleader can be a deceiver, they will say, in whatever sense a self-deceiver is a deceiver. It is not easy to see how to resolve this dispute. Our common

45

Self and Deception

conception of self-deception may be too indeterminate to allow us to settle it without engaging in some stipulation.[45]

Suppose that, as many nonskeptics have insisted, certain kinds of unintentional self-misleading suffice for self-deception. Suppose that the skeptic is wrong in claiming, for instance, that there is no such thing as unintentional deceiving. Suppose that acts of deception need not be done with the intention to deceive. Given my interests, it is still worthwhile investigating whether the kind of self-deception the skeptic seems to have in mind is possible. For by seeing how that kind of self-deception is possible, if it is, or why that kind of self-deception is not possible, if it is not, I may learn something about how desire can and cannot affect belief-fixing mechanisms, and, thereby, about the architecture of our minds. Therein, for me, lies the interest in investigating the possibility of self-deception, both its conceptual possibility and its nomological possibility. Thus, for me, the interest of investigating the possibility of self-deception lies elsewhere than in a concern to completely vindicate the notion of it. It lies in what such an investigation might reveal to us about how desires can bias belief-fixing mechanisms, and, thereby, reveal to us about the *architecture* of our minds.[46]

I am thus interested in the toughest sorts of cases the skeptic draws out attention to, even if they are not the only kinds of cases of self-deception, and even if they are quite atypical. Thus, for example, whether one can lie to oneself by thinking that *P* is of interest, even if this never happens in a case of self-deception. For we can learn something about the architecture of the mind by investigating whether one can lie to oneself by thinking that *P.* And, as I keep saying, it is because investigating kinds of self-deception can reveal aspects of the architecture of the mind that I find the exploration of the possibility of self-deception interesting. It is to me only of secondary interest if there is a kind of self-deception that does not require the contradictory belief or knowing-dupe conditions. If, for instance, certain kinds of wishful thinking count as self-deception yet do not require either of the conditions in question, then all well and good. There are cases of self-deception that are possible. But, to me, the real interest of self-deception is whether certain tough cases are possible, and how they are if they are, and why they are not, if they are not.[47] Even if certain kinds of cases of self-deception can be seen to be possible, even straightforwardly possible, whether the tough cases are possible remains of theoretical interest. Thus, even if the skeptic is wrong in claiming that self-deception is possible, we owe the skeptic a debt of thanks for calling our attention to the really tough cases. Investigating those may reveal something of importance about mental architecture.

In sum, it is of mild interest to be told that certain cases that would ordinarily count as cases of self-deception involve neither the contradictory belief nor the knowing-dupe conditions and are straightforwardly possible. Of far greater interest is whether some of the sorts of cases the skeptic draws our attention to are possible.[48]

NOTES

1. A. W. Wood, "Self-Deception and Bad Faith" in *Perspectives on Self-Deception*, ed. B. McLaughlin and A. Rorty (Berkeley: University of California Press, 1988), 207.

2. Two unrelated points: first, I get the term *excluder* from R. Nozick, *Philosophical Explanations* (Cambridge, MA: Harvard University Press, 1981). Second, when I speak of "the skeptic," I have no particular skeptic in mind, nor do I have a particular nonskeptic in mind when I speak of "the nonskeptic" below. However, skeptical positions concerning the possibility of self-deception can be found in S. Palach, "Self-Deception," *Inquiry* 10, 1987, 268–78; D. Kipp, "On Self-Deception," *Philosophical Quarterly* 30, 1980, 305–17; and M. Haight, *A Study of Self-Deception* (Sussex: Harvester Press, 1980). I refer below to various papers in which a nonskeptical view is defended.

3. We often speak of someone as self-deceived about himself, or about another (e.g., a spouse or a child) or about a situation (e.g., a marriage or a health condition). However, self-deception about oneself or another or a situation will invariably involve self-deception about something's being the case with respect to oneself, or the other, or the situation; indeed, it will typically involve self-deception about various things being the case. This is *not* to say that every kind of self-deception reduces to self-deception about something being the case. I claim only that every kind of self-deception *requires* self-deception about something being the case.

4. Robert Audi holds that one can be self-deceived about P without believing that P; someone self-deceived about P may, he says, sincerely avow that P or be disposed to avow sincerely that P, yet not believe that P. But someone who *sincerely* avows that P is at least of the opinion that P; and I take opinions, even fleeting, superficially held opinions, to be beliefs. Moreover, someone who is disposed to avow sincerely that P has, I would take it, at least the implicit opinion that P, and thus at least the implicit belief that P. In any case, I will use the term *belief* in a broad sense to include short-lived, superficially held, and even implicitly held, opinions. And I will concede to the skeptic that someone who is self-deceived about P is deceived in believing that P, in this broad sense of belief. Audi seems to use *belief* in a more restricted sense. My difference here with Audi is, I believe, merely verbal. If you find my broad use of belief at all strained, consider the discussion to follow one about whether it is possible to be self-deceived in believing that P, rather than a discussion about whether it is possible to be self-deceived about P. See R. Audi, "Self-Deception, Rationalization, and Reasons for Acting" in McLaughlin and Rorty, *Perspectives*.

Self and Deception

    5. Cf. B. McLaughlin, "Exploring the Possibility of Self-Deception in Belief" in McLaughlin and Rorty, *Perspectives*.

    6. Cf. ibid. This condition is similar to what Mele calls "the strategy paradox," a paradox he takes to be one of the two paradoxes of self-deception. The other is the belief paradox, which is, literally, the contradictory belief condition. See A. Mele, *Irrationality: An Essay on Akrasia, Self-Deception, and Self-Control* (New York: Oxford University Press, 1987) and "Recent Work on Self-Deception" in *American Philosophical Quarterly* 34, 1987, 1–17.

    7. Cf. D. Davidson, "Deception and Division" in *Actions and Events: Perspectives on the Philosophy of Donald Davidson*, ed. E. LePore and B. McLaughlin (New York: Blackwell, 1985), and McLaughlin, "Exploring the Possibility of Self-Deception in Belief."

    8. See, for example, K. Bach, "An Analysis of Self-Deception" in *Philosophy and Phenomenological Research* 41, 1981, 351–70, Mele *Irrationality*, Audi, "Self-Deception, Rationalization, and Reasons for Acting," McLaughlin, "Exploring the Possibility of Self-Deception in Belief," and M. Johnston, "Self-Deception and the Nature of Mind" in McLaughlin and Rorty, *Perspectives*.

    9. Adding the word *falsely* here is not redundant. One can deceive someone into believing something that is true. This is not to say that one can be deceived in believing something that is true; one cannot. For being deceived in believing something requires that the belief in question be false. But one can get someone to believe something that is true by deceitful means and, thereby, deceive the person into believing something that is true. (For an example and discussion, see McLaughlin, "Exploring the Possibility of Self-Deception in Belief," 35). However, that will require that one also get the person to believe or to continue to believe something that is false. For one cannot deceive someone into believing something without getting him or her to believe or to continue to believe something false. Nonetheless, one can, as I said, deceive someone into believing something that is true. I will hereafter ignore this complication.

    10. McLaughlin, "Exploring the Possibility of Self-Deception in Belief," 31–32.

    11. D. W. Hamlyn discusses similar cases in "Self-Deception," *Proceedings of the Aristotelian Society* 45, 1970, 45–60. See also R. Sorenson, "Self-Deception and Scattered Events," *Mind* 94, 1985, 64–69 and M. Johnston "Self-Deception and the Nature of Mind." Davidson in "Deception and Division" mentions essentially the same case presented above and says that it is not a "pure" case of self-deception since the belief in question is not *sustained* by an intention to deceive. I address the issue of whether the appointment example is an example of self-deception below.

    12. What about cases of deceiving oneself into continuing to believe something? Such cases are straightforwardly possible too and require neither the contradictory belief nor the knowing-dupe condition. For an example that involves a modification of the appointment example, see McLaughlin, "Exploring the Possibility of Self-Deception in Belief," 32.

    13. Cf. Ibid. 30.

14. M. Johnston "Self-Deception and the Nature of Mind," 77.
15. Ibid., 67.
16. Cf. McLaughlin, "Exploring the Possibility of Self-Deception in Belief."
17. Cf. R. Demos, "Lying to Oneself" in *Journal of Philosophy* 57, 1960, 588–95; Davidson, "Deception and Division;" and McLaughlin, "Exploring the Possibility of Self-Deception in Belief."
18. Motives for believing that P are motives for being a that-P believer. One can, of course, have motives for being a that-P believer; belief states have causal consequences and thus can further or frustrate our ends. Cf. McLaughlin, "Exploring the Possibility of Self-Deception in Belief."
19. For further discussion, see ibid.
20. But, as I argued in "Exploring the Possibility of Self-Deception in Belief," following G. Graham, "Russell's Deceptive Desires" in *Philosophy*, 1985, there seems to be a continuum of cases from cases of mere wishful thinking to those of self-deception. I have found that intuitions differ on where in the continuum we reach self-deception. I doubt that there is any fact of the matter as to where on the continuum we reach self-deception; our common conception of 'self-deception' is, I believe, somewhat indeterminate. I will not pursue that point here, however. And I will not assume it.
21. Cf. McLaughlin, "Exploring the Possibility of Self-Deception in Belief."
22. M. Johnston in "Self-Deception and the Nature of Mind" correctly notes that desiring that P will be a motive for believing that P only in cases of so-called positive thinking, cases in which one believes that believing that P will increase the chances of P's being true. (For a discussion of the relationship between wishful thinking and positive and negative thinking, see McLaughlin, "Exploring the Possibility of Self-Deception in Belief."
23. Bach in "An Analysis of Self-Deception" calls this phenomena "jamming" and notes an analogy with procrastination: when the question of whether to do something (the thing the procrastinator is procrastinating about) arises, the procrastinator typically immediately thinks of a reason for not doing it, and then, whether or not the reason is a good one, drops the issue. (Procrastination is habit forming. So is wishful thinking.)
24. For detailed discussions of how desire influences belief in wishful thinking, see Bach "An Analysis of Self-Deception"; Mele *Irrationality*, chapter 9; and McLaughlin, "Exploring the Possibility of Self-Deception in Belief," 42–44.
25. See, for example, Bach "An Analysis of Self-Deception"; Davidson, "Deception and Division"; Mele, *Irrationality*; Audi, "Self-Deception, Rationalization, and Reasons for Acting"; G. Rey, "Toward a Computational Account of Akrasia and Self-Deception," in McLaughlin and Rorty, *Perspectives*; and McLaughlin, "Exploring the Possibility of Self-Deception in Belief."
26. Cf. McLaughlin, "Exploring the Possibility of Self-Deception in Belief."
27. M. Johnston, "Self-Deception and the Nature of Mind," 75.
28. Stephen L. White, "Self-Deception and Responsibility for the Self" in McLaughlin and Rorty, *Perspectives*, 453. D. Pears in *Motivated Irrationality*, (Oxford: Oxford University Press, 1985) also proposes a homuncular model of self-deception;

he speaks of subsystems of a person deceiving the person's main system into holding the "quasi-altruistic" intention of protecting the main system from painful truths. However, I will discuss Stephen White's statement of homuncularism below, rather than Pears's, since White's statement is simple and straightforward and will serve to illustrate the points I want to illustrate.

29. On Pears's account, the subsystem in control of the speech center and gross motor skills is called the "main system."

30. To avert misunderstanding, I should note that while White has the self-deceiver self-deceived about not-P, I have spoken of the self-deceiver as self-deceived about P. This is just a verbal difference. One can be self-deceived in believing something is the case or self-deceived in believing something is not the case.

31. Mele *Irrationality*, chapter 10, and M. Johnston, "Self-Deception and the Nature of Mind," are extensive critiques of Pears's homuncularism. My discussion of homuncularism below draws from these critiques.

I should mention that Pears has responded to Johnston. Pears says that Johnston's criticisms mistakenly presuppose that the deceiving subsystem is conscious. However, not all of Johnston's objections presuppose that. Moreover, Pears offers no explanation of how a deceiving subsystem can do all he says it can without being conscious. See D. Pears, "Self-Deceptive Belief-Formation." *Syntheses* 89, 1991, 393–406.

32. This is not to deny, of course, that one agent's intentionally doing something can be part of the means by which another intentionally does that something. If one agent orders another to kill a certain individual, and the second obeys the order, they both kill the individual in question; and the orderer kills, in part, by means of the person ordered to kill. This is not the sort of transmission of intentional agency we are rejecting as incoherent. What we are rejecting as incoherent is the notion that one agent's intentionally doing something could be another agent's intentionally doing that something.

33. M. Johnston in "Self-Deception and the Nature of Mind" makes this point.

34. McLaughlin, "Exploring the Possibility of Self-Deception in Belief."

35. It may well be that all beliefs of nonverbal animals are inaccessible beliefs (cf. ibid.).

36. Cf. ibid. In a superb review of McLaughlin and Rorty, *Perspectives*, Kent Bach mistakes my notion of an 'inaccessible belief' for the notion of an 'unconscious belief' and criticizes requiring an unconscious belief in cases of self-deception. See Kent Bach, Review of McLaughlin and Rorty, *Nous*, 1992, 495–504. But Bach's own account of self-deception that P implies that one who is self-deceived about P is disposed not to have the "sustained and recurrent" thought that not-P, and this is closely related to my notion of an inaccessible belief that not-P (see Bach, "An Analysis of Deception"). If the thought that P occurs, it may quickly cease to occur and the belief become inaccessible, at least for a time. A belief can slip back and forth from accessibility to inaccessibility. Moreover, my notion of an inaccessible belief is different from any notion of an unconscious belief of which I am aware (as I pointed out at length in McLaughlin, "Exploring

the Possibility of Self-Deception in Belief," 49–50). Unconscious beliefs are inaccessible, but inaccessible beliefs can fail to be unconscious if that requires that they be repressed (think of the Freudian notion of an unconscious belief) or that they be at the subpersonal level (think of the 'cognitive science' notion). A person's belief may be inaccessible due to dissociation (of a much milder sort than is involved in multiple personality disorder, for instance).

37. Moreover, beliefs involved in the recognition of the evidence against P may likewise be inaccessible. For elaboration and argumentation, see McLaughlin, "Exploring the Possibility of Self-Deception in Belief."

38. M. Johnston, "Self-Deception and the Nature of Mind," 75.

39. Ibid., 65. The claim is also made by Mele, *Irrationality*, and McLaughlin, "Exploring the Possibility of Self-Deception in Belief."

40. M. Johnston, "Self-Deception and the Nature of Mind," 65. Johnston credits O'Shaughnassey with explicating the notion of a purposive but unintentional action. O'Shaughnassey speaks of "subintentional actions" which are purposive. See B. O'Shaughnassey, *The Will* (Cambridge: Cambridge University Press, 1981), vol. 2, chap. 10.

41. M. Johnston, "Self-Deception and the Nature of Mind," 65.

42. Davidson, "Deception and Division," 45.

43. McLaughlin, "Exploring the Possibility of Self-Deception in Belief," W. Ruddick, "Social Self-Deceptions" in McLaughlin and Rorty, *Perspectives*. The analogy between self-deception and being self-taught is Ruddick's.

44. I tried to offer an explanation of how self-deception is possible in "Exploring the Possibility of Self-Deception in Belief." However, whether I actually succeeded in giving a sufficient condition for self-deception depends on whether a self-deceiver must perform an act of deception. My conditions imply that a self-deceiver must have misled herself, but they do not imply that she must have intentionally misled herself. So, my conditions do not imply that a self-deceiver must have performed an act of deception. I tried to argue that intentional misleading is not required by appealing to the considerations discussed above about a self-deceiver not playing the full role of a deceiver.

45. As I mentioned (see note 20), there seems to be a continuum of cases from mere wishful thinking to self-deception, and I have found that intuitions vary on where on that continuum one reaches self-deception. Some hold that one reaches self-deception before there is any intentional misleading. As I said, I suspect that there is some indeterminacy in our common conception of self-deception.

46. Of course, some philosophers are interested in self-deception for other reasons. Some philosophers are interested in the implications of it for moral theory. (See S. Darwall, "Self-Deception and Duty Based Ethics" and M. Baron, "What is Wrong with Self-Deception?" in McLaughlin and Rorty, *Perspectives*.) But if self-deception is impossible, then it has no implications for moral theory.

47. In "Exploring the Possibility of Self-Deception in Belief," I tried to explain how a particularly problematic kind of self-deception is possible, one that involves the contradictory belief, albeit not the knowing-dupe condition.

48. I wish to thank Kent Bach and Al Mele for helpful comments.

TWO

THE VITAL BUT DANGEROUS ART OF IGNORING

Selective Attention and Self-Deception

Annette C. Baier

Any confident generalization about self-deception is bound to display metaself-deception, or at least an ignoring of some important cases. But a common form of self-deception seems to consist in a motivated forgetting of what, at an earlier point, we chose to ignore. In such cases ignoring turns into a sort of false ignorance, and the falsity of it is where the deception lies. Margaret Atwood, in her gripping and scary novel *The Handmaid's Tale,* reminds us of the difference between ignoring and being really ignorant: "We lived, as usual, by ignoring. Ignoring is not the same as ignorance, you have to work at it."[1] At least at first, one does have to work at ignoring, and it is cognitively important work, for example when one ignores the irregularities of the figure drawn on a board to represent a perfect circle, whose properties, not those of the irregular figure, are the ones one is concerned with. Ignoring is the same art as concentrating, seen from the side of what gets excluded from one's main focus of attention.

What one ignores are things one knows are there—the background chatter in a room where someone is talking to one, the weird facial distortions of the pianist whose hands are producing the wonderful music one is listening to, and so on. At times like these we ignore things that threaten to distract us from giving our full attention to some important matter; at other times we seek out distractions from supposedly important matters which we are choosing to escape from—we concentrate on the pattern of leaves or clouds outside the window and ignore the boring lecture that we continue to hear, and that maybe we could even give some sort of summary of later. We know what we are ignoring. As Atwood reminds us, to ignore something is not to maintain, let alone to produce, a state of ignorance about that thing—it is simply to refuse it the status of what we focus on, on the occasion when we ignore it. Later we may choose to focus on it, as we recall it, and we may choose to focus on our earlier ignoring of it. We may now highlight what we earlier pushed into the background.

Self and Deception

    This versatility of focus, this ability to obey the instruction "Ignore *x*, and concentrate on *y*," is not only a crucial cognitive ability, but also an important moral skill. When we are trying to achieve impartiality, we try to play down the sorts of facts that might bias our judgment in our own or our friends' favor. Hume writes that we "over-look" our own interest when we make a properly moral judgment about, say, the bravery of soldiers in the army of our current enemy.[2] We try to ignore the fact that their courage may lead to our own defeat, so as to be able to recognize it as courage, rather than to demote it to, say, ruthlessness. (Or, alternatively, we may recognize that what we are giving medals for, on our own side, is simply ruthlessness). To "over-look our own interest" is not to fail to realize where it lies, but rather to attempt not to bring that awareness into play in making our moral evaluation.

    John Rawls in *A Theory of Justice* calls what protects his reasoners in "the original position" from self-serving bias "the veil of ignorance," and some of the problems that critics have found in his account stem from this metaphor, suggesting as it does that real ignorance of where one's own particular interest lies is an appropriate idealization of what we try for in the real moral world, namely a conscious ignoring of our own special interests. Actual reasoners know, or think they know, where their own interest lies, and they are most unlikely to achieve ignorance of, say, whether they are men or women, when for example they do their moral reasoning about who should have the say about whether a woman terminates a pregnancy. They may try to ignore the fact that, as males, they will never experience pregnancy and the choices it presents. They might in theory succeed in ignoring that fact, though I doubt that they in fact often do succeed. We can realistically aim at ignoring or overlooking most bias-introducing factors, whereas it would be crazy to aim at becoming ignorant of them, even if we saw that as a real possibility, and just as crazy to regret knowing them. The morally ideal cases of ignoring will not even approximate to being or becoming ignorant.

    Our rational and moral arts of selective attention and inattention, of highlighting and of ignoring, can easily slip into pseudorational and morally dubious arts.[3] We risk self-deception whenever we engage, as we constantly do, in more or less voluntary sharpening of our mental focus on some matters, along with a consequent blurring of focus on others. Self-deception is the occupational danger of those capable of selective attention. I say "danger," since for the moment I will stick with the normal usage which takes deception to be morally dubious, and takes self-deception to be some sort of failure. But my interest is in the very thin line between what is an achievement, namely, keeping out of full mental view what it is reasonably judged for the moment best kept dark, or at least blurry, and what is usually a fault or a failure, namely, disowning one's own pushing of these things into obscurity, and so mistaking one's ignoring of them for one's ignorance of them. Self-deception is often the failure to achieve or to maintain consciousness of one's own successes at selective attention. It is then a disowning of one's own mental activities of overlooking and highlighting. Such disowning will be natural whenever it is some disreputable unconscious wish or fear that controls the focus of one's selective attention. One may notice only what one is on the watch for, while the rest of what one sees recedes into a blur and maybe eventually becomes lost to memory or lost to any recall except that assisted by some psychiatric expert. There is nothing especially paradoxical about the phenomenon of self-deception, when it can be seen as a motivated failure to attend to or to recall all of what one knows or once knew, as motivated failure to acknowledge one's own past highlighting and lowlighting of things that one knew. As Jorge Luis Borges' character Funes the Memorious finds out, forgetting, like sleeping, is something we need to be able to do. If what we forget is simply the clutter, the details that are of no special relevance for our main life concerns, either at the time we first knew them or later, then it will be healthy but uninteresting forgetting. If what we forget is what *did* have attention-grabbing power, but was pushed into the background out of escapism or some other form of wishful thinking, rather than because then was not the best time to attend to it, then the forgetting will be of more moral interest and will deserve the morally loaded label *self deception*. It will especially deserve it if we had to make an effort to ignore it at the time, since it presented some threat to our self-esteem, or to our sense of security, and if we have succeeded then and since in keeping it from painful attention, until others accuse us of turning a blind eye on it. For the accusation of self-deception is not usually, in the first instance, a self-accusation.

These phenomena, of sensible selective attention, of selective recall, of imperfect record keeping or cover-up of our own past selective control, are normal human phenomenology, both for individuals and for groups. Nations attend to some calls on their attention more than to others, write selective histories, and rewrite them as establishments and ideologies change. Also, social mechanisms of many kinds assist individuals in their individual self-deceptive activities, especially when these are coordinated with the maintenance of the preferred collective memory, that needed for a group's current self-esteem. War veterans' memories of what slaughter they participated in or witnessed may be uncomfortable memories both for them personally and for the national record. Psychiatric services help soothe and play down such memories as could be disruptive. In a free nation, the press, the film industry, and the book trade can serve as important curbs on this smoothing over of the blemishes on our shared past, can serve to revive uncomfortable memories and to stir up painful awareness of what we would understandably prefer to forget, or to continue to ignore. Of course they can equally serve to assist in the job of soothing and blurring. The skills needed to highlight overlooked facts are not so different from those needed to maintain the highlighting of selected facts, so that attention be diverted from others. Both skills are needed for any interpretation of complex data and for revision of past interpretations, for new looks and for reinterpretations.

Earlier I wrote of the arts of highlighting, lowlighting, ignoring, and forgetting as liable to become pseudorational arts. I take that term from Adrian Piper. In her paper, "Pseudorationality," she treats self-deception as a case where it is our near-rational capacities themselves that are at work, albeit in achieving "the illusion of rationality." The close-to-rational strategies that she takes the typical self-deceiver to employ are denial, dissociation, and rationalization, when these are used to protect a personal self-conception.[4] Her example is the self-conception of Sigismond in the novel *The Margin*, by André Pieyre de Mandiargues.[5] On Piper's interpretation, Sigismond believes himself to be lovable and loved by his younger, more vivacious wife, Sergine. Leaving wife and child in France, he travels from France to Barcelona to do some business for his cousin. On his arrival, he receives a letter from home, from his old servant. He opens it and reads enough to know that it reports the suicide of some woman who threw herself from a tower on his property. He reseals the letter, puts it aside on a table in his hotel room, and for two more days explores the city's red-light district, sleeping each evening with a pretty young Castilian prostitute, Juanita. Eventually, he reads the letter properly, learns that it is indeed his wife who has killed herself, after their little son's accidental death by drowning in a pond in their garden. He then shoots himself through the heart. As Piper interprets his series of reactions to the letter, they involve denial that he has received tragic news, during the days of distraction when he left the letter half-read, and also dissociation of himself from the letter—it becomes just part of the decor of his hotel room, lying on the table, weighted down by a glass bottle in the shape of the Colon (Columbus) tower. It is regularly seen, thought about, even caressed, but for two days not read. The denial and the dissociation are special to the time following the letter's arrival, but the rationalization needed during this time to sustain his half-belief that he has a loving wife,

that he is the centre and meaning of her life, is, as Piper interprets the
novel, merely a continuation of his long conscious or unconscious policy
of construing her mockery of him as a fact about her temperament, rather
than a sign of her lack of love for him. As Piper construes the novel,
Sergine's suicide makes it clear that it was her child, not her husband,
who gave central meaning to her life.[6] Sigismond's self-deception about
his role in her life is revealed for what it is, and he cannot bear the
realization. His self-conception as an adored and indulged husband, whose
faults were lovingly accepted, is effectively destroyed, and he then opts for
self-destruction.

Piper believes that the pseudorational strategies that we employ to
maintain our favored self-conceptions are aimed at what she calls "literal
self preservation," the preservation of the rational intelligibility of a version
of ourselves and our experience which is needed for self-conscious agency.
To lose one's self-conception does therefore threaten one's ability to continue as a self-conscious agent, one who has some acceptable story about
who she is and what she is doing. If self-deception is needed to keep one's
self-conception intact, then self-deception becomes a life-preserving skill.
The nonlethal alternative to it, Piper briefly suggests, is what she calls
"epistemic audacity," greater flexibility in revising self-conceptions, more
toughness in putting up with the shocks of periodic disturbances to one's
self-esteem, even putting up with "a little madness." We engage in self-deception, on her version of it, to the extent that we are "dogmatists" about
ourselves, unwilling to correct and update (and perhaps downgrade) our
self-conceptions. Had Sigismond had this audacity, he would presumably
have said to himself, "I never was the adored husband I took myself to be.
I was intending adultery here in Barcelona. I was a neglectful father, and an
escapist self-deceiver. So be it. And now I must either settle for becoming
a merry widower (after a due period of mourning) or else (perhaps after a
brief madness), try to change my self-indulgent ways. But I can go on." He
apparently was not flexible about living with a revised, updated self-conception, nor able to keep his old self-deceptive self-conception going
(by, say, attributing "a little madness" to his wife, a temporary but lethal
insanity brought on by the shock of her son's drowning, perhaps by guilt
that she had been so absorbed in her book that she had let her little son play
too near the water).

Piper's account of the near-rationality of the typical self-deceptive
strategies, their link with our self-consciousness and need for a self-conception, for some version of what we are doing that coherently relates
it to what we have previously done, is in line with many other recent

analyses of self-deception that emphasize its positive role and near-rational methods, rather than just the reasons why we do not give it full rational or moral marks. After all, if the alternative to self-deception can be a little madness, or be self-destruction, we surely cannot be content to classify it, as Pears[7] and Davidson[8] do, as necessarily a form of irrationality (unless we think that there are rational madnesses, and rational suicides. And those of us who do think that suicide can be rational would reasonably hesitate to take Sigismond's suicide, construed as Piper construes it, as a good example of suicide for good enough reasons.). As Amélie Rorty puts it, given the choice between being unable to retain the capacities that are exercised in self-deception, and being prey to self-deception, "one might well and even perhaps rationally choose to retain the capacities."[9]

Rorty takes the relevant capacities to be self-manipulation in situations of indeterminacy ("I can do it!"), and the strong conservation of beliefs and motives in the face of some reason to suspect them. ("Let us not be too hasty in thinking we have disconfirmation of our theory. The testube may have been dirty.") What Piper calls "denial," "dissociation," and "rationalization" are all procedures often used in conserving some theory from threatening counter-evidence. We "deny" when we refuse to attend to the awkward data, when we act on the hope that later data will cancel the force of the unwelcome data, often using some self-manipulation to sustain this hope. We "dissociate" when we simply put aside, under some mental paperweight, the data that we choose not yet to attend to, treating it as not our current concern. We "rationalize" when we invent Ptolomaic explanations to accommodate awkward data that is forced on our attention. We may rationalize our earlier denials and dissociations as warranted postponements and sensibly selective attention. Piper's three strategies are all typically used by the strong belief conserver, who is very close to what Piper calls the "dogmatist." Belief conservation, even in the face of some apparently recalcitrant evidence, is not an irrational strategy, but a part of normal scientific procedure, what Adam Morton calls scientific "partisanship,"[10] commitment to a theory and its research program. As Piper sees the matter, it is precisely in order to hang on to some account that makes the world and one's role in it "rationally intelligible" that one resorts to the ploys of self-deception. She may exaggerate when she writes that "we cannot possibly make rationally intelligible everything that happens to us, or everything that we feel and do, without threatening the coherence of what we *do* think we understand rationally,"[11] but it takes an unusually benign life experience (or else unusually low standards of rational intelligibility) to avoid what Piper sees as the "necessity" of resorting to pseudorationality. We need very good luck, or very low ambitions as understanders and self-understanders if we are to avoid having to make do with something less than perfect rationality. Pseudorationality is the saving consolation of would-be rational animals who are fairly well equipped to understand the world they are part of, but not perfectly so, particularly when it comes to understanding their own motives and aspirations. We have only finite depth of mental field and fallible memories for our own past decisions about what to leave for sharper focus later.

René Descartes wrote very interestingly about deception and self-deception[12] long before the rush of twentieth-century attention to this topic, and what he writes indicates that he was well aware of the positive epistemological and moral role that selective attention, bordering on judicious self-deception, could play. He may not have been as well aware of their dangers. Indeed, a case can be made for the charge that he succumbed to the dangers inherent in the self-conscious employment of these techniques of deliberately putting some matters out of mental sight. For he may be accused of forgetting or repressing the memory that this is what he had done, purportedly for a particular purpose and for a limited time, with the avowed original intention of eventually going back and rescuing from inattention the matters that he had deliberately put on mental hold. This Cartesian venture in self-manipulation is instructive for us, both to illustrate the cognitive and moral gains of selective attention and inattention and to show their risks.

In the *First Meditation,* after producing a series of progressively stronger reasons for not resting full confidence in the beliefs that he had naturally (and by the natural influence of his native culture?) come to have, the meditator concluded that doubt was the appropriate response for him then to adopt toward these now-suspect beliefs. Doubt, not rejection. But because he fears that his old habits of belief will prove too strong for him to succeed in maintaining a doubting attitude to all the impugned beliefs (virtually all the beliefs he took himself to have had), he instead deliberately changes the outcome of his doubt-inducing reasonings. Instead of regarding all these beliefs as doubtful, he will deliberately regard them as false, until any of them get established as certain truths. "I think it will be a good plan to turn my will in completely the opposite direction, and deceive myself, by pretending for a time that these former opinions are utterly false and imaginary. I shall do this until the weight of preconceived opinion is counterbalanced, and the distorting force of habit no longer prevents me from perceiving things correctly. In the meantime, I know that no danger or error will result from my plan, and that I cannot possibly go too far in my distrustful attitude. This is because the task in hand does not involve action, but merely the acquisition of knowledge."[13]

This famous passage sets for us many of the puzzles that have dominated later literature on self-deception. Does it make a difference if the matter in hand is practical or not?[14] Can one coherently resolve to let oneself be deceived by oneself? An open-eyed adoption of a "let's pretend" strategy, for a limited time and for a particular purpose, surely is anything but deception; it seems to involve an attempt to be quite honest, to evade nothing, to enter into the record just what one is doing and why. Should Descartes' meditator have used the word *deceive* here at all? Pretence need not be false pretence, if control is kept and if the announcement, "This is a deliberate pretence," is so clearly made. It is no more a deception, surely, than an actor would deceive himself and his audience if he gets really inside a part that he is playing, such as that of Othello, or of Hamlet. We may willingly suspend our disbelief that he really has the character of the Moor, or of the Dane, but we are not therefore deceived. We can keep apart the question, Who is that? to which the right answer is Othello, and the other question, Who is that? whose right answer may be Olivier. So we may read Descartes' *First Meditation* words about intending to deceive himself as a bit of rhetorical hype, replacing them with blander words about his intending to suppose, for a limited time, that certain claims, those whose truth is not yet known to him, are in fact claims that he has reason to deny.

But we will soon be halted in this smoothing out of what Descartes wrote. We will be given pause by subsequent moves even within the *First Meditation*. For, having said that he will deceive himself, Descartes' meditator then shifts (or reverts) to supposing that someone else is trying to deceive him—an evil genius. Is this a special bit of the intended self-deceit— the particular self-deception that one has reason to suspect that one is the intended victim of another's deception? Or is it a less intended dissociation of the deceiving intent in himself, a displacement of the will to deceive onto an alien will? And what are we to make of the last sentence of the *First Meditation*, where the state of "deception" by the forces responsible for one's precritical ordinary beliefs is said to be an agreeable state of imaginary liberty, a state which one conspires with the deceiver to prolong? The meditating "I" is at one point the purposeful (self-)deceiver, then the victim of an alien would-be deceiver, trying self-deceptive counter-ploys in order to outwit him, then finally the conspirator with the successful alien deceiver, afraid to awake from agreeable worldly illusion into the excessive darkness of wakeful critical undeluded consciousness.

In the *Second Meditation*, we read, "I have no senses and no body,"[15] as the pretend version of what is really warranted, namely, "I am not yet really sure that I have senses and a body," and other such not fully serious denials. In that *Meditation* the pretence is acknowledged as a deliberate strategy, but what is worrisome is that in the later *Meditations* it is neither acknowledged nor ever declared officially to be over.

In the above summary, I have in fact oversimplified the shifts in the roles of deceiver and deceived within the *First Meditation,* by omitting the first charge of deception, levied against the senses when they mislead us about the shape of very small or distant objects, and the later worry over the possibility that the all-powerful God, belief in whose existence had long been fixed in the meditator's mind, might allow him to be deceived, might as it were authorize his deception, by encouraging his self-deception by his senses or his free will, or by empowering some powerful deceiving force external to him. Indeed it is this possibility, that the power of God lies behind the forces that could deceive the meditator, which leads him to the near all-encompassing doubt that he sets out to preserve through the extreme measure of his deliberate pretence that he has reasons not merely for doubt but for denial of all his former beliefs. So he invents the imaginary, powerful nondivine deceiver to keep alive his uncertainty concerning God's responsibility for any state of deception that he may have been or have come to be in. This occasion for his strategy might suggest that the deliberate pretence that the doubtful beliefs are known-to-be-false beliefs should come to its end the moment the meditator proves that God is not a deceiver (namely, at the end of the *Third* or the beginning of the *Fourth Meditation*). In fact, however, there is no such announcement, no official reinstation of all the original pretend-denied beliefs to the status of "highly probable opinions," no explicit dropping of the moral myth of the to-be-outwitted evil genius. There is simply silence about the demon and the counterdemon denials. There seems to have been a forgetting that a morality play was supposedly in progress, needing some curtain to drop to signal its ending.

What is more, the fear of deception seems to persist right to the end of the *Meditations*. Immediately after establishing that God is not a deceiver, the meditator faces the worry of God's involvement in his human errors, in the false beliefs of the finite meditator who depends upon God. Late in the *Sixth Meditation* "true errors of nature,"[16] in the form of dropsical thirsts and phantom limb experiences, are acknowledged to occur. "Notwithstanding the immense goodness of God, the nature of man, as a combination of mind and body, is such that it is bound to mislead him from time to time."[17] God's free decree lies behind this inevitably self-misleading human nature, behind this fact of our embodiment, and our imperfect moment-by-moment information about the needs and condition of the bodies with which our souls are so closely intermingled as to form "a unit."[18] The *Meditations* end with apparent resignation to "the weakness of our nature." In the earlier discussion of whether an all-powerful God could possibly be a deceiver, deception had been closely linked with weakness (as well as with subtlety and cleverness), so the final resignation may include resignation to some inevitable self-deception.

Do the *Meditations* demonstrate (in the sense of "exemplify") deception and self-deception? One of the earliest criticisms made of Descartes' dualism of the mind and the body of his proof that "I am really distinct from my body," was that of Mersenne, in the *Second Set of Objections.* He wrote that the "vigorous rejection of the images of all bodies as delusive was not something you actually and really carried through but merely a fiction of the mind enabling you to draw the conclusion that you were exclusively a thinking thing. We point this out in case you should perhaps suppose that it is possible to go on to draw the conclusion that you are in fact nothing more than a mind, or a thinking thing."[19] Descartes in reply points out that it was not until the essence of body had been shown to be intellectually comprehensible spatial extension, in the *Fifth,* and the essences or natures of body and of mind compared, in the *Sixth,* that the real distinction of himself as a thinker from any body was inferred. But Mersenne's implicit gentle charge, that what began as a "fiction" had not been clearly concluded as a fiction, and so the transition from pretend denials of the (in fact) doubtful to serious denials of the false had not been clearly signaled within the *Meditations*—this still stands unanswered. Gassendi and Bourdin, in the *Fifth* and *Seventh Sets of Objections,* are less gentle. Gassendi suggests that Descartes' policy amounts to adopting a new prejudice, rather than relinquishing old prejudices, and says that critics will accuse Descartes of artifice and sleight of hand.

Both Arnauld in the *Fourth Set of Objections* and Gassendi in the *Fifth Set of Objections* join Mersenne in querying the move from "I can know I am a thinking thing without yet knowing whether I am an extended thing, that is, while pretend-denying that I have a body," to "I know I am a thinking and unextended thing," which is what is asserted in the *Sixth Meditation* proof of the real distinctness of mind and body. Now if Descartes in fact makes this move from "I could be and was certain I was a thinker while still uncertain that I had a body, that is while I was pretend-denying that I had a body, as a counter-ploy to any powerful beings who might be trying to deceive me into uncritical belief that I did have a body," to "I am certain that I am a thinker who does not need (even if he in fact has) a body in order to be a thinker," then he has indeed taken himself in, has done what he said he intended to do, deceived himself. For he has confused his pretend denials, those of the *Second Meditation,* with serious denials, those needed for the reasoning of the *Sixth* to succeed. He seems to have forgotten that his denials are untrustworthy, or rather that some of them need decoding.

What happens in the *Fourth Meditation* muddies the waters still further, for there the meditator adopts a rule which, while it would restrain the urge to deny as much as it restrained the urge to affirm anything that was not yet clear and distinct to intellect, gives no permission to recognize any distinction between what is "highly probable" (in the words of the *First Meditation*, "more reasonable to affirm than to deny"), and what is conceivably possible. Suspense of judgment is what is decreed for all less-than-certain claims. This may be the point at which the policy of exaggerating doubts into denials is in fact ended by being forbidden, and the spectre of the evil deceiving genius implicitly declared to have been successfully exorcised. But this ending and this exorcism are implicit only.[20] A note to the effect that "Up till now some of my apparent denials ('It is not the case that . . . ') have really had the force 'I do not (yet) know that . . . ,' but from now on all my denials are real denials," would have helped the reader, and perhaps the meditator too, to keep cognitive track of what has been and is going on. We really need to go through the *Meditations,* from the announcement of the intention to deny whatever there is any good reason to doubt onward, subscripting each negative claim with either a *p* for *pretend,* or an *s* for *serious.* And we might have some difficulty sorting the negative claims, especially those that the *Fourth Meditation* is packed with. Perhaps the demon was exorcised by the end of the *Third,* rather than later when God is freed of responsibility for human error at the end of the *Fourth.* Is the meditator still counteracting his former, too hasty assents with exaggerated dissents during the *Fourth Meditation's* reasonings about the explanation of human error? Might the *Fourth's* denial of any epistemic justification for assenting to what is highly probable be itself only a pretend denial, taken back in the *Sixth,* when "the exaggerated doubts of the last few days" are dismissed as "laughable"? (The meditator then adopts the policy of risking error, as long as it is corrigible error, in place of his former method of taking extreme measures to avoid ever having to correct himself.) We do not know how to answer such questions, since we are not told clearly just when the meditator stopped his methodological play acting, when all his nays became real.

In the light of recent literature, what is especially interesting about Descartes' treatment of the would-be rational person's reaction to the recognition of the real possibility of deception and of self-deception, is the fact that his mediator turns his self-deceptive (or *possibly* self-deceptive) skills onto some of the very cognitive operations that constitute these skills—in particular on denial and dissociation. What he sets out to do is precisely to dissociate himself from his possibly deceiving senses, which he knows all

Self and Deception

along are "one unit" with his intellect and his will. He achieves this dissociation, this putting of his own living body to one side for a few days, by a special sort of self-conscious pseudodenial, by saying "I have no body" ("I am not awake," "Two and three are not five," "There is no earth, no heavens,"), instead of saying what he knows himself warranted to say: "I am not yet certain that I have a body and so on, but I have better reasons to affirm than to deny it." He denies what he has better reason to affirm, telling himself that this is a good idea, since his reasons for affirming are not yet good enough, that his habit-dominated will to affirm needs some contrived counterwill if it is to be resisted. He concocts an unwarranted denier to balance a not-sufficiently warranted affirmer of these commonsensical claims. He effectively denies the normal force of a denial.

Dissociation occurs often, and perhaps the most striking metadissociation occurs during the *Second Meditation* when, immediately after the successful separation of thinking from life, after "I am not that structure of limbs which is called a human body," we get: "And yet may it not perhaps be the case that the very things which I am supposing to be nothing, because they are unknown to me, are in reality identical with the 'I' of which I am aware? I do not know, and for the moment I shall not argue the point."[21] Here the agnostic, controlling, self-conscious pretender dissociates himself from the self-certain negative thinker who is still denying embodiment, as he later dissociates himself from the different part of his mind which is given "free rein" in the examination of the piece of wax.

Does his deliberate self-deception take as its subject matter not only his intended denials and dissociations, in the subsequent meditations, but also his reason-giving there? Is there intentional metarationalization, as well as intentional metadenial and metadissociation? There is of course no doubt that the whole of the *Meditations* takes as its question what the reasons are to take certain things (sense perception, memory, clear and distinct intellectual perception, mathematical constructibility and demonstrability) as good enough reasons for one's beliefs. And the uncritical believer who lets "the weight of preconceived opinion" serve as rational weight might be said to have been decreed to be a rationalizer, one who is too accepting of not-good-enough reasons. What is not so clear is whether all the reasoning used in counteracting this natural sloppy believer in one's breast is itself taken to be of the highest standards of rationality. When, for example, it is asserted in the *Fourth Meditation* that when one affirms or denies what is not clear and distinct one is not using one's free will correctly, that the only good reasons for assent are absolutely compelling reasons ("a great light in the intellect followed by a great inclination of the will"), the reason that is given for this conclusion is that this will be a reliable way to avoid error. But should the avoidance of error be one's overriding cognitive aim? At the very end of the *Fourth* we get a hint of what the *Sixth* makes clear, that the answer in fact is no. Avoidance of error is distinguished from gaining of truths: "Today I have learned not only what precautions to take to avoid ever going wrong, but also what to do to arrive at the truth. For I shall unquestionably reach the truth, if only I give sufficient attention to all the things which I perfectly understand, and separate these from all the other cases where my apprehension is more confused and obscure. And this is just what I shall take care to do from now on."[22] "Separating" these two sorts of cases need not involve refusing any sort of assent to the slightly indistinct, and in the *Sixth Meditation* a new revised rule is adopted which effectively cancels the over-cautious rule adopted in the *Fourth*. A policy of error correction is adopted, wherever the policy of super-cautious error avoidance would be ruinous in its epistemic costs (that is, in all judgments about particular bodies). The fact that God is not a deceiver is now to be taken to mean not that one can, if one tries, avoid all error, but rather the "impossibility of there being any falsity in my opinions that cannot be corrected by some other faculty supplied to me by God."[23] We now are encouraged to dismiss the exaggerated doubts of the earlier meditations as "laughable" and to content ourselves with our ability to detect and correct our sometimes inevitable errors, to use all our faculties, "all the senses as well as my memory and intellect" in order to verify our naturally fallible truth claims. The way the *Meditations* ends does not seem to amount to a retrospective correction of the purportedly sound epistemic conclusions drawn earlier. Yet they were there quite deliberately drawn. So if the last word on what we have good reasons to assent to carries most authority, then some of the earlier conclusions were not sufficiently strongly supported and so may count as deliberate rationalizations or half truths about how to get truth, rather than as good reasons for firm conclusions concerning good reasons. Some of the earlier epistemological certainties, as well as earlier doubts, become laughable.

I have reminded us of this famous stretch of selective attention, of the Cartesian ploy that is advertised as deliberate self-deception, because it displays both the attractions and the risks of these mental manoeuvres. It displays the fact that what begins as justifiable ignoring of certain matters can end as confusion about what exactly was and is known and when it became known. It displays the fact that selective attention to matters of any type most typically becomes self-deception when the selective attention is directed to facts about oneself and one's doings. If not always, at least very often, "self deception involves deception of the self, by the self, for or about the self."[24] When the meditator ignores all beliefs except those that he can know with certainty, he is not thereby deceiving himself into thinking that those ignored beliefs are false. But when he ignores the fact that this was his announced deliberate strategy, supposedly for a definite limited time, and leaves it a matter of doubt when the strategy is completed and finished with, then the charge of self-deceit becomes appropriate. All self-deceit invites self-deceit about oneself. That is one way in which it may differ from plain deceit. Ordinary deceit often does include deceiving the victim about the belief state of deceiver, but it is not necessary that it do so, nor is it necessary that the deceiver takes herself in. A clever deceiver will avoid not merely outright lies, but even any sort of direct or indirect commitment to false claims about what she herself believes. One way to deceive you into believing that my feelings for you are stronger than they in fact are would be to express worries of the form Do I care enough? Am I perhaps undeserving of your love? I count on your plausibly supposing that a really uncaring person would not have or voice such worries, and so be reassured, and deceived, by my speaking this way. Suppose a person repeatedly expresses suicidal wishes to her family, and eventually acts on them, having counted on the sheer repetition to induce a dismissal of the seriousness of any one such announcement, so that she can be left free of any restraining measures, left free to do what she intends. Does she deceive her family about her state of mind? She misleads them about what she will in fact do, precisely by the frequency of her announcements. Crying wolf for weeks before the wolf arrives is a good ploy for the wolf's inside man to employ. Telling the truth, in this case about what one believes that one wants and intends, can be the best deceptive strategy. For we communicate, and we deceive, not just by what we do and do not say, but by why, when, and how often we say it. But such a strategy would not work for the self-deceiver.

Self-deceit has important differences from plain deceit (even if they are not sharp enough differences to make the term into what William Ruddick calls a "pseudo reflexive,"[25] like "self-instruction"). One of these distinctive features is its tendency to confuse itself with plain deceit. Descartes' moves from "My senses have deceived me," to "Perhaps a powerful God is deceiving me," to "It will be a good idea to deceive myself for a while," to "I will suppose that a malicious demon is out to deceive me, so deny whatever may be being suggested to me by him or her" involve this slippage from deceit by part of oneself, to deceit by another, to deliberate self-deceit, and back again to deceit by another, perhaps one with whom one may be oneself conspiring. There is a tendency to disown the role of deceiver, to project it outside oneself, but equally a tendency to prefer being deceiver to being deceived. Descartes' meditator is torn between pride in the cleverness needed to carry a deception through successfully, and shame that he needed to resort to such tactics to outwit any who might be exploiting his weakness. He alternately claims and disclaims the deceiving role. To be merely the deceived is unequivocal weakness. To be a self-deceiver is at least to call the tune, to show some power, to exhibit some cleverness.

The temporal stretch of the action of the *Meditations* is ideal for displaying the sort of alienation of one's past self and some of its intentions that helps to explain how many cases of self-deception come about. Many contemporary discussions (Pears,[26] Davidson,[27] Wood[28]) struggle to find in the self-deceiving person two contemporaneous psychic "systems," one duping the other. This may occasionally happen, but surely the more common cases involve the passing of time and, as Pears recognizes, the complicity of selective memory. With good reason does Descartes at the beginning of the *Second Meditation* refer to his lying memory,[29] for if his project of pretending that everything that he can doubt is in fact false is to really amount to a project of deceiving himself, he will have to have the help of convenient forgettings. It is because both our cognitive and our practical projects do typically take time, and that memory can heighten and dim its spotlight differently at different times, that it is so easy to seem to produce multiple temporary selves out of one persistent complex self. So it is easy to find something like the structure of deception of one person by another within the temporal stretch of one person. And something a bit like that structure can surely be there.

Harry Frankfurt, in *Demons, Dreamers, and Madmen*,[30] suggests that Descartes treats his relationship to himself at earlier times as if it were the relationship of one thinker to other thinkers; that he displaces the problems of trust between different thinkers onto a supposed problem of trust for one's own earlier clear and distinct perceptions, of acceptance today of the conclusions proved yesterday (a problem supposedly solved for the theist but insoluble to the atheist). Since there is no community of ordinary human thinkers explicitly recognized in the *Meditations*, not even as a partial source of those commonsense beliefs on which doubt is cast in the *First Meditation*, the only way that the question of trust can arise is either as a question of the meditator's relation to supernatural beings, gods or demons, or as a matter of self-trust, trust by the meditator of his own past findings (and of his memory of them), or of one part of himself, say intellect, or intellect-guided will, for another part, such as the senses. We might choose to read his musings on self-trust, trust of earlier selves, and trust of the senses, as displaced discussions of really interpersonal trust and distrust, of pupils for teachers, of citizens for governors, of lay persons for the church and its spokesmen, and so on. But we can just as plausibly read the discussions of reasons for trust or distrust of powerful gods and powerful demons as also discussions of trust and distrust for various powers within the individual psyche. The meditator's preferred idea of God is generated by looking toward the unreachable limit of the powers that he himself aspires to and finds himself possessing to a finite but increasing degree. Demons, correlatively, will be taken to exemplify qualities such as malice, which one may acknowledge that one does possess, but scarcely aspires to have more of. When it comes to the power to deceive, to take control of a mind and shape it in such a way that one remains superior to it, knowing more than it knows, Descartes and his meditator are ambivalent: "The ability to deceive appears to be a mark of cleverness or power, the will to deceive . . . of malice and weakness."[31] A weak will is the last thing that Descartes' meditator appears to fear that he has—his boast is that his free will, or power of choice, is so great that not even God's will could be greater "when considered as will in the strict and essential sense" (i.e., distinguished from power and knowledge). It is his intellect that he finds to be weak and finite. So, inasfar as he has aspirations for improvement, they will include aspirations to grow in intellectual subtlety and cleverness, thus in ability to deceive. Whether or not he chooses to use this improved ability will depend upon his will, on what his goals are at particular stages along his way. From the internal evidence of the *Meditations,* Descartes' will to deceive the reader cannot be entirely ruled out. The will to deceive himself for a while, in a supposedly good cause, was avowed by Descartes' meditator early on and never explicitly disavowed. The final self-description we get from him is of an embodied thinker whose Godgiven nature inevitably includes a source of deception and of self-deception. So it may well be that, far from declaring the temporary self-deception over, the meditator ends by accepting his deceiving and self-deceiving nature for what it is, resigned to the fact that when we are self-deceived we will not at that moment know that we are, however clear we may have been at earlier points that self-deception was then our aim, and however clear we may later be that we succeeded, for a while, in that aim. We may end by acknowledging both the cleverness and the only limited success of our self-deceptive strategies. Or did the overseeing[32] one, who was to decide how long the self-deception ideally should continue, himself fall victim to the deception? Did the original plan include or accept this? Does the pseudo denier get caught in his own toils when he tries to say "Enough, let my nays no longer be fake nays," leaving us all in persistent doubt as to when, in the *Meditations,* we are supposed to be in doubt and when in rational or less rational denial? Was this metadoubt perhaps the intended outcome?

Until the *Objections,* Descartes' self-deceiver has no human friend to remind him of what he set out to do, and of the need to declare an ending to the time when his denials may be only pretend denials. He supposedly has God on his side, but not a God who intervenes to remind him of unfinished business. For that he has only his possibly lying memory—and of course his written record. However, even if this record is re-read by its author, it no more serves the purpose that watchful co-meditating friends could have served than the clock that struck four, but was heard as defectively striking one o'clock four times,[33] succeeds in telling its hearer what the time is. An enemy, or at least a partly hostile acquaintance like Bourdin, might be even better than a friend like Mersenne for this vital monitoring purpose, but only if one could share one's self-deceptive intentions with that enemy. Once we do take the fact that we have watchful acquaintances noting any apparent discrepancies between what we announce we will do and what we go on to do, we soon see that the chances for sustained, rationally motivated self-deception in the real world are not great. Only if our fellows have the same motives for the very same deception that we have, so that there is concerted selective forgetting as well as concerted selective attention, will they fail to correct most of our self-deceptions. Normally, the selectivity and bias of one person's memory gets corrected by the different selectivity of her fellows' memory. Normally there *are* "objections" to reply to. One needs to retire from the human world if one really wants sustained success in personal self-deceptions.

Usually, rationalization and self-deception concur with wishful thinking. Piper's version of Pieyre de Mandiargues' Sigismond wanted to believe that he was the meaning of his loving wife's life. (He was engaged in what Piper calls "self aggrandisement," which is typical of the self-deceiver.) Wishful thinking need not be satisfying only hedonic forms of self-promotion. Hume noted that "a person of a sorrowful and melancholy disposition is very credulous of every thing that nourishes his prevailing passion."[34] Prevailing passions need not be pleasure-bent. But it is not so easy to see what ruling passion might be served by the questionable rationality of many of the meditator's moves in Descartes' *Meditations*. Is it that he wants, above all, to think of himself as an immortal soul? He seems just as strongly if not more strongly to want to think of himself as "one unit" of body-soul, an intelligent self-controlled interpreter of the sensory data that he needs in order to form his scientific views about the earth, the heavens, living bodies, human health, automata, light, and rainbows. So why the elaborate self-deceptions? What self-conception do they serve and protect? The self-conception of one who can be both a pious if unorthodox believer in the church's doctrines and also a scientist? The self-conception of a very clever person who was pretty sure he could outwit any merely human adversaries, so he thought he could afford to "go masked" without fear of inviting uncomfortable unmaskings? Or just someone very interested in deception and self-deception and trying to explore these human capacities the cleverest and subtlest way he knew how?[35]

Amélie Rorty has written that, since self-deception presents severe problems for certain theories of rational agency, there has been "an astonishing exercise in philosophic self deception in denying the phenomena, redescribing them in ways that preserve the theories they jeopardize,"[36] but Descartes stands as an equally astonishing example of the reverse philosophical exercise, of taking self-deception as both theme and avowed method, and maybe succeeding better than he really intended in showing us what it is, what we risk by engaging in it, and what we would risk were we to try at all costs to avoid it. Who is to know who is the more self-deceived, the philosopher who purports to find self-deception a paradox, or the Cartesian (on this interpretation) who purports to accept the inevitability of self-deception, the superior rationality of learning to live with it, and of milking it for all it can yield? Even if self-deception is, as I have agreed that it is, no paradox but part of normal life, and something that most of us, helped by our critics, can find in our lives if we look back (and with the aid of sterner critics find also in the present), there still remains some paradox in avowed current and future self-deception. Descartes challenges us to ponder the rationality of the decision that it will be a good plan to deceive oneself for some indeterminate period of time from this time on, to ponder the success of his meditator's implementation of his plan, and to ponder the criteria for judging its success.

The recent Western philosophical literature on self-deception displays very nicely the near-inevitability of selective attention. Some of us choose to attend to the closeness of the self-deceiver's typical ploys to the defining characteristics of rational procedure. Others of us select to attend to how the self-deceiver falls short of perfect rationality (and perhaps of moral ideals such as honesty[37] and integrity). Neither group usually ignores the other side of the story, we simply play it down a bit. So Descartes may have started a fashion when he wrote about self-deception in a way that exhibits the skills it needs and risks exemplifying the thing itself.

NOTES

1. Margaret Atwood, *The Handmaid's Tale* (New York: Ballantyne Books, 1985), 74.

2. David Hume, *A Treatise of Human Nature*, ed. L. A. Selby-Bigge and P. H. Nidditch (Oxford: Clarendon Press, 1975), 582.

3. For a subtle exploration of the links between the rational and the self-deceptive arts, see Rebecca Holsen, "Self-Deception, Reason, and Fiction," unpublished Ph.D. dissertation, University of Pittsburgh, 1984.

4. Adrian Piper, "Pseudorationality" in *Perspectives on Self Deception* ed. Brian P. McLaughlin and Amélie Rorty (Berkeley: University of California Press, 1988). "Denial" in this sense perhaps has as its paradigm case St. Peter's denial, that favourite theme of painters in Descartes' lifetime.

5. André Pieyre de Mandiargues, *The Margin*, trans. from the French by Richard Howard (New York: Grove Press, 1969) (winner in 1967 of the Prix Guncourt).

6. On my reading, Sigismond's despair is actually more naturally taken as refusal of life without his adored wife, rather than shock at the significance of her suicide for his self-conception. But for our purposes, I will pretend to agree with Piper's interpretation. For my own interpretation of this fine novel, see "How to Get to Know One's Own Mind: Some Simple Ways," in *Philosophy in Mind*, ed. Michaelis Michael and John O'Leary-Hawthorne (Dordrecht: Kluwer, 1994): 65–82.

7. David Pears, *Motivated Irrationality* (Oxford: Clarendon Press, 1984); "The Goals and Strategies of Self Deception," in *The Multiple Self*, ed. Jon Elster (New York: Cambridge University Press, 1986), 59–77.

8. Donald Davidson, "Paradoxes of Irrationality," in *Philosophical Essays on Freud*, ed. R. A. Wollheim and J. Hopkins (New York: Cambridge University Press, 1982); "Deception and Division," in Elster, 79–92.

9. Amélie O. Rorty, "Self-Deception, *Akrasia*, and Irrationality," in Elster, 125.

10. Adam Morton, "Partisanship," in *Perspectives on Self Deception*, ed. Brian P. McLaughlin and Amélie O. Rorty (Berkeley: University of California Press, 1988), 170–82.

11. Adrian Piper, "Pseudorationality," 298.

12. André Gombay, in "Lying, Now and Then: Descartes and the Ethics of Deceit," unpublished book mss., ch. 1, refers to the popularity of the topic of deceit among Descartes' contemporaries. Arnauld was expelled from the Sorbonne for his views on St. Peter's denial, and that denial was a favorite subject for painters such as de la Tour and Rembrandt.

13. *The Philosophical Writings of Descartes*, vol. 2, trans. John Cottingham, Robert Stoothoff, Dugald Murdoch (New York: Cambridge University Press, 1984), 15 (this volume will henceforth be referred to as C.S.M.); vol. 7, trans. Adam and Tannery, 22 (henceforth A.T.).

14. Robert Audi begins his discussion of "Self Deception, Rationalisation and Reasons for Acting," in McLaughlin and Rorty, 92–120, by drawing a similar distinction, and takes "states" rather than "acts" of self-deception as primary.

15. C.S.M., 16, A.T., 24.

16. Ibid., 59, A.T., 85.

17. Ibid., 61, A.T., 88.

18. Ibid., 56, A.T., 81.

19. Ibid., 87, A.T., 122.

20. It might be taken to have occurred earlier, at C.S.M., 37, A.T., 53, when the meditator says, "I now have no difficulty in turning my mind away from imaginable things, and towards things that are the object of intellect alone."

21. C.S.M., 18, A.T., 27.

22. Ibid., 43, A.T., 62.

23. Ibid., 56, A.T., 80.

24. Amélie O. Rorty, "Self-Deception, *Akrasia* and Irrationality," in Elster, 125. Rorty seems to have changed her mind about this as indicated in her chapter in this volume.

25. See William Ruddick, "Social and Self-Deceptions," in McLaughlin and Rorty, 380–89, esp. 384–85.

26. David Pears, *Motivated Irrationality;* "The Goals and Strategies of Self Deception," in Elster, 59–77.

27. Donald Davidson, "Paradoxes of Irrationality," in *Philosophical Essays on Freud;* "Deception and Division," in Elster, 79–92.

28. Allen W. Wood, "Self-Deception and Bad Faith," in McLaughlin and Rorty, 207–27.

29. C.S.M., 16, A.T., 24.

30. Harry G. Frankfurt, *Demons, Dreamers, and Madmen* (Indianapolis and New York: Bobbs-Merrill, 1970), 169.

31. C.S.M., 37, A.T., 53.

32. Our words and their history are revealing. To "oversee" originally was to fail to see, while to "overlook" was to achieve a higher viewpoint, a more panoramic one. (This is Hume's sense.) But now to oversee is to take charge, make sure nothing is overlooked (in the new pejorative sense). "Oversight," however, retains the old bad meaning of overseeing. So now we can almost say the reason we have overseers is to prevent oversights.

33. The example is Bourdin's, in *The Seventh Set of Objections* to Descartes' *Meditations.* C.S.M., 306, A.T., 437.

34. Hume, *Treatise,* 120.

35. I am much indebted, for my understanding of Descartes' near-obsession with deception, to André Gombay, "Lying, Now and Then: Descartes and the Ethics of Deceit."

36. Rorty, "Self Deception, *Akrasia,* and Irrationality," in Elster, 115.

37. See my "Why Honesty Is a Hard Virtue," in *Identity, Character and Morality: Essays in Moral Psychology,* ed. O. Flanagan and A. Rorty (Cambridge, MA: MIT Press, 1990), 259–82.

THREE
USER-FRIENDLY SELF-DECEPTION
A Traveler's Manual

Amélie Oksenberg Rorty

I

Since many varieties of self-deception are ineradicable and useful, it would be wise to be ambivalent about at least some of its forms.[1] It is open-eyed ambivalence that acknowledges its own dualities rather than ordinary shifty vacillation that we need. To be sure, self-deception remains dangerous: sensible ambivalence should not relax vigilance against pretence and falsity, combating irrationality and obfuscation wherever they occur.

The animus against self-deception has an honorable origin: the motto Know Thyself was inextricably linked to the Socratic enlightenment project, to the systematic critical examination of belief, its clarification and justification.[2] But the dangers of self-deception were nevertheless magnified by those who misunderstood the fundamental conviction of the later Enlightenment that we shall know the truth, and the truth will make us free. Because the narrow and naive interpretations of that project assigned a central role to self-consciousness and self-knowledge in the complex tasks of liberation through knowledge, self-deception seemed threatening to the primary tasks of rational inquiry. The denial of a systematic tendency toward various forms of irrationality, to self-deception, akrasia, and the conservation of emotions is, in effect, the Enlightenment's attack on the epistemological remnants of the doctrine of original sin. It is finitude—the limits of our epistemological equipment—rather than constitutional malformation that makes us subject to error. Kant complicated the Enlightenment story: self-critical rationality can recognize but not prevent its disposition to self-deceptive illusions. Ironically, it is the fundamental project of rationality—its articulating the conditions that make experience possible—that lures it to treat its postulates as if they were possible objects of experience.

We cannot avoid self-deception. Even open-eyed ambivalence is subject to the self-deceived conviction that although it is conflicted, the appropriate attitude will emerge in the right way at the right time. But we should not—and cannot—wish to do without the active, self-induced illusions that sustain us. Nor can we do without second-order denials that they are illusions, the second-order and regressive strategies that we self-deceptively believe rationalize our various self-deceptive activities. The question is, How can we sustain the illusions essential to ordinary life, without becoming self-damaging idiots? Are there forms of user-friendly self-deception that do not run the dangers that falsity, irrationality, and manipulation are usually presumed to bring?

II

The phenomena of self-deception are extremely various: they encompass an arbitrarily selected section of a spectrum of closely related activities of ritualized forms of self-manipulation; their identification presupposes theories about normal patterns of perceptual, emotional, and evidential salience, norms of rationality and transparency. We distinguish self-deception from its cousins and clones—compartmentalization, adaptive denials, repressed conflicts and submerged aggressions, false consciousness, sublimation, wishful thinking, suspiciously systematic errors in self-reflection—in whatever ways sustain our favorite theories.

And there is an evaluative element as well: The hidden politics of the attribution of self-deception and false consciousness masks their frequency and advantages. When we deplore what we regard as misplaced loyalty or highly focused concentration that resists expansion or correction, we pejoratively classify it as "self-deception." But when we admire persistent and dedicated single-minded attention that systematically resists the distraction of fringe phenomena, we call it "courage" or "purposeful resolution." The person who does not have our favored reactions is open game for the charge of self-deception, if not of a more serious form of psychological abnormality, or worse, a culpable form of political subversion.

To be sure, if the pronouncements of common opinion and ordinary speech are at all clearly identifiable and reliable, there are constraints and directions on the analysis of self-deception. Like virtually all the concepts that concern us ('self,' 'belief,' 'conflict,' and even 'rationality'), self-deception elusively moves between latitudinarian ordinary speech and a strict, theory-and-value-dependent technical vocabulary.[3] Enlightenment philosophers attempting to explain the possibility of knowledge focus on the primacy of cognition and construe their analyses of other psychological activities in the terms set by those concerns. To be sure, all the phenomena must be accounted for in one way or another, but the exigencies of elegant theory construction play a large role in categorizing and describing fringe phenomena that are not, in the first instance, a philosopher's primary explanatory concern. An ambitious philosophy of mind, designed to conjoin and support a theory of knowledge does not initially propose a theory of self-deception or akrasia. It classifies these as deviant phenomena and explains them in the terms that best suit the directions of its primary theory.

If we characterize self-deception narrowly, as requiring the strict identity of deceiver and deceived about beliefs in propositional form, the phenomena of self-deception seem to evaporate. After all, the conditions for strict personal identity are so stringent as to cast doubt on the continued temporal identity of the self, let alone the identity of a self deliberately lying to itself. As strict constructionists working with a technical vocabulary, we may get some understanding of the mind as an epistemic instrument, but little understanding of its psycho-social functioning and the popularity of other presumptively deviant activities like weakness of will and the irrational conservation of emotions. We nevertheless characterize these phenomena inclusively, with the broad latitudinarian hand that encompasses common practice and common speech, the phenomena that appear on the fringes of our presumptive rationality play a significant role in virtually all our activities. Beyond the constraints set by constructing a comprehensive theory of intellectual and psychological functioning—one that explains extremely diverse cognitive, motivational, and affective phenomena—there is no fact of the matter about whether we should be strict or latitudarian constructionists about the criteria for the identity of the deceiver and the deceived or about the conditions that identify cases of deception. Because we typically position ourselves dialectically, emphasizing the conceptions that have been neglected by our immediate predecessors, we can expect a continuous (re)cycling of latitudinarian and strict characterizations of self-deception.

We are in the awkward position of stipulating definitions that will satisfy our technically exacting colleagues in the cognitive sciences, while also carrying on with what passes for common sense and ordinary language. In analyzing and evaluating self-deception, we are engaged in the method of reflective equilibrium, attempting to balance our (common) considered judgments and practices with our principle-laden theories, as if our ordinary judgments and practices are not already theory-laden.[4]

III

Like deception, self-deception is a species of rhetorical persuasion; and like all forms of persuasion, it involves a complex, dynamic, and cooperative

Self and Deception

process. Successful deceivers are acute rhetoricians, astute seducers who know how to co-opt the psychology of their subjects. They begin with minute and subtle interactions designed to establish trust, with a manner of approach, certain gestures and intonation patterns, intimations of directed and redirected attention. Astute deceivers like Iago engage the cooperation of their victims. Othello's psychology—his sensitivity, his pride, his sense of being a stranger—was a collusive instrument in his being deceived and eventually in his being self-deceived. These strategies reveal the political complexity involved in drawing the boundaries between deception and socially induced self-deception. Deception and self-deception are not merely detached conclusions of invalid arguments: they are interactive processes with a complex cognitive and affective aetiology.

What Self-Deception Is Not

It is illuminating to track self-deception negatively, characterizing its varieties by noting what it is *not*. By exposing common misconceptions about self-deception, we shall arrive at a better understanding of its dynamics and its popularity.

Self-deception is typically not episodic. It rarely occurs as a single, momentary event, a kind of epistemic sneeze. The popularity of self-deception is not explained by its episodic propositionalized structure, but by its functional activity as a magnetizing disposition. A disposition is magnetizing or tropic just when "it promotes and even constructs the occasions that require its exercise."[5] For instance, a person who self-deceptively denies the estrangement of her affection typically does not await the occasion to affirm or proclaim it. Her self-deception consists largely in her active disposition to produce the occasions—the scenarios and events—that elicit the conventional expressions of affection: a term of endearment, a caress. Similarly, the Roman Catholic who denies that she has lost her faith sustains her self-deception by following routine habits, attending mass, continuing the rituals of religious observance. In both cases, the evidence for self-deception is a pattern of behavior: the caress is unconvincing, and participation in the ritual of the service is wooden. But one abstracted caress or absent-minded credo doesn't mark a self-deceiver. Self-deception is characterized by a continued and complex *pattern* of perceptual, cognitive, affective, and behavioral dispositions.

Self-deception is typically not a solitary activity. Like other intentional activities, it works through sustaining social support.[6] As standard ordinary beliefs are elicited and reinforced by our fellows, so too are our primary self-deceptive strategies. The canny self-deceiver puts herself in situations where her deflected attention will be strongly supported by her fellows. "How wonderful that you are beginning your Spiritual Retreat (or going to Lower Slobovia)," the world says to the uncertain and frightened traveler. Though she may be aware that she is more apprehensive than pleased by the prospect of her journey, she attempts to block her resistance by using conventional social forms to distract or submerge her attention.

Self-deception need not involve false belief. Just as the deceiver can attempt to produce a belief which is—as it happens—true, so too a self-deceiver can set herself to believe what is in fact true. A canny self-deceiver can focus on accurate but irrelevant observations as a way of denying a truth that is importantly relevant to her immediate projects.

Moreover, self-deception need not involve any belief at all. The process and the outcome can be protointentional or subdoxastic.[7] When someone systematically deflects the natural direction of her gaze, ignoring phenomena that she would normally find salient, her ignorance can be an instance of self-deception as well as an instrument designed to achieve it. Systematic, persistent resistance to correction can be internal to the processes of believing: it can indicate the functional role of a relatively trivial belief or a subdoxastic intentional disposition, rather than its epistemic status.[8]

Further, stylized or ritualized actions—culturally specific actions that conventionally express complex attitudes—can deceive. We adopt certain postures and gestures to show a self-confidence that we do not actually possess. The inclination of the head, a way of gazing, an intonation pattern can deceptively suggest intimacy.[9] Similarly, self-deception can be expressed in gesture and action: the gestures of an aging coquette—the head at angle, the languorous eyes, the flirtatious smile—are not only designed to help create and sustain an illusion, but they can also be its primary expression. But the beliefs that are implicated in such action—beliefs that such gestures retain whatever charm they might once have had—are sometimes mistaken without being self-deceived. The coquette's anxious look in the mirror as she applies layer after layer of lipstick and rouge indicates that she also knows better.

Self-deception need not focus on important matters. It can range from the momentous to the minute, from the sublime to the ridiculous. It can focus on the primary projects of a life (those of a politician or of a parent) . . . or on a new hairdo.

Self-deception need not be self-centered. To be sure, self-deception is—along with other epistemic and psychological attitudes—explained largely by the deceiver's system of beliefs, habits, and desires; but although it is of course always *by* the self, self-deception is not on that account always *for* or *about* the self: a person can be self-deceived about the honesty of her distant political allies or opponents.

Indeed the individual need not always initiate his self-deception. Like the members of any sports team, the president's cabinet can collectively acquire grandiose attitudes that they could not sustain as individuals. Affected by one another's influence, by the luxurious appointments of the cabinet room, and supported by the army of their secretaries and assistants, they so collude in magnifying one another's tendencies to self-importance that the memoranda on which they consensually agree are stronger than the views that they would accept individually, in isolation. And yet it was as distinctive individuals that they participated in the work of the cabinet.

Self-deception need not be motivated by a desire or a wish. A man who self-deceptively believes that his wife's professional success far outshines his own might be moved by a chronic, painful envious disposition, rather than by a desire for her flourishing.

Indeed self-deception is not always directly motivated. Like many psychological activities, it can continue as an entrenched habit long after its original impetus has been extinguished. The nervous novice teacher who self-deceptively ignores the boredom of her students can retain the habit of ignoring their reactions long after she has become a self-confident, and even self-important, but still boring teacher. We can also acquire specific self-deceptive habits in just the same way that we imitatively acquired other psychological and intellectual habits. Fearful about their health, our parents self-deceptively ignored or denied their ailments. Without the same fears, we can acquire the same strategies of denial.

Even when manipulative deception is morally suspect, its outcome is not always harmful. Indeed, deception and self-deception are often benevolently and insightfully motivated. By convincing themselves that a desired self-transformation is within relatively easy reach, canny self-improvers can use self-deception as an energizing instrument.

Strategies of Self-Deception

Clever deceivers rarely tell outright falsehoods. It is too risky. The art of deception is closely related to the magician's craft: it involves knowing how to draw attention to a harmless place, to deflect it away from the action. Deeply entrenched patterns of perceptual, emotional, and cognitive dispositions serve as instruments of deception. A skilled deceiver is an illusionist who knows how to manipulate the normal patterns of what is salient to their audience. He places salient markers—something red, something anomalous, something desirable—in the visual field, to draw attention just where he wants it. The strategy of perceptual self-deception is identical: the trick is to place oneself where patterns of salience are likely to deflect attention away from what we do not wish to see. The best way for a gambler to deceive herself—to avoid noticing her lover's roving eye—is to schedule their assignations at the casino or the race track instead of at the disco.

Opacity, vagueness, and over-determination are the deceiver's friend.[10] Just as we use the ambiguity of polite ritualized speech to mislead others ("I had a wonderful time." "I've been hoping to run into you so we could arrange to have lunch."), so we fuse the multiple functions of speech acts when we talk to ourselves. In hopes of levering ourselves to our desks, we gloss a vague thought as if it were a firm intention, we say "I'll spend the weekend finally getting to all those letters I must write." The more publicly such pronouncements are made, the more force the lever can exert.

Any experience is open to an indefinite number of true and even relatively salient descriptions. To recommend a brash and hostile student, we call attention to her energetic initiative in discussion. In the interest of maintaining our loyalty to our unreliable or treacherous friends, we praise their originality. While such cases do not involve lying, they typically do intend to deceive by distraction. Of course we might well have a second-order policy that rationalizes and justifies strategies of this kind. But they are nonetheless deceptive for having been rationalized and justified.

Shifting the level of generality of descriptions and explanations is also an excellent strategy of deception and self-deception. To deflect attention from the sordid, exasperating, and frustrating details of our major projects—parenting, teaching, political action—we move to general abstractions, lumping these details together under the heading of "No Pain, No Gain; it's all worth it in the end," forgetting that when we are making important decisions, it is often this—whether there is something about the activity that outweighs the trouble it brings—that is in question. Or we move in the other direction: we can deceive someone (including ourselves) into accepting an undesirable job by focusing on a few genuinely attractive details, drawing attention away from a general, all-things-considered evaluation.

Second-order policies that legitimate specific self-manipulative strategies are sometimes also canny instruments of self-deception:

—We rationalize compartmentalization as a generally efficient and efficacious way of advancing the diversity of our competing and potentially conflicting projects. (But we are half aware that we do not—indeed that we cannot—compartmentalize as thoroughly as our projects require. If the subsystems do not actually overlap, then they are certainly in close communication. However great their differences, Dr. Jekyll and Mr. Hyde both knew their way home. More significantly, if Dr. Jekyll had not been so righteous, Mr. Hyde might well not have been so venial.)

—We often justify epistemically dubious cognitive, emotional, and behavioral habits by policies assigning high priority to the social utility that such habits are meant to serve. (But in their details, such policies are often manifestly no more defensible than the strategies they are meant to support. Moreover, a person's self-deceptive strategy is a way of specifying his ends rather than a method for achieving them. For instance, Pascal's wager—the gamble of faith—can express and reinforce rather than assuage the horror of infinite spaces.)

—We construct general philosophical theories about human nature, specifying intrinsically valuable activities or activities that we declare to be "essential to a fully human life" as a way of helping ourselves through some of our more difficult and onerous activities. Or we invent something we call our identity, resting our self-respect on our engaging in its projects, independently of any other measure of their merits. (In such cases, it is typically not the theory or the commitment that is self-deceptive, but the belief that philosophic theories or projects of identity-engagement justify or ground rather than express our fundamental choices.)[11]

—Recognizing the distance between our best intentions and the activities that actually engage us, between the expected and the actual outcomes of our activities, we deflect our attention away from the horrors of contingency, away from the moral luck that attends everything we do. We characterize what we are pleased to think happens for the most part. (But we disguise from ourselves the extent to which contingency surrounds intentional activity and the extent to which "standard or normal" experience embeds questionable but self-fulfilling normative claims.)

—For the sake of promoting cherished ends, we rationalize self-manipulative strategies designed to produce beliefs, desires, or habits that we do not initially possess.[12] (But we are often self-deceived about the strength of our commitments; and when responsibility is weighty, we have reason to magnify or diminish the indeterminacy of the power of our agency.)

Is all this necessarily self-deceptive? Can we not maintain and indeed justify tactfully manipulative strategies without actually deceiving ourselves? We often deliberately mimic confidence and wholeheartedness in the hope of acquiring them; and indeed we can sometimes succeed in internalizing an attitude that was initially only mimetically expressed. But even the most successful of such manipulations often preserves traces of the original attitude in disguised or repressed ambivalence: the sarcastic remark, the verbal slips, the taut and guarded manner, the submerged hostility. Ambivalence of this kind is not necessarily self-deceptive, but the more we are intent on achieving a self-transformation, the more likely we are to deny traces of older attitudes. In any case, since method acting requires finding the projected character within oneself, the profoundly diffident are ill-equipped to help themselves to confidence by that method, particularly when their lines are not provided by a playwright. As a strategy for self-transformation, relatively contained, temporary self-deception is often more efficient and effective than method acting.

Taking a very different tack, we might, in the interests of high-minded enlightenment, attempt to persuade our fellows that openly acknowledged ambivalence may be at least as reliable as forced wholeheartedness. Practically speaking, however, we are often better served by self-deceptively undertaking to be wholehearted (by whatever the going standards are), than by attempting to persuade our fellows that ambivalence is a mark of reliability. All things considered, we are probably better served by acceding to the irrational desire for self-deceptive wholeheartedness rather by attempting the quixotic and self-deceptive project of curing our fellows' irrationality.

The Benefits of Self-Deception

Self-deception is sometimes construed as an effective measure against the despair of global skepticism. To be sure, we have, as Bas van Fraasen has argued, other ways of dealing with generalized uncertainty about the worth of our projects or about the reliability of those on whom our welfare depends.[13] Van Fraassen charts the advantages of the voluntarist strategy of affirming the trust or faith that he argues is implicit in every observation. Hume omits the voluntarist step. He observes that we just *naturally* believe beyond strict evidence; we trust beyond strict proof of reliability; we actively persist in our manifestly questionable projects. Despite our philosophic doubts about the continued existence of objects or the legitimacy of philosophic arguments, hunger guides us out of the study and out of skeptical philosophy at mealtimes, and after dinner, we are sociable and even affectionate, despite our clear-eyed assessment of the foibles and follies of our fellows. Some interpreters take Hume's solution to mark a final ironic skeptical turn: the operations of nature are identical with those that philosophers call "self-deception." Others see it as evidence of Hume's pragmatic naturalism: nature has so atuned us that what some philosophers call "self-deception" is actually a trustworthy sign of the natural health of the mind. At this point, we have returned to the rhetorical politics of philosophical terminology. The result is the same: some forms of self-deception are by-products of the standard operations of belief and the imagination. Although they run serious dangers, we could not do without their contributions to our intellectual and psychological activities. But it is natural psychology rather than a second-order rational policy that prompts accepting the self-deceptions that accompany standard modes of imagining and believing. We would engage in these activities even if we did not approve of our doing so.

The more interesting forms of self-deception are local rather than global. Without some species of self-deception, our dedications, our friendships, our work, and our causes would collapse. In deciding to have children, we ignore the travails of parents, obliterating our otherwise keen awareness of the typical relations among parents and children; in devoting ourselves to writing philosophy, we conveniently forget how little philosophy we ourselves are willing to read; in the interest of sanity and joy, we sidestep our deep ambivalence about our kith and kin.

The benefits of individual self-deception are obvious to its practitioners; the benefits of its socially induced forms are often more compelling.[14] The appearance of earnest and wholehearted conviction about our projects—defending a philosophic position, proposing a curricular reform, raising funds for a cherished cause—is commonly taken as an indication of trustworthy reliability. Disguising and submerging the ambivalence that is natural to most of our enterprises not only brings us the energy, verve, style, and ease that successful action requires, but it also helps to assure the social cooperation that is equally essential to our individual and collective projects. A good deal of the polite conversation of social life—the public description of the joys of our social roles and functions (friend, mother, teacher, scholar)—channels and streams us to play our parts without the mess, confusion, and upheaval that would occur if we openly expressed our natural and sensible ambivalence about these roles. It is virtually impossible to imagine any society that does not systematically and actively promote the self-deception of its members, particularly when the requirements of social continuity and cohesion are subtly at odds with one another and with the standard issue psychology of their members.[15] Socially induced self-deception is an instrument in the preservation of social cooperation and cohesion.

The Beneficiaries of Self-Deception

Who is served by socially induced self-deception? And who bears the primary responsibility when an individual's self-deception depends on social collusion? It's no news to post-Hegelian post-Freudian post-Marxist post-Wittgensteinians that the individual is not always the primary epistemic agent: like all epistemic activities, self-deception occurs within a social frame, one that not only defines but actively channels patterns of categorization, salience, and motivation.[16] But while we recognize the social influences on individual belief, we do not have a clear account of how they occur and where they stop. Locating epistemic responsibility with the individual—the last in a network of contributory of epistemic agents—derives from a forced parallel to voluntary behavior. Despite their repudiating Cartesian philosophical psychology, contemporary epistemologists still treat belief as voluntary: the individual is presumed to be a responsible epistemological agent, capable of identifying—and suspending assent to—any and all unwarranted beliefs.

Distinctions will help us. We can, to begin with, distinguish (1) the immediate, (2) the contributory, and (3) the primary agents of epistemic attitudes. The immediate agent of self-deception is the last active link in a causal chain that generates the work of deception. That work is not always carried out by individual persons: its agents can be subsystems of the self. Such subsystems are extremely various: they can range from subpersonic protointentional perceptual dispositions to internalized idealized group identifications.

Neo-Freudians,[17] cognitive psychologists,[18] and social theorists[19] differ in their analysis of the components that constitute the self, but they agree in characterizing it as constituted by relatively independent subsystems whose interaction is often only precariously integrated. For them, the explanation of the phenomena of self-deception lies in our complex psychological organization: the immediate agent and presumptive beneficiary of self-deception is a subsystem of the self. Social psychologists join many neo-Freudians in identifying the subsystems of the self as the internalized representatives of social personae who have formed—and who continue to influence—individual psychology.

In the interest of avoiding such regressive homuncular explanations, many cognitive psychologists have introduced subpersonic subsystems, capable of nonpurposive but intentional operations. When a subsystem is (by some measure) central to an aspect of a person's identity, its strategies are considered to be *self*-deceptive, though that "self" neither is nor has a central panoptical scanner or manipulator. There is no need for reductive zeal here, no need to determine—as if there were a theory-neutral fact of the matter—whether the subsystems engaged in self-deception are all homuncular or subhomuncular, whether they are all intentionally deceptive or subintentionally misleading, or whether self-deception reduces to subsystem deception.[20] When the deceiving and the deceived subsystems are interdependent, extensionally intersecting "parts" of a psycho-biological individual, the problem of whether self-deception is coherent becomes a verbal puzzle.

Of course, the immediate agents of epistemic attitudes need not be its primary agents. Typically the primary agents of deception and self-deception are its presumptive beneficiaries. As the primary agent of Othello's eventual self-deception, Iago orchestrated and directed the immediate and the contributory agents of the deceptions that generated Othello's eventual self-deception. Not only Emilia and Cassio, but also Othello's own subpersonae—the Moor's sense of honor, the soldier's quick reactions—were brought into play as agents of the work of deception.

Like other epistemic attitudes, successful self-deception typically requires the collusion of contributory agents. Whether it be an individual or a subpersonic system, the last agent in a causal chain of deception could not do its work without antecedent and conjoined support. It is extremely difficult to sustain self-deception without a little help from our friends, often rendered by observant, but tactful, silence. Once begun, the process of Othello's self-deception would have been difficult to sustain without the manipulated contributions of Emilia and Cassio. Sometimes the contribution is rendered by the silence of tactful friends.

Active cooperation in self-deception is more readily assured when it brings widespread secondary gains. For instance, normal science is served by training scientists to follow a conservative epistemic policy, one that makes them susceptible to self-deceptive denials of evidence contrary to dominant theories.[21] But collaborative contributions to self-deception need not always serve larger gains: sometimes self-deception just happens. A society can systematically contribute to the self-deception of its members even when there are few benefits from such patterned misapprehension. The explanation of self-deception is often global and structural: it does not lie in its occasions, but in its being an unintended by-product of functional activities.[22]

Why the Best Solution Is Not Available to Us

In a way, the virtues required for astute self-deception are those required for astute and righteous lying: deception in the right way at the right time for the right reason. But what does *phronesis* about self-deception require? How do we determine the properly atuned balance between persistence and fallibility, one that deflects correction as long as closure is beneficial, generating self-deception in love and work but not in self-defence?

In principle, an acute philosophical logician could formulate a context-sensitive set of policies for determining the cut-off points for beneficial self-deception, specified for distinctive measures of benefits, distinctive agents and beneficiaries, appropriate time spans. But while the theorist can distinguish benign from maladaptive cases of self-deception and other irrational psychological activities, the practitioner is not, in the very nature of the case, in a position to do so. If the practitioner always casts herself as theorist, scanning and testing her psychological activities for their legitimacy, she would rarely be in a position to benefit from their exercise. Complex psychological activities best function at a precritical and prereflective automatic or autonomic level. The utility of many of our presumptively self-deceptive responses—like those moved by fear and trust, for example—depends on their being relatively undiscriminating, operating at a deeply entrenched habitual precritical level.[23]

Ambivalence in the Service of the Enlightenment

Having argued that self-deception is inevitable and distinguished its layers and beneficiaries, have we joined the ranks of postmodern social constructionists? Certainly not. Masked as a presumptively egalitarian attitude to the various personae of the self, a laissez faire attitude toward self-deception runs the danger of giving intrapsychic power politics full and unchecked play: it endorses the actions of the self's most powerful, rather than those of its most justified, personae. Self-deception is only as good as the person who has it.

If the difference between deception and self-deception is arbitrary, and if the deceived typically collude in their deception and the self-deceived depend on the complicity of their fellows, the allocation of responsibility for the harms of deception seems arbitrary. We might well be uneasy that such an openhanded latitudinarian way of subscripting the various agents, benefits, and beneficiaries of self-deception runs the danger of blaming the victim. Self-deception does not monitor its own use: it doesn't know when or where to stop. It is specifically constructed to ignore and resist correction. The danger of self-deception lies not so much in the irrationality of the occasion, but in the ramified consequences of the habits it develops, its obduracy, and its tendency to generalize.

But this is equally true of many of our other, more superficially rational intellectual activities.[24] Consider the various Platonic recommendations for dialectical analysis offered in the *Sophist* and the *Statesman*: the method of division is designed to construct a taxonomy of (what became) genus, species, and varieties to "catch the meanings of general terms." When that method is astutely used, it charts the geography of a conceptual field. But it is clear—it was certainly clear to Plato—that when the method of division is globally or grossly applied, when it is entrenched as a primary and exclusive mode of analysis, it can be deceptive and even self-deceptive. Like Socratic self-knowledge, the Platonic method of division is only as good as the mind that uses it.

It was for reasons like these that Descartes wanted to find a method so simple that any mind could use it, a method that presupposes no ability or knowledge beyond the capacity to test its ideas for their logical consistency, using reductive proofs, moving only a step at a time. Here again, a method which is rational if any method is, brings the fruits of rationality—a clearly demonstrated knowledge of the world—only when it is supplemented by a wide range of other, shadier intellectual and psychological activities. Without the generous support of suspect nonrational intellectual and psychological activities, Descartes' method is sterile and useless.

Even though its authority rarely carries executive power, it is the active, permanent possibility of asking critically evaluative questions that preserves us from dangerous folly: When is self-deception self-defeating? What is really beneficial and to whom? There are, to be sure, a variety of context-dependent criteria for such evaluations, and each psychological or political subsystem has its own claims for special privilege. Still, at any given level, for any subscripted measure of utility or rationality, intrapsychic might does not make intrapsychic right or even intrapsychic utility. Socratic inquiry—actively pressing for self-critical evaluation—is the only safeguard against the damaging uses of self-deception, or indeed or any of our intellectual or psychological devices.

In evaluating the self-deception of our friends and enemies, in retrospectively gauging our own, we are directed by judgments about the merits of the ends it serves, as well as judgments about whether those ends could have been better served by other means. In making such evaluations, we need to think laterally as well as linearly, systematically as well as episodically. We need to consider the global effects of all our epistemic and psychological activities—their addictive qualities as well as their immediate benefits. When they are successful, psychological and intellectual activities typically tend to become rapidly entrenched, ramified, and generalized.

But we have very little latitude in monitoring our psychological activities, and still less in forming them. Our epistemological strategies become habitual before we are aware of their patterns and consequences. As philosophers, the best thing we can do about self-deception is what we should do about our other psychological and intellectual activities: engage ourselves in the Stoic task of understanding the minute details of its operations. Since we are highly susceptible to socially induced self-description, the wisest practical course is to be very careful about the company we keep. But it is no easy task to determine where our best protection lies. On the one hand, prudence counsels avoiding the company of charismatic rhetoricians who might mislead us. On the other hand, it is not easy to identify epistemic seducers, particularly when we benefit from hospitality to a wide range of opinions, each with a distinctive beneficial and critical perspective on our favorite illusions. Unfortunately, self-deception is just the thing that prevents us from seeking its best therapy: it does not know when to expand and when to limit its epistemological company. Fortunately, we have many other kinds of reasons for being astute about the company we keep. With luck, a canny self-deceiver's other psychological and intellectual habits—a taste for astringency and a distrust of hypocrisy, for instance—can prevent the wild imperialistic tendencies of self-deception from becoming entrenched and ramified.

But that is a matter of luck, and as we know, ambivalence is the best attitude toward luck.[25]

NOTES

1. One variety of self-deception: X is self-deceived about p when
    1. X believes that p at t (where t covers a reasonable span of time);
    2. Either (a) X believes not-p at t or (b) X denies that he believes p at t;
    3. X recognizes that p and not-p conflict;
    4. X denies that his beliefs conflict, advancing an improbable ad hoc reconciliation, making no attempt to suspend to judgment or to determine which belief is defective.

Since conditions 1 and 2 are parallel to 3 and 4, the attribution of self-deception is regressive. It is typically justified by an inference to the best explanation, an account of what X would normally believe, perceive, notice, infer. For more elaborate formulations of these conditions, see Leon Festinger, *Cognitive Dissonance* (Stanford: Stanford University Press, 1957); B. McLaughlin, "Exploring the Possibility of Self-Deception in Belief"; R. Audi, "Self-Deception, Rationalization and Reasons for Acting"; and A. O. Rorty, "The Deceptive Self: Liars, Layers and Lairs," in *Perspectives on Self-Deception*, ed. B. McLaughlin and A. Rorty (Berkeley: University of California Press, 1988).

2. After having raised the paradox of analysis in the *Meno* and come to the brink of skepticism, Socrates says, "we shall be better, braver and more active if we believe we should inquire than if we believe we cannot discover what we do not already know. That is something for which I am ready to fight in word and deed to my utmost ability" (86B).

3. See "Persons and Personae," 27–98; A. O. Rorty, *Mind in Action* (Boston: Beacon Press, 1988); A. Mele, *Irrationality: An Essay on Akrasia, Self-Deception and Self-Control* (New York: Oxford University Press, 1987); A. Mele, "Recent Work on

Self-Deception *APQ*, 1987; D. Pears, *Motivated Irrationality* (Oxford: Claredon Press, 1984); M. Martin, ed., *Self-Deception and Self-Understanding* (Lawrence: University Press of Kansas, 1985); M. R. Haight, *A Study of Self-Deception* (Sussex: Harvester Press, 1980); Jon Elster, *Sour Grapes* (Cambridge University Press, 1983).

4. Ordinary language is Protean in this area: it has incorporated the terminology of psychoanalysis and popular cognitive science. And as it becomes increasingly cosmopolitan, it adds "mauvaise foi" and "false consciousness." We can expect that considered judgments derived from French ("Je me trompe" for "I made a mistake," "Je m'en fiche" for "I don't care") would not coincide with those influenced by languages that are less generous with reflexive pronouns.

5. Cf. "The Two Faces of Courage," in *Mind in Action* (Boston: Beacon, 1988), 301.

6. See William Ruddick, "Social Self-Deceptions," and Ron Harré, "The Social Context of Self-Deception," in *Perspectives on Self-Deception*.

7. See Annette Baier, "The Vital but Dangerous Art of Ignoring" in this volume; Mark Johnston, "Self-Deception and the Nature of Mind," *Perspectives on Self-Deception*. Since many pre-intentional activities can sometimes function in a fully intentional form, I prefer to speak of *protointentional* rather than subintentional activities.

8. Following the model of analyses of justified belief, analyses of self-deception typically specify necessary and sufficient logically distinct conditions—reified as independent psychological states—whose conjunctive presence constitutes cases of self-deception. If the conditions of justified belief can be condensed in one activity, so can those of self-deception. "The same liberty may be permitted to moral, which is allowed to natural philosophers; and 'tis very usual with the latter to consider any motion as compounded and consisting of two parts separate from each other, tho' at the same time they acknowledge it to be in itself uncompounded and inseparable" (Hume, *Treatise* 493).

9. Cf. Bruce Wilshire, "Mimetic Engulfment and Self-Deception," in *Perceptions on Self-Deception*.

10. Cf. Iris Murdoch, "The Idea of Perfection," in *The Sovereignty of the Good* (London: Routledge and Kegan Paul, 1970).

11. See Sartre, *Sketch for a Theory of the Emotions* (London: Methuen, 1962); *Existentialism and Humanism, Anti-Semite and Jew* (New York: Grove Press, 1948).

12. Cf. William James, "The Will to Believe"; Pascal, *Pensees;* Bas van Fraassen, "The Peculiar Effects of Love and Desire," in *Perspectives on Self-Deception*.

13. Bas van Fraassen, "Peculiar Effects."

14. Cf. A. O. Rorty "Some Social Uses of the Forbidden," *Psychoanalytic Review* (1972).

15. Since they do not involve beliefs in propositional form, such conflicts are not, of course, technically speaking contradictions. (Cf. R. Marcus, "Moral Dilemmas and Consistency," in *Moral Dilemmas,* ed. C. W. Gowans (Oxford, 1987). Other essays in this volume provide a useful background for understanding some of the motivation for self-deception. See also L. Festinger, *Cognitive Dissonance.*

16. See Tyler Burge, "Individualism and Psychology," *Philosophical Review* (1986); "Intellectual Norms and the Foundations of Mind," *Journal of Philosophy* (1987). Burge argues that the individuation of intentional states essentially refers to social practices. See also Alvin Goldman, "Varieties of Cognitive Appraisal," *Nous* 13, 22–38 for a useful discussion of the variety of criteria by which beliefs are assessed.

17. See Freud, "Repression," "The Unconscious," SE, 1915, and "Splitting the Ego in the Service of Defence," SE, 1938; R. Schafer, *A New Language for Psychoanalysis* (New Haven: Yale University Press, 1976); D. Sachs, "On Freud's Doctrine of the Emotions," *Freud*, ed. R. Wollheim (New York: Anchor Books, 1974); H. Kohut, *The Search for the Self* (New York: International Universities Press, 1978); R. Wollheim, *The Thread of Life* (Cambridge, Ma.: Harvard University Press, 1984).

18. Cf. D. Dennett, "Three Kinds of Intentional Psychology," in *Reduction, Time and Reality*, ed. R. Healey (Cambridge: Cambridge University Press, 1981); articles in H. Kornblith, ed., *Naturalizing Epistemology* (Cambridge, Ma.: MIT Press, 1994); D. Davidson, "Paradoxes of Irrationality," *Philosophical Essays on Freud*, ed. J. Hopkins and R. Wollheim (Cambridge: Cambridge University Press, 1982); "Deception and Division," rep. in *Action and Events*, ed. E. LePore and B. McLaughlin (New York: Blackwell, 1985); M. Johnston, "Self Deception and the Nature of Mind," in *Perspectives on Self-Deception;* S. Stich, "Beliefs and Subdoxastic Systems," in *Philosophy of Science*, 1978; and *Fragmentation of Reason* (Cambridge, Ma.: MIT Press, 1990). See also footnote 9 in "The Deceptive Self," and *Mind in Action*, 217–19.

19. For an account of the distinctive aspects and features of identity, see Alfred Schutz, *Collected Papers* (The Hague: Wijhoff, 1962), esp. 16–18, 221–222; G. H. Mead, *Mind, Self and Society*, esp. 144–45, 149–52 (Chicago: University of Chicago Press, 1934); A. Rorty and D. Wong, "Aspects of Identity and Agency," in *Identity, Character and Morality*, ed. O. Flanagan and A. Rorty (Cambridge, Ma.: MIT Press, 1990).

20. See Mark Johnston, "Self-Deception," and Brian McLaughlin, in this volume for discussions of the presumed incoherence of self-deception and its reduction to other-deception.

21. See Adam Morton, "Partisanship," in *Perspectives on Self-Deception*.

22. See Jon Elster, *Sour Grapes*.

23. Cf. "Fearing Death," *Mind in Action*, 202–7.

24. Cf. Roy Sorensen, *Thought Experiments* (New York: Oxford University Press, 1992). Sorensen remarks that the standard modes of argumentation have their shortcomings as well as their strengths. He recommends what he calls a "diversified portfolio" of argument forms.

25. An early version of this chapter was delivered at colloquia at the East-West Center and at Williams College. I am grateful to Annette Baier, Brian McLaughlin, Sam Fleischacker, and Steven Gerrard for their comments. This article was previously published in *Philosophy* (April, 1994) by Cambridge University Press.

FOUR

SELF, DECEPTION, AND SELF-DECEPTION IN PHILOSOPHY*

Robert C. Solomon

> "I have done that," says my memory. "I cannot have done that," says my pride, and remains inexorable. Eventually, memory yields.
> —Friedrich Nietzsche, *Beyond Good and Evil*

Nietzsche once asked, "Why must we have truth at any cost anyway?"[1] It was an odd question, coming from the philosopher who prided himself, above all, on his brutal honesty, and it is an obscene question, in any case, for the profession that sees itself as solely seeking the truth. Even those philosophers who challenge the very idea of truth, not just Nietzsche and Nāgārjuna, but Jacques Derrida and Richard Rorty, are scrupulous and unforgiving when it comes to deception, misrepresentation, and so-called creative misreadings, at least of their own work.[2] Philosophers in general insist on the truth even if they do not believe in "the Truth." They despise deception, and they ridicule the self-deception of the "vulgar," which it is their mission to undo. Australian philosopher Tony Coady probably speaks for most philosophers when he writes, "Dishonesty has always been perceived in our culture, and in all cultures but the most bizarre, as a central human vice. Moreover the specific form of dishonesty known as lying has generally been scorned, and the habitual liar treated with contempt. There are perfectly good reasons for this." But, he adds, "we should note that this perception is consistent with a certain hesitancy about what constitutes a lie and with the more than sneaking suspicion that there might be a number of contexts in which lying is actually justified."[3] Plato defended "the noble lie," and the ultrarespectable English ethicist Henry Sidgwick suggested that a "high-minded lie" in the direction of humility might do us all a great deal of good.[4] Of course, philosophers have often fantasized whole cultures composed of liars, if only as a possible counter-example to the categorical imperative or as a source of self-referential paradox. The neo-Marxist notion of 'false consciousness' and one common use of the word *myth* have reinforced the idea that a whole society could be in self-deception. But the possibility of such pervasive self-deception already presupposes some ideal and independent criterion for the truth while at the same time giving considerable recognition to the legitimacy and the necessity of deception. In this essay, I want to further muddy these already treacherous waters without denying what I take to be obvious, that in general—indeed, more than in just general—we have to trust what people tell us and that lying, without some further specification, is wrong.[5] Whatever the pronouncements of the philosophers, the case against deception both in and out of philosophy is clouded, not only by questions about consequences but by questions of culture and the intricacies of self-deception.

We could, of course, delimit the use of the word *deception* and especially the use of *lying* to just those cases in which an untruth is knowingly and maliciously told with the intention to deceive, but this would eliminate a good deal of our subject matter. In particular, it would eliminate what I shall suggest is a very large proportion of cases in which deception and self-deception function together and support one another. It would also eliminate all of those cases in which cultural considerations clearly dictate deception, whatever the truth may be. To define lying as wrong or to limit lying to just cases of wrongful deception begs important questions, one of which is Nietzsche's, "Why must we have truth at any cost anyway?" And Nietzsche is not alone. Plato and Sidgwick both defend the high-minded lie, and one of the beliefs advocated for novice monks, I am told, is the obvious falsehood: I am the worst person in the world. In Buddhism, the demand for truth and truthfulness seems to include acquiescence in the face of the most astounding "truths," all in the name of their salutary affects, harmony, and eventual "liberation." Nietzsche is pursuing a very different program, of course, defending desirable untruths that are most inspiring and conducive to the "will to power," but the point, it seems to me, is the same. Truth is in the service of ethics, not the other way around.

"Dishonesty is a form of injustice, a vice," Coady says, echoing the harsh condemnations of Augustine and Kant. "It deforms the liar and debases the currency of language." But not all untruths are malicious, and not all deceptions are lies. The truth hurts, and sometimes it destroys. Lies can protect and inspire, and deception can serve noble ends. Self-deception sustains the illusions that sustain us, and though conducive to pathological dysfunction it is self-deception and not the truth alone that shall set us free.[6] Indeed, in many if not most cases of self-deception (and deception too) the question of truth can be a source of considerable consternation, not just for the perplexing reasons long advocated by epistemological skeptics, but rather because of the self-fulfilling (and sometimes

Self, Deception, and Self-Deception in Philosophy

self-denying) features of our beliefs about ourselves and those aspects of the world that matter most to us. A saintly man considers himself wicked. What is the truth of the matter? A mass murderer with strong political beliefs, a "terrorist" in the eyes of the press, considers herself a noble freedom fighter. Who is right, and who is wrong? A lover trusts and defends the beloved, no matter how hideous the evidence to the contrary. Is this self-deception, or is it just—love? The truth in such matters is rarely a matter of "the facts" alone.

When it comes to the large questions of philosophy—the meaning of life, the nature of morality, the existence and personality of God, and the teleology of nature, it is by no means clear what it means to seek "the truth," whatever the rhetoric. And yet, for over two thousand years, both in the East and in the West, the problem of truth seems not to have jeopardized the status of truthfulness as a definitive moral and intellectual virtue. If this is a paradox, it is not a very interesting one, but it gives rise to a fascinating if neglected set of questions about the self-aggrandizing language of philosophy and the variety of deceptions and self-deceptions among philosophers. There is no doubt, for example, that philosophers have almost always deceived themselves if not others about the importance of philosophy, a fact made manifest only occasionally by some iconoclast such as Nietzsche or Wittgenstein or a Zen master like Dōgen. On a more parochial level, philosophers generally deceive themselves and try to deceive others about the superiority of this school or method as opposed to that one, typically ripping one thread out of a fabric and defending it alone as the whole truth. More personally, philosophers often deceive themselves about their supposed love and pursuit of the truth—not to mention wisdom—when ignoring the centrality of such concerns as their reputation in the agora and their status in the profession. Thrasymachus has in fact remained as much of a presence in philosophy as Socrates, though he is rarely recognized.

The roles of deception and self-deception in philosophy are not unrelated to the ways that deception and self-deception have been discussed by philosophers. It is often assumed, for example, that deception is a peculiarly linguistic activity, having to do with the assertion of false propositions, and that self-deception is therefore a paradoxical if not impossible lie to oneself.[7] However, I can effectively deceive someone by driving or walking off in the wrong direction, without saying a word, and there is good evidence that many animals systematically practice deception.[8] And it is wrong to suppose that self-deception is simply the application of deception to oneself, not only because that generates paradoxes, but because it represents a misunderstanding of the phenomenon. If one explores the strange realm of self-directed psychological attitudes (and various "self-" prefaced ascriptions of psychological attitudes) what immediately becomes evident is that rarely are self-ascription and ascription to others just different applications of the same psychological description. (Consider, just as a small sample, self-love, self-pity, self-respect, and self-loathing.) Indeed, if one were to think of self-deception as deception *about* the self as well as deception directed to the self, there would be less of a temptation to assimilate the first-person cases to the third-person.[9] But what this also means is that the nature of the self is part of our inquiry, along with the various conventions and conceptions concerning deception. Insofar as the self is a social being and not merely a locus of self-reference, the characters both of the self and of self-deception depend on the character of the society or culture in question. What we are depends only in part on what we think of ourselves, and what we think of ourselves is rarely free of the opinions of others and free of the ethical values of our society. We want to think well of ourselves, and so the need to convince and the strong temptation to deceive others about ourselves and to fool ourselves as well is always with us. The various social conventions that dictate the rules about lying and deception are the same conventions that dictate the acceptable nature of one's self. What gets praised as good character and what gets condemned as deception are by no means the same in different contexts and cultures. In the pages that follow, I am concerned with some of those connections between contexts, cultures, deception, and the self, beginning with the rather odd status of the truth and deception in philosophy.

DECEPTION IN PHILOSOPHY

> Call me a truth-seeker, and I will be satisfied.
> —Wittgenstein, letter to his sister, in Ray Monk,
> *Ludwig Wittgenstein*

Throughout the history of philosophy, deception has been assumed to be a vice, and honesty a virtue. Of course, one might tactfully suggest that the very nature of the subject, namely, the articulation of profound truths, requires such a commitment. If philosophers didn't seek and tell the truth, what would distinguish them from poets and myth makers, apart from their bad prose? Philosophers seek and tell the truth, the *whole* truth, and nothing but the truth. Or so they would have us believe. Diogenes strolled the city looking for an honest man, not expecting to find another, but never doubting that he himself was one. He would not have fared much better, we suspect, if he had toured the philosophers' hall of fame. His predecessor Socrates insisted that he was telling the truth when he claimed to know nothing, an argumentative strategy that was doubly a lie. For many philosophers and scientists too, we readily recognize that the search for truth may be something of a cover, a noble façade for working out personal problems, pleasing their parents, or pursuing personal ambition. Nietzsche suggested that every great philosophy is "the personal confession of its author and a kind of involuntary and unconscious memoir."[10] But unconscious revelation is hardly the same as telling the truth, and when philosophers such as Nietzsche go on to argue that there is, in fact, no truth, refusing to tell the truth then becomes a kind of truthfulness and insisting on the truth becomes a philosophically venal sort of lie.[11]

And yet, Socrates, we are told, died for the sake of his honesty. Epictetus, the early Stoic, defended above all the principle "not to speak falsely." In more modern times, Immanuel Kant took the prohibition against lying as his paradigm of a "categorical imperative," the unconditioned moral law.[12] There could be no exceptions, not even to save the life of a friend. Even Nietzsche took honesty to be one of his four "cardinal" virtues, and the "existentialist" Jean-Paul Sartre insisted that deception is a vice, perhaps indeed the ultimate vice.[13] Sartre argued adamantly on behalf of the "transparency" of consciousness, thus enabling him to argue (against Freud) that all deception is in some sense willful and therefore blameworthy. Today one reads American ethicists, for example, Edmund Pincoffs, who insists that dishonesty is so grievous a vice that its merits cannot even be intelligibly deliberated.[14] In this, unlike in many other matters, philosophy and common sense seem to be in agreement. And whether philosophy merely follows and reports on the *zeitgeist* or actually has some hand in directing it, it would be safe to say that the philosophical championing of honesty is an accurate reflection of popular morality. Lying, for philosophers and laymen alike, is wrong.[15]

But what does it mean to insist that lying is wrong, and how wrong is it really? Is a lie told to embellish an otherwise tedious narrative just as wrong as a lie told in order to cover up a misdeed and avoid punishment? Is a lie told in desperation any less wrong than a calculated, merely convenient lie? Is a lie told out of self-deception more or less wrong than a clearheaded, tactical lie? (Is the former even a lie?) Are all lies wrong—is lying as such wrong?—or do some lies serve an important function not only in protecting one another from harm (especially emotional harm) but in developing and protecting one's own sense of individuality and privacy?

Self and Deception

One could think of lying as diplomatic, as fortification, as essential protection for a necessarily less-than-candid self. Or, one could just think of honesty as merely one virtue among many, not a fundamental virtue at all. It is worth noting that Aristotle, in his catalog of moral virtues, lumped "truthfulness" together with "friendliness" and "wit," important traits to choose a friend or colleague, to be sure, but hardly the cornerstone without which the entire edifice of morality would fall down. Moreover, what Aristotle meant by "truthfulness" primarily concerned the telling of one's accomplishments, "neither more nor less"—in contemporary terms, handing in an honest resumé.[16] He did not seem at all concerned about social lies, "white lies," or, for that matter, even political lies, except insofar as these contributed to injustice or corruption.[17] Critics have often challenged Kant's analysis of honesty as a "perfect duty," appealing to our natural inclination to insist that it is far more important to save the life of a friend than it is to tell the truth to the Nazis who are after him. But if there is even one such case in which it is right to lie and honesty can be overridden, then the "perfect" status of the duty not to lie is compromised, and the question is opened to negotiation. It is in the light of such dogmatic ("a priori") condemnation too that we can understand the perennial controversy surrounding the seemingly innocent "white lie," the lie that saves instead of causing harm. And, to say the obvious (though it is often neglected by philosophers), lies can also entertain, for example, as theater and as fiction. Indeed, lies can also be useful and fascinating in philosophy. Not only do they provide promising "heuristic" goads to further thinking, but also they provide some of the essential subject matter as well. How many dozens of professors are now employed because some Cretan, years ago, supposedly declared that "all Cretans are liars" and thus generated the most basic paradox in logic and philosophy. (If he told the truth, then he was lying, but if he was lying, then . . .) Is there anything wrong with a lie when it causes no harm? Is it always true that we should tell the truth "even when it hurts"?

Behind the blanket prohibition of lying, we can discern the outlines of a familiar but glorious philosophical metaphor, the truth as bright, plain, and simple, standing there as the Holy Grail of Rationality, while dishonesty is dark and devious, the ill-paved path to irrationality and confusion. In revealing the truth, we think of consciousness as transparent through and through; in deception we detect an opacity, an obstacle, a wall within consciousness. The honest man and the true philosopher know all and tell all (except in Socrates's case, since he insists that he does not know anything). Nevertheless, Socrates's student Plato offers to lead us out of the shadows and into the light, even at great peril. The philosopher illuminates that which the liar and the layman leave in the dark, including his or her own inner soul.[18] Truth and light are good; deception and darkness are bad or evil, leading not only to ignorance and harm, but to the degradation of rationality, the abuse of language, and the corruption of the soul. But philosophy, one begins to suspect, has overrated these metaphors of clarity and transparency. The obvious truth is that our simplest social relationships could not exist without the opaque medium of the lie.

In his novel *The Idiot,* Fyodor Dostoevski gave us a portrait of a man who had all of the virtues, including perfect honesty.[19] He was, of course, an utter disaster to everyone he encountered. More recently, Albert Camus presented us with an odd "antihero" who was also incapable of lying.[20] It is not surprising that he comes off as something of a monster, "with virtually no human qualities at all" (as the prosecutor points out at his murder trial). On a more mundane and "real life" philosophical level, one cannot imagine getting through an average budget meeting or a cocktail party speaking nothing but the truth, the whole truth, and nothing but the truth. If one wished to be perverse, he or she might well hypothesize that deception, not truth, is the cement of civilization, a cement that does not so much hold us together as it safely separates us and our thoughts. We cannot imagine social intercourse without opacity.

Steve Braude, a philosopher who works extensively in parapsychology, illustrates the utter importance of deception with a simple experiment. He asks his audience if anyone would take a pill (which he has supposedly invented) which would allow them to read the minds of everyone within a hundred-yard radius. Not surprisingly, no one accepts the offer. We can all imagine the restless thoughts flickering through a friend's mind as we describe our latest trauma or the adventure of the day, the distracted and hardly flattering thoughts of our students as we reach the climax of the lecture two minutes before the class bell rings, the casual and not at all romantic thoughts of a lover in a moment of intimacy. "What are you thinking?" is an extremely dangerous and foolish question, inviting, if not usually requiring, the tactical but flatly deceptive answer: Oh, nothing.

The threatening nature of the truth has long been whitewashed by philosophers, often under a pseudosecularized version of the religious banner The Truth Shall Set You Free.[21] But, against the philosophers, we all know that sometimes the truth hurts and the harm is not redeemed, that the truth is sometimes if not often unnecessary, that the truth complicates social arrangements, undermines collective myths, destroys relationships, and incites violence and vengeance. Deception is sometimes not a vice but a social virtue, and systematic deception is an essential part of the order of the (social) world. In many societies, social harmony is valued far more than truthfulness as such, and to tell the other person what he or she wants

Self and Deception

to hear rather than what one might actually feel or believe is not only permitted but expected. In such circumstances, do we still want to speak of "deception" at all? And could we not begin to see our own enlightened emphasis on "seeking the truth at all costs" (as Ernst Jones wrote admiringly of Sigmund Freud) as one more ethnocentric peculiarity, another curious product of our strong sense of individualism and a particularly unsociable conception of "the truth"?

WHAT IS WRONG WITH DECEPTION?

> Why should one tell the truth if it's to one's advantage to tell a lie?
> —Ludwig Wittgenstein (age 8 or 9), in Ray Monk, *Ludwig Wittgenstein*

Philosophers usually agree that lying is wrong, but they are by no means in agreement about why lying is wrong. There have been at least three more or less mutually antagonistic philosophical positions which have woven their way through the history of philosophy and come to define the current discussion. There is the idea that the exhortation *Do not lie* has the special "deontological" status of a moral law, a "categorical imperative," which means that it is always wrong to lie, no matter what the circumstances. In Kant's words, it is a "perfect duty," never to be excused or overridden. Utilitarians, by contrast, insist that lying is wrong only because a lie does, in fact, cause more harm than good. There is no absolute prohibition here, rather perhaps a "rule of thumb," and there may well be many cases such as the infamous "white lie" in which lying causes no harm and therefore is not wrong. It may even be commendable. More sophisticated utilitarians ("rule utilitarians") offer a more thoroughgoing objection to lying by insisting that the consequences of lying *in general* (not in every particular case) weigh the balance against lying, white lies not withstanding. By emphasizing rules instead of particular acts and their consequences, the "rule utilitarians" thus move closer both in temperament and in conclusions to the Kantian deontologists. Indeed, the Kantian purely hypothetical question *What if everyone were to do that?* is not so obviously different from the rule utilitarian's empirical question *What if everyone did that?*

In addition to deontology and utilitarianism, there is a new contender (in fact a very old contender, promulgated at length by Aristotle) that rejects both the rigidity and the centrality of moral rules and principles governing our actions and the emphasis on utilitarian consequences and instead concerns itself with the *character* of the person who performs the actions in question. What counts are not the principles according to which one behaves or the consequences of what one does, but rather one's *virtues*. Do not lie, accordingly, becomes not a principle but an expression of a certain character trait, honesty. The honest man is not so much one who refrains from lying, much less one who resists the temptation to lie because he or she knows that it is wrong to lie. Telling the truth is built into his or her character. (He could no more tell a lie than break the law of gravity.) Thus Aristotle insists that truthfulness must be cultivated, habitual, "second nature," not a battle between conscience and temptation, and not the outcome of a consequentialist calculations.

The ideal of honesty as a well-cultivated virtue may well seem more appealing than the usual insistence on honesty as a matter of principle or the outcome of utilitarian calculations, but it still remains to be seen why honesty should be such a virtue and why lying—not just once but habitually—constitutes a vice. The explanation of many contemporary virtue ethicists is as vacuous as it is appealing: honesty enhances individual character, and dishonesty corrupts it. But what do enhancement and corruption mean in an individualistic context? One might argue on behalf of Aristotle that his analysis presupposes the social framework of his ethics, not only in the sense that the "right amount" of truthfulness would be a matter of shared agreement among his aristocratic peers, but in the more currently agreeable sense that truthfulness like all virtues becomes a virtue and gains its significance only within a social context in which people are inextricably tied together in their pursuit of the good life. One could, presumably, make a similar argument in terms of Confucian "harmony," for truthfulness is a personal virtue, not only because it is good for the individual soul, but because it is to some extent essential to the well-being of the community as a whole.

What gets left out of the overly individualistic philosophical accounts of telling the truth and lying is what Aristotle takes for granted: the effect of lying and deception (also self-deception) in interpersonal relationships. As Nietzsche so wisely complains, in characteristic opposition to Kant, "Not that you lied to me, but that I no longer believe you, has shaken me."[22] It is not the breach of principle against lying that is so troublesome, nor is it the consequences of a lie which might in themselves be wholly benign. Nor is it that the character of the liar is necessarily compromised or impugned (he or she may already be a rotter), but rather that his or her relationships are compromised, corrupted. The problem, here as elsewhere in philosophy, is that knowledge and truth telling are not taken seriously as a *social* phenomenon, in terms of the way that people interact. The standard philosophical emphasis on principles, consequences, and the isolated concept of 'individual character' de-emphasizes or even ignores social relations and relationships between particular people (as opposed to the general notions of 'the public good' or 'society'). Of course, any philosophical theory worthy of the name will be sufficiently flexible to claim to encompass and include such personal and social implications, whether as part of the preconditions of the theory or by way of subtle and extended calculation (as, for example, an economist might claim to explain all of human behavior by way of "cost/benefit" analysis and utility maximization). The problem is not that social and personal relations cannot be included in such theories, but rather that they are sidelined, de-emphasized, reduced at best to mere "instances." But the thesis I want to pursue here is that the wrongness of lying does not have to do primarily with breaches of principle or miscalculations of utility, even if these weigh heavily in particular cases—in a court of law or congressional hearing, for example. Lying is wrong because it constitutes a breach of *trust,* which is not a principle but a very particular and personal relationship between people.[23]

Neither is the wrongness of lying primarily a matter of "character," although, to be sure, questions of character and integrity do arise, not so much in the relationship itself as when one steps back to reconsider, "sizing up" one's friend or colleague anew in light of a recent deception or betrayal. Furthermore, one might argue that this concept of character is at best probabalistic and not deterministic. It allows us at most a tentative summary of what an individual has done and a prediction based on less-than-perfect knowledge about what he or she will probably do in the near future. And, of course, this notion of 'character' tends to ignore or make light of those all-important "out-of-character" performances, and it also neglects that important dimension of willpower or resolve so celebrated by many of the existentialists, notably Sartre.[24] The problem with the emphasis on character in most virtue ethicists is that it does not get at the intricacies of human relationships, the way different traits are expressed and stimulated (or inhibited) when two or more people get together. Virtue ethics presupposes a measure of psychological autonomy and constance of character that is probably implausible, in part, one surmises, because of moral philosophy's obsession with talking about more or less isolated ("autonomous") individuals and the equally misleading tendency to talk about relations with *strangers,* rather than friends, family, neighbors, or lovers. Social interchange may be presupposed and implied in any discussion of the virtues (one cannot be "generous" or "charming" if there is no one else to give to or to charm), but it is not the social dynamic itself that gets highlighted in current studies of virtue. In traditional philosophical ethical theories, notably in deontology and utilitarianism, the dynamic and the social nature of ongoing activities and relationships typically gets ignored in favor of what Pincoffs rightly calls "quandary ethics," an emphasis on particularly difficult situations and dilemmas.[25] But shifting that focus from situations and the principles that govern them to the character of the individual does not recapture the lost social dynamics that have been so long ignored or dismissed as mere "psychology" by philosophers.

Lying is essentially a social activity. It not only involves other people (which is obvious), but it is also part of the intercourse that binds people together. Thus lies to strangers are a peripheral concern. Official lies by politicians and professional lies by doctors and others in positions of authority are a special case. Lying is first of all a matter of interpersonal trust, and to say that lying is wrong is to point out that a lie breaches the very trust it necessarily presupposes, not in the abstract sense argued by Kant, but in the very personal and concrete sense that usually goes by the name of *betrayal*.

Therefore, is it always wrong to lie? The question here is not the "perfect" nature of the imperative not to lie nor is it a cost/benefit analysis according to which most lies are harmful and a few white lies may be harmless. If lying is first of all a matter of breaching the trust of a relationship, it follows that the severity of the lie depends on the nature of the relationship and the understanding that forms that trust. This is by no means a simple matter. There are relationships that are built on lies, relationships that thrive on lying, relationships in which only the participants know where the truth begins and ends, and relationships where uncertainty rather than trust as such is the glue that holds them together. There are willing suspensions of trust which presuppose an underlying trust in turn, explicitly in the case of fictional story-telling and performances of various kinds, tacitly in the case of the "sore spots" in any relationship where deception may be the better part of valor. No, lying is not always wrong, and the seemingly simple difference between right and wrong becomes rightly muddled once we appreciate the personal rather than the abstract moral implications of deception.

DECEPTION, SELF-DECEPTION, AND THE SELF

> The difficulty making such distinctions [between real and only apparent truthfulness] is almost as great for liars as for their dupes, because self-deception enters into such estimates to such an extraordinary degree. Hypocrites half believe their own stories, and sentimentality makes fraud take on the most innocuous tints.
> —Sissela Bok, *Lying*

Self and Deception

> It takes two to lie, one to lie and one to listen.
> —Homer Simpson

It is one thing to self-consciously and intentionally tell what one knows to be a falsehood, but it is something quite different to tell what one sincerely believes which turns out to be false. Thus the phenomenon of self-deception further muddies the supposedly transparent waters of truth telling and knowledge. What is it to know the truth? And what if one doesn't seem to know but nevertheless *ought* to know the truth? The presence of that "ought" suggests that self-deception and deception have a normative as well as a factual basis. We are taught that the truth is of primary importance, more important than social harmony. But surely this is itself a normative judgment, cultivated in some societies and not in others. What of those many societies (and is ours so obviously excepted?) in which saying what one is supposed to say is deemed more important than saying what one believes to be the truth? In so many discussions of deception, and especially self-deception, it is simply assumed that in lying one is clear about the truth oneself and then purposefully and directly misleads the other about its nature.[26] Lying, accordingly, is fully intentional and malicious, at least insofar as it willfully deprives another of something extremely important: the truth. But this presupposes a degree of autonomy, rationality, and transparency that just does not hold up to scrutiny. There are, of course, cold-blooded, self-interested lies, knowingly false answers to such direct questions as Where were you last night? and Who ate all the cookies? But one might consider the claim that such lies are the special case rather than the rule, like cold-blooded murder for profit in the bloody complex of accidental, negligent, desperate, and passionate homicides. Our fascination with lying and deception will not be satisfied by the straightforward cases favored by the philosophers. What we are after is a drama of truth and falsehood in the complex social and emotional webs we weave, compared to which what is often singled out as "the lie" tends to become a mere epiphenomenon, an ethical "dangler" of comparatively little philosophical interest.

Self-deception, like deception, is a dynamic social phenomenon, not only an internal drama or a pathological condition. However, the "social" nature of the phenomenon is often less than obvious, but part of the reason for this is that philosophers tend to think of self-deception as an odd and even paradoxical version of deception, as a "lie to oneself," not involving other people in any way at all. Of course, the lie may well be "about" other people—as in a lover's self-deceptive vision of his or her beloved, and other people may be *affected* by one's self-deception, as they themselves are deceived in turn. But a conception of self-deception that begins with the idea that the dynamics of self-deception are individually self-contained will lose the essential thread, which is not merely terminological, between deception and self-deception, namely, their shared role in our social and personal relationships. So, too, it is important to get away from the static "knowing and not knowing" conception that characterizes many philosophical studies of self-deception.[27] As an integral part of an ongoing relationship both deception and self-deception are necessarily dynamic, unstable (or, perhaps, "metastable")[28] and a continuous effort of enormous complexity.[29]

Deception and self-deception, I want to argue, are conceptually distinct but thoroughly entangled phenomena. Superficially, one essentially involves other people, the other does not. But to treat them as different versions of the same phenomenon in two very different settings or to treat them wholly differently (as lying and lying to oneself, respectively) is to miss the dynamic that motivates both (and to miss the very important differences between them). To fool ourselves, we must either fool or exclude others; and to successfully fool others, we best fool ourselves. Philosophical discussions of lying too often take as the paradigm example, the straightforwardly cynical, self-interested lie, and ignore the more common species of lying that includes self-deception. Transparency to ourselves can be just as intolerable as transparency to others and for just the same reason. The self, with its flaws and failings, is all too evident. The recognition of one's own motives and the significance of one's own thoughts can be devastating to one's self-image and sense of self. Part of the self is self-presentation and self-disclosure, but an aspect of equal importance is the need to disguise or to hide, those facets of the self that are less than flattering, humiliating, or simply irrelevant to the social context or interpersonal project at hand. To a certain extent, this is merely a matter of attention, of editing, of selective self-presentation, but it is not just (or even for the most part) in our own hands. The self is essentially a social construct, and our sense of ourselves depends on other people, or what Jean-Paul Sartre called (with more than a touch of paranoia) "our Being-for-Others."[30] One can hide or refuse to disclose oneself to oneself in many ways, notably by ignoring or distracting oneself, but none of these ploys has a ghost of a chance if others cannot be distracted or fooled—or at least put off—as well. Deception and self-deception are intimately intertwined. We fool ourselves in order to fool others, and we fool others in order to fool ourselves. And to make it more complicated (as it should be), we do not always know which is which, who is self and who is other.

Deception between persons is rarely so cynical that it does not involve more than a trace of sincerity and belief, in most cases the belief that even if this particular "fact" is false, the truth that the lie is protecting is far more

Self and Deception

significant than the act of lying. Thus we have the lover who lies to protect his love, or the scientist who fudges her results to "prove" a hypothesis she just "knows" to be true. Sissela Bok rightly suggests that there is a thin line at best separating the lie for the sake of the truth and the lie that marks one a liar. Lying for the sake of the truth is a paradox that already requires a considerable amount of self-deception. Deception between persons is rarely if ever unmotivated, and even a mischievous lie "for its own sake" (the familiar "shaving" of one's age, for example) is typically a cover-up for other lies, insecurities, and distrust. Thus Samuel Johnson wrote, of self-deceptive men who would be virtuous, "Having none to recall their attention to their lives, they rate themselves by the goodness of their opinions, and forget how much more easily men may shew their virtue in their talk than in their actions." As we start to understand deception and self-deception as essential aspects of self-consciousness and not as willful violations of principle or antisocial acts, we begin to lose that sense of blanket condemnation of "lying as wrong" and understand deception and self-deception as part of the matrix of human relations, neither good nor evil as such, but open to sympathy and understanding rather than blame. Amélie Rorty recites the touching case of a talented young doctor who refuses to recognize in herself all of the evident symptoms of cancer. Her behavior makes it obvious that, in some sense, she does know of her condition, but the explicit recognition would be devastating. And so she pretends, to herself and to others, convincing no one but herself, perhaps, but maintaining the desperate deception nonetheless. Is there anyone at all who would call such behavior blameworthy?[31]

People tell lies not only to avoid punishment or to impress others but because they need to define and protect themselves (their selves) and cope with difficult social situations. Within the limited realm of self-knowledge, in particular, deception is almost always a matter of coping rather than a celebration of falsehood as such. Indeed, what it means to be false to oneself is a rather complex ethical problem; our knowledge of ourselves is not only incomplete but undergoing continuous revision, often along the lines of ideals and ambitions, that are themselves ill-conceived, inappropriate, or merely borrowed. It is within this continuing co-authorship of self and self-esteem that both deception and self-deception must be appreciated. Even the most cynical interpersonal intrigues are first of all shared productions of the self, involving both conspiracy and vulnerability in more or less equal measure. Consider, for example, the web of affections and deceptions in Chodoros Laclos's *Liasons dangereuses,* which deceptively presents itself to us as an aristocratic game but soon reveals itself as a life-or-death theater of mutual self-deception. And as in *Liasons dangereuses,* (whose author felt it necessary to produce a lengthy preface morally denouncing and distancing himself from the psychology he so insightfully represented), what is too often presented as a morality tale becomes a study in interpersonal psychology and the mutual, surreptitious, social construction of the self.[32] It is not as if ethics is (or should be) absent from such a study, but our evaluations can no longer be of the Manichean "truth is good, deception is evil" variety.

In self-deception, telling the truth can easily become a vice parading as a virtue. In the name of integrity, one can use truth as a weapon and honesty as a strategy. Children and lovers, as authors on the subject often point out, frequently tell the truth precisely in order to hurt and to humiliate. Such truth telling can be manipulative, even vicious. In Camus's last novel, *The Fall,* an extremely devious character named "Clamence" confesses to an acquaintance (the reader, of course) the truth about his life, including first and foremost the many lies he had always told himself.[33] However, what becomes obvious is that he is still deceiving himself by way of seducing the other, and even his truths are only a ploy. What Clamence is after, we learn in the last pages, is neither truth nor total disclosure but a subtle vengeance, and his confession is a subversive expression of a deeply felt resentment. But who is the victim, and who is the villain in such tales of deviousness? Why do we think that victims and villains must be part of the structure of deception? As often as not, deception and self-deception combine to form the most sincere belief among co-conspirators, not victim and villain. Virtually every faith and religion is a large-scale example of such belief, but so too is almost everyone's self-image and every society's sense of itself, including the scientific and philosophical communities as well as every ethnic group or culture. Nietzsche and later Jung wrote extensively on our need for myths and warned against an age that would try to do without them. But what is a myth if not an elaborate self-defining collective self-deception, and if all such deceptions are wrong, then would there be any truth that is ultimately worth defending?

THE TANGLED WEB:
DUPLICITY AS A HOLISTIC PHENOMENON

> O, what a tangled web we weave
> When first we practice to deceive.
> —Sir Walter Scott

If deception and self-deception are to be understood first of all as interrelated dynamic interpersonal and social phenomena, then it is a mistake to try to understand them in terms of one or another artificially isolated aspect

Self and Deception

of the relationship. For example, in most modern discussions of lying, much of the focus has been on the alleged victim, the person who is misled or betrayed by the lie. The evaluation thus tends to trace out the obvious and the not so obvious effects of even the "whitest" lie, its ability to undermine trust and render the victim helpless when the truth might well have allowed some significant action. Sissela Bok, for example, pursues such a quest in wonderful detail, tracing the consequences of professional lies, political lies, loving lies, paternalistic lies, therapeutic lies, experimental lies, and so on.[34] Bok discusses at length the complications of authoritarian deception and the manufacture of excuses, including the notorious slippery-slope argument from the very plausible claim that "the whole truth" is impossible to tell down to the insidious thesis that the truth is not necessary. That is the challenge and the fun of philosophical investigations of lying, of course; first we recognize the obvious immediate consequences: hurt feelings, a tragically un- or ill-informed patient (client, friend, public). Then the devastating penalties for an unsuccessful "cover-up" become evident. Finally, there are the more subtle implications of spreading distrust, increased cynicism and consequent withdrawal, a corruption of language and public discourse. However, what gets left out of many of those discussions of deception is the need to focus on the liar and not just the consequences facing the liar. For if deception and self-deception are so intimately involved, then the assumption that the perpetrator of the lie is not also its victim becomes less plausible. The lie is a matter of mutual engagement and not just a malevolent act perpetrated by one person upon another.

Alternatively, when philosophers have fixed their gaze on the nature of the lie instead of its consequences, they have tended to even further deny the interpersonal and social nature of deception. Kant in particular was adamant about the logical inconsistency of the "maxim" of any and every lie, established by the fact that one could not universalize the allowability of lying without undermining the very possibility of language (assuming, that is, that the primary purpose of language centers around such activities as describing true facts and making promises). Of course, because lying is (by definition) the *intentional* telling of a falsehood, some attention must be focused on the liar who has and exercises that intention. But Kant quite explicitly dismisses and ignores the motives and the character behind the lie, preferring to emphasize the immorality of lying rather than to understand the psychological and social dynamics. But even as ethics, it is certainly not unimportant what motivates lying and what kind of characters we are dealing with when we point our fingers at liars. Here is where "virtue ethics" gains its hold. But to overemphasize the character of the liar is just as misleading as an isolated emphasis on the lie or its consequences. Deception is, to employ an over-used and much abused word, a *holistic* phenomenon. One cannot break it up into parts and expect to understand its vital organic unity. One cannot try to understand or evaluate the lie, the liar, the victim, and the consequences and then put these together in some "multi-dimensional" analysis which adds up to an adequate understanding.

One of the most distinctive and most neglected features of lying is that it is surprisingly hard to do. As anyone who has tried to protect even a small casual lie can tell you, the amount of thought and care that are required to keep in mind all of the logical implications and possible contradictions (If I was at Sam's place, then I couldn't have seen Thelma at the Casino, but if I didn't see Thelma, then how could I have known about the party at Shelby's house?). It is always easiest, the old adage tells us (with considerable truth), to tell the truth. But next easiest is to believe your own lie, to become so submerged in its network of details and implications that the continuation of the lie—as Aristotle argued for honesty—becomes but second nature, without further thought or deliberation. In either case, however, neither ease nor difficulty is a dependable mark of morality, and one might (like a novelist or any other storyteller) delight in the intrigue and self-conscious tension that artful lying requires. Part of the pathology of compulsive liars may well be the high-adrenalin challenge of holding a number of lies together as a high-risk acrobat might juggle a number of brightly-lit torches or razor-sharp knives—along with the sometimes psychotic need to cover-up not just something but (by logical implication) almost everything. Here, of course, there is some temptation to scissor off the liar from any particular lie or any particular audience, but a moment's reflection makes it clear that this too is a distinctively and often compulsively public performance, part of a possibly rich and probably very deep pattern of self-deception as well as a way of relating to other people, despite the fact that the nature of the relationship may be quite puzzling or offensive to them. So, too, with more innocent and straightforwardly strategic lies. Lying involves a complex logic that reaches across and cuts through our various social relationships and sometimes with great difficulty weaves a portrait of the self and its relations. And even in self-deception, it is the inconsistencies in our stories discovered or discoverable by other people that motivate our continued efforts at duplicity. After all, if self-deception were a matter of mere internal consistency, would anyone but a logician feel compelled to avoid inconsistency at all costs? Would "cognitive dissonance" ever become an issue, much less a motivational force, if it did not also become subject to the scrutiny of others?[35]

No matter what the challenge or the logical complexity of the lie or the effects of the lie on the liar and his or her social entanglements, the

Self and Deception

primary concern always seems to be the benign or harmful effects of the lie on the listener. But here again there is a social matrix and a set of interpersonal presumptions that generally go unnoticed. What renders most lies odious is that they occur in a context in which one expects the truth, most obviously, in response to a direct inquiry. But even there the odiousness of the lie depends on the context and the nature of the question (What are you thinking?), and there are circumstances in which only a Kantian or a paranoid would insist that the truth is essential and lying immoral. Imagine yourself on an inter-city bus or a short-hop plane next to a somewhat tedious fellow passenger who insists on knowing what you do? One can readily imagine offering up the most banal and boring answer as an alternative to an utterly offensive reply, or, alternatively, one can with slightly more effort imagine constructing a fascinating but wholly false account of one's life as a KGB double agent or a Texas Ranger. In the first case, one gets a chance to get some reading or sleeping done, while in the second, there would seem to be no harm done but rather a welcome entertainment for both of you during an otherwise tedious voyage. There is, of course, the odd chance that one's fellow passenger may (contrary to all expectations) show up again, wreaking the sort of havoc that only old movies can fully appreciate, and it is true, no doubt, that every lie opens one up to possible complications of this sort. But this is hardly a moral objection to lying, and in the absence of harm such elaborate lies seem unobjectionable. (So, too, one could argue, for the "big lies" that hold most cultures and religions together—myths of origin, shared fantasies of moral right and manifest destiny, illusions of favored status in the eyes of the divine, delusions of grandeur.[36]) But here again the attention should be on the social context and the relationship—in the above case essentially transient—and not on the lie or the consequences of the lie exclusively.

It is a mistake to think about and condemn deception and self-deception *sui generis*. There are legitimate lies in literature, heuristics in science, myth in religion and philosophy, but these are not just isolated fictional frames with at most metaphorical connections to considerations of self or extremely tenuous "expressions" of ourselves and our relations with other people. Quite the contrary, these are the "myths and metaphors we live by," according to many authors from the ancients to our contemporaries.[37] Once we give up the philosophical tendency to generalize about deception and self-deception in the abstract and focus instead on the whole phenomenon of lying, the intentions and motives behind it, the context as well as the consequences and the interpersonal relationship between the participants, it becomes increasingly obvious that most lies are not merely lies but also self-deception and part of a larger matrix of beliefs and emotions that define not only this relationship but a community or a culture. The lies of love (or pretended love) depend for their credibility on a remarkable institution that defines and gives structure as well as elaborate discourse to a seemingly "primitive" emotion.[38] Consider how much cultural apparatus goes into the simple but vicious lie, when someone falsely utters "I love you." And how often the felt truth is uttered with the knowledge (or in many cases a host of doubts) that it may in fact be a lie? Self-deception, like deception, is motivated not by self-interest, cold and calculating, but by our engagement in an emotionally charged world in which things *matter* to us, in which the truth is by no means clear and wishful thinking and the expectations of others matter more to us than that abstract metaconception known to us as "the Truth."

Deception and self-deception are part and parcel of our engagements in the world including, not least, the development and maintenance of our image and sense of ourselves. Deception is first of all a way of relating, a not-entirely-accurate presentation of self to others and to oneself. There is no juncture where presentation becomes deception, where pretense becomes sincerity, where play becomes the real thing. Self-presentation is always deception, but whether or not it counts as deception or whether or not it is blameworthy depends on the context, the performance, and the expectations.[39] Some deception is harmful and even immoral, but some of it is neither. Indeed, an extremist might even argue that there is no such phenomenon as lying as such, only various ways in which we relate to one another as insecure social creatures surrounded and infiltrated by an inevitably equivocal language. Perhaps we are not only capable of lying but virtually incapable of not doing so.[40] Deception and self-deception, according to such a kinky view, may not be perversions so much as they are the very stuff of human intercourse.

SELF, SOCIETY, AND CULTURE: A "CHINESE" CONCEPTION OF SELF-DECEPTION

> The same illusion that the East labored for thousands of years to abandon, is the one that the West has laboured just as long to maintain.
> —Hermann Hesse, *Steppenwolf*

But how "human," that is, how universal, is "human intercourse"? And how universal, accordingly, are the phenomena of deception and self-deception? It is evident that some people lie more than others, and so, too,

Self and Deception

different peoples treat deception—for example, the misleading or cheating of strangers—very differently. Does it make sense to suppose that some cultures might not recognize the category of the lie, might not condemn or for that matter even have a concept of deception, might not be capable of self-deception? I earlier suggested (following a comment by Annette Baier) that we at least consider the hypothesis that self-deception is not only deception *of* the self but *about* the self as well. The "self" is not merely an indication of direction but of content as well. Strictly construed, of course, the hypothesis is palpably false. One can fool oneself about the future of one's children or the fate of the economy or the prospects for war, and none of these are "about" the self. But they are all, to various degrees of abstraction, self-*involved,* and the nature of the self that is involved is an essential ingredient in the deception. But just as deception and self-deception are interpersonal and social phenomena, so too is the self a social phenomenon. This is a controversial suggestion, and it is complicated enormously by the (even more controversial) claim that the self is differently construed in different societies and cultures. Moreover, it is one thing to claim that the self is socially contrued, another to insist that it is socially constructed, and still another to maintain that it is socially constructed as a social self. I find these three claims often linked or conflated, and I think it is extremely important to separate them. So the question I want to ask, in conclusion, is What is the role of the self in self-deception? What does one's culture have to do with the seemingly autonomous relation between a person and his or her beliefs?

It is too often simply assumed in discussions of self-deception that the self in question is merely a "formal indicator" (Heidegger's term), a peculiarity of the first-person view, which is then variously hypostatized along various ontological lines, most of them in accordance with the internalist model. But even this minimalist conception of the self—and the first-person viewpoint it assumes—is a distinctively "Western" conception, and it is very much a part of the individualist, independent, autonomous vision of the person that is part and parcel of Western philosophy from Descartes to Sartre and Rousseau to Rawls. It has been pointed out—and I now take at least the anthropological claim to be no longer controversial—that other cultures construe the notion of the self quite differently. In a summary article that is receiving widespread attention in psychology and anthropology, Hazel Rose Markus and Shinobu Kitayama suggest that "divergent contruals of self, others and the interdependence of the two" suggest deep implications for the understanding of different cultures, their systems of knowledge, ways of behaving, and the relativity of emotions. The authors limit themselves to a somewhat unspecified discussion of two different modes of self-construal: "Western" and "non-Western," exemplified, for example, by American and Chinese (and other Asian) societies respectively. They refer to the essential difference between these two construals of selves as "independent" and "interdependent." What they say throws a dark shadow across the universal pretensions of the "so-called Western view of the individual as an independent, self-contained, autonomous entity who (a) comprises a unique configuration of internal attributes . . . and (b) behaves primarily as a consequence of these internal attributes."[41] So, too, the notion of an interdependent construal of self puts the internalist model of self-deception—if not the very notion of self-deception—in jeopardy. Who is being fooled? about what? and why should anyone care?

The claim that there is a difference between the Western individualist conception of self and various alternative "social" conceptions of the self has often been made, with various degrees of evidence, sophistication, and persuasiveness. So, too, it has been claimed (for instance by Roger Ames) that in China there is no such phenomenon as self-deception.[42] But my claim is that the "Western" conception of self has itself been misconstrued, that whatever individualist ontologies may serve as the premises for philosophers and provide the catchphrases for politicians, our conception of self is in fact far more social as well as socially constituted than we are usually willing to recognize. And, therefore, so is the phenomenon of self-deception. As well as numerous suggestions by other "Western" philosophers, I would consider superindividualist Jean-Paul Sartre's emphasis on the ineluctable importance of "Being-for others" as one piece of evidence for this hypothesis. Hegel and Schopenhauer defended notions of the nonindividual self (as "Spirit" and as "Will" respectively) on more or less a priori grounds, taking their departure from Kant.[43] Almost two centuries earlier, Spinoza defended an equally cosmic conception of the self, arguing too that the individual self is an illusion. Heidegger described a conception of the "anonymous" self under the rubric of Das Man in his *Being and Time* (1928), and the Cartesian conception of the unified self has suffered a severe case of fragmentation if not pulverization under the auspices of his current Parisian progeny.[44] The self is, as the French anthropologist Mauss suggested in 1938, a "delicate cateory," subject to substantial variation.[45] It is, in other words, by no means obvious that philosophy in the European tradition has assumed without question the autonomous individuality and independence of the self. And insofar as philosophy is a reflection of the thinking of more ordinary folk, I would suggest (though not only on those grounds) that our Western conception of the self is far more interdependent in practice, if not always in theory, than the usual self-caricature would allow.

Self and Deception

In China, in particular, the self is explicitly social or "interdependent," in the vocabulary of Markus and Kitayama. One consequence of this is that telling the truth is not of primary importance. It is much less important than social harmony, showing respect, playing one's role and "getting along." Accordingly, deception is a very different concept, when it is applicable at all. Saying what one is expected to say, acting as one is expected to act, is essential. There is no inner drama, no inner conflict between integrity and expectation. Where there is conflict, it is a confrontation of loyalties, a conflict of expectations. So, then, we can understand why Ames might want to claim that self-deception is impossible. But why should we assume that the Chinese view is all that foreign to us? In other words, the conceptual gap between ourselves and the Chinese is not so profound, so "incommensurable," at least along this dimension.[46] I do not want (and am not able) to explore the Chinese conceptions of self and self-deception here, but I do want to challenge our Western view of the "Western" view of the self. I would like to end by rendering our conception of ourselves—and consequently our understanding of self-deception, more "Chinese."

I want to distinguish here between two quite different models of self-deception, which in turn depend on two quite different models of the self. I have already referred to them, uncreatively, as the *internalist* and the *externalist* models of self-deception, and they are based respectively on similarly internalist and externalist accounts of the self. An internalist views self-deception as a relation between a person and a set of beliefs (broadly construed, which may or may not involve the contradictory "believing p and not-p" paradox that preoccupies so much of the analytic literature). Accordingly, internalist models of self-deception tend to be concerned with the internal structure or architecture of the self. Thus Freud divides the self into consciousness and an unconscious, a troubled house with an inaccessible basement, and later into "agencies." Amélie Rorty ingeniously suggests that the self is something like a medieval city, a virtual labyrinth of pathways and neighborhoods functioning independently and without knowledge of the others.[47] Less architectural theorists look to gerry-mandering belief, or by-passing belief altogether, by way of "avowals" or other acknowledgements.[48] The problem for the internalist, perhaps but not necessarily made more intractable by paradox, is to understand how one can in some sense "know and not seem to know." Self-deception, in other words, is first of all an epistemological problem.

The externalist, on the other hand, sees self-deception as a social phenomenon. It has to do not so much with a person and his or her beliefs as with a person and his or her roles and relationships. Self-deception is a consequence of wanting to be thought of and treated in certain ways and not others, by other people. One's self-conceptions are the product and not the source of the opinions of others, and self-deception is thus an attempt to manipulate those opinions, not just one's own. I think the idea that we fool ourselves in order to fool others, more often than not, is backwards, and the idea that in self-deception we first of all lie to ourselves is just plain wrong. Self-deception begins and continues by playing a part, by acting the good husband, the responsible citizen, the competent, healthy professional. This may or may not be accompanied by self-avowal. It may or may not be accompanied by rationalization or denial. Self-deception is thus first of all a performance, if sometimes a performance enjoyed only by oneself. Thus Sartre considers being for others an essential ingredient of the self, even when others are not around.[49] It is also within the perspective of being for others that we can understand why Sartre comes down so hard on "sincerity," which is only a "display" of the truth, a show, another self-presentation, a mode of deception and not genuine self-reflection.[50] Here, too, we can understand why Roger Ames can claim that the Chinese have no conception of self-deception. He is appealing to the clearly externalist model of the Chinese self and with it an externalist account of self-deception. But, again, why should we assume that the internalist model so accurately portrays the European self, or that the externalist view is all that foreign to us? On the externalist model, self-deception is contextual, and the context is paradigmatically a social context. I would claim just this for our Western conception of self-deception. Indeed, at the extremes of this view, there is no self without others.[51] (St. Exupery: "Man is but a network of relationships, and these alone matter to him."[52]) According to the externalist model, one might, half tongue in cheek, say that the "inner self" is social.

However, what does it mean to say that the self is social? I mentioned earlier that it is one thing to claim that the self is socially contrued, another to insist that it is socially constructed, and still another to maintain that it is socially constructed as a social self—three claims often conflated. To say that the self is socially contrued is by far the weakest of the three, the one understandably adopted by most social scientists, and it leaves entirely open to what extent the nature of the self is determined, for example, by biological and noncognitive social forces and attitudes. To have a construal of the self is to adopt a perspective, to look at it a certain way, but this has minimal ontological commitments. For example, it might be that as a teacher I construe the selves of my students as "student selves," that is, defined in terms of their behavior, preparation for and performance in class. I do not pretend that they do not have other, most likely more pressing, conceptions of self themselves, as I find immediately and perhaps rudely when meeting them in the local beer hall. To claim that different cultures construe the self in different ways is to make a minimal claim, one that is just as true of various subcultures in our own culture. Self-deception, so understood, would consist in part of adopting an inappropriate construal of self in certain contexts.

To say that the self is socially constructed, by contrast, is to make a much more radical claim. It is to insist that there is no self apart from its construction in particular social contexts (although one might distinguish here between a very general claim that one will have no concept of self at all unless he or she grows up in some society and the more particularist claim that a person learns to cultivate a particular self—a Texan, a Kuangchou, or a Maori self, for example—only by growing up in Texas, Kuangchou, or Tanderoa [New Zealand]).[53] However, to insist that the self is constructed is not yet to claim that the construction is of any particular typology; in particular, it does not mean that the self so constructed is a social self. The American "rugged" individualist is a socially constructed self, as is the infamously antisocial Ik.[54]

To say that the self is socially constructed as a social self is to make a very particular kind of claim, which must be distinguished from the other two. The Chinese self is socially constructed as a social self, an interdependent self, but, again, we need to make at least one further problematic distinction. The social construction of self proceeds in part by way of a language, a language which includes a certain vocabulary of selfhood. In this language we learn to talk about ourselves in certain ways. A self-consciously individualist culture will naturally emphasize the importance of such notions as 'individuality,' 'autonomy,' and 'independence.' A self-consciously communitarian culture will naturally emphasize the importance of such notions as 'community,' 'loyalty,' 'duty,' and 'kinship.' But how we talk about ourselves is only a partial indication of how we *think* about ourselves and how we actually behave. The social construction of self also proceeds without language, without self-description, by way of ten thousand nonverbal cues and examples, everything from a mother's refusal to leave her infant alone even for a minute and the fact that people tend not to look each other in the eyes, to the waging of war and the celebration of religious rituals. Therefore, it is perfectly possible for a culture to cultivate a way of talking about themselves and the self, that is somewhat at odds with the ways in which they actually conceive of themselves and their relationships to one another. Indeed, in times of social tension or dislocation, or in order to distinguish oneself from an alien culture, such divergence of self-conception from practice may be extremely common.[55]

It is this that I claim about some of our own self-conceptions. After two hundred years of self-conscious "enlightenment" and "romantic" thinking and works of imagination, after a century of war against aboriginal tribal cultures in the name of progress and "The American Dream," after three-quarters of a century of confrontation with societies which we generically condemned as "Communist" and "Collectivist," and after decades of philosophically doltish political campaigns in which the language of individual autonomy and rights eclipsed all other figures of speech, we not surprisingly have come to believe our own rhetoric, not as rhetoric but as the most profound of philosophies. We have come to accept a concept of ourselves and the self which is quite at odds with our communal way of life, our insistence on affection, friendship, and family, our life in communities, organizations, and institutions that belies our myth of the autonomous individual. But, of course, self-conceptions, no matter how false, influence and eventually determine the construction of self, which is a constant process and not a fait accompli. There are no "national types," only selves in progress. And so, on the evidence of the last decade or so, we are becoming what we have long celebrated, but as monsters not as men and women. We are starting to live according to the rhetoric of individualism, and we are in the midst of destroying ourselves. This is our most troublesome source of self-deception, not the relatively harmless lies to oneself that perplex the philosophers, but the great lie of a philosophically and politically misunderstood conception of self. It is not the denial of multiculturalism in the name of an ethnocentric, universalist notion of self that is troubling, but the nature of that self. We are by nature, as Aristotle wrote two and a half millenia ago, social animals, and we could not and cannot be otherwise. To believe anything else is the most insidious self-deception, and one of those places where we learn, at our peril, that we must master some truths, at any cost, any way.

NOTES

*Portions of this chapter are adapted from a chapter I wrote for M. Lewis and C. Saarni, eds., *Lying in Everyday Life* (New York: Guilford Press, 1992).

1. Nietzsche, *Beyond Good and Evil.*
2. Consider Nietzsche's late lament, "Has anyone understood me?" *(Ecce Homo)* Consider too Derrida's indignant response to widespread criticism of his work when he was offered an honorary degree at Cambridge in the spring of 1992. "I have never written any such thing!" he insisted to the press and against his critics, hardly indifferent to the truth of the matter. Of course, this is not a refutation of the position (any more than the perils of Pyrrhus constituted a refutation of ancient skepticism). But it is a pragmatic paradox of considerable interest, what Bernd Magnus (following Fish) calls a "self-consuming concept."
3. C. A. J. Coady, "The Morality of Lying."

Self and Deception

4. Indeed, Sidgwick further suggested that philosophers might be well instructed to lie systematically to their readers. While he firmly believed in the truth of the doctrine of utilitarianism, he also believed that public knowledge of that doctrine might have results that would be disastrous. Accordingly, the promotion of the utilitarian doctrine in practice required its systematic deception.

5. For example, one might deny that a person has a *right* to the truth in question. Do Nazis have a right to know where their innocent victim is hiding? Does an eavesdropper have the right to overhear only truths? It is said that dishonesty is a form of injustice, but in that case greater injustices may excuse or override the injustice of a lie. One might even refuse to call unjust lies "lies." This maneuver would presumably also eliminate jokes and fictions as lies, at least where the audience does not expect to hear the truth. Of course, one critical concern here is the case of "white lies," often based on social conventions. See C. A. J. Coady, *Testimony* (New York: Oxford University Press, 1992). Even more interesting are those cases and cultures in which social convention is considered mandatory and "trump," even at the expense of what we would consider an outright lie.

6. Amélie Rorty, "Adaptivity and Self-Knowledge," in *Mind in Action;* "User-Friendly Self-deception: A Traveler's Manual," in this volume.

7. This is the formulation discussed in the analytic literature, for example, in Brian McLaughlin, "Self-Deception and the Structure of the Self," in this volume, and it is the point of departure even for those who reject the paradox, e.g., Herbert Fingarette in his excellent *Self-Deception.* It is also used by Jean-Paul Sartre at the beginning of his famous discussion of "bad faith" *(mauvaise foi)* in *Being and Nothingness (L'etre et le neant),* 86–116, but this is unfortunate, as bad faith is clearly a much broader and richer concept than self-deception. In fact, Sartre uses the paradox only to set up a show-trial against Freud's psychological determinism and attack his notion of the 'Unconscious.' The "knowing p and not-p" paradox plays virtually no role either in his examples or in his subsequent arguments. I would suggest that the examples in the early (part 1) chapter on bad faith might better be looked at in the light of the concept of 'being for others' and the all-important notions of 'freedom' and 'responsibility' in parts 3 and 4 respectively. Indeed, I would argue that Sartre's attack on Freud and his casual treatment of the paradoxes of self-deception are at most secondary if not incidental to his overall aim, which is to attack what Kathleen Higgins has called the "atmosphere" of irresponsibility that he perceived in Parisian society. (Of course, as so often, the same charge has been turned on Sartre himself, by Herbert Lottman, in his detailed chronicles of the actual (lack of) involvement of Sartre and his comrades in the Resistance and in the war.)

8. E.g., Carolyn Ristau on broken-wing displays by waterbirds in "Aspects of the Cognitive Ethology of an Injury-Feigning Bird, the Piping Plover," in *Cognitive Ethology: The Minds of Other Animals,* ed. C. Ristau (Hillsdale, NJ: Erlbaum, 1991). See also D. Cheney and R. Seyfarth, *How Monkeys See the World* (Chicago: Chicago University Press, 1990) on deceptiveness among primates.

9. I owe this tentative suggestion to Annette Baier.

10. Nietzsche, *Beyond Good and Evil.*

11. Nietzsche, "On Truth and Lie in the Extra-Moral Sense" (1873), in *The Portable Nietzsche*, ed. W. Kaufmann (New York: Viking, 1954).
12. Kant, *Grounding of the Metaphysics of Morals*.
13. Sartre, *Being and Nothingness*, "Bad Faith."
14. Edmund Pincoffs, *Quandaries and Virtues*.
15. Nor should this be assumed to apply only to "advanced" and philosophical cultures. The ancient inhabitants of the island of Maui used to throw the umbilical cords of their newborn infants into the (then active) crater of the volcano Haleakale to assure that their children would grow up to be honest. On my way to the East-West Conference on Self and Deception, I was particularly struck by the fact that, of all the virtues, honesty was singled out as exemplary.
16. Aristotle, *Nicomachean Ethics*.
17. Aristotle, *Politics*.
18. Plato, *Republic*, book 7.
19. Fyodor Dostoevski, *The Idiot*.
20. Albert Camus, *The Stranger*. Camus's commentary on his novel was published over a decade later, in the preface to Germaine Greer's 1955 edition. Camus's judgment is compromised by the fact that Meursault does lie in the novel, indeed, commits outright perjury, and his obliviousness to matters of morals make it highly unlikely that he can be said to "refuse to lie."
21. It is perhaps not without intentional ambiguity that this originally religious injunction (John 8:32) is engraved on the administration building of the University of Texas at Austin.
22. Nietzsche, *Beyond Good and Evil*.
23. Laurence Thomas, *Living Morally*.
24. Sartre. *Being and Nothingness*.
25. Pincoffs. *Quandaries and Virtues*.
26. Sartre, *Being and Nothingness;* Fingarette, *Self-Deception*.
27. Robert Audi, "Self-Deception, Rationalization, and Reasons for Acting," in *Perspectives on Self-Deception*, ed. B. McLaughlin and A. Rorty.
28. A term that Jean-Paul Sartre borrows from chemistry in *Being and Nothingness*, 99f. Metastability has a tentative stability, an appearance of stability, but the slightest intrusion or misstep brings about total disaster. Consider a waiter carrying an overly full tray of cups of hot coffee. All goes smoothly until the first jiggle, and a single boiling hot drop touches his bare skin. He flinches slightly, and . . .
29. Ibid., 112ff.; cf. Marcia Baron, "What Is Wrong with Self-Deception?" in *Perspectives*, ed. McLaughlin and Rorty.
30. Sartre, *Being and Nothingness*, part 3. Philosophers typically talk as if our sense of personal identity were just an internal affair (of self-revelation, memory, or the transcendental unity of consciousness). Indeed, Sartre's analysis of the self in *Being and Nothingness* too readily appears to be such an "internalist" account. (Even the name *for itself* has obvious Cartesian credentials.) But in our obligatory reading of Sartre in the context of discussions of self-deception, I would like to urge that three textual points be kept in mind. (1) The famous, often-reprinted chapter on bad faith is one (remarkably short) early chapter in an eight-hundred-page book,

and the subject is rarely mentioned again. (2) Sartre insists the "being-for-others" is on an "ontological par" with the other two modes of being, "being-for-itself" and "being-in-itself." He is not, therefore, a traditional Cartesian dualist, and his concept of 'self' is not an internalist account. In fact, Sartre's argument and his examples are quite at odds with the ontological apparatus he has provided for us in that early chapter of his humongous book. The examples, which have been rightly criticized as inadequate by Allen Wood (in *Perspectives,* ed. Rorty and McLaughlin) involve "being-for-others" as well as the categories of "facticity" and "transcendence" he explicitly employs there. Thus construed, they escape many of Wood's (and other traditional) objections. (3) In an earlier work, *The Transcendence of the Ego,* Sartre insists that the self is not "in" consciousness but is "outside of us in the world, like the consciousness of another. His is, therefore, what I will call an "externalist" account of the self, not a Cartesian account at all.

31. Amélie Rorty, "The Deceptive Self, Liars, and Layers" in *Perceptions,* ed. McLaughlin and Rorty.

32. Chodoros Laclos, *Liasons dangereuses.*

33. Camus, *The Fall.* In many ways, *The Fall* is the opposite of *The Stranger.* Meursault (the "stranger") is the very portrait of transparency, all experience and virtually no reflection or self-consciousness. Clamence, by contrast, is all reflection and painful self-consciousness. One tells the truth because he is too simple-minded to lie, the other because he wants to seduce his listeners. In what sense is either of them "not lying"?

34. Sissela Bok, *Lying.*

35. Leon Festinger, *Cognitive Dissonance.*

36. In Fiji, before the arrival of the British, Viti Levu was considered, with some reason, the center of the earth, its largest land mass, surrounded by ocean and a few hundred modest islands. When confronted with a map of the world, nineteenth-century Fijians reacted first with predictable denial, then humiliation. It was then that the story of the great African canoe *Kannitow* became established among the Fijians, despite its dubious veracity. Our British commentator scoffs. But then thinking of the standard stories of our own culture (Columbus's discovery, the conquest of the West, the beacon of democracy and freedom in the world), are our stories any more reasonable?

37. George Lakoff and Mark Johnson, *Myths We Live By.*

38. Roland Barthes, *A Lover's Discourse.*

39. This is the point where proposition-minded philosophers too readily isolate false verbal self-ascriptions of such presentations and point to them as the paradigm of deception—lying, in effect, about who one is. (Aristotle treats "truthfulness" this way, *Ethics,* bk. 4 ch. 9.). But a more typical and more interesting case is the person with some limited knowledge who acts as if he or she is an expert without ever claiming to be so. As casual conversation and social self-presentation, this is innocent enough. But in a context in which a real expert is or becomes urgently needed, it becomes not only deception but also fraud and betrayal. So, too, it is not deception to "act friendly" with a person for whom one has no special affection. Nor is it even obvious that proclaiming one's friendship in such circum-

stances, as encouragement or a friendly gesture, for example, is deception or in any way blameworthy. It is only when the expectations of the so-called friend (or in rare cases, other people) are such that the true devotion of a friend is called for and not forthcoming that, in retrospect, the entire performance gets indicted.

40. Nietzsche, "Truth and Lie in the Extra-moral Sense"; Jean Baudrillard, *Selected Writings*.

41. H. A. Markus and S. Kitayma, "Culture and the Self," 224.

42. Roger T. Ames, "The Classical Chinese Self and Hypocrisy," in this volume.

43. I.e., Kant's "Paralogisms of Rational Psychology." I have examined and defended this connection between Kant and Hegel in "Hegel's Concept of *Geist*" in my *From Hegel to Existentialism* (New York: Oxford University Press, 1988).

44. I am thinking, of course, of Jacques Derrida and Michel Foucault, in particular, as well as several other authors who have engaged in the "death of the author" controversy. On first glance, the fragmentation of self-hypothesis would seem to be exactly the opposite of the "interdependent" conception of self that is evident in many other cultures. But, first, any breaking of the boundaries of the autonomous individual self is already a giant step in the direction of recognizing the optional quality of that conception of self and, second, the ground on which these radical claims are being made is uncontrovertibly a social constructionist view, quite compatible with the multicultural perspective of the self suggested here. However, it is a mistake to simply deny that a unified self is "real," on the grounds that it is in fact socially constructed.

45. M. Mauss, "A Category of the Human Mind," 1–25.

46. It is certainly not my intention to adopt a "universalist" perspective here and defend the obviously false empirical claim that all cultures are essentially alike. But the idea of "total difference" and incommensurability are so pervasive in these disputes that it is sometimes healthy to minimize rather than maximize differences. Indeed, the language of "alternative conceptual schemes" in which so many of these disputes are cast too readily lends itself to such exaggeration. Donald Davidson, in a much-quoted article "On the Very Idea of a Conceptual Scheme," in *Actions and Events*, ed. E. Lepore and B. McLaughlin conscientiously throws such claims into conceptual confusion. But there is nothing in the notion of "alternative conceptual schemes" that requires incommensurability. It is quite sufficient that there is or could be systematic mutual misunderstanding. If one "raises the ante" such that incommensurability becomes the criterion for alternative schemes, however, then, of course, the pressing problems of multicultural understanding get compacted into an impenetrable philosophical paradox.

47. Rorty, "The Deceptive Self, Liars, and Layers."

48. Fingarette, *Self-Deception*.

49. Sartre, *Being and Nothingness*, pt. 3, ch. 1, esp. sec. 4, "The Look."

50. Ibid., 110–11.

51. E.g., Hegel in *Phenomenology*, "Lordship and Bondage"; P. F. Strawson in *Individuals*; and grudgingly even Sartre in "The Reef of Solipsism," *Being and Nothingness*, 303ff.

Self and Deception

52. *Pilote de Guerre* (quoted by Merleau-Ponty in *The Phenomenology of Perception*).

53. Both the general and the particularist claims are developed, for example, by Clifford Geertz in his *Interpretation of Cultures*. Both are suggested, at least, by Hegel *(Phenomenology)*.

54. Colin Turnbull, *The Mountain People*.

55. For two good philosophical discussions of this, see Alasdair MacIntyre's *After Virtue*, especially the opening chapters, and Nietzsche's classic discussion of the Greeks in his *Birth of Tragedy*.

REFERENCES

Aristotle. 1981. *Nicomachean Ethics*. Trans. T. Irwin. Indianapolis: Hackett.
———. 1941. *Politics*. Trans. B. Jowett in R. McKeon, ed. *The Works of Aristotle*. New York, Random House.
Audi, Robert. "Self-Deception, Rationalization, and Reasons for Acting." In B. McLaughlin and A. Rorty, eds. *Perspectives on Self-Deception*.
Baron, Marcia. "What Is Wrong with Self-Deception?" In McLaughlin and Rorty.
Barthes, Roland. 1977. *A Lover's Discourse*. New York: Farrar Straus and Giroux.
Baudrillard, Jean. 1988. *Selected Writings*. Stanford: Stanford University Press.
Bok, Sissela. 1978. *Lying*. New York: Random House.
———. 1983. *Secrets*. New York: Random House.
Briggs, Jean. 1981. *Never in Anger*. Cambridge: Harvard University Press.
Camus, Albert. 1946. *The Stranger*. New York: Random House.
———. 1957. *The Fall*. New York: Random House.
Coady, C. A. J. 1992. "The Morality of Lying," unpublished paper, Melbourne.
deSousa, Ronald. 1988. *The Rationality of Emotions*. Cambridge: MIT Press.
Dostoevski, Fyodor. 1969. *The Idiot*. Trans. Henry and Olga Carlisle. New York: New American Library.
Ekman, Paul. 1990. *Why Kids Lie*. New York: Scribner.
Festinger, Leon. 1957. *The Theory of Cognitive Dissonance*. Stanford: Stanford University Press.
Fingarette, Herbert. 1969. *Self-Deception*. New York: Humanities Press.
Freud, Sigmund. 1929. *Standard Edition of the Collected Works*. London: Hogarth.
Geertz, Clifford. 1966. *Interpretation of Cultures*. New York: Basic Books.
Gur, Ruben C., and Harold A. Sackheim. 1979. "Self-Deception: A Concept in Search of a Phenomenon." *Journal of Personality and Social Psychology*, no. 2.
Johnson, Samuel. 1987. "Self-Deception." In M. Sommers, *Virtue and Vice*. San Diego: Harcourt Brace Jovanovich.
Kant, Immanuel. 1981. *Grounding the Metaphysics of Morals*. Trans. J. Ellington. Indianapolis: Hackett.
Laclos, Chodoros. 1962. *Liasons dangereuses*. New York: Penguin.
Lakoff, George, and Mark Johnson. 1980. *Myths We Live By*. Chicago: University of Chicago Press.

MacIntyre, Alasdair. 1978. *After Virtue*. Notre Dame: University of Notre Dame Press.
Markus, H. A., and S. Kitayama. 1991. "Culture and the Self." *Psychological Review*. 98, no. 2, 224–253.
Martin, Michael W. 1986. *Self-Deception and Morality*. Lawrence: University Press of Kansas.
Mauss, M. 1985. "A Category of the Human Mind: The Notion of Person, the Notion of Self." Trans. W. D. Halls. Ed. M. Carrithers, S. Collins, and S. Lukes, *The Category of the Person: Anthropology, Philosophy, History*. Cambridge: Cambridge University Press.
McLaughlin, Brian B., and Amélie Rorty, eds. 1988. *Perspectives on Self-Deception*. Berkeley: University of California Press.
Merleau-Ponty, Maurice. 1962. *Phenomenology of Perception*. New York: Humanities Press.
Monk, Ray. 1990. *Ludwig Wittgenstein: The Duty of Genius*. London: J. Cape.
Nietzsche, Friedrich. 1979. "Truth and Lying in the Extra-moral Sense." In *Philosophy and Truth*. Trans. D. Breazeale. Atlantic Highlands, NJ: Humanities Press.
———. 1996. *Beyond Good and Evil*. Trans. W. Kaufmann. New York: Random House.
Pincoffs, Edmund. 1986. *Quandaries and Virtues*. Lawrence: University Press of Kansas.
Plato. 1974. *Republic*. Trans. G. M. A. Grube. Indianapolis: Hackett.
Rorty, Amélie. 1988. "Adaptivity and Self-Knowledge." In A. Rorty ed. *Mind in Action*. Boston: Beacon Press.
———. 1972. "Belief and Self-Deception." *Inquiry* 15 (Winter).
———. 1988. "Deception, Liars, and Layers." In Rorty, Amélie, and Brian B. McLaughlin, eds., *Perspectives on Self-Deception*.
———. "Self-Deception, Akrasia and Irrationality." *Social Science Information* 19: 905–922; reprinted in B. McLaughlin and A. Rorty.
Sartre, Jean Paul. 1938. *The Emotions*. New York: Philosophical Library.
———. 1956. *Etre et l'neant*. Trans. as *Being and Nothingness*, by Hazel Barnes. New York: Philosophical Library.
———. 1957. *The Transcendence of the Ego*. New York: Noonday.
Solomon, Robert C. 1990. "In Defense of Sentimentality." *Philosophy and Literature*, 14.
———. 1976, 1993. *The Passions*. New York: Doubleday-Anchor, and Notre Dame: Notre Dame Press. Revised edition, Indianapolis: Hackett.
———. 1987. "Sartre on Emotions." In P. Schilpp, ed., *The Philosophy of Jean-Paul Sartre*. LaSalle: Open Court.
Thomas, Laurence. 1989. *Living Morally*. Philadelphia: Temple.
Turnbull, Colin. 1974. *The Mountain People*. New York: Simon and Shuster.

FIVE

BAD FAITH AND KITSCH AS MODELS FOR SELF-DECEPTION

Kathleen Marie Higgins

Self-deception, as philosophers describe it, seems a type of logical problem. How can a person deliberately disbelieve a proposition that he or she knows to be true? So expressed, self-deception appears a puzzle of theoretical interest, not obviously linked to the passions of everyday life.

Yet as Amélie Oksenberg Rorty suggests, self-deception is a matter of heated practical interest. "Why is it," she asks, "the subject of such passionate indignation—and sometimes envy—among friends and enemies?"[1] What is it that annoys us when we encounter self-deception in another? Are we offended because the person has adopted an attitude that will resist our every effort to clinch an argument?

I propose in what follows that the aesthetic category of kitsch may help us to understand the strong emotions that self-deception inspires. Kitsch, while often alleged to *involve* self-deception, has not typically been taken as a model of self-deception. I shall suggest that kitsch as a model is in several respects superior to that offered by Sartrean "bad faith."

I

Bad faith, as Sartre characterizes it, is a flexible term relevant to the analysis of various cases of self-deception. His examples include a group of pathologically frigid women, a woman who misinterprets flirtation, a waiter who enjoys playing the role of being a waiter, a homosexual who refuses to characterize himself as one, and a "friend" who tries to persuade the homosexual to admit that he is gay. Allen W. Wood notes that Sartre manufactures his examples for his own purposes: "Sartre describes these examples so skillfully and vividly that it is easy to overlook the fact that they do not tell us much about self-deception. . . . In fact, they are little more than a series of illustrations of Sartre's own radical and idiosyncratic views about human freedom."[2] I shall later discuss the peculiarities of Sartre's first two examples. For the moment, however, let us simply consider the features of bad faith that emerge from Sartre's discussion. These include the following:

1. *The person in bad faith **knows very precisely** what he or she is concealing.* Sartre alleges,

> I must know in my capacity as deceiver the truth which is hidden from me in my capacity as the one deceived. Better yet I must know the truth very exactly *in order* to conceal it more carefully—and not at two different moments . . . —but in the unitary structure of a single project.[3]

2. *The content the person is concealing is **propositional** and specifiable.* Sartre contends that "the one who practices bad faith is hiding a displeasing truth or presenting as truth a pleasing untruth."[4] Wood sees Sartre's discussion as straightforwardly propositional: "Sartre's problem about self-deception arises because it seems that in order to deceive myself I must simultaneously believe and disbelieve the same proposition at the same time, and this looks like a contradiction."[5]

3. *Bad faith is a project with a very **particular goal**.* "There must be an original intention and a project of bad faith," Sartre insists.[6] In the case of the woman who is self-deceived about her suitor's amorous intentions, "The aim is to postpone the moment of decision as long as possible."[7]

4. *Given these constraints, the **mechanisms** of bad faith are extremely **flexible**.* Of the woman conversing with her suitor, Sartre concludes, "We see immediately that she uses various procedures in order to maintain herself in this bad faith."[8]

5. ***Denial of freedom and responsibility** is fundamental to the character of bad faith.* "The very first act of bad faith," claims Sartre, "is to flee what it cannot flee, to flee what it is. The very project of flight reveals to bad faith an inner disintegration in the heart of being, and it is this disintegration which bad faith wishes to be."[9]

6. *Quite often, the person in bad faith is self-deceived about the respective ranges of his or her **facticity** and **transcendence**.*[10]

> The basic concept which is thus engendered utilizes the double property of the human being, who is at once a *facticity* and a

transcendence. These two aspects of human reality are and ought to be capable of a valid coordination. But bad faith does not wish either to coordinate them or to surmount them in a synthesis. Bad faith seeks to affirm their identity while preserving their differences. It must affirm facticity as *being* transcendence and transcendence as *being* facticity, in such a way that at the instant when a person apprehends the one, he can find himself abruptly faced with the other.[11]

II

Sartre's analysis of bad faith involves a number of dubious presuppositions. In the first place, it is based on a *radical subject/object dichotomy.* The typical case of bad faith, Sartre suggests through his examples, depends on self-deception regarding the extent that one is a free, transcendent subject and the extent to which one is an object, determined by external conditions. Human beings are in bad faith when they dodge their freedom by pretending that their characteristics are objectively determined or that their objective behavior is a fact beyond their control.

Insofar as bad faith is mostly a function of self-awareness and self-understanding, third-person observations regarding bad faith have only limited reliability. However, Sartre simply asserts the truth of his observations. "We shall say that this woman is in bad faith,"[12] he tells us. But on what grounds shall we say this? The more radical the separation of the individual's free consciousness from the realm of objecthood, the more problematic is Sartre's insinuation that he, as third-person observer, knows more of the woman's mental state than she does.

Still, the woman resides in Sartre's example, so perhaps her transcendence is not as recalcitrant to observation as that of an actual woman. Sartre thinks he has grounds for saying that she is in bad faith, the grounds of logical paradox. Sartre analyzes what is ignored in bad faith terms of *specific propositional content,* which he can relate to other, similarly specific propositions: "What unity do we find in these various aspects of bad faith? It is a certain art of forming contradictory concepts which unite in themselves both an idea and the negation of that idea."[13]

I question whether self-deception usually involves atomistically statable, definite propositional content. (Indeed, I suspect that we imagine that we deceived ourselves about some specific *fact* in retrospect only to convince ourselves that we have resolved our problem. Perhaps we are often self-deceived in "overcoming" self-deception.) When one *can* specify a proposition—for example, that a colleague voted against one in a secret ballot—its significance depends on a whole background. An atomistic statement tells but a small part of the story. The resisted knowledge in Sartre's example appears to be an atomistic proposition only because he supposes that heterosexual male desire has a singular, literally propositional aim. He characterizes the man's intention, after all, as a "desire cruel and naked" which would "humiliate and horrify" his date.[14]

However, the meanings of most claims that might be made regarding human affairs depend on many varied factors. Among the relevant contextual features are the interests of the individuals involved and the significance that they ascribe to other individuals' behavior, many of which may not be propositionally specifiable. In Sartre's example, the "troubled and unstable harmony which gives the hour its charm" dictates the significance the man's behavior has to the woman. This is hardly a propositional content, but it does describe what is of present interest to the woman. However, Sartre is not concerned with such interests or such enjoyments. He is more concerned with the "proposition" that the woman is ignoring.

Sartre's third-person characterization of the woman here is suspect. The "charm" that occupies her consciousness is presented as a mere front for the "true" perspective on the situation, namely the man's intention. This intention is treated as the unproblematic and unswayable motive for the entirety of the man's behavior. Sartre's account does not do justice to the extent to which the significance of both parties' behavior is negotiated over the course of the evening. Oddly, though claiming that the woman is in bad faith because she conceives of *herself* as pure facticity, Sartre treats both her and her companion as precisely that.

The preponderance of sexual examples in Sartre's list is noteworthy. Such examples are convenient for displaying his analytical moves of preference, for sexual interactions often do render problematic the notions of 'subjective independence' and 'objectification.' However, Sartre exploits the reader's ability to identify with fictional sexual desire—the sole feature through which the man in his example is characterized—to present the woman's response and behavior as unwarranted.

Indeed, Sartre's accounts in his first two examples depend on insensitivity to female sexuality. Consider his dismissive treatment of Steckel's female patients "whom marital infidelity has made frigid":[15]

> Here we find a pattern of *distraction*. Admissions which Steckel was able to draw out inform us that these pathologically frigid women apply themselves to becoming distracted in advance from

the pleasure which they dread; many for example at the time of the sexual act, turn their thoughts away toward their daily occupations, make up their household accounts. Will anyone speak of an unconscious here? Yet if the frigid woman thus distracts her consciousness from the pleasure which she experiences, it is by no means cynically or in full agreement with herself; *it is in order to prove to herself* that she is frigid.[16]

Sartre apparently considers pleasure to be a mere facticity of someone engaged in sexual intercourse. Thus, the frigid woman is dreading *pleasure,* and indeed, Sartre goes on to say, "experiencing" pleasure. It does not strike him that what the woman dreads may indeed be dealing with her husband. Given the allusion to marital infidelity, however, she may well associate her husband with feelings of betrayal, emotional abuse, rejection—strong emotions that bear little relation to pleasure.

Even if one were to agree with Sartre that the woman is avoiding pleasure as such, it does not follow that she is in bad faith. Her strategy, whether consciously or unconsciously adopted, may be the best emotional recourse she has available to her, and indeed one that she might rationally adopt. Very likely, she no longer trusts her husband. In general, it is a reasonable strategy to avoid depending on an untrustworthy person for anything, pleasure included. Sexual pleasure also renders many women emotionally vulnerable to their partners. Such vulnerability would put the woman in this example at risk of future hurt should her husband be unfaithful again. She might very reasonably be inclined to forgo physical pleasure in order to avoid such emotional risk. Moreover, deliberate distraction from potentially pleasurable activity may be much more easily achieved than the distraction she would require for enjoyment—distraction from awareness of her husband, her emotions in response to him, her disturbance over the condition of her marriage, and so on.

None of this is intended to suggest that Steckel's patients do not have problems. Indeed, their strategy may be misguided with respect to certain of their goals. For example, a woman's evident sexual disinterest might motivate her husband to seek sexual applause elsewhere—very likely not the result desired by a woman who responds with such distress to infidelity. Nevertheless, in a situation that might strike a woman as far from ideal, it is not obvious that self-deception is involved in her sexual resistance.

Sartre's account is deficient in that he does not seek to understand the concerns of these patients. Sartre's notion of bad faith, so far as it emerges from this example, seems to have nothing to do with their emotional reality

Self and Deception

but instead to be entirely a matter of logical paradox (and indeed, one imposed from the third-person point of view): "We have in fact to deal with a phenomenon of bad faith since the efforts taken in order not to be present to the experienced pleasure imply the recognition that the pleasure is experienced; they imply it *in order* to deny it."[17]

Again, oddly, Sartre treats the subjective states of the individuals involved as matters of facticity, unaffected by their own transcendent interpretations.

Sartre has omitted from his analysis what would be transparent were he to take the first-person point of view seriously—the images involved in the woman's interpretation of sexual activity with her husband and her marriage. Given his own biography, he would likely have little sympathy for the images involved; but this does not justify Sartre in ignoring them. Analyzing bad faith through the mutually exclusive terms of transcendence and facticity—the dimensions of individual independence and external determination—Sartre ignores the arena which mediates most *intersubjective* relationships, the arena of images and myths.[18]

Sartre's account of bad faith is also questionable in that its focus is thoroughly *momentary*. Just as his analyses of transcendence and facticity portray individuals atomistically, he takes an atomistic approach to the temporality involved in choice. The decision to adopt bad faith, like all choices, seems to be a function of each particular moment: "She does not want to see possibilities of temporal development. . . . The aim is to postpone the moment of decision as long as possible. We know what happens next."[19] At every moment, in Sartre's examples, an individual is guilty of denying freedom.

Here as elsewhere, Sartre seems to see every moment as a moral dilemma. At this given moment, the Sartrean examination of conscience would be, Am I deceiving myself or not? But self-deception is not so momentary. Normally, it is a pattern of some duration. Certainly, self-deception becomes practically problematic only if it endures. For example, I may self-deceptively believe that a friend is not in danger, despite considerable evidence that she is. Such self-deception is problematic if it prevents my taking appropriate action with the requisite haste. However, if my disbelief lasts only a moment, after which I actively respond, my self-deception is scarcely a problem. Indeed, it would be odd for anyone but myself to describe this as a case of self-deception. At most, *I* may be worried that I *can* mistake urgent situations, a reflection that might jar me to a stance of greater responsiveness in the future.

The momentary character of Sartrean bad faith is obscure in Sartre's example because he equivocates on the temporal character of seduction.

The process of the seduction is temporally extended, but the evidence that seduction is accomplished is a specific, momentary act. Thus the woman appears to be in bad faith because she *continues* to deny the man's obvious advances. However, presumably she must eventually say yes while denying all responsibility if bad faith is a just accusation. If a sexual encounter does not take place, then it seems unfair to describe the woman as deceived throughout the evening about its ultimate destination.

Can Sartre fairly complain that the woman has been in bad faith throughout the evening, even if she does consent to a sexual liaison? He suggests that she is in bad faith for not reflecting on the evening's outcome. Yet should she spend the evening focused, not on the charm of conversation but on the way the night will end? Indeed, comedy scripts have been written about characters obsessing about how to respond to a proposition that never occurs. Sartre describes the woman's behavior as the outcome of a self-deceptive decision. But why does he think that she has made any decision, and made it in advance of further developments? He himself asserts that "she does not quite know what she wants."[20] The only basis for claiming that she has decided is Sartre's own doctrine that not deciding is a form of decision.

Sartre's story treats the man's every gesture a "moment of choice" for the woman, during which she abandons her responsibility for what follows. Sartre's account is a less humorous analogue of the remark by comedian Paul Rodriquez, "Women are psychic. They always know if you're going to get laid." The man in Sartre's example does not know whether she will say yes until he asks (and perhaps does not know if she means yes until later). But neither does she know whether he will ask until he does. And neither does she know for sure how far his flirtations signal a preamble to sexual encounter until they reach a moment of choice that is *intersubjectively* recognized.

Sartre treats the process of flirtation like the Freudian "ordeal of civility." The woman is in bad faith, he suggests, because she avoids confrontation with "the desire cruel and naked." In other words, the understatement and ambiguity that are fundamental to flirtation generally are a bad faith camouflage unless seen cynically as the prelude to the business at hand. This seems an extreme conclusion!

Why does Sartre emphasize the moment of choice despite the ongoing character of his examples? An obvious candidate is the effort to locate points of *moral failure*.[21] Beginning with its name, bad faith is a thoroughly moral concept. By making bad faith essentially a matter of the present moment, Sartre locates a precise site of moral failure. "And what is the goal of bad faith? To cause me to be what I am, in the mode of 'not being what

Self and Deception

one is,' or not to be what I am in the mode of 'being what one is.' "[22] Sartre's model makes self-deception appear positively diabolical. The self-deceived person is Iago-like in focus, willing to employ virtually any mental maneuver in order to achieve a given aim.

But does self-deception deserve this villification? Often in everyday self-deception, one's avoidance of unpleasant knowledge is not so much a consequence of systematic deceit as of *focusing on unrelated matters*. Rorty emphasizes the extent to which self-deception is achieved by means of selective focus:

> *Being aware of something* does not occur at a single glance, at an instant. It takes place over time; it integrates distinctive actions of focusing, scanning, refocusing, and reconstructing a series of interpretations derived from shifting the foreground and the background of attention. Standardly, marginal information corrects the distortions of attention that arise from intensive focusing.
>
> But when a person is afraid or absorbed in love or grief, or concentrated on some form of hierarchical combat, she can fail to integrate the relevant material that is at the periphery of her strong, attentive focusing.[23]

Allen Wood similarly observes that self-deception is largely a matter of manipulated focus; and he contends that the mechanisms utilized even in Sartre's examples are themselves "restricted to what Harry Stack Sullivan calls 'selective inattention.' In bad faith, I maintain my belief by consciously attending to those aspects of the world that the belief integrates, and directing my attention away from those aspects that clash with my belief."[24]

Far from being a symptom of diabolical falsehood, self-deception is often a function of everyday attention and inattention. Indeed, Rorty contends, the possibility of self-deception proceeds directly from our survival-related abilities to shift and narrow our focus. "The structures and capacities that enable us to manipulate ourselves in situations of indeterminacy allow self-deception as an unintended, tangential consequence." Moreover, while not defensible on grounds of accuracy or conscientious honesty, self-deception may be useful in connection with a number of reasonable goals.

> In the interests of generating a self-fulfilling prophecy, we intentionally shift our epistemic policies. We can speak to ourselves as the friendly neighborhood demagogue, cannily conning ourselves into believing that we can do things that are only distantly or marginally within our repertoire. Self-deception is

an effective, if irrational, cure for melancholia. . . . Effective focusing enlarges what is directly present and blurs what is on the periphery: what is blurred falls out of sight and becomes irrelevant. Writing philosophy papers, devoting ourselves to political causes, taking the minutiae of our friends' tribulations seriously, and believing in the futures of our students do not, of course, require self-deceptive manipulation. But it helps.[25]

Sartre is less concerned with the positive contents of consciousness in cases of self-deception than with particular contents avoided. This explains, in part, his lack of concern for what might realistically be on the mind of a woman enjoying a date. The phenomenon described as "kitsch" by Milan Kundera, by contrast, offers a basis for exploring the contents of self-deceived consciousness. I shall now consider self-deception from the perspective of kitsch.

III

Kitsch has been variously defined, but most commentators agree that it is bad. Not only is kitsch "bad art," according to many observers, but it also promotes or necessarily involves self-deception. Karsten Harries, for example, sees kitsch as engendering a self-deceptive atmosphere:

> What is enjoyed or sought is not a certain object, but an emotion, a mood, even, or rather especially, if there is no encounter with an object which would warrant that emotion. Thus religious Kitsch seeks to explicit religious emotion without an encounter with God, and erotic Kitsch seeks to give the sensations of love without the presence of someone with whom one is in love. But even where such a person is present, love can itself be said to be Kitsch if that person is used only to stimulate a feeling of love, if love has its center not in the beloved but within itself. Kitsch creates illusion for the sake of self-enjoyment. It is more reflective than simple enjoyment in that it detaches itself from the original emotion in order to enjoy it. On the other hand, this reflective distance may not become so great as to force man to see his emotion for what it really is—self-deception.[26]

Milan Kundera similarly sees kitsch as involving a project of self-deception, which he describes as a "categorical agreement with being." Kitsch

Self and Deception

is dangerous, in his view, because it screens out all that is objectionable in life.

> The aesthetic ideal of the categorical agreement with being is a world in which shit is denied and everyone acts as though it did not exist. This aesthetic ideal is called *kitsch*. . . . kitsch is the absolute denial of shit, in both the literal and the figurative senses of the word; kitsch excludes everything from its purview which is essentially unacceptable in human existence.[27]

Theorists of modernity have made multiple efforts to determine what class of objects falls into the category of kitsch. I have argued elsewhere that many of these efforts are misguided.[28] Nonrelational features of objects are not in themselves sufficient to render a given object an instance of kitsch. Instead, kitsch is a function of the way an object is used.

What lends an object to kitsch employments is its "iconicity"—its ability to assimilate considerable emotional impact by gesturing toward a body of unstated mythological material.[29] An object functions as kitsch when it gestures toward archetypical human and/or cultural experiences that its audience can be expected to find emotionally powerful, and when the object is utilized solely as a means of evoking an emotional atmosphere that can be enjoyed. Kundera points to the kinds of archetypal images that are suitable for kitsch:

> The feeling induced by kitsch must be a kind the multitudes can share. Kitsch may not, therefore, depend on an unusual situation; it must derive from the basic images people have engraved in their memories: the ungrateful daughter, the neglected father, children running on the grass, the motherland betrayed, first love.[30]

Kundera goes on to conclude, with Harries, that kitsch involves an emotional atmosphere:

> Kitsch causes two tears to flow in quick succession. The first tear says: How nice to see children running on the grass!
>   The second tear says: How nice to be moved, together with all mankind, by children running on the grass!
>   It is the second tear that makes kitsch kitsch.[31]

The relations that an object's properties bear to basic images of cultural and human experience determine whether or not that object can function as kitsch. A souvenir plate from a notoriously "romantic" location, for example, might evoke in an individual who enjoys it a plethora of romantic and nostalgic emotions largely independent of the plate's "objective" characteristics. A disparity occurs between the kitsch object's presentational features (which may be artistically feeble) and the depth and intensity of the feelings aroused in conjunction with it.

Kitsch has more to do with the melánge of emotions elicited in the viewer than with the nature of the object or objects involved. A natural panorama can function as kitsch, as can any object kept for sentimental reasons. A recognized masterpiece of painting can also function as kitsch. It might be utilized by some viewers as an occasion for enjoying emotions of satisfaction or inspiration in the face of human achievement, patriotic admiration for the culture that produced it, charm over reveries that its content arouses, and so on.

Because it depends on the beliefs and orientations of the observer, the appearance of kitsch objects can differ markedly from observer to observer and from culture to culture. Kitsch is culture- and subculture-specific. As Denis Dutton has observed, it is easy to scorn other people's kitsch, while our own and "the kitsch that hangs in university presidents' offices" might tell us more about kitsch as a phenomenon.[32]

Because kitsch depends on basic beliefs and attitudes regarding fundamental kinds of human relationships and experiences, however, the enjoyment of kitsch atmospheres is a possibility for everyone (although the objects individuals find evocative will vary). Moreover, the images and myths which are basic to the kitsch experience are the very images that we utilize to form our sense of human relationships and basic situations. Kundera concludes, "The brotherhood of man on earth will be possible only on a base of kitsch."[33]

The following characteristics of kitsch are important in assessing it as a model of self-deception: (1) Kitsch involves an *emotional atmosphere.* (2) Kitsch utilizes *images,* or *icons,* that are central to human and cultural experience. (3) Kitsch is a function of an object's *relations* to broader, intersubjective attitudes and emotional landscapes. With these characteristics in mind, we can observe several points of contrast between kitsch and Sartrean bad faith.

Like the project of bad faith, the project of kitsch obscures certain realizations. However, in the case of kitsch, the *contents of the screen*—what one is actually attending to—are structurally more important than the details of what is being concealed. One takes delight in children running on the grass. What this vision conceals is not straightforward.

The kitsch user *need not know* what is being concealed with any degree of specificity. What is concealed might be fairly nebulous, as Kundera suggests when he describes it as the "essentially unacceptable." The shaping mechanism that determines what one does and does not

Self and Deception

notice is atmospheric. One fails to observe anything that is incompatible with the emotional atmosphere, so long as the atmosphere prevails.

Employment of kitsch is *not* linked to any *particular project*. The kitsch atmosphere is therefore compatible with many projects—indeed, any that is not directly at odds with the atmosphere's emotional tone. The versatility of kitsch in this connection is what makes kitsch useful as propaganda for politicians of all countries and creeds. Harries suggests that the effort to avoid boredom itself can be the "project" behind kitsch: "The need for Kitsch arises when genuine emotion has become rare, when desire lies dormant and needs artificial stimulation. Kitsch is an answer to boredom. When objects cannot elicit desire, man desires desire."[34]

Kitsch totalizes. Kitsch involves a whole interpretive atmosphere that is brought to bear on one's vision of reality.[35] It is deceptive because it screens out any insight that is inimical to the atmosphere. (At least, it does so as long as the spell endures. When an inimical insight does come to consciousness, instead of the kitsch atmosphere, it may survive the confrontation. Kundera notes the force of notions contrary to the kitsch atmosphere: "In the realm of totalitarian kitsch, all answers are given in advance and preclude any questions. It follows then, that the true opponent of totalitarian kitsch is the person who asks questions.")[36]

By means of totalizing one's interpretation of reality, kitsch *shapes propositional content* in accordance with the screen. On this model, so long as the kitsch atmosphere endures, one interprets all evidence in light of it. Thus, one does directly not shove a particular proposition out of consciousness.

Moral failure, if it is involved, is not a matter of making an irresponsible decision at every moment, as Sartre's model suggests. The problem with kitsch, when it is a problem, is that over time the user of kitsch fails to look beyond the kitsch atmosphere. The *kitsch life,* not the *kitsch experience,* is the basis of moral failure.

IV

Some examples may help to show how kitsch can function in self-deception.

Sexual Infidelity Is a Stereotypical Scenario for Self-Deception

A character in Amy Tan's recent novel *The Kitchen God's Wife*[37] describes a situation in which she was self-deceived. Returning from the hospital, this woman discovered another woman in her bed. She was horrified to think that her husband (no moral hero) would betray her while she was hospitalized. She found his infidelity all the more degrading if, as it appeared, he had not even made an effort to hide his misdeeds.

The distraught woman went to a nearby neighbor's apartment and there met the neighbor's aunt. When it was mentioned that the aunt had a daughter, the woman concluded that it must have been the daughter she discovered in her bed. She was relieved. However, we soon discover that she was also self-deceived. In fact, the situation was exactly what she initially interpreted it to be.

Such a case might seem to involve the conscious avoidance of definite propositional content. Tan's character wants not to know that her husband has been flagrantly unfaithful. This "fact" is being deliberately avoided. The woman goes out of her way to focus on any shred of evidence that might help her to avoid this conclusion.

However, at issue for the woman is more than a particular "propositional content." Her sense that unveiled infidelity is more degrading than veiled infidelity shows that she is not solely concerned with the truth of a given suspicion. For this woman, as for many individuals, marital fidelity has many symbolic overtones.[38] It is an element of vital importance in her whole interpretation of her place in the world.

In telling her story over the course of Tan's novel, the woman makes recurrent references to the notion of a "good marriage." The image of a good marriage established the emotional atmosphere through which the woman functioned in her married life. This atmosphere served as a kitsch screening device that gave events in her marriage their "spin." She believed that her marriage at least had the potential to be a "good marriage," and she interpreted counterevidence in ways that remained compatible with this belief.

Perceiving the presence of the woman in her bed as incompatible with having a decent marriage, the woman was in emotional crisis. By recognizing the evidence of her husband's infidelity for what it was, she faced the dissolution of the entire interpretive scheme on which she had constructed her adult life. She was not merely contending with a proposition deliberately banished from mind, but with the salvageability of her entire interpretive framework. Eventually, the woman comes to recognize her self-deception. But in so doing, she simultaneously abandons a whole mythology of marriage, her place in the world, and so on. The price for overcoming self-deception is for her extremely high.[39]

Unrequited Love Is another Common Type of Self-Deception

Gabriel Garcia Marquez provides an account of extremely self-deceived unrequited love in *Love in the Time of Cholera*.[40] Although the unrequited lover eventually does gain the love of his fantasy object, the actual relationship between these two elderly people has little in common with his lifelong fantasy. Moreover, the fantasy has so little bearing on his actual behavior for most of his life that he sees no conflict between it and his obsessive pursuit of amorous conquests. This fantasy, however, for years provides the unrequited lover with a "meaning" in life, as well as motives (however bizarre) for behavior in virtually all of his activities.

One could interpret such unrequited love as a straightforward repression of true propositional content. One deceives oneself in unrequired love that the beloved is not really indifferent, perhaps, or that the beloved will come to love one with the intensity of one's own desire. Nevertheless, unrequited love is inadequately understood in terms of avoidance of a given proposition.

Unrequited love is a highly textured phenomenon. The image of the beloved's love is central to a whole counter-factual texture. The lover believes that the beloved's love would make life completely good. The entire atmospheric schema is mobilized in self-deceptive interpretations. Any evidence that one's love is not reciprocated is interpreted as a mere setback to the attainment of a future situation that one positively believes and expects. Perhaps, the lover imagines, the beloved is only testing his love.

The love of the fantasy beloved provides a basis for an atmosphere of life interpretation. The fact that the scheme is characterized by the modality of possibility rather than actuality does not interfere with its effectiveness. Indeed, as Kundera suggests, such a subjunctive character is typical of a kitsch state of mind. The involvement of a subjunctive atmosphere is suggested by the fact that an individual in such a condition often prefers the frictionless fantasy relationship to an actual relationship with actual tensions. Indeed, this is so for Marquez's character. His unrequited love, in his imagination, is unsullied by his string of amatory conquests. These conquests are designed specifically to minimize the chances of romantic love toward another object. In this case, fidelity to an atmosphere is the precondition to practical promiscuity.

Many of Sartre's Writings Suggest that the Situation of Bad Faith that He Is Most Concerned with Is the Stance of Political Bad Faith

Certainly he is most offended by the bad faith of those who pretend to be victims of the political situation, as though they are powerless to affect it. Given the context in which Sartre was writing, this moral indignation does not seem misplaced.

However, Sartre's examples do seem misplaced. The dating woman's bad faith, for instance, does not obviously correspond to the type of bad faith of the politically apathetic person. Political responsibility may require one's recognition that one could act differently. But responsible dating surely does not require that one actively consider at every moment the possibility of being elsewhere.

Sartre's suggestion that particular propositional content is ignored in bad faith does not seem well suited to the political situation. In the political arena, a particular proposition is not usually being denied unless one considers "The world is not in good shape" to be a specific proposition. Indeed, Sartre seems to claim that one denies the proposition that one is free. But this is an empty abstraction unless one considers specifics that one is actually free to do.

The politically apathetic individual during World War II denied not *a* particular proposition or particular responsibility. This individual denied *any* particular relationship or responsibility. But such denial was accomplished by means of the kind of atmosphere that Kundera describes. The emotional atmosphere was the stance of a victim, which enabled such individuals to imagine that *nothing* in particular obliged them because they were not in a position to do *anything*.

Kundera finds fault with kitsch atmospheres like this because they serve as on-going obstructions to confrontations with important human problems. This seems to be the most reasonable basis for Sartre's complaints against bad faith as well. However, the kitsch model strikes me as more serviceable than Sartre's model for clarifying such atmospheric self-deception.

The self-deceived person considers the kitsch atmosphere unfalsifiable. Tan's woman in her "good marriage" can't see the abusiveness of her husband because it is incompatible with her interpretive scheme. No slight of the beloved will convince the unrequited lover that they are not made for each other. A kitschified view of the fatherland prevents its adherent from recognizing cases when the nation is at fault. In each case, the self-deceived individual places absolute faith in an interpretive scheme that is immune, in his or her view, to qualification or question.

For this reason, the atmosphere of kitsch interferes with intersubjective human negotiation. This, I think, is the sound basis for our irritation at others' self-deception. Another's self-deception, so long as it endures, thwarts any communicative gesture that would counter or qualify relevant content. It undercuts our sense that we have genuine contact with the person, for some of our messages do not get through.

However, entertaining fantasies is not intrinsically evil. Nor is kitsch, although it may be a shallow perspective from which to view the world. Kitsch becomes a problem when it actually becomes a life style, involving the kitsch-enjoyer in a completely fantastic life, obstructing awareness of the conditions of real relationships. Kitsch is bad in such a case, not because a *specific* content is not noticed, but because *any* propositional content can be translated and absorbed without provoking reflection on the atmosphere itself.

One can reasonably criticize kitsch when it functions as an entrenched interpretive schema. Beyond this, however, can one fairly criticize from a third-person point of view? Can one really be sure of what *specific* realizations an individual must have in order to avoid irresponsibility or pathology?

Occasional enjoyment of kitsch is not an obstruction either to responsibility or to human encounter. Kitsch is not, like the red scare, something always to beware. By contrast, Sartre hints that one ought always to be on guard against bad faith, making the avoidance of bad faith itself a life project.

If one were really to act on this suggestion, the search for bad faith would easily become a self-fulfilling, paranoid project. One can always imagine possible horrors just beyond the horizon of one's attention, yet this hardly seems a healthy ideal. Indeed, the project of exposing bad faith might itself be a bad-faith endeavor. The project involves a prior commitment to edit one's observations in accordance with a global interpretive scheme which one does not evaluate or criticize. The hunt for bad faith can also support self-satisfaction in one's own heroism at the expense of compassion toward others. It easily degenerates into a self-righteousness that accuses everyone else of dishonesty.

To see people as kitschifying, by contrast, while not exactly complimentary, is not so accusatory. To kitschify sometimes is to be human, as Kundera contends: "None among us is superman enough to escape kitsch completely. No matter how we scorn it, kitsch is an integral part of the human condition."[41]

Moral interpretations, claims, Nietzsche, are symptoms. Although Sartre follows Nietzsche in seeking naturalistic accounts of behavior, he does not successfully transcend moralizing descriptions. His account of bad faith is extremely moralistic. I think we would do well to investigate, not the morals, but the aesthetics of self-deception.

NOTES

1. Amélie Oksenberg Rorty, "The Deceptive Self: Liars, Layers, and Lairs," in *Perspectives on Self-Deception*, ed. Brian P. McLaughlin and Amélie Oksenberg Rorty (Berkeley: University of California Press, 1988), 22.

2. Allen W. Wood, "Self-Deception and Bad Faith," in *Perspectives on Self-Deception,* ed. McLaughlin and Rorty, 213.
3. Jean-Paul Sartre, *Being and Nothingness,* trans. Hazel E. Barnes (London: Methuen, 1958), 49.
4. Ibid., 49.
5. Wood, "Self-Deception and Bad Faith," 215.
6. Sartre, *Being and Nothingness,* 49.
7. Ibid., 55.
8. Ibid., 56.
9. Ibid., 70.
10. Wood contends that Sartre makes this distinction fundamental to his entire notion of bad faith. "Does Sartre really expect us to believe that every case of self-deception involves attributing a contradictory concept to something? And does he think that all contradictory concepts derive from the facticity-transcendence relation? Neither claim has much plausibility, and neither receives any real defense from Sartre" (Wood, "Self-Deception and Bad Faith," 215). However, Sartre seems not to require that the facticity-transcendence relation be basic to the mechanism of bad faith. "Although this *metastable* concept of 'transcendence-facticity' is one of the most basic instruments of bad faith, it is not the only one of its kind. We can equally well use another kind of duplicity derived from human reality which we will express roughly by saying that its being-for-itself implies complementarily a being-for-others" (Sartre, *Being and Nothingness,* 57). However, Sartre goes on to conflate the two dualities in his examples. Wood is certainly right to claim that, whatever allegations Sartre makes regarding the role of the transcendence-facticity duality in bad faith, he employs it in each of the examples that he uses to explicate the "patterns of bad faith." Nevertheless, the example of the frigid women, discussed in the section prior to the "patterns of bad faith" section, seems to fall outside of the transcendence-facticity scheme. Indeed, this scheme might be turned against Sartre in connection with this example, for reasons that I shall discuss below.
11. Sartre, *Being and Nothingness,* 56.
12. Ibid.
13. Ibid.
14. Ibid., 55.
15. Sartre, *Being and Nothingness,* 54. I assume in my further discussion that the infidelity described here has been that of the women's husbands. However, if infidelity on the part of the women themselves rendered them frigid, presumably guilt is the basis of their inability to enjoy sex. An analysis comparable to that which I give below could be presented, taking guilt, rather than hurt, as the incitement of the problem. Again, a whole complex view of the significance of fidelity to marriage would be involved in an explanation of their condition. If a woman took fidelity to be a sine qua non for marriage, then her own infidelity might strike her as proof that she was not suited for the pleasures that accompany marriage. Distraction during sex with her husband would, at the same time, be distraction from an activity that

would, were she attentive, cause her to think about the tattered condition of her marriage (at least from her own point of view).

16. Sartre, *Being and Nothingness*, 54.

17. Ibid.

18. Wood cites Sartre utilizing the term *mythology* as a scornful synopsis of Freud's theory of instincts and drives. See Wood, "Self-Deception and Bad Faith," 209.

19. Sartre, *Being and Nothingness*, 55.

20. Sartre, *Being and Nothingness*, 55.

21. Fingarette observes that Sartre "is deeply concerned with analysing the moral context of self-deception" (Fingarette, *Self-Deception* [London: Routledge & Kegan Paul, 1969], 92).

22. Sartre, *Being and Nothingness*, 66.

23. Rorty, "The Deceptive Self," 18.

24. Wood, "Self-Deception and Bad Faith," 222.

25. Rorty, "The Deceptive Self," 17.

26. Karsten Harries, *The Meaning of Modern Art: A Philosophical Interpretation* (Evanston: Northwestern University Press, 1968), 80.

27. Milan Kundera, *The Unbearable Lightness of Being*, trans. Michael Henry Heim (New York: Harper and Row, 1984), 248.

28. Kathleen Higgins, "Sweet Kitsch," in *The Philosophy of the Visual Arts*, ed. Philip Alperson (New York: Oxford University Press, 1992), 568–81.

29. In this context, I am using the terms *archetype* and *mythological* quite broadly. While I have sympathy for the theories of others who employ such terms—C. G. Jung, for example—I do not intend in this context to endorse or utilize these theories.

30. Kundera, *The Unbearable Lightness of Being*, 251.

31. Kundera, *The Unbearable Lightness of Being*, 251.

32. Denis Dutton in response to Mary Mothersill, "Bad Taste," presented at the meeting of the American Society for Aesthetics, Portland, Oregon, November 1991.

33. Kundera, *The Unbearable Lightness of Being*, 251.

34. Harries, *The Meaning of Modern Art*, 79–80.

35. Sartre does maintain that bad faith has its own characteristic *weltanshauung*, which Wood characterizes as "to behave as if the function of believing is as much to cater to our desires and feelings as it is to conform to the evidence and produce an integral response to the world" (Sartre, *Being and Nothingness*, 68; Wood, "Self-Deception and Bad Faith," 221).

36. Kundera, *The Unbearable Lightness of Being*, 254.

37. Amy Tan, *The Kitchen God's Wife* (New York: Putnam, 1991).

38. Kundera's *The Unbearable Lightness of Being* indicates the extreme differences that individuals have in their interpretation of the significance of marital infidelity (even if these differences are largely conditioned by a societal double standard).

39. Cf. Fingarette: "What the self-deceiver specifically lacks is not concern or integrity but some combination of courage and a way of seeing how to approach his dilemma without probable disaster to himself." (*Self-Deception*, 143).

40. Gabriel Garcia Marquez, *Love in the Time of Cholera*, trans. Edith Grossman (New York: Alfred A. Knopf, 1988).

41. Kundera, *The Unbearable Lightness of Being*, 256.

SIX
UNLOADING THE SELF-REFUTATION CHARGE

Barbara Herrnstein Smith

Philosophers, logicians, and those whom they have instructed demonstrate recurrently—in classrooms, at conferences, in the pages of professional journals—the "incoherence" of certain theoretical positions, for example, relativism, skepticism, perspectivism, constructivism, and postmodernism. They often do this by exposing to their audiences—students, colleagues, and readers—how such positions are self-refuting. The positions so exposed are generally those that diverge from the relevant philosophical orthodoxy. Though presumably not impossible, it is certainly not common to find a neo-Platonist or neo-Kantian charged with self-refutation. Defenses of orthodox positions are, to be sure, charged with hollow arguments, but the charge here is characteristically petitio principii, begging the question: that is, circular self-affirmation rather than specular self-refutation. The classic agents and victims of self-refutation, however, are Protagoras, the relativist; Hume, the epistemological skeptic; Nietzsche, the perspectivist; and, in our own era, postmodernists such as Kuhn, Feyerabend, Foucault, Derrida, Lyotard, Goodman, and Rorty, whose individual and collective incoherence, self-contradiction, and self-refutation have been demonstrated by, among others, Davidson, Putnam, and Habermas.[1]

As the foregoing list suggests, the agents/victims of self-refutation are also usually philosophical innovators: that is, theorists who have articulated original substantive views on various matters of philosophical interest: knowledge, language, science, and so forth. When their self-refutation is being exposed, however, they are seen primarily in their role of negative critics of orthodox thought: that is, as deniers, rejecters, and abandoners of views that are widely experienced as intuitively correct and manifestly true. Indeed, even prior to and independent of any formal demonstration of their self-refutation, the views of such theorists tend to be experienced by disciplinary philosophers—and those whom they have instructed—as self-evidently absurd.

Because various elements of the orthodoxies in question—that is, those from which the views of the skeptic/relativist/postmodernist di-

Self and Deception

verge—are also widely seen as sustaining important communal goods (e.g., the authority of law, the possibility of moral and aesthetic judgment, the progress of science) and as averting corresponding evils (e.g., social anarchy, moral paralysis, aesthetic decline, intellectual chaos), the questioning or denial of those elements is also widely seen as, at the least, communally perilous and often morally criminal as well. It is not surprising, then, that the theoretical innovators mentioned above have often been demonized. Nor is it surprising that much of the energy of disciplinary philosophy has been and continues to be devoted to demonstrating—as the self-refutation charge itself proclaims—that the apparently dangerous demons are actually impotent, self-deceived fools. That, in fact, seems to be the point of the self-refutation charge: to show, so to speak, that the devil is an ass.

What officially justifies the charge of self-refutation is a manifestly self-canceling, self-disabling statement: All generalizations are false, Relativism is (absolutely) true, It is wrong to make value judgments, etc. What more commonly elicits the charge, however, is some set of analyses and arguments that is said to "come down to" such a statement or, duly paraphrased, to have the "logical form" of such a statement. The justice of the charge, in either case, may be more or less readily acknowledged by the person accused, who may then attempt to eliminate the problem through some appropriate self-qualification. For example, the relatively alarming "All generalizations are false" may be amended to the relatively unexceptionable "Most generalizations have exceptions." Or, more strikingly, acknowledgment of the justice of the charge of self-contradiction has had important effects on the development of the sociology of science.[2]

Charges of self-refutation do not always, however, yield genial or self-transformative resolutions. On the contrary, although a particular charge may be manifestly on target from the perspective of many members of some immediate audience, it may also appear empty and irrelevant to the alleged agent/victim and to his or her partisans. Indeed, a charge of self-refutation is, often enough, a sign of head-on intellectual collision and also an occasion of mutually frustrating nonengagement or impasse. Accordingly, it provides an instructive illustration of what could be called the microdynamics of incommensurability.

Although I am sympathetic to many of the views of the unorthodox theorists mentioned above (and have developed some relatively unorthodox views myself),[3] my purpose here is not to defend any of them (theorists or views) per se or to "refute" any specific charges leveled against them. It is, rather, to examine the more general rhetorical and psychological operations of the charge itself and, to some extent, its institutional operations as well.

Though necessarily limited, the examination will, I hope, illuminate some issues of broader current interest and, perhaps, make the charge of self-refutation, in some quarters, somewhat less *automatic*.

TRICKS OF THOUGHT

In the dialogue that bears his name, the good-natured, mathematically precocious Theaetetus offers, in reply to Socrates' questions about the nature of knowledge, the teachings of Protagoras: "Man is the measure," and so on. Through cross-questioning, certain implications and difficulties of the doctrine are explored. Protagoras himself is imagined risen from the grave and arguing in his own defense. Other difficulties, notably an "exquisite" self-contradiction, are drawn out. These are acknowledged by Theaetetus, now delivered to better understanding.[4]

This is the archetypal exposure of self-refutation, both in its dramatic, triangular form—student, false teacher, true teacher—(to which I return below) and in the logical/rhetorical details of the turnabout. Through the explications and applications of subsequent commentators, Socrates' exposure of self-refutation becomes the authority for charging, and the model for exposing, the incoherence of latter-day Protagoreans.

Man is the measure of all things, says the Protagorean, or *Each thing is as it is perceived.* Thus he denies the possibility of (objective, absolute) truth and (objectively) valid knowledge. But then he cannot claim that his own doctrine is (objectively, absolutely) true or the product of (objectively valid) knowledge. Thus also he declares the (objective, absolute) truth of the views that disagree with his own. But, then, he acknowledges that what he says is false and worthless. His doctrine refutes itself.

These moves are simple enough. So also is the problem with them, namely that they hinge on dubious paraphrase and dubious inference. For the self-refutation charge to have logical force (as officially measured), the mirror reversal it indicates must be exact: What the self-refuter explicitly, wittingly denies must be the same as what she unwittingly, implicitly affirms. Accordingly, the charge fails to go off properly, and the supposed demonstration is declared a trick or an error, if the restatement diverges too obviously or too crucially from the original[5] or if the supposedly implied affirmation is itself questionable: if, for example, Protagoras had actually said "*It appears to me that* man is the measure of all things," or obviously meant his doctrine to be taken as only *relatively* true, or obviously meant to affirm only that each thing is as it is perceived *to those who perceive it that way.* Similarly, in the case of

Self and Deception

the related tu quoque charge, the trait evidently condemned by the self-refuter must be the same as that thereby exhibited, as in the (social-) scientific theory that claims: "Scientific theories are (mere) reflections of the social interests of those who produce and promote them." Here the charge fails if the supposed self-refuter disavows the "mere" and the presumably self-*excepting* claim is revealed as (or transformed into) an explicitly and flagrantly self-*exemplifying* one: "You charge my theory of the social interests of all theories with reflecting social interests? But *of course* it does: it could hardly prosper otherwise!" Thus, as in the schoolyard exchange, the target of the taunt ("You, too. So *there!*") turns the tables back again ("Me, too. So *what?*").

An error or perhaps trick of this kind—that is, dubious paraphrase and/or dubious inference—occurs, according to most classical scholars, in the course of Socrates' examination of Protagoras' doctrine in *Theaetetus*.[6] Almost all of those scholars, however, read the charge of self-refutation as redeemed—both there and more generally—on shifted grounds. Thus it is said that Protagoras *must* claim the *absolute* truth of his doctrine because all assertions are implicit claims of absolute truth and/or that otherwise there would be no point to anyone's listening to or believing them. One commentator, for example, after extensive consideration of the text, concludes that Protagoras' doctrine and "relativism" more generally are self-refuting "for reasons that go deep into the nature of assertion and belief."[7] "No amount of maneuvering with his relativizing qualifiers will extricate Protagoras from the commitment to truth absolute which is bound up with the very act of assertion. To assert is to assert that *p*— . . . that something is the case—and if *p*, indeed if and only if *p*, then *p* is true (period)."[8] Another commentator assures his readers, " 'Relative rightness' is not rightness at all. . . . The relativist cannot regard her beliefs, or her relative truths, as warranted or worthy of belief."[9] Yet another, acknowledging Socrates' dubious paraphrase of Protagoras' thesis, insists on the ignominious outcomes of the examination: for, he observes, "if what [Protagoras] says is right he has no claim on our attention."[10]

It will be noted that, in all these recuperation, the assumption is that the particular conceptions of 'truth,' 'assertion,' 'rightness,' and so on, to which they appeal are not themselves contestable, that those concepts and also the discursive/conceptual ("logical") connections among them could not be seen, framed, or configured otherwise. I return to this matter below.

Logic is not my primary concern here, but one point deserves emphasis in view of its significance in contemporary debates and also because it opens into the more general questions of psychology and cognition that are my main interest here. In explications of *Theaetetus* and elsewhere, the supposed self-refutation often hinges on what is taken to be an *egalitarian* (claim implied by the unorthodox doctrine at hand: that is, a claim seen as erasing all differences of (presumably inherent, objective) better and worse, superiority and inferiority. A commentator writes: "[T]he point of Protagoras' theory which is to be attacked [in the dialogue] is its implication that no man is wiser than any other." This supposed implication leads to a self-refutation because, "according to his own theory [Protagoras] cannot himself be any better judge of truth than the ignorant audience he mocks."[11] Indeed, the familiar image of "relativism" as a fatuous, sophomoric demonism and, accordingly, the rhetorical force of the epithet itself derive largely from a supposed implication of this kind: that is, the idea that, according to the (unorthodox) doctrine in question, everything—every opinion, every scientific theory, every artwork, every moral practice, and so on—is "just as good" as every other.

I discuss this general supposition and argument elsewhere as the egalitarian fallacy.[12] It is a fallacy because, if someone rejects the notion of validity in the classic sense, what follows is not that she thinks *all* theories (etc.) are *equally* valid but that she thinks *no* theory (etc.) is valid *in the classic sense*.[13] The non sequitur here is the product of the common and commonly unshakable conviction that differences of better and worse must be objective or could not otherwise be measured. When appealed to in the argument, the conviction is obviously question begging. Thus, the supposed relativist could observe that her point is, precisely, that theories (etc.) can be and are evaluated in *other* non-"objective" ways. Not all theories are equal because they (including her own) can be, and commonly will be, found better or worse than others in relation to measures such as applicability, connectability, stability, and so forth. These measures are not objective in the classic sense, since they depend on matters of perspective, interpretation, and judgment, and will vary under different historical conditions. Nevertheless, they appear to figure routinely, and operate well enough, in scientific, judicial, and critical practice.

Close kin to the egalitarian fallacy is the idea that any theory that does not ultimately affirm the "constraints" of "an objective reality" or "nature itself" implies that "anything"—any practice, any belief, and so on—"goes." The assumption here is that there can be no other explanation for why we do not all run amok or believe ridiculous things: that is, that no alternative accounts of the dynamics of social behavior and cognition are possible. The logic of "anything goes" is identical to that of "everything's just as good as everything else." Both depend on taking for granted as *unquestionable* the classic concepts that *are being questioned* in the theory at hand. Hence the recurrent (and technically proper) countercharge of question begging; hence the recurrent deadlocks, nonengagements, and impasses[14]—or, one could say, incommensurabilities. Which brings us to what is, in my view, the heart of the matter.

The classical scholars cited above, though close readers and scrupulous interpreters, operate within the closures of traditional epistemology and philosophy of language. The confinement is reflected in the strenuously self-affirming and self-absolutizing formulations that recur in their arguments. We recall, from one, "the commitment to truth absolute which is *bound up* with *the very act* of assertion."[15] He cites in support Husserl: "The content of such [relativistic] assertions rejects what is *part of the sense . . .* of *every assertion.*"[16] For another commentator, it is "*the very notion* of rightness" that is undermined by Protagoras and latter-day relativists.[17] He cites in support Hilary Putnam: "It is a *presupposition of thought itself* that some kind of objective 'rightness' exists."[18] A passage in the recent work of Jürgen Habermas is relevant here, but I would note that his intricate arguments and far from epigrammatic prose make extraction difficult. In any case, he writes as follows: In the process of "convincing a person who contests the hypothetical reconstructions [of the *inescapable presuppositions* of argument] . . . that he is caught up in performative contradictions[,] . . . I must appeal to the *intuitive preunderstandings* that *every* subject competent in speech and action brings to a process of argumentation."[19]

Two related ideas are notable in these formulations. One is that certain meanings, contents, forces, claims, or commitments inhere in (or are "bound up with," or are "part of the sense of") particular terms (or "concepts") and strings of words per se. The other is that certain concepts, claims, and commitments are deeply connected with ("presupposed by" or "fundamental to the nature of") our mental and discursive activities. Both ideas are recurrent; both, in my view, are dubious; and both, I think, are the product of cognitive tendencies—tricks of thought—that may be (as *tendencies*) endemic.[20]

It appears from the formulations cited above and from the arguments in which they figure that the discursive/conceptual elements in question (concepts, meanings, claims, commitments) and also their interconnectedness are experienced introspectively by those who appeal to them as self-evident—intuitively right. This is not remarkable, I think, in view of the particular conceptual traditions in which, as philosophers, logicians, and classicists, they were presumably both formally educated and professionally disciplined, and in view also of the particular idioms with which, as scholars in those disciplines, they presumably operate more or less every day of their lives. What is worth remarking, however, is the move from *experiencing* one's own cognitive activities and their conceptual and discursive products (that is, one's own thought, beliefs, and linguistic usages) as self-evident or intuitively right to *positing and claiming* them as prior, autonomous, transcendentally presupposed, and (properly) universal.

It appears (on the evidence of, among other things, alternative introspections) that ideas such as 'inescapable presuppositions,' 'intuitive pre-understandings,' and 'truth absolute' are neither universal nor inescapable. On the contrary, it is possible to believe—as I do, myself—that such concepts and the sense of their inherent meanings and deep inter-connectedness are, rather, the products and effects of rigorous instruction and routine participation in a particular conceptual tradition and its related idiom. It is also possible to believe, accordingly, that instruction (more or less rigorous) in some other conceptual tradition, and familiarity with its idiom, would yield other conceptions and descriptions of "the fundamental nature" of "thought itself" and of what is "presupposed" by "the very act of assertion." Or—as I would myself be more inclined to say, in the alternative idiom of one such alternative tradition—a different personal intellectual/ professional history would make other descriptions and accounts of the operations of human cognition and communication more cognitively comfortable and congenial.[21]

I pursue these points further below. First, however, a brief trip to the theater and to school, which are, in this neighborhood, not too far apart.

THEATERS OF INSTRUCTION

Foiled, exposed, and rejected, the devil in the old morality play exits stage left, muttering curses. The evocation of theater is not irrelevant here. The archetypal, exemplary self-refutation, *Theaetetus,* is, of course, dramatically scripted, and theatricality remains central to its re-productions. The dramatis personae are certainly among the most compelling in cultural history: the callow, showy, scoffing, hubristic truth-denier; the seasoned, gently ironic, ultimately martyred truth-deliverer; plus, as crucial parties to the scene, the mixed chorus of disciples and occasional interlocutors and, not insignificantly, the audience itself, motley representatives of the community at large.[22] The self-refuting skeptic recalls other self-deluded, self-destroying heroes and villains: Oedipus unwittingly condemning himself in his sentence on the killer of Laius; Rosencrantz and Gildenstern "hoist with their own petard";[23] Satan, self-corrupted and self-damned, his engines of unholy warfare recoiling upon himself.

Self and Deception

The structural principle of self-refutation is turnabout, reversal—in logic, *peritrope*. It is the counterpart of *peripeteia*, the turn of fortune that Aristotle thought most conducive to the effects of tragedy: fear, pity, catharsis. The emotional effects of both—classical tragedy and classic self-refutation—are complex: anxiety and satisfaction, as fear yields to pity and terror to relief; the pleasure of formal symmetry (revenge and justice coincide, the punishment both fits and mirrors the crime) joined with knowledge of a threat averted, an outlaw brought to book, order restored, orthodoxy vindicated. There is in self-refutation the satisfaction, too, of cognitive and pragmatic economy: the exposure and defeat of an adversary accomplished neatly, at his own cost. And, certainly, the frequency of suicides and self-mutilations in tragedy indicates that *self*-destruction has, as such, a certain frisson.

Self-refutation dramas—like all great artworks, or so we are told—can be experienced repeatedly without satiety. The effects are endlessly renewable here, perhaps, because the threat involved is itself so strong and ineradicable. Every Orthodoxy is to some extent unstable, vulnerable. And the skeptic's denial or counter-truth is appalling: All is flux, It is as each man perceives it, No knowledge is certain, God is dead, There is nothing outside of the text. A thrill of horror: What if it's *right?* Everything would be lost—rational argument, objective knowledge, truth itself, *and my life's work for naught*. But also, perhaps, another thrill, closer to desire: What if it's *right?* Everything would be permitted—anarchy, murder, mayhem, *and I, free at last of my life's work.*

The full tragic effect, it has been said, requires the spectator's identification with the hubristic hero: at least a moment of sympathy with him—or her—in opposition to all those gods, seers, kings, courtiers, and choruses of the orthodox. It may be that, among the audiences of self-refutation dramas, even among the disciples themselves, there are flashes of identification with the skeptic, even, sometimes, secret hopes for his triumph. Indeed, although the two lead figures described above—truth-denier and truth-deliverer—are familiar, their respective characterizations tend to blur (scoffer and ironist, tragic hero and martyr), and their respective roles can seem as reversible as the self-refuter's own argument. Thus Socrates can be seen as trickster and, perhaps, as the most radical of skeptics.[24]

Nor is it irrelevant here that the drama of self-refutation was originally produced as a pedagogic exercise for the betterment of the young. The "brilliant" (as he is called) but philosophically immature Theaetetus arrives in a state of enthrallment to dubious doctrines. He is delivered to better understanding—if not to the knowledge of knowledge itself—by witnessing and participating in the exposure of the self-refutation of those doctrines, thereby undergoing, through Socrates' midwifely ministrations, his own intellectual rebirth. The model is powerful and itself proves enthralling, the drama still re-produced, more than two millennia later, for the delivery of similarly bright, abashable seventeen- and eighteen-year-olds.[25] Are the doctrines not, after all, still the same, still seductive, and still false? Perhaps. In any case, the classic pedagogic exposure merges, along the way, with other stagings of demonic exposure and spiritual salvation, including exorcism.

As often observed, the enlightenment of the young in formal education operates through a process not dissimilar from other inductions into orthodoxy, from boot camp to monastery: a process of ordeal, alternating public punishment and public reward, that concludes with a welcoming by and incorporation into the special community. Given the institutional conditions under which this commonly occurs, that is, the regular convening in a theater of instruction of young men and women[26] in quasi-familial and semi-erotic relationships to—and rivalry with—both each other and the supervising master or mistress of the mysteries, it is not surprising that public humiliation has emerged as a favored technique. Moreover, in a company where status is measured by the development of intellectual prowess, there is probably no instrument of instruction more effective in that respect than the demonstration that one has unwittingly *refuted oneself*—the counterpart, no doubt, of the exposure, in other companies (athletic or military, for example), of more bodily self-disablings or self-foulings. It is no wonder, then, that the effects of such exposures (however gently, subtly, wittily, or ironically administered) remain, for those who receive or witness them, so powerful and profound, or that fear of a charge of relativism can haunt the spirits and buckle the knees of grown men and women, even the most sophisticated of them, even the most otherwise unorthodox of them.

DREAMS OF REASON

Like the devil, the skeptic is never finally vanquished or finally triumphant. No matter how decisively her self-refutation is demonstrated, she does not acknowledge or indeed believe that she has refuted herself. Nor does the orthodox believer regard the skeptic's evasion of his charge as proper, or acknowledge the justice of her countercharge that he has begged all the questions.[27] Alternatively, of course, it could be said that skepticism triumphant *is* orthodoxy.

But the question may still be asked: If orthodoxy is that which is manifestly true, self-evidently right, and intuitively and universally preunderstood, then how is it that its truth and rightness elude the skeptic? The orthodox answer to this question is familiar: profound defects and deficiencies of intellect and character—an innate incapacity for logical thinking, unregenerate corruption by false (or French) doctrine, domination by personal resentment and political ideology, or unfamiliarity with the best work on the subject in analytic philosophy.

The explanatory asymmetry here—that is, the orthodox believer's conviction that he believes what he does because it is true while skeptics and heretics believe what they do because there is something the matter with them—is a general feature of defenses of orthodoxy: political, aesthetic, and scientific as well as philosophical (or religious). Its recurrence seems to reflect the cognitive tendencies alluded to above: that is, the tendency to experience one's own beliefs as self-evident and, sometimes, to posit them as prior, necessary, and properly universal. The failure to believe what is self-evident is self-evidently folly; the failure to believe what is necessarily presupposed is necessarily irrational—or perverse.

The tendency to experience one's own thinking as inevitable and to experience its products as prior and autonomous is, in the conceptual traditions and idioms I find congenial and cognitively comfortable, not a foundational intuition to be affirmed but a more or less intriguing phenomenon to be explained. To summarize all too briefly:

Certain configurations of perceptual/behavioral tendencies ("beliefs") are strengthened and stabilized by our effective-enough and predictable-enough interactions with our environments (including other people and what they produce, e.g., institutions and discourses). To the extent that this occurs, we (human, social, cultural, verbal organisms) may experience and interpret those configurations reflexively as "referring to" or "being about" specific, determinate features of an autonomous reality: features, that is, seen as (simply) "out there," prior to, quite separate from, and quite independent of, our own interactions, past or current, with our environments. This experience, so interpreted, is not, I would say, either "illusion" or "delusion." Nevertheless, it could be *otherwise*—and, for some purposes, from some perspectives, more usefully, interestingly, coherently, and appropriably—described and interpreted.[28]

We recall that, with some disciplined effort (by, for example, mystics, Buddhists, and deconstructionists), the experience of an autonomous reality may be subjected to reflexive scrutiny and to temporary de-naturalization, de-stabilization, and dis-integration.[29] Descriptions of technologically induced "virtual reality" also make alternative interpretations of the experience easier to entertain. Subjects report that, after a certain amount of interactive feedback from computer-generated sensory stimuli—goggle-generated images that shift their shapes and size as the subject turns her head, glove-induced pressures that vary with the subject's hand motions—these modally diverse sensations will seem suddenly to integrate themselves and to surround the subject as a distinct and autonomous environment.[30] The cognitive dynamics of our ordinary experiences of "real" reality are, perhaps, not too different from the dynamics of such reported experiences of "virtual" reality.[31]

Human beings appear to have a tendency to protect their particular beliefs from destabilization, even in the face of what strike other people as clearly disconfirming evidence and arguments. I have termed this tendency "cognitive conservatism."[32] Though it often operates in technically "irrational" ways (as assessed by, say, economists),[33] cognitive conservatism is better regarded, I think, not as a flaw or failing but, rather, as the *ambivalent* (sometimes/ways good, sometimes/ways bad) counterpart of an (also endemic and ambivalent) tendency to cognitive flexibility and responsiveness.[34]

For better and for worse, cognitive conservatism yields intellectual stability, consistency, reliability, and predictability; it also yields, for better and for worse, powerfully self-immuring, self-perpetuating systems of political and religious belief. At its extreme, when played out in specifically theoretical domains, it can become *absolute epistemic self-privileging:* that is, the conviction that one's convictions are undeniable, that one's assumptions are established facts or necessary presuppositions, that the entities one invokes are unproblematically real, that the terms one uses are transparent and the senses in which one uses them inherent in the terms themselves, and, ultimately, that no alternative conceptualizations or formulations are possible at all, at least no "adequate," "coherent," or "meaningful" ones—at least not for beings claiming to be "rational." Cognitive conservatism is an endemic tendency and a mixed blessing. Its hypertrophic development, epistemic self-privileging, is a human frailty, common among common folk—but, in rationalist philosophy, honed to a fine art.

For those well instructed in traditional foundational epistemology, everything—each concept, each opposition, each link, and each move—hangs together, comfortably and, it seems, self-evidently. It hangs together in part because, perhaps, that's the way human cognition works, but also because the major project and achievement of foundational epistemology is the maintenance, monitoring, and justification of precisely that interdependency: the rigorous interorganization of everything that fits and the vigorous rejection (and "refutation") of everything that doesn't. Indeed, disciplinary philosophy *as such* (I do not say every philosopher or every philosophical work) can be seen as the cultural counterpart and institutional extension of individual cognitive conservatism—again, for better and for worse.

Self and Deception

The routines—rituals, habits—of rigorously taught, strenuously learned conceptual production and performance come to operate virtually automatically, to be experienced as necessary and autonomous, and, sometimes, to be posited as prior to and independent of the activities of any mortal human agent.[35] The resulting coherence and interdependency of concepts, connections, distinctions, and moves is what Derrida and others speak of, with regard to the history of Western philosophy, as "the closure of metaphysics."[36] It is not, however (as such theorists commonly stress), altogether closed, nor could any conceptual system ever be. Both individually and culturally, there is always noise and uncontrollable play in the system. Individually, our beliefs are heterogeneous and, though more or less effective and coordinated ad hoc, not globally coherent and always potentially conflicting. Moreover, there are always glitches in cultural transmission. We never learn our lessons perfectly. The rigorous training is never rigorous enough. There is always someone who missed class that day, or got distracted, or came from somewhere else, or heard something else that she liked better first, or just didn't care: the class misfit—outlaw, heretic, devil, skeptic, spoiler.

None of this is to say that the postmodern skeptic has "discovered the objective truth of the inherent wrongness" of traditional epistemology. To an epistemological traditionalist, any skeptic who claimed that would refute herself on the spot. To a postmodernist, any postmodernist who claimed such a thing would be a pretty problematic postmodernist.

The postmodern skeptic does not say or think that traditional epistemology is inherently wrong, an error, or a delusion. She observes and believes that the conceptual systems it sustains operate well enough for a good many people. Nevertheless, she also knows that those systems and that epistemology do not operate as well for her as other conceptual systems and theories of knowledge. That does not make them, in her eyes, all "equally valid" or "equally invalid." All are, and will be, measured and judged by, among other things, their applicability, connectibility, and stability. By such measures, different epistemologies and conceptual systems are found, and will be found, better or worse or, sometimes, congruent enough. But the measurements themselves, taken under differing conditions, interpreted from different perspectives, will vary. Equivalence and disparity, like commensurability and incommensurability, are, in her view, not absolute but contingent matters. As Protagoras might have put it, man is the measure of all the measures that man has.

The postmodern skeptic thinks that the interest and utility of all theoretical formulations are contingent. She is not disturbed, however, by the idea that, in order to be self-consistent, she must "concede" the "merely" contingent interest and utility of her own theoretical formulations. Nor is she embarrassed by her similar "obligation" to "concede" the historicity—and thus instability and eventual replacement—of the systems and idioms that she finds preferable to traditional epistemology and that she would, and does, recommend to other people. She is not disturbed or embarrassed—or, to her own way of thinking, self-refuted—by these things because she believes, in comfortable accord with the conceptual systems and idioms she prefers, that that's the way all disciplinary knowledge—science, philosophy, literary studies, and so forth—evolves. And she also believes that, all told (as she tallies such matters), that's not a bad way for it to happen.

Although the postmodern skeptic is not affirming (self-contradictorily) "the (objective) truth of the (inherent) wrongness" of traditional epistemology, a traditionalist may hear her affirming it, just as if those words were coming right out of her mouth. That is because, by his logic, that is just what it means for someone to *deny* something. Thus, he hears her contradicting (and, in his terms, refuting) herself. By the postmodern skeptic's own logic, the traditionalist is mistaken. The traditionalist will not see his mistake *as* one so long as he remains a traditionalist. He may, however, become a postmodern skeptic himself—or, of course, the skeptic a born-again believer.[37]

This last point is significant: not the conversion (or corruption) of the believer (or the skeptic) per se, but, despite the reciprocal impasses indicated here, the general possibility of the transformation of belief. Nothing said here implies a permanent structure of deadlock.[38] On the contrary, what has been said explicitly and implied throughout is that no orthodoxy—or skepticism—can be totally stable, no theoretical closure complete, no incommensurability absolute.

By the same token, one cannot *interact* with a theoretical closure and remain totally "outside" of it, even if the interaction is skeptical or adversarial. Thus one disputes "logic" with logic (or logic with "logic"), neither identical, but each, over time, shaped by the other.[39] The process—that is, skeptical, adversarial interactions with traditional conceptual systems—is both rhetorical and cognitive: played out in public theaters (classrooms, conference halls, the pages of journals) and also in the private theater of the mind, where the "self" takes all the roles—truth-deliverer and truth-denier, master and disciple, chorus of mixed voices and motley audience—and every self-refutation is, simultaneously, the self's triumph and transformation.

NOTES

*A version of this article appeared in *Common Knowledge* 2:2 (Fall, 1993): 81–95.

1. Individual instances are cited where discussed, below. For recent rehearsals, collections, and surveys, see Harvey Siegel, *Relativism Refuted: A Critique of Contemporary Epistemological Relativism* (Dordrecht: Reidel, 1987); Michael Krausz, ed., *Relativism: Interpretation and Confrontation* (South Bend: University of Notre Dame Press, 1989); and Larry Laudan, *Science and Relativism: Some Key Controversies in the Philosophy of Science* (Chicago: University of Chicago Press, 1990).

2. The crucial charge here has been tu quoque, that is, unwarranted self-exception and thus (if condemnations are involved) implicit self-condemnation. See Steve Woolgar, ed., *Knowledge and Reflexivity: New Frontiers in the Sociology of Knowledge* (London: Sage, 1988); Malcolm Ashmore, *The Reflexive Thesis: Writing Sociology of Scientific Knowledge* (Chicago: University of Chicago Press, 1989); Andrew Pickering, "From Science as Knowledge to Science as Practice," in *Science as Practice and Culture*, ed. Pickering (Chicago: University of Chicago Press, 1992), 1–28.

3. *Contingencies of Value: Alternative Perspectives for Critical Theory* (Cambridge: Harvard University Press, 1988).

4. Plato, *Theaetetus* (170a–172c, 177c–179b). The translation by M. J. Levett is appended to Myles Burnyeat's study of the text, *The Theaetetus of Plato* (Indianapolis: Hackett, 1990). I draw here also on the following: Edward N. Lee, " 'Hoist with His Own Petard': Ironic and Comic Elements in Plato's Critique of Protagoras (Tht. 161–71)," in *Exegesis and Argument*, ed. Lee, A. P. D. Mourelatos, and R. M. Rorty (Assen: Van Gorcum, 1973), 225–61; Myles Burnyeat, "Portagoras and Self-Refutation in Plato's Theaetetus," *The Philosophical Review* 85 (April 1976): 172–95; David Bostock, *Plato's Theaetetus* (Oxford: Clarendon Press, 1988); and Rosemary Desjardins, *The Rational Enterprise: Logos in Plato's Theaetetus* (Albany: State University of New York Press, 1990).

5. When the texts of fertile and original theorists (Nietzsche or Foucault, for example) are paraphrased as one-line "theses," "claims," or "*p*'s," the assumption is that specific analyses, examples, and counter-proposals are irrelevant to the identity of a theoretical position, and also that particulars of verbal idiom—diction, voice, imagery, style, etc.—are irrelevant to its force, uptake, interest, and appropriability. This assumption, fundamental to the operations of formal logic, is implicitly contested by the rhetoricist/pragmatist line in contemporary theory. See, for example, Stanley Fish, *Doing What Comes Naturally: Change, Rhetoric, and the Practice of Theory in Literary and Legal Studies* (Durham: Duke University Press, 1989), and, of course, the works of Nietzsche and Foucault.

6. G. B. Kerferd, "Plato's Account of the Relativism of Protagoras," *Durham University Journal* 42 (1949): 20–26; Gregory Vlastos, ed., *Plato's Protagoras*, trans. B. Jowett (Indianapolis: Liberal Arts Press, 1956), intro. The trick or error is noted and discussed in all the commentaries cited in n. 4, above, and also by Siegel, *Relativism Refuted*.

7. Burnyeat, *Theaetetus of Plato*, 30.

8. Burnyeat, "Protagoras and Self-Refutation," 195. See Smith, *Contingencies*, 112–14, 205, for a (self-exemplifying) reply to this formulation and argument.

9. Siegel, *Relativism Refuted*, 8, 20.

10. Bostock, *Plato's Theaetetus*, 95. Lee, " 'Hoist with His Own Petard,' " argues the same point.

11. Bostock, *Plato's Theaetetus*, 89, 85.

12. Smith, *Contingencies*, 98–101, 150–52. For the related idea that a rejection of classic conceptions of objective validity amounts to a rejection/forswearing of all value judgments (and thus to moral/political paralysis or quietism), see Smith, "The Unquiet Judge: Activism without Objectivism in Law and Politics," *Annals of Scholarship* 9 (1–2) (1992): 111–33. For the idea that relativists who observe circularities, fallacies, and non sequiturs in their adversaries' arguments are caught in a "performative" self-contradiction, see n. 39, below.

13. "Validity" is especially pertinent here, but the analysis applies to the rejection of any classic measure—truth, beauty, virtue, etc.—in an absolute or objectivist sense.

14. Since those who assume the unquestionability of ideas such as "intrinsic value," "universal moral norms," and "constraints of an objective reality" foreclose the possibility of alternative—nonobjectivist, nonaxiological—accounts of judgment, motivation, and cognition, it is not surprising that they have great difficulty entertaining or, it could be said, grasping such accounts.

15. See Burnyeat, above (italics added).

16. Edmund Husserl, *Logical Investigations*, 2d ed. (1913), trans. J. N. Findlay (London: Routledge and Kegan Paul, 1970), 139 (italics added), cited by Burnyeat, *Theaetetus of Plato*, 30.

17. Siegel, *Relativism Refuted*, 4 (italics added); similarly, later: " 'Relative rightness' is not rightness *at all*. . . . To defend relativism relativistically is to fail to defend it *at all*," 8–9 (italics added).

18. Putnam, *Reason, Truth and History* (Cambridge: Cambridge University Press, 1981), 124.

19. Habermas, "Discourse Ethics: Notes on a Program of Philosophical Justification," in *Moral Consciousness and Communicative Action*, trans. Christian Lenhardt and Shierry Weber Nicholsen (Cambridge: MIT Press, 1990), 89–90 (italics added).

20. The emphasis here is meant to distinguish this suggestion from the idea of cognitive universals in a classic (e.g., Kantian) sense.

21. Disciplinary instruction is not, of course, simply determinative. All education is complexly interactive and the effects of formal/professional education are always diversely mediated by personal temperament as well as by other aspects of personal history.

22. We may recall, in *Theaetetus*, the figures Theodorus, senior mathematician and occasional participant in the dialogue, and Eucleides (142a–143c), its continuous witness and scrupulous recorder.

23. The appropriateness of Shakespeare's phrase to Protagoras is remarked by Lee, " 'Hoist with His Own Petard.' " Lee reads *Theaetetus* as fundamentally comic and, via the supposed punishment-fits-the-crime image of Protagoras reduced to a cabbage-like vegetable, as related in impulse to the *Divine Comedy*.

24. The irony in *Theaetetus* is exceedingly complex. Commentators note that it concludes with its ostensible central question—What is knowledge?—unanswered. Desjardins (*Rational Enterprise*, 85–90) goes further, reading Socrates/Plato as ultimately endorsing the Protagorean thesis, appropriately interpreted.

25. See Hadley Arkes, *First Things: An Inquiry into the First Principles of Morals and Justice* (Princeton: Princeton University Press, 1986), 78–80, for an unselfconscious report of triumphs along these lines by a professor of philosophy at a small, elite college.

26. Mostly young men, of course, in disciplinary philosophy. For original and instructive discussions of the significance of that bias, see Michèle Le Doeuff, *The Philosophical Imaginary* (London: Athlone Press; Stanford: Stanford University Press, 1989); Andrea Nye, *Words of Power: A Feminist Reading of the History of Logic* (New York: Routledge, 1990).

27. See James L. Battersby, "Professionalism, Relativism, and Rationality," *PMLA* 107 (January 1992): 63, for the (awkwardly stated) counter-counterargument that "self-refutation" (i.e., presumably, the charge) does not beg the question because it is (i.e., presumably, it appeals to) "a standard" that "belongs to the class of transparadigmatic criteria." Of course this re-begs the question, though at a more elevated level. Similarly, Siegel argues (*Relativism Refuted*, 187) that the charge by epistemological "naturalists" that the "incoherence argument" is question-begging "founders on the confusion . . . between truth and certainty," thus appealing (question-beggingly, as charged) to the classic conception of "truth" at issue.

28. Whether or not "it" is the same when otherwise conceived and described is a puzzle of which much has been made. It figures, for example, in the "dualism of [variable] conceptual scheme and [fixed] empirical content" alleged by Donald Davidson to be "essential to"—and thus, perhaps, crucially damaging of—certain views of Kuhn and Feyerabend (Davidson, "On the Very Idea of a Conceptual Scheme," in *Inquiries into Truth and Interpretation* [Oxford: Clarendon Press, 1984], 189). Here as elsewhere, however, part of the issue is what sort of puzzle one thinks it is: whether "essentially" logical, as Davidson's term seems to indicate, or contingently discursive, conceptual, and rhetorical, as it could also be seen (and, accordingly, handled quite differently). Davidson's own position on the question appears ambivalent. It is certainly more elusive than is suggested by recurrent citations of this essay as decisive for debates over the epistemological claims of "conceptual relativism" and "postmodernism" and the implications of the idea of incommensurability (cf. S. P. Mohanty, "Us and Them: On the Philosophical Bases of Political Criticism," *Yale Journal of Criticism* 2 [1989]: 1–31, and Christopher Norris, *What's Wrong with Postmodernism: Critical Theory and the Ends of Philosophy* [Baltimore: Johns Hopkins University Press, 1990], 186–87).

29. For descriptions of the effort among Buddhists, see Francisco Varela, Evan Thompson, and Eleanor Rosch, *The Embodied Mind: Cognitive Science and Human Experience* (Cambridge: MIT Press, 1991), 59–81.

30. Howard Rheingold, *Virtual Reality* (New York: Summit Books, 1991).

31. It should be stressed that "cognitive" is not confined here to activities above the neck (i.e., the entire organism is involved) and also that the stabilization and naturalization of belief are the product of interacting psychophysiological, social, political, and technological dynamics and practices. For recent discussions, see "Irreductions" in Bruno Latour, *The Pasteurization of France* (Cambridge: Harvard University Press, 1988), and Andrew Pickering, *The Mangle of Practice: Time, Agency, and Science* (Chicago: University of Chicago Press, 1995).

32. Cf. Smith, "Belief and Resistance: A Symmetrical Account," *Critical Inquiry* 18 (Autumn 1991): 125–39.

33. Cf. Daniel Kahneman, Paul Slovic, and Amos Tversky, eds., *Judgment under Uncertainty: Heuristics and Biases* (Cambridge: Cambridge University Press, 1982).

34. Cf. Joan S. Lockard and Delroy L. Paulus, eds., *Self-Deception: An Adaptive Mechanism?* (Englewood Cliffs, NJ: Prentice-Hall, 1988).

35. Cf. Brian Rotman, *Ad Infinitum: The Ghost in Turing's Machine—Taking God out of Mathematics and Putting the Body Back In* (Stanford: Stanford University Press, 1993).

36. Cf. Jacques Derrida, *Positions,* trans. Alan Bass (Chicago: University of Chicago Press, 1981), 6–7, 13, 22. For relevant discussion of the idea, see Arkady Plotnitsky, *Reconfigurations: Critical Theory and General Economy* (Gainesville: University of Florida Press, 1992), 194–211.

37. "Traditionalism" and "postmodernism" (each of which comes in a variety of sizes and colors, not all represented here) are not, to be sure, the only stances possible. Numerous transcendences and via medias have been proposed (e.g., Richard J. Bernstein, *Beyond Objectivism and Relativism* [Philadelphia: University of Pennsylvania Press, 1983]; Hilary Putnam, *Realism with a Human Face* [Cambridge: Harvard University Press, 1990]; Joseph Margolis, *The Truth about Relativism* [Cambridge, MA: Basil Blackwell, 1991])—and one must not forget the multitudes of people who lead rich, full lives without any articulated positions whatsoever on issues of epistemology. It must be added, however, that the psychological and social/political dynamics that operate to stabilize beliefs seem also, under a wide range of conditions, to *polarize* them (cf. William E. Connolly, *Identity/Difference: Democratic Negotiations of Political Paradox* [Ithaca: Cornell University Press, 1991]). Also, while some transcendences and via medias are, from the present perspective, more congenial or interesting than others, it seems that most of them strive to hunt with the hounds and run with the fox(es), that is, to exhibit the solid home virtues of orthodoxy but seek credit for the cosmopolitanism (as it may be seen) of postmodernism. It is no coincidence that the pages in which they are developed are commonly strewn with charges of the "incoherence" and self-refutation of more unambivalently unorthodox positions.

Self and Deception

38. Nor is it implied, more generally, by critiques of the traditional idea of ultimate "determinations" of which side is/was ("essentially," "objectively") right ("all along").

39. The quotation marks here distinguish what are commonly seen as the fixed canons of formal logic from what could otherwise be seen as contingently (though very broadly) effective discursive/conceptual practices. The parenthetical reversal acknowledges the claims of each of these logics to priority: "logical" priority for the traditionalist; pragmatic/historical/psychological priority for the postmodern skeptic. Habermas and Karl-Otto Apel, among others, would see in this disputing of logic with "logic" a "performative [self-]contradiction" and, accordingly, validation of the "inescapably presupposed rules of argumentation" (Habermas, "Discourse Ethics: Notes on a Program of Philosophical Justification") and of "reason itself" (Apel, "The Problem of Philosophical Foundations in Light of a Transcendental Pragmatics of Language," in *After Philosophy: End or Transformation?* ed. Kenneth Baynes, James Bohman, and Thomas McCarthy [Cambridge: MIT Press, 1987]). In a sequel to this chapter, I examine (as ["]rationally["] and ["]logically["] as seems necessary, under current conditions, to be persuasive) the questionable logical/rhetorical operations of such arguments.

SEVEN

FALSITY, PSYCHIC INDEFINITENESS, AND SELF-KNOWLEDGE

Joel J. Kupperman

The poem of the *Tao Te Ching* that traditionally has been numbered 18 (and in the new translation by Mair is 62) describes in an amusing and cynical way our descent from primitive integrity. After the mighty Way declines, kindness and morality take its place. The advent of wisdom and shrewdness/intelligence (Mair has cunning and wit) is accompanied by a great *wei* 偽. Some translators (e.g., Legge and Blakney) render this as hypocrisy; Mair has "falsity."[1] These are different views of the territory of what is not genuine or is insincere, and it is this territory that I wish to explore. Someone who is false to others may well be false to herself or himself, so that we may pursue the links among hypocrisy, self-deception, and insincerity, as well as the connections between these qualities and the genuine ones (if there are any) of which they are counterfeits.

The least interesting part of this territory is falsity that is fully conscious hypocrisy or dishonesty. Bloggs tells us that he has done *X* when he knows full well that instead he has done *Y*, or he misdescribes his attitudes or a pattern of his behavior, knowing that he is misdescribing. The motives for this kind of deception are usually clear enough: they may have to do with a desire for popularity, or respect, or not to be bothered or pressured. The context is usually Bloggs's awareness that there are certain things, such as kindness, morality, wisdom, and intelligence, that are thought highly of, and that he has been falling short. None of this generates philosophical puzzles.

Sometimes Bloggs convinces himself, as we say, of the story he is telling us. This is more interesting. How could Bloggs start out knowing the truth, and in the end forget or blur it? Or, even if we cannot specify a time at which it is clear that Bloggs fully knew the truth, we might posit that in some sense he did—and does—know the truth. Or, at least, the truth is readily available to him, and it is as if he chooses not to know. So *he,* who knows (or knew, or could know) the truth, is deceiving himself as well as us, even though in his case the deceiver and the deceived are one and the same person. That is the philosophical problem.

Self and Deception

It should be pointed out that this summary is too neat for the continuum of real-world cases, in which Bloggs may "sort-of" know that the story he is telling us is not an accurate one; he may think though that the story is not too misleading (or that it is, but that it really makes no difference), or it may be that at some moments he is very well aware that the story he has been telling is inaccurate but that at other moments he convinces himself, and so on.[2] There are many patterns of self-deception, not merely one. Rather than pursue this, though, we will return to the philosophical puzzle of how the truth can be available to Bloggs and yet (at least seemingly) not known by him.

We can approach this by means of some comments on a recent book, Stephen White's *The Unity of the Self,* which approaches self-deception in a way that has become increasingly influential, and also links to the topic an interesting (and I think wrong-headed) account of the psychological context of responsibility. White sees a person as an interacting system of homuncular subsystems, which are conscious but not self-conscious. This way of viewing a person will seem bizarre to some, but the idea of homuncular subsystems (as pioneered by Daniel Dennett and William Lycan) has played an important part in the recent philosophy of psychology literature; and, as some commentators point out, Freud's account of self-deception is in a way an account in terms of homuncular subsystems. If the subsystems, while meeting the standards of consciousness, are not self-conscious, there is a sense in which none of them avows (to use a word crucial in Herbert Fingarette's account of self-deception) the truth, which they are shielding the system from. This, at the least, lessens the apparent paradox in self-deception.

White's account of responsibility is more novel. It centers on the ascription to any individual of an ideal reflective equilibrium (IRE), which is "the most coherent extension of the subject's noninstrumental or intrinsic desires that the subject could and would produce . . . in eliminating conflicts among his or her noninstrumental desires."[3] This prepares the way for the following dilemma. If someone acts on a desire, either that desire is or is not in that person's IRE. The former case is like that of a psychopath, in that blame can find "no footing in the person's motivational makeup." In the latter case the agent is like someone who is compulsive: both act on a desire whose motivational strength is out of proportion to its evaluational strength. In this case, then, like that of compulsive behavior, blame seems irrelevant and unnecessary.[4]

White's solution to this dilemma, which grounds ascriptions of responsibility in the importance and value we give to authorship of actions, seems to me ingenious and plausible. But the dilemma itself can seem plausible only if we can accept an exceedingly simple a priori psychology of human desire. Some sense of empirical complications is required if we are to begin to understand self-deception and more generally the *wei* referred to in the *Tao Te Ching*.

This discussion must include profuse apologies. First of all, I am not a psychologist. And, in any event, it would be impossible to develop an adequate account of human conative attitudes in a single, not very long chapter. Second, the psychological inadequacy of what I will say is conjoined with crudity at one important linguistic point. The recent philosophy of psychology literature is marked by reliance on a small number of simple category words, so that the single world *desire* is used—artificially and contrary to ordinary usage—for a wide variety of positive conative attitudes. Annette Baier has made this clear in a sensitive essay on desire.[5] Reliance on an artificial all-purpose use of the word *desire* would be disabling in an essay that centered on Buddhism. Here it is merely embarrassing, but convenient; and I will follow in this usage the authors I am commenting on.

The most important thing that White's attractively simple model of human motivation leaves out is the indefiniteness of many desires. (This is the conative counterpart of the image of a speckled hen, of which one can ask futilely, How many speckles are there?) It also leaves out the fluidity of desire. Most of us do not know, much of the time, entirely what we want; and any attempt at arriving at an IRE will depend in part on how the questions are put and the context in which they are raised. Most of us also are suggestible in at least some of our desires. How else could philosophers such as Charles Stevenson ascribe with any plausibility emotive effects to ethical judgments? It is now a commonplace among psychologists that almost everyone often is, at least to some slight degree, "situational" in her or his behavior, which means that context (including other people's recommendations or expectations) influences behavior.[6] As Robert Solomon points out, character (to the extent that one has one) is played out in human relationships in such a way that different traits are expressed, stimulated, or inhibited in different company.[7] Roles that one is expected to play also can make a difference. In some cases the influence on behavior is a matter of conscious compromise, but often it is a matter of the modification of desire or the shaping of unformed desire.

A dramatic illustration of the point is the Stanford prison experiment.[8] College-age subjects were randomly assigned roles as prisoners and guards in a simulated prison. Guards became arrogant and brutal, and prisoners became apathetic and demoralized. The experiment had to be cut short because of the surprisingly quick, thorough, and excessive adaptation of the subjects of their roles, which suggested risks of psychological damage. What were the real desires of the pretend guards and the pretend prisoners? It is far from clear that there is a definite answer to that question or a single-solution IRE for each of them.

It should be added that the indefiniteness and fluidity of many desires is linked to an indefiniteness and fluidity in most people's sense of self, which allows them to dream or fantasize about themselves (i.e., someone they identify with) doing things that are drastically out of character. Part of the key here is Kant's idea that the self is a constructed, synthesizing concept by means of which the mind's "I" spreads itself on a range of experiences, thoughts, and actions. Not only do we unhesitatingly identify people as the same even after they have switched political, moral, and religious allegiances, but also people very often have no difficulty in thinking that they would be the same despite drastic changes in values. This gives us a self which is fluid and to which it is difficult to assign definite character.

It then does not seem all that puzzling that we hold people responsible for things they did which, in some sense, they wanted to do. Even if it makes sense to speak of the operative desire as part of their current IRE, blame can nudge them in the direction of a new (and better) IRE. Even if we can say flatly that they have a current IRE that does not include the operative desire, we still can hope to nudge them in the direction of an IRE that includes desires that are strong and reasonable enough to outweigh or control the wayward desire.

The fluidity of the self also provides the key, I think, to accounts of self-deception that are superior to White's homuncular analysis. Here I follow Mark Johnston. I accept his argument that the phenomena of self-deception are better viewed in terms of "subintentional tropisms" than in terms of homuncular subsystems.[9] Whether these tropisms can be grouped under the heading of wishful thinking is a complicated question, into which I do not propose to go. There may be forms of self-deception which are to the general category as nightmares are to dreams, and even an elastic treatment of "wish fulfillment" may not do justice to the varieties of self-deception.

A deeper question is whether the fluidity of the self, marked by psychic tropism and shifting influence of situations, allows for any knowledge that can be contrasted with self-deception. Some readers may think of Jean-Paul Sartre here and may think of remarks in the section on "bad faith" in his *Being and Nothingness* which indicate an answer of no. Those who have

Falsity, Psychic Indefiniteness, and Self-Knowledge

read to the end of the book know that Sartre's answer is in a way yes. We can work toward our own answer in this second half of this chapter, at the same time considering Sartre's view and also the Confucian view of the virtuous person's self-knowledge.

First, though, we can return to the poem of the *Tao Te Ching* with which we began. One way of reading it is as a caution against positing too simply a self-knowledge that can be contrasted with self-deception. At the very least, the poem gives an account of what is presupposed by (and must be in place for) self-deception. But the poem also can be taken to suggest that conventional attempts to overcome self-deception bark up the wrong tree and that indeed one should not be (so to speak) barking up any tree at all.

One analytic point the poem makes is that the motivation for falsity, at least in normal cases, presupposes normative standards. It is imaginable that Bloggs might represent himself as X when really he is Y even if X is not thought better than Y, but it does not seem likely. (And thus what is arguable is that self-deception could not exist as a culturally recognized practice—although there could be isolated cases—if there were not normative standards that people would like to satisfy.) If X is thought better than Y, then Bloggs has a clear incentive to convince the rest of us that he is X rather than Y. To the extent that he accepts, or at least goes along with, this normative judgment, he also has an incentive to convince himself that he is X rather than Y. Eliot Deutsch has a point when he suggests that if a self-centered and ungenerous Bloggs describes himself as generous, this can be understood (if one knows how to interpret it) as expressing a desire to be generous . . . as he is.[10] Bloggs may, as we say, fudge the evidence, even when he is reviewing it for himself, or he may manage to forget or to not notice key bits of evidence. Herbert Fingarette's notion of 'avowal' is useful here: whatever Bloggs may have once known or noticed, or have been in a position to know, need not be avowed by him.[11] However we tell the story, normative standards can provide strong motivation for Bloggs's self-deception. When the mighty Way declines, people no longer behave toward one another in a natural, unselfconscious manner; instead, there are good ways (kind, moral) and bad ways of acting. Bloggs will try to convince himself, as well as others, that he is a kind and moral person.

A key element in this story is that Bloggs not only is motivated to misrepresent himself, but also that misrepresentation has become possible in a world in which people are busily representing themselves. This is a world of wisdom and intelligence, or cunning and wit. Perhaps, before the mighty Way declined, people did not try to formulate who or what they were, either to others or to themselves. They simply were. Now they are busily presenting avowals, which very possibly vary according to mood, circumstance, and audience. The sociologist Erving Goffman wrote a very clever book related to this theme, *The Presentation of Self in Everyday Life*, examining how what is displayed can be different within a circle of intimates from what it is for a wider public; presumably there can be related differences in avowals. Any inner narration of one's thoughts and behavior can differ from the avowals presented to various groups, but it would be surprising if it were not influenced (at least for most people) by the outward avowals.

Inner presentations can fulfill a variety of functions. They can be reminders of what one thought one was doing or choosing, something especially useful for those of us who are easily distracted or confused. It scarcely need be said that, before the Tao declined, this help would have been much less needed, especially if one assumes that *then* behavior was natural and unreflective. A second function of inner narrative may be to give a sense of structure and meaning, and hence of value, to what is going on in one's life.[12] This obviously supposes that normative categories have emerged and that we live in a world in which we can ask if a life is meaningful. A third function is that of nudging desires, as well as behavior, in the direction indicated by the inner presentation. We need to bear in mind that (as Johnston emphasizes, and perhaps over-emphasizes) a great deal of self-deception is wishful thinking, that people usually want to be what their self-deceptive inner presentations suggest that they are. For that matter, in many cases people seem "sort of" to know that the inner presentation is not entirely true, but they think that there is some truth to it and that, with effort, it could become more true. The inner presentation can be a way of nudging one's desires and one's character in a certain direction.

One should not entirely fault this. If it is true that desires are (for almost all of us, most of the time) both indefinite and fluid, then a little self-deception in some contexts might be a good thing. This would be a little like the cases in which unwarranted self-confidence turns out to enable someone to achieve more than what she or he otherwise would have done. In short, there is room for a case that a limited degree of self-deception can have advantages, and philosophers such as Amélie Rorty (who presents self-deception as being a good adaptive strategy at times) and Bas van Fraasen (who links it to courage) have made such a case.[13] Indeed self-deception need not be fantasy: it can be recognition (and exaggeration) of what is already there, encouraging a person to build on that. It is relevant to note that, from the point of view of a puritan or a Jansenist, any statement *I am a good person* will be this kind of self-deception.

Falsity, Psychic Indefiniteness, and Self-Knowledge

In a world in which desires are indefinite and fluid, various forms of nudging can be useful. What was it like before the mighty Way declined? One hesitates to answer, in part because there is a great deal about which the *Tao Te Ching* is far from explicit. But part of the answer surely is that desires were still. Indeed—if one pays proper attention to the ordinary use of the English word *desire*—one would have to say that, strictly speaking, there were no desires. So what is there to nudge? Also, in this prelapsarian world, inner presentations would be neither possible nor useful. Why would anyone want to mar the unity of praxis by introducing the double-mindedness of self-representations as accompaniments of thought and action? Hence self-deception could not exist.

II

Of course self-deception does exist in our world. To the extent that it is undesirable, and can be viewed as a blemish on human life, there are two main ways of responding to it. One is to view it as a poor way of playing a game that cannot in any case be won and should not be played at all. As we have seen, that is the view of the *Tao Te Ching*. Skepticism about self-representation also emerges in a famous chapter on "bad faith" in Sartre's *Being and Nothingness*. The alternative way of responding to self-deception is, of course, to insist that the game of self-representation can be won, or at least played successfully and that there is self-knowledge which can be contrasted with self-deception.

Sartre's skepticism in chapter 2 of *Being and Nothingness* is based on the ascription of nothingness to the *pour soi*. Anyone who tries to fit his or her true nature to a formula is willfully disregarding the fact that choices that do not fit the formula are possible. Thus self-representation is an attempt to evade the discomfort and responsibility of freedom. Insofar as freedom involves anguish, each of us would like to say, This is the way I am; I cannot be anything else. But even if the formulas we use for ourselves are honest in the sense of fitting accurately what has been the pattern of our thought and behavior, this "good faith" is in a way just a subtle form of bad faith, because it denies something important about us: our ontological openness and our freedom.

This is a beguiling argument, presented by Sartre with considerable panache. It is not easy to discuss, in part because (like much in Confucius, Hume, and Nietzsche, to mention other great philosophers who are also not easy to discuss) it is a mixture of analytic and empirical (psychological) points. One analytic point is that if there were such a thing as self-knowledge, it would involve not only description or analysis of facts but also decision (or something related to decision). That is, to say I am an *X* kind of person not only makes a claim about the way I am thinking and behaving, or have been thinking and behaving, but it also implies a decision to continue thinking and behaving in an *X* kind of way, or at least the absence of a decision to stop. I have explored this elsewhere at some length.[14] If decision, or a failure to decide, is an essential component, then it is fair to ask, By what necessity does she/he have to decide to continue as an *X* kind of person (or fail to decide not to continue)? There is also the question of how bindingly one can decide what one's decisions will be next week or next year. All of this suggests that, when a person defines himself or herself, what is presented as definite is in reality up for grabs; it also suggests that what is a matter for decision is being dishonestly presented as merely a matter for description.

The ontological openness or "nothingness" of human beings is presented by Sartre simply as an insight, but clearly it is related to what I have called the "fluidity of desire," for which there is considerable psychological evidence. However, two problems suggest themselves. One is that (as already noted) many psychologists will agree that most people are "situational" in their behavior, and on this account alone, fluid in their desires. But *most* need not equal *all*. It may be that people vary enormously in the degree to which they have Sartre's ontological openness; and for that matter it may be that an individual can vary within a lifetime, becoming say more rigid in her or his old age. In short, it could be that there is a continuum of degrees of "nothingness," with the average conformist teenager at the high end and perhaps someone like Cato the Elder at the low end. (Public figures who are eager to please also could be toward the high end; Kierkegaard sometimes joked about people losing their selves, but when it happens it is no joke.) One need not look at the low end for someone as distinguished (and odd) as Cato the Elder; some literary characters seem to fit the pattern of *en soi* more than *pour soi*, in a way that suggests the question of whether there are any real people like that. In a very revealing remark, Sartre commented that he did not believe there could be real people like some of Faulkner's characters.[15] It would be interesting to unpack the basis for this skepticism, and to assay the role of empirical evidence.

A related problem is that if Sartre wishes to maintain that it is always possible for Bloggs (or anyone else) to do such-and-such, we need to look at various senses of the word *possible*. Does saying that it is possible that Bloggs will do *X* mean that we cannot have 100 percent certainty that Bloggs will not do *X*? In this sense, perhaps it is possible that President Clinton will suddenly order a nuclear attack on Great Britain: as astonishing as this would be, it is difficult to see how we can rule it out with absolute certainty. But perhaps this is more a comment on human knowledge, and specifically on the kind of knowledge provided by the social sciences, than on anything else. (It is often said that the social sciences are much better at predicting mass phenomena than the actions of an individual. A standard example is the ability to predict, within some limits, the number of "dead" (unable to be delivered) letters that will be posted in London in a given year; this does not yield complete certainty about whether the next letter I post in London will be delivered, nor does the National Safety Council's ability to predict traffic fatalities during the next holiday weekend include an ability to predict whether Bloggs will be one of them.) There is a sense of "possibility," in short, in which we say (of an individual's future behavior), Anything is possible—in relation to what we can know. The thesis of ontological openness seems to lose something in interest if it is interpreted in relation to this sense of possibility.

Another sense is one linked to phrases such as *real chance* or *live option*. William James first pioneered the use of the phrase *living option* in a discussion of religion.[16] There are some religious allegiances that might be living (or live) options for me, in the sense that it would not be entirely surprising if I considered them as possibilities (and not "beyond belief" that I ultimately adopted them); in this sense, it would not be a live option for me to become a Mithras worshipper or a Sikh. What does this mean in terms of probabilities? One would certainly say that the probability of my becoming a Mithras worshipper or a Sikh is vanishingly small. But is there any basis for saying that it is zero?

Enough has been said to make it clear that the concept of 'live option' is hardly a scientific one, especially if one's idea of science is modeled on the physical sciences. (But perhaps the social sciences in general fall short of being "scientific" by *that* standard?) Nevertheless, the concept is a useful one in accounts of human choice. The most obvious points to begin with are that no one's live options are, at a given time, unlimited, and second, that someone's live options can change drastically with circumstance. Even the conformist teenager, whom I placed at the upper limit of ontological openness, will not have a live option of becoming a Mithras worshipper, at least if he or she lives (let us say) in Iowa in the late twentieth century. But the same teenager, transported in time and place to the heyday of the Mithras cult, could become an enthusiastic Mithras worshipper. If we look purely at moral choices, a number of studies, including Stanley Milgram's *Obedience to Authority* and Hannah Arendt's *Eichmann in Jerusalem*, indicate that for most people the range of possible live options can be very wide.

What might serve to limit someone's live options? As the example of the Iowa teenager and Mithras worship suggests, one limit might be that some putative possibilities are seen (in the situation one is in) as too outlandish, too difficult to present persuasively. Plato, in the myth of Er in book 10 of the *Republic*, suggests another source of limits. Commenting on the story of a man who had led a virtuous life within a well-ordered community, and in the underworld chooses his next life to be that of a tyrant, Plato deconstructs the man's previous "virtue" as a matter of habit but not philosophy.[17] The idea seems to be that education can provide some understanding of values, or of the reasons for moral norms, such that a properly educated person will not regard certainly morally unacceptable choices as live options.

Something like this appears to be central to Confucianism. It enables Herbert Fingarette to title the second chapter of his book on Confucius "A Way without a Crossroads."[18] Before we discuss Confucian moral education, and the kind of self-knowledge for which it would seem to clear the way, it is worth taking another look at Sartre. He too, after all, seems to allow for a kind of self-knowledge, at least as a knowledge of limited personal live options.

Sartre's view is that someone's live options are structured by two phenomena of childhood. One is simply the emergence of a sense of self. He speaks of "the fortuitous and shattering advent of self-consciousness," illustrating it by means of a long quotation from Richard Hughes' novel *A High Wind in Jamaica*.[19] The other is the formation in that self of an "original project," which as circumstances develop will yield particular projects (and presumably, as circumstances change, will yield new projects).

A simple example of the intersection of original project with particular decision is the case in which Sartre, out for a long hike with companions, has to decide whether to stop to rest.[20] Sartre yields to fatigue but recognizes that there is a sense in which he did not have to; he could have continued with his companions to the designated resting place further ahead. The question, Sartre says, really should be

> Could I have done otherwise without perceptibly modifying the organic totality of the projects which I am; or is the fact of resisting my fatigue such that instead of remaining a purely local and accidental modification of my behavior, it could be effected only by means of a radical transformation of my being-in-the-world?[21]

What is at stake is Sartre's original relation with his body, and more generally with the in-itself of the world via his body. Particular actions, mannerisms, and gestures fall out from the original project: "A gesture refers to a *weltanschaung* and we sense it."[22]

Falsity, Psychic Indefiniteness, and Self-Knowledge

An original project, Sartre says, is not a deliberate choice: "This is not because the choice is *less* conscious or *less* explicit than a deliberation but rather because it is the foundation of all deliberation and because as we have seen, a deliberation requires an interpretation in terms of an original choice."[23] However, the original project can be deliberately reconsidered, either in the context of existentialist psychoanalysis, or perhaps by an adult who has the power and insight to rethink the orientation that had been conditioned by childhood circumstances. (This seems to be one of the themes of Sartre's *Saint Genet*.) Insofar as existential psychoanalysis is available to everyone, we can say of anyone that she (or he) does not have to be like that. But how "genuine" or strong a possibility this points toward may vary from individual to individual.

In any case, *Being and Nothingness*, taken as a whole, points toward a kind of self-knowledge which differs from the dishonest good faith of chapter 2 in embodying recognition of a component of commitment, and the accompanying possibility of change of commitment. Bloggs can say: This is the kind of person that I appear to have chosen myself to be; insofar as I intend to carry on being that kind of person, I can say that that is what I am like, although I have to recognize that I could (in some sense of "could") choose to change. Self-knowledge, in this view, is not a matter of finding a summary formula for a series of choices. It is rather like linking a number of dots on a page and suddenly discovering a picture and deciding that one does not mind living by that picture, or that one feels unable to change one's orientation (which is not the same as saying that it is impossible). In a classic case of existentialist psychoanalysis, that of "Ellen West," chronic overeating was analyzed in terms of a project of "the metamorphosis of life into mold and death."[24]

That an original project, which usually is then decisive throughout a person's life, is adopted in childhood is an empirical claim, one that calls for research on the formation and role of childhood self-images. Sartre did not do this research, and, in that I also am not a research psychologist, I will not argue for a view of my own on this topic. Some philosophers have suggested, though, that willed change of character is highly difficult, or is likely to consist at most of limited modifications of a basic structure rather than fundamental redesign.[25] This fits common sense and, if true, supports the view that who we are is largely formed in childhood. It may be though that what is largely formed are patterns of attention and emotional response, attitudes toward our bodies and other people, and so on; and it may be that what is largely formed in an individual will be consistent with a variety of moral policies, ranging from the virtuous to the vicious. In other words, it is possible to believe that a large part of who someone is will be formed by the end of childhood, and also to believe that whether that person is good or not will typically *not* have been determined by the end of childhood. Both of these beliefs seem to me to be plausible.[26] They will look inconsistent only to someone who assumes that moral virtue is a matter of deeply embedded instinct (rather than requiring moral judgment), or that moral virtue simply depends on one's being a "nice" person or having been brought up to respect the right set of moral rules. Confucius's observation that "The 'honest villager' spoils true virtue" is a pungent comment on the latter assumption.[27]

Let us agree with Confucius that a pattern of doing the right thing in ordinary circumstances is not enough to make someone genuinely a good person, and with Plato that it may take something as extraordinary as a ring of invisibility, or a choice of reincarnation—or life under an evil regime, or participation in an experiment such as the Stanford simulated prison or Milgram's—to find out. What would make someone a reliably good person in all of these circumstances? It may well be that we do not have enough hard evidence to answer this question with great confidence. One study, of Gentiles who risked their lives to save Jews during the holocaust, suggests a conclusion that may be disconcerting to those who would like the answer to involve roots in a community. Nechama Tec puts first among the common features of the "rescuers," "They don't blend into their communities."[28]

Probably most of us would like the key ingredient of genuine goodness to be the one Plato spoke of: philosophy. However, our response may depend on whether we take "philosophy" to refer to formal training in the subject or merely the acquisition of a reflective sense of personal values and the ability to engage other points of view. If it is the case that there is some form of cultivation that can turn an adolescent with a wide range of moral possibilities into a genuinely good person, then this cultivation must have, as one of its accomplishments, that some immoral things will seem personally unthinkable even when all around one are saying, Go ahead; it's the normal thing to do; it's really nothing.[29] How philosophy-based this process of cultivation must be is a question I will not attempt to answer. Indeed, the appropriate answer might vary from individual to individual. Rather, we can look at the form genuine goodness will take. This will bring us back to the topic of self-knowledge.

The connection is that genuine goodness, by definition, includes a strong tendency to act virtuously even in situations in which it might no longer seem the "normal" or "expected" thing to do. The data—from My Lai to Stanford—indicate that habits and a conventionally acceptable upbringing are not enough. Sometimes the virtuous person must think, I am different from the others; *my* values dictate different behavior. However it

Falsity, Psychic Indefiniteness, and Self-Knowledge

is arrived at, one element of this is what might be termed a "sense of self": an awareness of oneself as a distinct individual, with her or his own values. In a television documentary on the My Lai massacre, a soldier who had refused to participate (to outward appearances an uneducated man) said retrospectively, "*I* don't do that kind of thing." This expresses a moral commitment, but it is also an element of self-knowledge. Knowing who one is is in some form implicated in genuine goodness.

So let us look again at self-knowledge. Thus far the image of it we have developed is that (pace Sartre) it includes an element of awareness of one's own psychic fluidity, and (insofar as self-knowledge is not merely knowledge of oneself up to this microsecond) an element of something like decision—either a decision to continue more or less as one has been, or at least the absence of any decision to the contrary. One respect in which this image still seems to me to be seriously defective is that, despite the factor of something like decision, it offers us (as the fruit of self-knowledge) a largely static picture of a person's thought and behavior patterns. It is instructive then to look at the self-knowledge reported by Confucius in the *Analects:* "The Master said, In a hamlet of ten houses you may be sure of finding someone quite as loyal and true to his word as I. But I doubt if you would find anyone with such a love of learning."[30] The Confucian self is always in process, at least to the age of seventy (and very probably beyond).[31] Confucius' self-knowledge is presented in terms of the leading vector of personal change.

The key assumption behind this is that of the fallibility even of a very good person. One always can learn. Furthermore, even a very good person repeatedly will encounter situations which function as a challenge to self-examination. Mencius presents this dramatically: if he encounters someone who treats him in an outrageous manner, the superior man "will turn round upon himself—'I must have been lacking in benevolence and courtesy, or how could such a thing happen to me?' " Hence, Mencius says, "While a gentleman has perennial worries he has no unexpected vexations."[32]

There is another dimension in the Confucian account of self, as Roger Ames points out.[33] The social context and interrelationships of individuals are an integral part of the story. In this context, the dilemma of the person of superior merit, such as Confucius himself, whose merit is not generally recognized, is in a way a dilemma of self-knowledge. It may be (as in Sartre's discussion of bad faith) that there is no straightforward solution that is ideal: for the unrecognized worthy to act as a high official would be presumptuous, but to act as a nobody would be (and should be) felt as demeaning.

Even if we focus on the individual, a final point is that what counts as self-knowledge depends on the focus of the inquiry. There is more to any person, including her or his response to various kinds of foods, emotions on seeing various kinds of imaginative enactments, and so on, than anyone could possibly have a firm grasp of. Self-knowledge must be predicated on a selective emphasis. The self-knowledge of Sartre and of psychoanalysts focuses on sources of desire, aversion, awareness, and inattention. Confucian self-awareness focuses on factors decisive to a person's goodness, and also to that person's effectiveness in the social and political world. The two are closely connected. Mencius links being true to oneself with the ability to move others (by winning their confidence and trust).[34]

Charles Taylor recently has argued that values provide the orientation or framework within which a person's sense of self assembles itself.[35] This is more clearly true of ethically oriented self-knowledge than of psychoanalytic self-knowledge. To the extent that it is true, ethical reflection is part of the process of achieving self-knowledge. And, as Confucius' remark about learning suggests, it is arguable that neither process will ever be complete.

NOTES

1. See James Legge, *The Sacred Books of the East, The Texts of Taoism*, pt. 1 (Oxford: Oxford University Press, 1891), 61; R. B. Blakney, *The Way of Life* (New York: Mentor Books, 1955), 70; *Tao Te Ching*, trans. Victor H. Mair (New York: Bantam Books, 1990), 80. I am grateful to Chenyang Li for discussion of the text.

2. The possibility that one can be self-deceptive, but not grossly so, about one's beliefs, desires, and intentions is relevant to Akeel Bilgrami's very interesting Strawsonian argument that there is a link between responsibility and self-knowledge. One reply is that, even if one accepts the argument, a low degree of self-knowledge, which is consistent with significant self-deception, will suffice.

3. Stephen L. White, *The Unity of the Self* (Cambridge, MA: MIT Press, 1991), 202.

4. Ibid., 206, 268.

5. See especially note 8 in "The Ambiguous Limits of Desire," in *The Ways of Desire* ed. Joel Marks (Chicago: Precedent Publishing Company, 1986).

6. Cf. David S. Funder, "The 'Consistency' Controversy and the Accuracy of Personality Judgments," *Journal of Personality* 51 (1983).

7. See Robert Solomon, "Self, Deception, and Self-Deception in Philosophy," in this collection.

8. See Craig Haney, Curtis Banks, and Philip Zimbardo, "Interpersonal Dynamics in a Simulated Prison," *International Journal of Criminology and Penology* (1973).

9. See Mark Johnston, "Self-Deception and the Nature of Mind," in *Perspectives on Self-Deception*, ed. Brian McLaughlin and Amélie Rorty (Berkeley and Los Angeles: University of California Press, 1988). To say that a mental process is

Falsity, Psychic Indefiniteness, and Self-Knowledge

subintentional is to say that it is purposive but not initiated for and from a reason. "Our over-rationalization of self-deception," Johnston says, "consists of assimilating subintentional processes to intentional acts, where an intentional act is a process initiated and directed by an agent because he recognizes that it serves a specific interest of his" (65).

10. See Eliot Deutsch, "Self-Deception: A Comparative Study," in this collection.

11. Cf. Herbert Fingarette, "Alcoholism and Self-Deception," in *Self-Deception and Self-Understanding*, ed. Mike W. Martin (Lawrence: University Press of Kansas, 1985).

12. See Hannah Arendt, *The Human Condition* (Chicago: University of Chicago Press, 1958), 181–88; Alasdair MacIntyre, *After Virtue* (Notre Dame, IN: University of Notre Dame Press, 1978), 202ff.

13. See the essays by Rorty and van Fraasen in *Perspectives on Self-Deception*, ed. McLaughlin and Rorty.

14. "Character and Self-Knowledge," *Proceedings of the Aristotelian Society* 85 (1984–85).

15. See "William Faulkner's *Sartoris*," in *Literary and Philosophical Essays*, trans. Annette Michelson (New York: Collier Books, 1962).

16. See "The Will to Believe," in *Selected Papers on Philosophy* (London: J. M. Dent, 1947).

17. *Republic*, bk. 10, st. 619, in *Dialogues of Plato*, trans. B. Jowett (New York: Random House, 1937), 1:877.

18. See Herbert Fingarette, *Confucius—The Secular as Sacred* (New York: Harper Torchbooks, 1972).

19. See *Baudelaire*, trans. Martin Turnell (New York: New Directions, 1950), 19–20.

20. See *Being and Nothingness*, trans. Hazel Barnes (New York: Philosophical Library, 1956), 453ff.

21. Ibid., 454.

22. Ibid., 457.

23. Ibid., 461–62; italics are Sartre's.

24. See Ludwig Binswanger, "The Case of Ellen West," trans. W. Mandel and J. Lyons, in *Existence. A New Dimension in Psychiatry and Psychology*, ed. Rollo May, Ernest Angel, and Henri Ellenberger (New York: Basic Books, 1958). The quotation is from p. 318.

25. See David Hume, *Treatise of Human Nature*, ed. L. A. Selby-Bigge, rev. P. H. Nidditch (Oxford: Clarendon Press, 1978), bk. 3, pt. 3, sec. 4, p. 608; Hume, "The Sceptic," in *Essays*, ed. Eugene Miller (Indianapolis: Liberty Fund, 1985), 169; Jonathan Glover, "Self-Creation," *Proceedings of the British Academy* 59 (1983); Glover, *I: The Philosophy and Psychology of Personal Identity* (London: Allen Lane, 1988), 135, 136, 179.

26. See the appendix on education of character in my *Character* (New York: Oxford University Press, 1991) for relevant discussion.

27. See *Analects of Confucius*, trans. Arthur Waley (New York: Vintage Books, 1938), bk. 17, ch. 13, p. 213.

28. See Gay Block and Malka Drucker, *Rescuers: Portraits of Moral Courage in the Holocaust* (New York: Holmes and Meier, 1992), 6. An earlier study is Nechama Tec, *When Light Pierced the Darkness: Christians' Rescue of Jews in Nazi-Occupied Poland* (New York: Oxford University Press 1986).

29. It may be that adolescents who have this possibility do not include the conformist teenager spoken of earlier. Second on Tec's list of common features of "rescuers" is "They are independent people and they know it." Other features are a long history of doing good deeds: "Because they have done the right thing for a long time it doesn't seem extraordinary to them," "They choose to help without rational consideration," and universalistic perceptions. See *Rescuers*, 6.

30. *Analects*, trans. Arthur Waley, bk. 5, ch. 27, p. 114.

31. See *Analects*, bk. 2, chp. 4, p. 88.

32. *Mencius*, trans. D. C. Lau (London: Penguin Books, 1970), bk. 4, pt. B, 28, p. 134. Legge has "The superior man has a life-long anxiety and not one morning's calamity." See *The Chinese Classics*, trans. James Legge (New York: Hurst & Co., 1870), 2:118.

33. See Roger T. Ames, "The Classical Chinese Self and Hypocrisy," in this collection.

34. See *Mencius*, bk. 4, pt. A, 12 (123 in Lau).

35. See *Sources of the Self* (Cambridge, MA: Harvard University Press, 1989).

EIGHT

A CONFUCIAN PERSPECTIVE ON SELF-DECEPTION

A. S. Cua

This essay is an inquiry into the possibility of a Confucian response to the problem of self-deception. Due to paucity of textual materials, such an inquiry requires extensive reconstruction and interpretation.[1] The specific aim of the following investigation is to sketch a Confucian perspective on self-deception, based mainly on my studies of Hsün Tzu's moral philosophy.[2] Section 1 treats the classical Confucian concern with self-deception in *Ta-hsüeh* 大學 (the Great Learning). Section 2 deals with both the diagnosis of self-deception in the light of Hsün Tzu's conception of *pi* (obscuration) and the problems surrounding the Confucian notion of the 'self.'[3]

I

In *Ta-Hsüeh* (adult education),[4] personal cultivation (*hsiu-shen*) is considered as the foundation of peace and order both in the world and in family life. Along with the investigation of things (*ko-wu* 格物), extension of knowledge (*chih-chih* 致知), and rectification of the mind or heart (*cheng-hsin* 正心), making one's thoughts sincere (*ch'eng-yi* 誠意) is said to be an essential step or component of personal cultivation. The so-called three principal items (*san-kang* 三剛) provide the objective of abiding in the highest good or excellence (*chih-shan* 至善) by manifesting clear character or virtue (*ming ming-te* 明明德) and loving the people (*ch'in-min* 親民).[5] The concern with self-deception is explicit in chapter 6, a gloss on what it means to make one's thought sincere (*ch'eng ch'i yi* 誠其意). Before attending to this text, something must be said about the notions of 'sincerity' (*ch'eng* 誠) and 'one's thoughts' (*yi* 意).

The Notion of Sincerity (*ch'eng*)

On the first occurrence of *ch'eng* in *Ta-hsüeh,* Chu Hsi (朱熹) says, without further explanation, that *ch'eng* means "genuineness" (*shih* 實).[6] A longer

Self and Deception

gloss on *ch'eng* in *Chung Yung* 中庸 (the Doctrine of the Mean) is more helpful.[7] According to Chu Hsi, *ch'eng* means *chen-shih wu-wang* 眞實無妄: roughly, "truthfulness (*chen* 眞), genuineness (*shih* 實), and freedom from falsity (*wu-wang* 無妄)."[8] I suggest that we regard *chen, shih,* and *wu-wang* as characteristics of *ch'eng* construed as an ideal, ethical condition of personhood. If a person possesses *ch'eng,* such characteristics would be expected to be present in his thoughts, beliefs, speech, and actions. In Wang Yang-ming's understanding of the term, such a person would embody the unity of thought and action (*chih-hsing ho-i* 知行合一).[9]

As regards *chen,* if we render it as "truthfulness," we may say that a *ch'eng* person (*ch'eng-che* 誠者) is one who is sincere in acknowledging his thoughts or beliefs to himself and to others. Presumed in this acknowledgement is a concern for the truth of the belief and for the explanation of factual claims and justification of normative ones. This presumption perhaps accounts for Hsün Tzu's recurrent emphasis on *li* 理 (reason, principle) and *lei* 類 (kinds, categories), and *fu-yen* 符驗 (accord with evidence) as standards of argumentative discourse.[10] However, for the Confucian, *chen* is more than a desirable epistemic attitude or disposition, since the agent must also express this concern with *kung* 恭 (respectfulness), *ching* 敬 (seriousness, reverence), and *chin* 謹 (caution, circumspection).[11] *Kung* is a virtue of *li* 禮 (ritual). At issue here is whether *chen* is expressed in a respectful manner. Often this respect takes the form of deference to the opinions and wishes of others, particularly the elders and more experienced persons in the community. *Ching* is seriousness in expressing one's convictions, especially those that affect the well-being of the family and the community. A related consideration is *chin* (caution, circumspection), since the expression of one's view must take account of the feelings of the audience. In the words of Hsün Tzu, "Words of praise for another are warmer than clothing of linen and silk. The wound caused by words is deeper than that of spears and halberds."[12] Even more important is "to consider the long view of things and think of consequences."[13] In sum, *chen* as truthfulness is more than just a matter of sincere avowal of one's beliefs and concern for their truth. It is oriented toward the proper expression of these beliefs in the context governed by *li* or rules of proper conduct.[14]

As regards *shih,* it can be rendered as "genuineness," or "reality" in the sense opposed to "counterfeit."[15] A genuine person, for example, is one who is devoid of any hypocrisy or pretence with respect to the expression of her thoughts or feelings.[16] In the case of ethical commitment, *shih* signifies that it is something concrete or substantial, that is, the committed person is one who is disposed to discharge her obligation in the appropriate situation. In the case of the commitment to the ideal of the good human life as a whole, say, to *tao* or *jen* (humanity) in the broad sense, such a commitment must not be half-hearted, though it does not preclude inquiry to dispel doubt in the course of the agent's endeavor to specify its concrete significance. The commitment to *tao* 道 or *jen* 仁 is one that calls for a creative task of clarifying what *jen* means in personal life. Chu Hsi's recurrent use of *shih-li* 實理, commonly rendered as "concrete principle," displays a concern with the concrete significance of *tao* in terms of action.[17] As an achievement word, however, *shih* pertains not so much to the genuineness of commitment but to its actualization. Thus Tai Chen (戴震) quite properly explains *ch'eng* in terms of *shih* in the sense of fulfillment.[18]

As regards *wu-wang*, it can be rendered as "freedom from falsity," but the emphasis lies not so much in the abstention from making false statements, which may indicate a disregard for truth, as in the manner in which such utterances are made. *Wang* is a characteristic of speech or action that is uttered or performed in a cunning or crafty fashion with the intention to mislead or deceive others; such deceit is not easily detectable, especially by trustful persons. It is perhaps for this reason that Ch'en Ch'un (陳淳), Chu Hsi's eminent disciple, remarks that "the word *ch'eng* is closely similar in meaning to *chung* 忠 (loyalty, doing one's best) and *hsin* 信 (trustworthiness, faithfulness), but it must be distinguished from *ch'eng*."[19] *Wu-wang* is perhaps best rendered as "freedom from deliberate and cunning deception." And when we add that such an ascription to persons also involves *chen* and *shih*, we have a Confucian conception of *ch'eng* as an ideal, ethical condition of personhood.[20]

The Notion of yi 意

As Ch'en Ch'un observes, the basic sense of *yi* pertains to thinking and estimation or consideration (*ssu-liang* 思量) with respect to feelings. "Feelings naturally arise from inside the mind." Their expression requires the direction of the heart-and-mind (*hsin* 心), the master.[21] *Yi* can be used concurrently to refer to will (*chih* 志):

> Take for example that something is encountered. The master inside that controls is the heart-and-mind (*hsin*). As it [the nature] is activated to become joy or anger, that is feeling. That which is inside that can be activated is nature. To operate the mind and to consider to whom the joy or anger is to be directed is *yi*. When the heart-and-mind is directed to the person who is the object of joy or anger, it is will (*chih*).[22]

Self and Deception

In another use, *yi* refers to intention (*yi-ssu* 意思). As Ch'en Ch'un points out, "People often talk about intention (*yi-ssu*). *Ssu* 思 is to think. Contemplation, consideration, and so on, all belong to *yi*."[23] In sum, Ch'en Ch'un offers us a way of explaining *yi* in terms of three possibly interconnected uses. In the basic sense, *yi* is thoughtful consideration of the proper expression of feelings, involving an appraisive judgment which furnishes the object of will, and it is often accompanied by the intention to carry it out in actual performance.[24]

Before turning to a discussion of "making one's thoughts sincere" (*ch'eng-yi*) and "self-deception" (*tzu-ch'i* 自欺), something must be said about the connection of *ch'eng-yi* to the Confucian ideal of ethical excellence (*chih-shan* 至善) which is the ultimate objective of *Ta-hsüeh*. A question naturally arises: What is its subject matter? The formal answer must involve such familiar notions as *jen* 仁 (humanity, benevolence), *yi* 義 (rightness, righteousness), and *li* 禮 (ritual, rules of proper conduct). But these are generic notions. There is a need to draw attention to the concrete setting in which these notions function in the lives of committed persons. Tai Chen rightly points out that there are two complementary ways of speaking about *ch'eng* as an effort to realize the highest good: "Speaking plainly (*chih-yen chih* 質言之), we mean human relationships, affairs and activities of everyday life. Speaking more accurately (*ching-yen chih* 精言之), we mean *jen*, *li*, and *yi*."[25] The former provide the concrete context, and the latter provide the objectives of our endeavor.

Ch'eng-yi 誠意 (*Making One's Thoughts Sincere*) and Tzu-ch'i 自欺 (*Self-Deception*)

Presupposing our explication of *ch'eng* in terms of *chen, shih, wu-wang* (truthfulness, genuineness, and freedom from falsity), and *yi* in terms of *ssu-liang* (thought), let me adopt for convenience of reference James Legge's rendering of *ch'eng-yi* as "sincerity of thought," and attend to the commentary in *Ta-hsüeh* enjoining avoidance of self-deception in making one's thought sincere (*ch'eng ch'i yi*). The analysis proceeds along the lines of Legge's division of chapter 6 into four sections.[26] The text runs:

> *Section 1.* What is meant by "making the thoughts sincere" (*Ch'eng ch'i yi*)? One must not allow self-deception (*wu tzu-ch'i yeh* 毋自欺也), as when we detest a bad smell or as when we love a beautiful color. This is what is called *tzu-ch'ien* 自謙. Therefore, the superior man (*chün-tzu* 君子) will always be watchful when alone.[27]

The difficulty of interpreting this section lies in the character *ch'ien* 謙 in the binomial *tzu-ch'ien*. According to Chu Hsi, *ch'ien* should be read in terms of *ch'ieh* 慊, which means *tsu* 足 (satisfaction or contentment). Thus *tzu-ch'ien* means "self-satisfaction."[28] This interpretation is puzzling, for what is the connection between detesting a bad smell or loving a beautiful color and self-deception? While the passage implicitly refers to avowal of aversion, preference, or desire, such an avowal hardly constitutes self-satisfaction. An alternative reading without substitution of *ch'ien* is more plausible. In *Shuo-wen*, *ch'ien* means *ching* 敬 (respect).[29] Accordingly, the binomial *tzu-ch'ien* can be rendered as "self-respect." In this sense, avowing one's preference, desire, or aversion is a matter of self-respect. Whether such a preference can be satisfied remains a separate issue. Of course, their realization may well lead to self-contentment or self-satisfaction (*tzu-tsu* 自足). The imperative "One must not allow self-deception," as Chao points out, appertains to *chen* (truthfulness) and *shih* (genuineness).[30] If a person really detests a bad smell, she will not pretend to herself or others to the contrary. Hence, the attitude of a self-respecting person is such that she will not deceive herself and others.

While Chu Hsi's substitution of *tzu-ch'ieh* for *tzu-ch'ien* is arbitrary, his explanation of *tzu-ch'i* (self-deception) is informative. The self-deceiver is "one who knows that he must do good and avoid evil, but what emanates from his mind contains something that is not yet genuine (*shih*)." Recall that a person concerned with *shih* is a genuine person devoid of any hypocrisy or pretense. Chu Hsi's explanation of *tzu-ch'i* thus suggests that the victim of self-deception may not be aware that he is in that state of mind. Says Chu Hsi, "The person who desires self-cultivation (*tzu-hsiu* 自修) knows quite well that if he is to do good and avoid evil, he must exert effort in order to prevent self-deception."[31] Elsewhere Chu Hsi remarks: "A person knows well that he must realize excellence or goodness (*shan-hao* 善好), that he must do good. Yet within heart and mind (*hsin*) he thinks that there is no urgency in doing so. This is self-deception (*tzu-ch'i*), this is mere pretension, lacking genuine conviction (*hsü-wei pu-shih* 虛偽不實)."[32]

In Chu Hsi's view, the self-deceiver lacks genuine ethical conviction. He persuades himself, as it were, to believe that there is no urgency in doing good and avoiding evil, and he persuades himself precisely in order to evade his responsibility. There is an element of purposiveness (*yi*) involved, but the self-deceiver need not be aware of his state of mind.[33] The lack of genuine conviction (*pu-shih* 不實) is contrary to the requirement of *ch'eng*. As *ch'eng* involves *chen* (truthfulness), the self-deceiver may also disregard relevant truth or evidence. When he thinks that there is no urgency for ethical performance, it is this *yi* (thought) that misleads him. Of course, Chu Hsi is assuming that the self-deceiver is committed to doing good and avoiding evil. Chu Hsi's account of self-deception suggests that it is a product of lack of discernment or insensitivity to the context of action. As we shall see later, there is likely to be a hidden, operative motive such as selfish desires (*ssu-yü* 私欲).[34]

Because of the possibility of self-deception, the *chün-tzu,* concerned with personal cultivation "will always be watchful when he is alone." For it is solitude that affords ample opportunity to examine his thoughts and feelings. As Chu Hsi says, "When a man is alone (*tu* 獨), he himself knows what others do not know. Hence he must be careful in examining his incipient tendencies (*chi* 幾)."[35] Since human relationships, as noted earlier, furnish the context of action, they are the principal topic of examination. Recall the remarks of Tseng Tzu, a Confucian disciple: "Everyday I examine myself on three counts. In what I have undertaken on another's behalf, have I failed to do my best? In my dealings with my friends have I failed to be trustworthy? Have I passed on to others anything that I have not tried out myself?"[36] Ideally, the result of self-examination is freedom from self-approach.[37] But this requires the person to engage in reflection detached from preoccupation with personal gain, especially when it is contrary to *yi* 義 (rightness). As Confucius reminds his pupils, the *chün-tzu* considers *yi* to be of the highest importance.[38] Moreover, "the right sort of self-examination . . . consists not in idle brooding over oneself but in examining the effects one produces. Only when these effects are good, and when one's influence on others is good, will the contemplation of one's own life bring the self-satisfaction of knowing oneself to be free of mistakes."[39]

The aim of self-examination is self-knowledge. At a minimum, self-knowledge consists in acknowledging one's knowledge and ignorance. This is perhaps the force of Confucius' saying: "To say you know when you know, and to say you do not when you do not, that is knowledge (*chih* 知)."[40] For Hsün Tzu 荀子, the cultivated Confucian (*ju* 儒) will be concerned with knowledge in this sense so that "within they do not delude themselves (*wu*), and without they do not deceive others."[41] This means that they will be true to themselves (*chen*) and avow their knowledge or ignorance to themselves and to others.[42] Self-deception in this light may thus be characterized as a sort of "evasion of full self-acknowledgement of some truth or of what one would view as truth if one were to confront an issue squarely."[43] Self-deception and deception of others is a sort of concealment.[44] Such concealment is unlikely to be successful in "the eyes of others." As the commentary continues:

Sections 2–3. When the small man is alone and at leisure, there is no limit to which he does not go in his evil thoughts. Only when he sees a superior man (*chün-tzu*) does he then disguise himself, concealing his evil thoughts and displaying his goodness. But what is the use? For other people see him as if they see his lungs and liver. This is what is meant by the saying that what is true in a man's heart will be shown in outward appearance. Therefore the superior man must be watchful when he is alone. Tseng Tzu said, "What ten eyes are beholding and what ten hands are pointing to–isn't it frightening?"

The metaphor of sight is a familiar one in Western philosophy.[45] But as Fingarette justly points out, in the *Analects,* the emphasis is on shame rather than guilt. Fingarette plausibly maintains that "there is developed in the *Analects* no notion of guilt and repentance as a moral response to one's wrongdoing."[46] But his thesis on the absence of a developed notion of 'choice' in the *Analects* cannot be generalized to apply both to classical and to Neo-Confucianism, for the notion *ch'üan* 權, ("weighing of circumstances or alternatives") is explicit in Mencius 孟子 and Hsün Tzu, as well as in Chu Hsi.[47] Thus the classical Confucian concern with shame (*ch'ih, ju* 恥辱) is not just a matter of disgrace, that is, the loss of honor in the "eyes of others." As Hsün Tzu insists, there is a distinction between intrinsic or just shame (*yi-ju* 義辱) and circumstantial shame (*shih-ju* 埶辱), and between intrinsic honor (*yi-jung* 義榮) and circumstantial honor (*shih-jung* 埶榮). A *chün-tzu* may have circumstantial shame, but not intrinsic shame, for the former is a matter of circumstance beyond one's power or control, while the latter has a source within oneself.[48] At any rate, self-deception is analogous to "self-presentation." The deception cannot succeed, "for other people will see him as if they see his lungs and liver" and "this is what is meant by saying that what is true (*ch'eng*) in a man's heart-and-mind (*hsin*) will be shown in outward appearance." As we shall see later, concealing one's thought and conduct before oneself or others is an example of *pi* 蔽 (obscuration, blindness).

The commentary continues:

Section 4. Wealth makes a house radiant and virtue (*te*) makes a person radiant. The mind is broad and the body at ease. Therefore, the *chün-tzu* always makes his thought or will sincere (*ch'eng ch'i yi*).

The analogy of *te* 德 (virtue) with wealth is instructive, for *te* is a sort of power or force. Thus a *chün-tzu* has the power or capacity to influence the

Self and Deception

course of human affairs. As Confucius once remarked, "Virtue (*te*) never stands alone. It is bound to have neighbors"; "The virtue of *chün-tzu* is like the wind. . . . Let the wind blow over the grass and it is sure to bend."⁴⁹ So also, no matter how a person conceals her wealth before others, it is likely to be evident to them. It is possible for a self-deceiver concerned with personal cultivation and in the course of time preoccupied with earnest self-examination to experience self-disclosure and accordingly, to disavow self-deception.⁵⁰

The preceding exposition of the commentary in *Ta-hsüeh* provides, I hope, a coherent Confucian perspective on self-deception. Self-deception must be avoided because it undermines the task of personal cultivation (*hsiu-shen* 修身), in particular, the task of making one's thoughts sincere (*ch'eng-yi* 誠意). Our discussion provides a picture of a person of ethical integrity or self-respect (*tzu-ch'ien*), who engages in constant self-examination in order to attain sincerity (*ch'eng*), involving *chen* (truthfulness), *shih* (genuineness), and *wu-wang* (freedom from falsity). However, self-examination cannot be carried out without some understanding of the potential sources of self-deception.

II

Diagnosis of Self-Deception

Given its primarily ethical orientation, the Confucian interest in self-deception lies in its use as an interpretive and diagnostic concept.⁵¹ Chu Hsi's explanation of the binomial *tzu-ch'i* (self-deception), for example, is a textual interpretation.⁵² Moreover, the interpretation is proffered in part as a diagnosis of failure to attain "sincerity in one's thoughts" (*ch'eng-yi*). For diagnosing the sources of self-deception, I shall attend to Hsün Tzu's conception of 'obscuration' (*pi*).⁵³

Let me briefly note the background of Hsün Tzu's concern with *pi*. For Hsün Tzu, *tao* is a holistic ideal of the good human life, comprising ritual (*li*), rightness (*yi*), and humanity (*jen*) as basic interdependent foci of ethical interest. The failure to comprehend the *tao* is due to obstruction (*pi*)—a common human liability. Philosophers are no exception. They err not so much because of mistaken doctrines, but because their doctrines represent only partial views of the whole. In his words, "Some of what they advocate has a rational basis enough to deceive [*ch'i* 欺] and mislead [*huo* 惑] the masses."⁵⁴ Yang Liang's 楊倞 gloss on *pi* is this: "The man beset by *pi* is one who is unable to see through things clearly. His view is impeded by one corner as if there were things that hindered his vision."⁵⁵

A *pi*, literally, is a screen, shelter, or cover. *Pi* is Hsün Tzu's metaphor for an obscuration of the mind. In this condition the mind is obstructed in its proper functioning—thinking, remembering, imagining, and judging. In short, a *pi* is any factor that obstructs the mind's cognitive task. When the mind is in the state of *pi*, reason is, so to speak, not operating properly. The opposite of *pi* is clarity of mind. Thus Hsün Tzu says, "If you guide it [the mind] with reason (*li*), nourish it with clarity, and do not allow external objects to unbalance it, then it will be capable of determining right and wrong and of resolving doubts."⁵⁶ In this light, *pi* can also be rendered as "blindness." As Watson reminds us, Hsün Tzu's use of *pi* "denotes here [in *chieh-pi p'ien* 解蔽篇] a clouding or darkening of the faculties or the understanding, and Hsün Tzu plays on the image of light and darkness throughout the chapter."⁵⁷

Humans beset by *pi* may be said to be in the state of *huo* 惑 (delusion).⁵⁸ For example, "A drunken man will try to leap a ditch a hundred paces wide as though it were a narrow gutter, or stoop to go through a city gate as though it were a low doorway. This is because the wine has disordered his spirits."⁵⁹ In *huo* a person's mind is misled or misguided in his belief or judgment;⁶⁰ it is a condition in which the person is responsible for assenting to misleading guidance—a failure in the exercise of reasonable judgment in accord with his sense of *yi* (rightness). A person in *huo* is a self-deceiver. The potential sources of *pi* may thus be construed as sources of self-deception.

According to *Hsün Tzu*, whenever we make distinctions among things, our minds are likely to be obscured (*pi*) by these distinctions. "This is a common affliction (*kung-huan* 公患) of our ways of thinking."⁶¹ For Hsün Tzu, all distinctions owe their origin to comparison and analogy of different kinds of things. They are made in accordance with our purposes, and thus are relative to the context of thought and discourse. Distinctions, while useful, are not dichotomies. In the case of *pi*, the person attends exclusively to the significance of one item without consideration of the significance of the other. Common people as well as philosophers are prone to exaggerate. For example, according to Hsün Tzu, Mo Tzu 墨子 is beset by *pi* in his exclusive attention to utility without recognizing the importance of culture (*wen* 文); Chuang Tzu 莊子 is beset by *pi* in his preoccupation with heaven without recognizing the importance of human beings.⁶² For Hsün Tzu, the common sources of *pi* are desire and aversion (*yü-wu* 欲惡), distance and nearness (*yüan-chin* 遠近), breadth and shallowness of knowledge (*po-ch'ien* 博淺), past and present (*ku-chin* 古今).⁶³ For present purposes, I shall discuss these sources of *pi* in terms of desires and aversions, or positive and negative desires. This course is based on the assumption that in all cases of *pi,* there is present a desire as a motive.[64]

Since the state of *pi* is contrary to reason (*li* 理), we may regard that state as one of irrational preoccupation with one side of the distinction at the expense of careful consideration of the other. Well aware of the distinction between desire and aversion, a person may pursue her current desire without attending to its possible unwanted consequences. That person's mind may be said to be in the state of *pi.* More generally, humans suffer because of their concern for acquisition of benefit and for the avoidance of harm. When they see something beneficial, they do not consider carefully whether it may lead to harmful consequences.[65] However, even if consequences are considered, the person may fail to attend to distant consequences (*yüan* 遠) and simply focus upon near or immediate ones (*chin* 近), well aware of the relevance of the distinction at issue. Conversely, a person may be so preoccupied with distant consequences without attending to immediate ones which may well bring disaster. Hsün Tzu cites examples of ancient rules preoccupied with their concubines, and ancient subjects preoccupied with the acquisition of power. Thus "their minds become deluded (*huo*) and their actions were thrown into confusion."[66] Similarly on matters of life and death, a person may be a victim of *pi* because of inordinate attention to one without regard to the other. So also as regards present and past, and the breadth and shallowness of knowledge.

Hsün Tzu's discussion of *pi* does not provide us any systematic scheme for diagnosis of self-deception. However, it does suggest that our desires are the main motivating impulses and that they cannot be reduced to just one factor such as selfish desires—a prominent view in neo-Confucianism. Wang Yang-ming 王陽明, for instance, thinks that selfish desires alone are the obscuring factor (*pi*) that accounts for moral failure, but the mind may be obscured (*pi*) in many ways.[67] We may expect that in the case of self-deception, such obscurations may be reflected in a variety of patterns, such as willful ignorance, emotional detachment, pretentiousness, and rationalization.[68] In regard to remedy, Hsün Tzu would recommend that the person concerned with self-cultivation be engaged in wise and informed deliberation (*chih-lü* 知慮). In such deliberation, the person weighs all relevant considerations so as to arrive at a unified preference in the light of *tao.* This is a topic I have examined elsewhere.[69]

The Confucian Notion of the Self

Recently some scholars have proposed different conceptions of the self for Confucian ethics. I take these proposals as primarily constructive interpretations of an aspect of some classics such as *The Analects* (*Lun Yü* 論語) and *The Doctrine of the Mean* (*Chung Yung* 中庸).[70] Before expressing my critical appreciation of these efforts, let me consider the more general question of whether there is a Confucian notion of the self in the classics.

In order to approach this question, following Stephen Toulmin, we may distinguish three different uses of the term *self* in English: (1) the use in everyday reflexive idions as a prefix or postfix, that is, "self-" and "-self," (2) the use in speculative psychology as "the name of a hypothetical entity, or intervening explanatory variable," and (3) the diagnostic use in "clinical psychotherapy and comparable, non-medical modes of psychological description."[71] Toulmin goes on to show how a careful extension of the reflexive use "provides grounding for, and in due course develops into, the fully-fledged terminology of the 'self,' as it figures in clinical theory, psychiatric diagnoses and/or psychoanalytic interpretation."[72]

Toulmin's three-fold distinction provides a useful approach to our question of the Confucian notion of the self. It is uncontroversial to note that one would search in vain for a theoretical use of self in Confucian ethics. Earlier I suggested that the binomial *tzu-ch'i* 自欺 (self-deception) is best construed as a diagnostic term. In light of Toulmin's essay, our question is perhaps best approached by examining reflexive binomials such as *tzu* 自-locutions, then exploring the possibility of the diagnostic use of some of these locutions, not as a means for developing a philosophical, psychological, or clinical theory, but as a means of articulating an aspect of personal cultivation, especially in attaining sincerity of thought (*ch'eng-yi*). My remarks here, of course, amount to no more than a suggestion for inquiry.

In *Lun Yü*, for example, we find *tzu-hsing* 自省 (examine oneself), *tzu-sung* 自訟 (reproach oneself), and *tzu-ju* 自辱 (disgrace oneself).[73] In *Meng Tzu* we find *tzu-pao* 自暴 (do violence to oneself), *tzu-yang* 自養 (nourish oneself), and *tzu-te* 自得 (realize [*tao*] in oneself);[74] and in *Hsün Tzu*, apart from *tzu-hsing*, we find *tzu-ts'un* 自存 (to preserve [goodness] in oneself), *tzu-chih* 自知 (know oneself).[75] In *Hsün-Tzu*, one passage on mind (*hsin*) as "the ruler of the body" contains a series of six different *tzu*-locutions: *tzu-chin* 自禁, *tzu-shih* 自使, *tzu-to* 自奪, *tzu-tsu* 自足, *tzu-hsing* 自省, and *tzu-chih* 自止, roughly "the mind itself issues its own prohibitions and commands, makes its own decision and choices, initiates its own actions and omissions."[76] Except for Hsun Tzu's series in one passage, all the other *tzu*-locutions, even in modern Chinese, are part of the language of practical, reflexive conduct. In section 1, we have drawn attention to *tzu-ch'i* (self-deception) and to the necessity of avoiding it in order to attain *tzu-ch'ien* (self-respect). Our earlier suggestion of *tzu-ch'i* as a diagnostic term perhaps can be applied to most of the other *tzu*-locutions with primary focus on

Self and Deception

tzu-hsing (self-examination) as the general context for constructive interpretation. The singular exception is *tzu-te,* but *tzu-te* (realize [*tao*]) in oneself) for some Chinese thinkers, for example, Ch'en Pai-sha (陳白沙), has a special significance, influenced by Mencius and Ch'eng Hao (程顥). And quite apart from the use of *tzu-te,* Wang Yang-ming's 王陽明 insistence on *jen* or *tao* as a matter of *t'i-jen* 體認 (personal realization) also reflects these influences.[77]

As self-examination (*tzu-hsing* 自省) is the keynote of the Confucian doctrine of personal cultivation (*hsiu-shen*), the other *tzu*-locutions may be construed as having primarily a diagnostic use; they call attention to the need of the learners of *tao* to preserve (*tzu-ts'un*) and nourish (*tzu-yang*) their ethical dispositions against the onset of wayward tendencies or proclivities that impede the pursuit of *tao,* in particular, those tendencies that do violence (*tzu-pao*) and bring disgrace to themselves (*tzu-ju*). Of especial importance in self-examination is a careful review of one's conduct in order to see whether one has done anything that merits self-reproach (*tzu-sung*). As Mencius says, "A *chün-tzu* differs from other men because he examines his heart-and-mind (*hsin*). He examines his heart by means of humanity (*jen*) and ritual (*li*)."[78] Suppose he is treated by someone in an outrageous manner. He will turn around and examine himself (*tzu-fan* 自反), and say to himself, "I must be lacking in *jen* and *li,* or how could such a thing happen to me?" When such a self-examination discloses that he has done nothing contrary to *jen* and *li,* and yet the outrageous treatment continues, he will say to himself, "I must have failed to do my best for him."[79] Yet the possibility of others' reproach or the concern with one's "face" (*mien-tzu* 面子) is also a proper subject of self-examination.[80] Ideally, intrinsic honor coincides with circumstantial honor (section 1).[81] In the end, if frequent self-examination is successful, one can then claim to have a modicum of self-knowledge (*tzu-chih*). It is hoped that the process of self-examination in conjunction with the constant practice of humanity (*jen*), ritual (*li*), and rightness (*yi*) will culminate in personal attainment or realization of *tao* (*tzu-te*).[82]

The foregoing suggestion on the possible connection between the reflexive and the diagnostic uses of *tzu*-locutions is not an adequate response to the question of the Confucian notion of the self. For it is a legitimate question for a Confucian philosopher today whether he can find a use of the term *self* other than as "a name of a hypothetical entity" in the construction of psychological or philosophical theory. Moreover, the suggestion does not seem to accommodate the insights into the use of 'self' in some writings of Tu Wei-ming, Fingarette, and Ames. A caveat is in order before presenting my provisional thesis. The thesis is not intended as a solution to the philosophical problem of the self, as though it constituted an alternative to the theses of an enduring self, a no-self, and a constructed self.[83]

A Confucian today may proffer a nominal use of 'self' by adapting Hsün Tzu's distinction between generic (*kung-ming* 共名) and specific terms (*pieh-ming* 別名).[84] Suppose we regard 'self' as a generic term (*kung-ming*). Such a term has a proper use in formal, abstract, theoretical discourse. The use of 'self' as a generic term in the title of Fingarette's essay, "The Problem of the Self in the *Analects*" is quite intelligible. However, the question naturally arises: How is such a use to be rendered intelligible in expounding an aspect of the *Analects* (*Lun Yü*)? This question can be handled by using specific terms such as those of the *tzu*-locutions we have considered. Put differently, the generic term *self* has its "cash value" in specific terms (*pieh-ming*), which function as possible specifications of the concrete significance of *self* as a general term. To translate *tzu-hsing* as in Tseng Tzu's remark cited earlier as "I examine my self," is a mistake,[85] for *tzu-hsing* as "self-examination" is a binomial, reflexive idiom, as Fingarette has later come to realize in his response to Ames' critique. This acknowledgment focuses on the use of the reflexive idiom in translating *tzu-hsing*.[86] Of course specific terms (*pieh-ming*), such as *tzu-sung* (self-reproach), are also terms that may need further specification, for example, in answer to the question What is the object or content of self-reproach?" In the context of practical discourse. We must note also that apart from *tzu*-locutions, specific terms such as *shen* (in one's own person) or *chi* as contrasted with *jen* (distinguishing oneself from others) can also function as specific terms for 'self' as a generic term.[87] The variability and degree of specification of *self* as a generic term depends on the purpose and context of practical discourse on a particular occasion.

Equipped with *self* as a generic term, we can appreciate Tu Wei-ming's claim that in Confucian ethics the conception of the self is "a center of relationships." In his essay on *Chung Yung*, Tu declares: "Since a person in the Confucian tradition is always conceived of as a center of relationships, the more one penetrates into one's *inner self*, the more one will be capable of realizing the true nature of one's human relatedness." Alternatively, "As the Confucians argue, it is more difficult to imagine ourselves as isolable individuals than as centers of relationships constantly interacting with one another in a dynamic network of human relatedness."[88] As noted earlier (section 1), human relationships (*lun* 倫) comprise the concrete setting for conduct in accord with humanity (*jen*), ritual (*li*), and rightness (*yi*). Tu's metaphor of a dynamic network quite rightly points to the complex, indeterminate, or changing character of the interconnection of varieties of role playing in an individual human life. From the standpoint of the individual concerned with self-cultivation (*hsiu-shen*), he is a center, the focal point around which interpersonal relationships revolve. The metaphor of center may be misleading in suggesting a self-centered or self-serving preoccupation, a potential source of *pi*. Moreover, Tu's use of the term *inner self* is best construed as generic subject to specification, for example, by the reflexive *tzu*-locutions, rather than as a name of some sort of abstract entity—a reification of concrete reflexive *tzu*-locutions in practical Confucian discourse. But Tu seems to be aware of the possible misleading use of 'self' when he shifts to the term *true self* as a convenient way of referring to "the Confucian *idea of the self* in terms such as self-cultivation (*hsiu-shen* or *hsiu-chi* 修己), in contrast to the idea of the 'private ego' in such terms as self-centeredness (*ssu* 私)."[89] But the retention of an idea of the self has force only if such an idea has implicit reference to reflexive *tzu*-locutions, otherwise the expression would be entirely freestanding without any concrete anchorage.

In his critique of Fingarette's essay on the self, Ames is implicitly committed to a process view of the self as contrasted with the substantive view, much reminiscent of Mead's thesis that "the self is not so much a substance as a process in which the conversation of gestures has been internalized within an organic form."[90] Indeed, Ames cites a passage from Mead on the relationship between the "I" and the "me" as elucidative of his thesis that "the conception of self in Confucius is dynamic as a complex of social roles." Ames points out that Fingarette fails to make the distinction between "autonomous individual and unique individual," that is, the distinction between individual as a member of a class of human beings and as "one-of-a-kind," like John Turner's "Seastorm." Ames maintains that *jen*, "a unique person-specific goal can also be taken as a term denoting 'self.'" For Ames, "given that *jen* is always a unique and particular achievement, it can only refer to a self. . . . 'Self' as Confucius defines it is irreducibly interpersonal. It is not the case that *jen* refers to 'other' in contradistinction to 'self.'"[91] Before attending to Ames's insights, we must note again that like Tu and Fingarette, Ames pays no attention to the crucial role of reflexive *tzu*-locutions in providing for his use of *self* as a generic term. Also, he gives no evidence for his claim that Confucius defines 'self' as "irreducibly interpersonal," though it is a plausible, interpretive claim acceptable to modern Confucians, since it is a community with a tradition such as *li* (ritual) that renders intelligible any individual claim for being a distinct, unique individual. Ames rightly maintains that *jen* is a "unique and particular achievement," since *jen* is more an ideal theme, a standard of inspiration, than an ideal norm. The realization of *jen* will thus be manifested in an individual's style or manner of performance and/or style of life.[92] As an ideal theme, *jen* is a quasi-aesthetic vision that provides a point of orientation. It is expected that the achievement of *jen* as an ideal theme will be a polymorphous exemplification especially in the lives of paradigmatic individuals.[93] Ames's insightful suggestion on the relevance of Mead to the Confucian notion of the self is a worthwhile project for further inquiry by anyone interested in comparative Chinese and Western ethics.[94]

The foregoing reflections on the ethical aspect of self-deception focus mainly on the Confucian conception of self-deception, its context and background, as well as the possibility of diagnosis and remedy. In the Confucian perspective, avoidance of self-deception is required in personal cultivation or character formation, especially in the task of attaining sincerity of thought (*ch'eng-yi*). Indispensable to the success of this task is constant engagement in self-examination, a process partially exemplified in the diagnostic use of reflexive *tzu*-locutions. Toward the end, a tentative thesis on the notion of the self is offered as a topic for further inquiry. In this sketch of the Confucian response to the problem of self-deception, no attempt has been made to respond to specific issues in current discussion. My aim has been solely to present some materials for comparative East-West dialogue.[95]

NOTES

1. This difficulty is compounded by lack of attention to our problem among Chinese and Western writers on Confucianism. To my knowledge, only one recent essay explicitly addresses the problem. See Chang Chung-hsing, "Tzu-ch'i chih t'i chi ch'i fang-chih," in *T'an tzu-chi'i ch'i-jen* 談自欺欺人 (Taipei: Commercial Press, 1991).

2. Textual references to *Hsün Tzu* in this essay are the following: Li T'i-sheng 李滌生, *Hsün Tzu chi-shih* 荀子集釋 (Taipei: Hsüeh-sheng, 1979), which is a careful and updated edition based on the standard one by Wang Hsien-ch'ien 王先謙, *Hsün Tzu chi-chieh* 荀子集解 (Taipei: World Publishing Co., 1961). Citations from Li's edition are indicated by the title of the essay followed by the page number. Translations adopted from existing works will be indicated in appropriate places.

3. The parentheticals for transcriptions of Chinese characters are not translations but convenient indicators of possible meanings and of Chinese characters. Analytical explication of some characters such as *ch'i* 欺, *ch'eng* 誠, *pi* 蔽, and *huo* 惑 provide my constructive interpretation independently of the initial use of convenient indicators.

4. According to Chu Hsi, in antiquity there were two kinds of education or learning: the learning for adults (*ta-jen chih hsüeh* 大人之學) and the learning for the young or children (*hsiao-tzu chih hsüeh* 小子之學). "Learning for children consisted in the chores of cleaning and sweeping, in the formalities of polite conversation and good manners, and in the refinement of ritual, music, archery, charioteering,

calligraphy, and mathematics. Learning for adults consisted in the way of probing principle [*ch'iung-li* 窮理], of establishing harmony in the household, or governing the state well, and of bringing tranquility to the empire. What this work treats is the learning for adults; hence it is named *Ta-hsüeh*" (translated by Daniel K. Gardner in *Chu Hsi and the Ta-hsüeh: Neo-Confucian Reflection on the Confucian Canon* [Cambridge: Harvard University Press, 1985], 51). For a different interpretation of *ta-hsüeh* 大學 as *t'ai-hsüeh* 太學 or education for the ruler, see Chao Tse-hou 趙澤厚, *Ta-hsüeh yen-chiu* (Taipei: Chung-hua, 1972), 119–20. Chao's interpretation, however, seems to contradict the statement in the text: "From the Son of Heaven, down to the common people, all must regard cultivation of the personal life [*hsiu-shen*] as the root or foundation." See Wing-tsit Chan, trans., *A Source Book in Chinese Philosophy* (Princeton: Princeton University Press, 1963), 87. It must be noted that *Ta-hsüeh* is a subject of historical controversy. Aside from issues pertaining to textual arrangement, there have been disputes over the interpretation of key terms that occur throughout this short essay and original commentary. Gardner provides an informative account of the issues until Chu Hsi's times. A more extensive and updated discussion is given by Chao. A recent rearrangement is given in Yen Ling-feng, *Ta-hsüeh chang-chü hsin-pien* (Taipei: Pamir, 1984). See Gardner, *Chu Hsi and the Ta-hsüeh*, ch. 3; Chao, *Ta-hsüeh*, chs. 3–6.

5. Unless indicated otherwise, I adopt Chan's translation of *Ta-hsüeh* in his *Source Book*. The original text I use is Yang Liang-kang, *Ta-hsüeh chin-chu chin-i* (Taipei: Commercial Press, 1977).

6. Chu Hsi, *Ssu-shu chi-chu* (Hong Kong): T'ai-p'ing, 1980), 2.

7. I shall not follow Chu Hsi's elaboration in terms of the distinction between *t'ien-li* 天理 and *ssu-yü* 私欲 or *jen-yü* 人欲 (human desires). For a discussion of this distinction see my "Between Commitment and Realization: Wang Yang-ming's Vision of the Universe as a Moral Community," *Philosophy East and West* 43 (no. 4) (1993): 611–49.

8. Chu Hsi, *Ssu-shu chi-chu*, 19. A different translation of *chen-shih wu-wang* is "Truth, reality, and freedom from error." See Wing-tsit Chan, trans., *Neo-Confucian Terms Explained (The Pei-hsi tzu-i) by Ch'en Ch'un* (New York: Columbia University Press, 1985), 97. For Ch'en Ch'un's text, see *Pei-hsi hsien-sheng tzu-i hsiang-chiang* (Taipei: Kuang-wen, 1979), 117.

9. See my *The Unity of Knowledge and Action: A Study in Wang Yang-ming's Moral Psychology* (Honolulu: University Press of Hawaii, 1982), esp. 1.

10. See my *Ethical Argumentation: A Study in Hsün Tzu's Moral Epistemology* (Honolulu: University of Hawaii Press, 1985), 26–36, 51–101.

11. The analysis below is suggested by a presumably common view of scholars in Ch'en Ch'un's times. Ch'en Ch'un rejects the view largely because it was supposed to describe the highest degree of *ch'eng* attainment in a sage. However, one would expect the characteristics of *chen*, *ching*, and *chin* to be present in different degrees of *ch'eng* attainment among ordinary people as well as the sage. See *Pei-hsi hsien-sheng tzu-i hsiang-chiang*, 117. Cf. Chan, *Neo-Confucian Terms Explained*, 97.

12. John Knoblock, *Xunzi: A Translation and Study of the Complete Works*, vol. 1, bks. 1–6 (Stanford: Stanford University Press, 1989), 186; *jung-ju p'ien* 榮辱篇, 55.

13. Knoblock, *Xunzi*, 195; *jung-ju p'ien*, 68.

14. When *chen* is rendered as "truthfulness," but qualified in terms of *kung, ching,* and *chin,* a Confucian would find agreeable Martin's notion of 'truthfulness': "Truthfulness is caring about truth and manifesting that care in belief, reasoning, speech, conduct and relationships. It should be distinguished from knowing particular truths (truth-awareness) and stating truths (truth-telling); we can be truthful while unintentionally believing and uttering a falsehood" (Mike W. Martin, "Honesty with Oneself," in *Rules, Ritual, and Responsibility: Essays Dedicated to Herbert Fingarette,* ed. Mary I. Bockover [La Salle: Open Court, 1991], 116).

15. For example, Bodde's translation of *chen* and *shih* as "truthfulness and genuineness" as used by Fung in his comment on Hsün Tzu's notion of *'ch'eng.'* See Fung Yu-lan, *A History of Chinese Philosophy,* vol. 1, trans. Derk Bodde (Princeton: Princeton University Press, 1952), 293; and Knoblock's translation of *ch'eng* as "truthfulness" in his *Xunzi,* 1:177. See *pu-kou p'ien,* 47. For translation of *shih* as "reality," see Chan, *Neo-Confucian Terms Explained,* 97.

16. It is interesting to note here that a genuine person may also be called a "true person," but in Chinese the latter is more commonly used in translation of *chen-jen* 眞人 as used by Chuang Tzu in his depiction of the Taoist sage. The Confucian counterpart is Hsün Tzu's characterization of *chün-tzu* as one who cherishes *ch'üan* 全 (completeness) and *ts'ui* 粹 (purity). See Burton Watson, trans., *The Complete Works of Chuang Tzu* (New York: Columbia University Press, 1968), ch. 6; *ch'üan-hsüeh p'ien,* 19; Knoblock, *Xunzi,* 1:142. For a different conception of genuineness as "being authentic and exerting effort in resolving personal problems," see Martin, "Honesty with Oneself," 116, 118–19.

17. For a highly tentative discussion of Chu Hsi's uses of *li* (reason, principle) as contrasted with Wang Yang-ming's, see my "Between Commitment and Realization," sec. 3.

18. See Ann-ping Chin and Mansfield Freeman, trans., *Tai Chen on Mencius: Explorations in Words and Meaning* (New Haven: Yale University Press, 1990), 159; Tai Chen, *Meng Tzu tzu-i* in *Tai Chen wen-chi* (Taipei: Ho-lo, 1975), 122.

29. *Ch'eng tzu yü chung hsin tzu chi hsiang chin.* See *Pei-hsi hsien-sheng tzu-i,* 116. Cf. Chan, *Neo-Confucian Terms Explained,* 97.

20. It is interesting to note that the whole expression *chen-shih wu-wang* has a modern Chinese use. One recent dictionary offers the following translation: "a really honest heart; genuinely honest without any guile." If our exposition of *chen, shih,* and *wu-wang* is assumed as the basis for elaboration, this entry could be used as a convenient summary of our discussion of *ch'eng* thus far. But adopting this entry leaves entirely open the question how the notion of honesty or self-honesty is to be analyzed. Martin's analysis may be a useful beginning, though a Confucian would be most reluctant to embrace his emphasis on candor, autonomy, and self-disclosure without proper qualification in terms of *li* (ritual). I shall say something about the Confucian notion of 'autonomy' in connection with *tzu* locutions. See Martin, "Honesty with Oneself," 116–21; and the *wang* entry in S. T. Lee, comp., *A New Complete Chinese-English Dictionary* (Hong Kong: China Publishers, 1980), 317.

21. This recalls Hsün Tzu's view: "The mind [*hsin*] is the ruler of the body and the master of its godlike intelligence [*shen-ming*]." See Burton Watson, trans., *Hsün Tzu: Basic Writings* (New York: Columbia University Press, 1963), 129; *chieh-pi p'ien*, 488. For a discussion of *shen-ming*, see Knoblock, *Xunzi*, 1:252–55. For further discussion of Hsün Tzu's conception of mind (*hsin*), see my *Ethical Argumentation*, 15–16, 30–37, 138–45.

22. This is Chan's translation with retention of characters *yi* and substitution of "will" for "purpose" for the character *chih*. See Chan, *Neo-Confucian Terms Explained*, 68; *Pei-hsi hsien-sheng tzu-i*, 66. It must be noted that *chih* can be used in the sense of memory. As noted in *Shuo-wen*, "*yi* means chih," that is, what the mind knows or is familiar with (*shih*). However, *chih* as will does involves memory, as it presupposes that the person is aware (*shih*) of the object of his will. See Tuan Yü-ts'ai 段玉裁, *Shuo-wen chieh-tzu chu* (Shanghai: Ku-chi, 1981), 513.

23. Chan, *Neo-Confucian Terms Explained*, 68; *Pei-hsi hsien-sheng tzu-i*, 67.

24. Apart from these three uses, *yi* is sometimes used to refer to motive or to desire in Wang Yang-ming. See my *The Unity of Knowledge and Action*, 21–26.

25. *Tai Chen wen-chi*, 122. Cf. Chin and Freeman, *Tai Chen on Mencius*, 159.

26. James Legge, *The Chinese Classics*, vol. 1 (Hong Kong: Hong Kong University Press, 1960), 366–67. Because of easy access, I adopt with modification Wing-tsit Chan's translation in *A Source Book in Chinese Philosophy*, 89–90. For the most part, my modification of Chan's translation is influenced by Legge.

27. Both Legge and Chan follow Chu Hsi. Gardner renders *tzu-ch'ien* properly as "self-respect," but this seems to be based on Chao's critique of Chu Hsi as we shall note shortly. See Chu Hsi, *Ssu-shu chi-chu*, 6; Gardner, *Chu Hsi and the Ta-hsüeh*, 106.

28. My remarks below are based mainly on Chao, *Ta-hsüeh yen-chiu*, esp. 294–95.

29. Tuan Yü-ts'ai, *Shuo-wen chieh-tzu chu*, 94.

30. Chao, *Ta-hsüeh yen-chiu*, 194.

31. Chu Hsi, *Ssu-shu chi-chu*, 6. Cf. Gardner, *Chu Hsi*, 105n.

32. Chu Hsi goes on to say that such a state of mind may be compared to a physical object that is "coated with silver on the outside, but with iron inside." See *Chu Tzu yü-lei*, ed. Li Ching-te (Taipei: Wen-chin, 1986), vol. 3, ch. 16, 328; Gardner, *Chu Hsi*, 105n.

33. These remarks are influenced by Herbert Fingarette, *Self-Deception* (London: Routledge and Kegan Paul, 1969), 28–29. We may note here that focus on purposiveness does not imply that the act of self-deception is intentional. For arguments on the subintentional as opposed to the intentional account of self-deception, see Mark Johnston, "Self-Deception and the Nature of Mind," in *Perspectives on Self-Deception*, ed. Brian P. McLaughlin and Amélie Oksenberg Rorty (Berkeley: University of California Press, 1988), 63–91.

34. The self-deceiver may be said to be a self-misleader. As Johnston points out, "To be deceived is sometimes just to be *misled* without being *intentionally* misled or lied to. The self-deceiver is a self-misleader. As a result of his own activity he gets

into a state in which he is misled at least at the level of conscious belief." Johnston, "Self-Deception and the Nature of Mind," 65.

35. Chu Hsi, *Ssu-shu chi-chu*, 6, my translation.

36. D. C. Lau, trans., *The Analects of Confucius* (*Lun Yü*) (New York: Penguin Books, 1979), 1:4.

37. This point seems implicit in Confucius' saying: "If, on examining himself, a man finds nothing to reproach himself for. What worries or fear can he have?" (Lau, *The Analects*, 12:4).

38. My reading is based on the original text of *The Analects*, 17:23, 4:16. See Mao Tzu-shiu, *Lun Yü chin-chu chin-i* (Taipei: Commercial Press, 1977), 281, 54.

39. This citation is Wilhelm's incisive comment on hexagram no. 20 (*kuan* 觀) in the *I Ching*. See the *I Ching or Book of Changes*, trans. Cary F. Baynes from the German version of Richard Wilhelm (New York: Pantheon Books, 1950), 1:90–91. I owe this citation to Martin, who draws attention to the affinity with his own view that "insight comes only as we look outward to the full social context that gives meaning to both our inner states and outward behavior." See Mike W. Martin, *Self-Deception and Morality* (Lawrence: University Press of Kansas, 1986), 136, 159 n. 55.

40. *Analects*, 12:17. Cf. Roger Ames, "Reflections on the Confucian Self," in Bockover, *Rules, Rituals and Responsibility*, 111.

41. *Ju-hsiao p'ien*, 149; Knoblock, *Xunzi*, 2:80. An alternative to the first part of Knoblock's translation is "within they have no cause for self-reproach," since *wu* literally means "to accuse falsely," thus the alternative translation of *nei pu tzu-i wu*. In either case, self-deception or self-delusion is implied. See *ju-hsiao p'ien*, 151n.

42. Indeed, *chih*, apart from knowledge, is sometimes used in the sense of "acknowledgement," especially in Wang Yang-ming's writings. For an examination of a related use of *chih* in the sense of "realization" in the *Analects*, see David L. Hall and Roger T. Ames, *Thinking Through Confucius* (Albany: State University of New York Press, 1987); for Wang Yang-ming, see my *The Unity of Knowledge and Action*, ch. 1.

43. Martin, *Self-Deception and Morality*, 13.

44. In *Shuo-wen*, *ch'i* 欺 (deception) means *cha* 詐. To my knowledge the earliest definition of *cha* is *ni-hsing* 匿行 (concealing conduct). See Tuan Yü-ts'ai, *Shuo-wen chieh-tzu chu*, 414; and *hsiu-shen p'ien*, 26; or Knoblock, *Xunzi*, 1:153.

45. For some samples in Greek thought, see John King-Farlow and Richard Bosley, "Self-Formation and the Mean (Programmatic Remarks on Self-Deception)," in Mike W. Martin, ed., *Self-Deception and Self-Understanding* (Lawrence: University Press of Kansas, 1985), 199–202. The closing section of this essay contains an interesting dialogue between Aristotle and Confucius, but, unfortunately, no specific textual reference is given. This presents a difficulty in locating their sources of interpretation, especially *Lun Yü* and *Chung Yung* (ibid., 215–19). We may note also the use of the sight metaphor in Butler and Kant. See "Upon Self-Deceit," in *The Works of Joseph Butler*, ed. Samuel Halifax (Oxford: Oxford University Press, 1850), 117, 124; Immanuel Kant, *The Doctrine of Virtue*, trans. Mary J. Gregor (New York: Harper Torchbooks, 1964), 92.

46. Herbert Fingarette, *Confucius: The Secular as Sacred* (New York: Harper Torchbooks, 1972), 28ff.

47. See A. C. Graham, *Disputers of the Tao: Philosophical Argument in Ancient China* (LaSalle: Open Court, 1989), 27, 29, 252. For Mencius and Chu Hsi on *ch'üan* (weighing of circumstance), see my *Dimensions of Moral Creativity: Paradigms, Principles and Ideals* (University Park: Pennsylvania State University Press, 1978), 72–76; and "The Idea of Confucian Tradition," *Review of Metaphysics* 45 (no. 4) (1992), 824–39. For Hsün Tzu, see my "The Possibility of Ethical Knowledge: Reflections on a Theme in the *Hsün Tzu*," in *Epistemological Questions in Ancient Chinese Philosophy*, ed. Hans Lenk and Gregor Paul (Albany: State University of New York Press, 1993).

48. See *cheng-lun p'ien*, 410–11; or Homer H. Dubs, trans., *The Works of Hsüntze* (Taipei: Ch'eng-wen, 1966), 209. It is often said that modern Chinese are concerned with "face." But as Hu points out, there is a distinction between *mien-tzu* and *lien*. The former pertains to social standing and does not necessarily have moral implications. The latter implies satisfaction of the moral standards of the society. A person concerned with *lien* is one who possesses a sense of decency and regard for moral virtues. This distinction seems to reflect Hsün Tzu's distinction between intrinsic and extrinsic honor. See Hsien Chin Hu, "The Chinese Concepts of 'Face,' " *American Anthropologist*, n.s., 46 (1944), 45–64. Cf. Ames, "Reflections on the Confucian Self," 111.

49. Lau, *The Analects of Confucius*, 4:25, 12:19.

50. Cf. Fingarette: "Self-deception is resolved when the disavowed engagement of the individual is avowed" (Fingarette, *Self-Deception*, 110).

51. Cf. "The concept of self-deception is more interpretive and diagnostic than predictive" (Robert Audi, "Self-Deception and Rationality," in Martin, ed., *Self-Deception and Self-Understanding*, 191). For a discussion of closely related use of *self* as a diagnostic term, see Stephen Toulmin, "Self-Knowledge and Knowledge of the 'Self,' " in *The Self: Psychological and Philosophical Issues*, ed. Theodore Mischel (Oxford: Blackwell, 1977): 291–317.

52. For an instructive discussion of Chu Hsi's hermeneutical method, see Yü Ying-shih, "Morality and Knowledge in Chu Hsi's Philosophical System," in *Chu Hsi and Neo-Confucianism*, ed. Wing-tsit Chan (Honolulu: University of Hawaii Press, 1986): 228–54.

53. Below I confine my exposition to the relevance of *pi* and its attendant *huo*. For an extensive discussion of the diagnosis of erroneous ethical beliefs see my *Ethical Argumentation*, ch. 4.

54. Knoblock, *Xunzi*, 1:233ff; *fei shih-erh tzu p'ien*, 94. For the notion of 'partial grasp of a whole,' see *t'ien-lun p'ien*, 381; *chieh-pi p'ien*, 472, 478; Watson, *Hsün Tzu*, 87–88, 121, 126.

55. Yang Liang, *Hsün Tzu*, *ssu-pu pei-yao* edition (Taipei: Chung-hua, 1976), ch. 15:1a. For similar use of *pi*, see *Analects*, 17:8.

56. Watson, *Hsün Tzu*, 131; *chieh-pi p'ien*, 490. These remarks on *pi* are based on *Ethical Argumentation*, 138–45.

57. Watson, *Hsün Tzu*, 121n. Thus Knoblock renders *chieh-pi p'ien* as "dispelling blindness" (Knoblock, *Xunzi*, 2:111). Consistent with the concern with self-deception, a Confucian philosopher will appreciate the view of self-deception as a

form of "blindness to self." See David W. Hamlyn, "Self-Knowledge," in *The Self: Psychological and Philosophical Issues*, ed. Mischel, 179–80.

58. In *Shuo-wen, huo* means *luan* and *luan* means "not in order (*pu-chih yeh*); when something is not in order, one then desires to put it into order." In other words, it is desirable to put into order what is in the state of disorder, chaos, or confusion. In the case of a mental state, we can properly construe *huo* as a state of delusion. Ascription of delusion, as Austin remarks, suggests that "something is really wrong, and what's more, wrong with the person who has them." See Tuan Yü-ts'ai, *Shuo-wen chieh-tzu chu*, 511, 740; J. L. Austin, *Sense and Sensibilia* (Oxford: Clarendon Press, 1962), 21–22.

59. Watson, *Hsün Tzu*, 134; *chieh-pi p'ien*, 495. This is one of a few examples of perceptual delusions. For discussion of the role of wise and informed deliberation (*chih-lü*) with respect both to perceptual and to ethical examples, see my "The Possibility of Ethical Knowledge," pt. 2.

60. For this use of *huo*, see also *Analects*, 12:10, 12:21, but note that there *huo* is part of the binomial *pien-huo* (misguided judgment). In the dialogue, it has no special connection with *li* (ritual) as Fingarette claims in his *Confucius: The Secular as Sacred*, 22–23.

61. *Chieh-pi p'ien*, 474, my translation. Cf. Watson, *Hsün Tzu*, 122; Dubs, *Hsüntze*, 260. Hereafter cited as Watson and Dubs.

62. For Hsün Tzu, only Confucius is free from *pi* as he embodied *jen* and wisdom, for his school alone has all-around understanding of *tao* (*chou-tao*). See *chieh-pi p'ien*, 478, 481n. Cf. Dubs, *The Works of Hsüntze*, 265; Watson, *Hsün Tzu*, 126.

63. *Chieh-pi p'ien*, 474. Cf. Watson, 122; Dubs, 260.

64. This proceeding is in part justified in terms of Hsün Tzu's conception of human nature as a basic motivational structure consisting of feelings and desires. Desires are responses to feelings. For further discussion, see my "The Conceptual Aspect of Hsün Tzu's Philosophy of Human Nature," *Philosophy East and West* 27 (no. 4) (1977): 373–89.

65. See *pu-kou p'ien*, 53; Knoblock, *Xunzi*, 1:180.

66. Translation based on Watson, 122, and Dubs, 260. See *chieh-pi p'ien*, 472.

67. See the conclusion of my "Between Commitment and Realization."

68. See Martin, *Self-Deception and Morality*, 6–11.

69. See part 2 of my "Possibility of Ethical Knowledge."

70. Herbert Fingarette, "The Problem of the Self in the *Analects*," *Philosophy East and West* 29 (no. 2) (1979): 129–40; Roger T. Ames, "Reflections on the Confucian Self: A Response to Fingarette," in *Rules, Rituals and Responsibility*, ed. Bockover, 103–14; Tu Wei-ming, *Centrality and Commonality: An Essay on Chung Yung* (Honolulu: University Press of Hawaii, 1976); or the revised and expanded edition entitled *Centrality and Commonality: An Essay on Confucian Religiousness* (Albany: State University of New York Press, 1989). My remarks below refer to this revised edition. Note that in a couple of places I have also made a distinction between the actual self and the ideal self and have made use of DeWitt H. Parker's distinction between matrix and focal self in discussing the Confucian notion of *tao*. See *The Unity of Knowledge*

and Action, 57; "Chinese Moral Vision, Responsive Agency, and Factual Beliefs," *Journal of Chinese Philosophy* 7 (no. 1) (1980): 3–26.

71. Toulmin, "Self-Knowledge and Knowledge of the 'Self,' " 291.

72. Ibid., 303f.

73. *Lun Yü*, 4:17, 5:27, 19:17. *Tzu-hsing* also occurs in Hsün Tzu's *hsiu-shen p'ien*, 23, and *wang-pa p'ien*, 251. In *Meng Tzu*, *tzu-fan* (to look within, to turn within and examine oneself) seems to be functionally equivalent to *tzu-hsing*. See *Meng Tzu*, 2A:2; 4B:28.

74. *Meng Tzu*, 4A:10, 3A:2, and 3A:4, 4B:14.

75. See *hsiu-shen p'ien*, 23; *jung-ju p'ien*, 59.

76. *Chieh-pi p'ien*, 488. The translation is based on Dubs, 269. For the problem of autonomy of mind in Hsün Tzu, see my *Ethical Argumentation*, 138–42.

77. See Paul Yun-ming Jiang, *The Search for Mind: Ch'en Pai-sha, Philosopher-Poet* (Singapore: Singapore University Press, 1980), esp. ch. 9. For Wang Yang-ming, see Tu Wei-ming, *Neo-Confucian Thought in Action: Wang Yang-ming's Youth* (1472–1529) (Berkeley: University of California Press, 1976), and my "Between Commitment and Realization."

78. *Meng Tzu*, 4B:28. My translation here reads *ts'un* as *cha* (examine) in accordance with Chiao Hsün's gloss. See Shih Tz'u-yün, *Meng Tzu chin-chu chin-i* (Taipei: Commercial Press, 1978), 233n.

79. *Meng Tzu*, 4B:28. The translation is based on D. C. Lau trans., *Mencius* (Middlesex: Penguin Books, 1970), 134.

80. See note 48 above.

81. For the Confucian, concern with one's "name" (*ming*) or reputation is always a just concern except in adverse circumstances of being placed in a situation of shame beyond one's control (*shih-ju*). In this way, she may concur with Hume's insightful remark on the love of fame: "By our continual and earnest pursuit of a character, a name, a reputation in the world, we bring our own deportment and character frequently in review and consider how the eyes of those who approach and regard us. This constant habit of surveying ourselves, as it were, in reflection, keeps alive all the sentiments of right and wrong, and begets in noble natures a certain reverence for themselves as well as others, which is the surest guardian of every virtue" (David Hume, *An Inquiry Concerning the Principles of Morals* [Indianapolis: Bobbs-Merrill, 1957], 96).

82. It is presumed that the learner of *tao* has at least some understanding and knowledge of ancient classics, say, the Four Books (*Lün Yü, Ta-hsüeh, Chung Yung,* and *Meng Tzu*). Ideally, the study of the classic aims at a comprehensive understanding of the concrete significance of *tao* as a thread that runs through the classics (*kuan-t'ung ching hsüeh*) with the view of becoming a sage. In terms of the highest attainment of *ch'eng*, such a sage would "assist in the transforming and nourishing process of Heaven and Earth," thus forming "a trinity with Heaven and Earth" (*Chung Yung*, sec. 22; translation adopted from Chan, *A Source Book in Chinese Philosophy*, 108).

83. These are terms used by Kupperman. I think that with proper qualification, a Confucian would find congenial the view of the constructed self favored by

Kupperman, especially as he thinks that it is virtually equivalent to the word *character* emphasizing "matters of importance." See Joel Kupperman, *Character* (New York: Oxford University Press, 1991), ch. 1, esp. 44.

84. This distinction is used extensively in my *Ethical Argumentation* (see the index of terms), but elaborated in my "The Problem of Conceptual Unity in Hsün Tzu and Li Kou's Solution," *Philosophy East and West* 39 (no. 2) (1989), 122–25.

85. See Fingarette, "The Problem of the Self in the *Analects*," 132.

86. It is puzzling that Fingarette focuses on the use of reflexive idioms in European languages, since reflexive idioms are quite familiar in colloquial English. See Fingarette, "Comment and Response," in Bockover, *Rules, Rituals and Responsibility*, 198–99.

87. Unless I am mistaken, these terms are not translatable as 'self,' though it is tempting, probably for economy, to translate them thus. I notice this, for example, in Knoblock's excellent work, *Xunzi*, 1:136, 143, 154, 166. Cf. Fingarette, "The Problem of the Self in the *Analects*," 131–35. Note that my critical remarks of Fingarette's essay are not meant as a general evaluation of the insights and issues he raised.

88. Tu Wei-ming, *Centrality and Commonality: An Essay on Religiousness*, 27, 95; my emphasis.

89. Ibid., 108; my emphasis. These remarks are from Tu's essay "On Confucian Religiousness" added to the second edition (1989) of his *Centrality and Commonality* (1976). Note the affinity of my use of "ideal and actual self" (*The Unity of Knowledge and Action*, 57), though my use has no special connection with the contrast of "the self" with "private ego."

90. George H. Mead, *Mind, Self and Society* (Chicago: University of Chicago Press, 1934), 178.

91. Ames, "Reflections on the Confucian Self," 105–8. Cf. my "Confucian Vision and the Human Community," *Journal of Chinese Philosophy* 11 (no. 3) (1984): 226–38.

92. See my *Dimensions of Moral Creativity*, chs. 7–8.

93. Ibid., 138–39.

94. These remarks are compatible with Ames's recent field-focus view of the self, and one can learn much from his incisive critique of four models of self: "the hollow man," "autonomous individuality," "the organic self," and "part of the whole self," though Ames would agree that the autonomous-individuality model may well be one way to deal with Hsün Tzu's conception of the person's mind as one who exercises the freedom of choice as indicated in the series of *tzu*-locutions (note 76 above). See Ames, "The Focus-Field Self in Classical Confucianism," in *Self as Person in Asian Theory and Practice*, ed. Roger T. Ames, Thomas P. Kasulis, and Wimal Dissanayake (Albany: State University of New York Press, 1994).

95. This chapter was a contribution to the East-West Center Symposium on Self and Deception, August 24–28, 1992. I am grateful to Daniel Dahlstrom for valuable suggestions in its preparation and to Eunice Rice for her patience in transforming handwritten drafts into readable form.

NINE

A CONFUCIAN CONSTRUCTION OF A SELF-DECEIVABLE SELF

Robert Cummings Neville

Construed in a narrow and uninteresting way, self-deception might be an impossibility, like affirming and denying a proposition in the same respects at the same time. In real life, however, there are many contexts in which we live with assumptions that we know at some level to be mistaken or misleading. These include psychological contexts, contexts determined by our sense of social realities, and contexts in which religious issues about the meaning of life are at stake. Self-deception is a common state of living in these contexts.

This chapter outlines some of the ways in which Confucians might understand self-deception in comparison with certain predominant Western ways of approaching the same topic. Although the chapter's genre is comparison, its emphasis is on explicating the Confucian side because of the Western orientation of the history of the problem of self-deception. The comparison involves two obvious topics, the self and deception. Although the former is a much richer topic, it shall be sketched here only to serve as background for the consideration of deception.

THE SELF

The self in Western philosophy is an idea based explicitly on self-reference, the word deriving from the self-reflexive pronoun in English. Although the idea of self bears connotations of "person," "human being," "human nature," "soul," "spirit," "heart," "mind," "consciousness," "character," and "personality," among others, each of which has cognate words and ideas in nearly all languages, including Chinese and other East Asian tongues, it adds to all of these ideas that of self-reference or self-relation. Furthermore, there is also a sense that the self-reference involves embracing or overcoming some internal contradiction in identity.

This Western concept, the self, shall be described here in a few historically oriented remarks. Then it will be possible to articulate what the Confucian tradition exhibits instead, which can be called, somewhat

Self and Deception

oxymoronically, "the Confucian conception of self." Although the Chinese language has words or phrases for most of the kinds of self-reference or self-reflexiveness found in Western languages—including self-cultivation, self-deception, and selfishness—it does not have a summary word for person, human being, or individual personal character that itself is constructed so self-consciously out of self-reference itself.[1]

Thomas J. J. Altizer has called attention to important origins of the Western notion of self in the ancient world.[2] One of these is the role of the divided will in St. Paul whose classic statement follows:

> I do not understand my own actions. For I do not do what I want, but I do the very thing I hate. Now if I do what I do not want, I agree that the law is good. But in fact it is no longer I that do it, but sin that dwells within me. For I know that nothing good dwells within me, that is, in my flesh. I can will what is right, but I cannot do it. For I do not do the good I want, but the evil I do not want is what I do. Now if I do what I do not want, it is no longer I that do it, but sin that dwells within me. So I find it to be a law that when I want to do what is good, evil lies close at hand. For I delight in the law of God in my inmost self, but I see in my members another law at war with the law of my mind, making me captive to the law of sin that dwells in my members. (Romans 7:15–23, NRSV)

Some thinkers leap to the conclusion that Paul was attacking the body in favor of the soul, and indeed that interpretation has been influential in some parts of Christianity. But *flesh* here is a metaphor for a bit of behavior that has a kind of autonomy of its own, a subroutine of life that is harmful or wicked when taken out of the context of integrated moral and spiritual behavior. Sexual passion, for instance, when running autonomously is lust, but when integrated into the wholeness of personal and social life before God is the image of the greatest virtue, love. The proper integrating principle is the law of God, or what Paul elsewhere calls the "mind of Christ," which is the person's own "inmost self." As strongly as any Confucian devoted to principle (*li*) in the heart (*hsin*), Paul believed that God's law or loving intentionality is innate to the mind. But the mind does not automatically effect its good intentions. Rather, the wholeness of human nature, according to Paul, includes also the will which is always "close" to evil. The *problem* of human nature is not the presence of the divine mind but the integration of that mind with voluntary actions, especially vis à vis other people. When one's will gives in to its subroutines and acts "in slavery to sin," then the authorship of the person over his or her own actions is lost: sin itself, the subhuman passions with wicked consequences, becomes the author. What is left of the person is merely the law of God which, by itself, is hardly the person. The ordinary state is that the person is dissolved into the innate law of God, which functions now only as condemning judge, and the nonpersonal acts of sin. In the ordinary state, for Paul, there is *no* self or personal authorship, only sinful acts and divine judgment. Thus the problematic of salvation is to reunite these, the sin and the divine nature, in a responsible human author.

St. Augustine reconceptualized Paul's problem with an idea of soul combining memory of the past, alertness to the present, and will for the future, all of which add up to love.[3] Furthermore, the human soul mirrors the divine soul, so that the wholeness of the human soul stands in reflective tandem with the wholeness of God. The individualism of Augustine in this move has not been entirely beneficial and is in contradiction to the moral and communal strain within Christianity; the Cappadocian fathers offered a better alternative for conceiving soul in interpersonal terms. But Augustine's idea has been more influential in the West. For him, sin consists in lying memory, faulty attention, and a bad will resulting from allowing the body to overwhelm the divine image within. But sin is not simply a falling away of the will with the loss of responsible authorship. It is a direct contradiction within the soul. Whereas Paul's soul dissolves away in bondage to sin, Augustine's becomes tortured in its self-contradiction. Moreover, for Augustine, memory, attention, and will are all functions of consciousness, and the deepest hurt of sin is self-consciousness. From Augustine's theory arose the Western conception of the self as in guilty self-conscious self-contradiction to itself, struggling to let the divine image express itself throughout the arena of concrete action.

Hegel made this point central to his whole philosophy, and he reversed the conceptual order of God and self. For Hegel, the self developing through unfolding self-contradictions becomes the model for God as Spirit unfolding through contradictions of nature and history. The self of Hegel's idealism is the result of overcoming negations. Some of these are external, and the grandeurs and pomposities of the bourgeois self and its religion of progress express this. Others of the negations are internal, rooted in the price paid in prior overcomings of negations. In both cases, the self is what the self itself has made of itself in overcoming, or swallowing whole, the negations that had defined its previous oppositions. The Western self as the overcoming of self-contradiction is individualistic in the sense that its becoming is its own project. God's self requires the overcoming and internalizing of all externality, for Hegel. The human self might not internalize all

Self and Deception

other selves, but it surely internalizes all its relations to other selves so that they function as roles within it, and nothing more. The Hegelian self shows no deference, save to its own image in the other.

Kierkegaard brought the point about the reflexivity of the self to its most abstract conclusion:

> Man is spirit. But what is spirit? Spirit is the self. But what is the self? The self is a relation which relates itself to its own self, or it is that in the relation [which accounts for it] that the relation relates itself to its own self; the self is not the relation but [consists in the fact] that the relation relates itself to its own self.[4]

The Western self, at least in the heritage traced here, can have physical, social, and psychological structures. Yet all these are integrated by and subjugated to the problems of internal self-contradiction and self-consistency. The Western self is *deep* because it involves self-conscious reflection of reflection of reflection, down to the infinity of God conceived as equally deep. In its depths, the Western self embraces, usually without clearing up, its own contradictions. If the Western self were ever to work it out that the law of God in the inmost mind automatically directed the will, the self would be bored.[5]

The Confucians conceive the self to be a product of its own cultivation, just as much as does the Western tradition. For the Confucians, the attainment of true selfhood is a matter of becoming the responsible author of one's own character and actions. But the underlying model is different from that of the West. The following account is based not on the explicit doctrine of a single text but on a series of powerful motifs that have shaped each thinker in the multiplicity of Confucian strands.

According to the *Doctrine of the Mean*, the heaven-given human Way is in a normative continuum of structured activities lying between two poles, *chung* and *yung*. *Yung* means the ordinary world, the "ten thousand things" that constitute our environment and to which everyone must relate directly or indirectly. People's ordinary worlds differ by context and circumstance, by geographical location, by historical place, and by one's associations. But everyone has an objective, ordinary world in which to live and with which to cope, and there is a great deal of commonality consisting of needs for nutrition, shelter, family, and social life.

Chung means centrality or equilibrium, "before the feelings of pleasure, anger, sorrow, and joy are aroused."[6] *Chung* is the readiness to respond normatively to the various ten thousand ordinary things. Mencius, in his famous illustration of what he took to be a universal response to a child about to fall into a well, asserted that everyone whatsoever has a readiness to respond to things appropriately; this readiness constitutes what he and the tradition have called the "Four Beginnings" of humanity, righteousness, propriety, and wisdom.[7]

The later neo-Confucians developed this idea of *chung,* or the incipience of right response in the Four Beginnings, into the doctrine of Principle (*li*). Principle is the very essence of heaven, and it is identical in all human beings. But it is only the readiness to respond that is universal, the incipience of normative reaction: the actual situation to which each person has to respond is unique. We differ not in the Principle in our heart but in that to which the Principle must direct action, in the ordinary objective world of *yung.*

Human nature or the self in the Confucian tradition is not *chung* by itself (one of the mistakes of Buddhism, according to the later Confucians, is meditatively to cultivate *chung* by itself as if that were worth something). Rather, the self is *chung* actually responding to the affairs of *yung.* Not mere readiness but the habits of response constitute the self. The self consists of all the structures in a person that mediate the connections between that person's ordinary objective world and the *chung* in that person ready to respond. So far, St. Paul might not disagree.

These structures, for the Confucian tradition, include physical, cognitive, and emotional elements (to introduce some crude distinctions) and can be conceived as perceptive on the one hand and action oriented on the other. Moreover, those structures need to be educated or cultivated. As *The Doctrine of the Mean* says, "What Heaven (*T'ien,* Nature) imparts to man is called human nature. To follow our nature is called the Way (Tao). Cultivating the Way is called education."[8] The body needs to be educated so that we perceive with sensitivity and discrimination, and also so that we can act effectively on what we intend. A person who does not pay attention would not notice the child on the lip of the well, and the physical klutz would tumble into the well with the child while trying to save it. A person's cognitive skills need to be developed as well; it is one thing to understand the simple danger to the child at the well, and another to understand the problems of economic competition; whereas the remedy for the child's situation does not need much learning, the remedy for economic problems does. Our emotions at any age can blind us to the true worths of the ten thousand things in our world to which we should respond appropriately; similarly, our emotions can bend our actions to selfish behavior even when we know what to do and are capable of it.

Two other points in the Confucian world view need to be lifted up to understand this sense of self. First, as just mentioned, each thing or person

Self and Deception

in the world is viewed as having a nature with a specific worth. The appropriateness of a person's responses to things depends on identifying that worth and acting accordingly. The *chung* or Principle or Four Beginnings does not itself have a moral content but is a kind of aesthetic sensitivity to the value content of other things and an innate taste regarding how to honor those values. Because in any situation there are even more than "ten thousand things" that need to be honored at once, the actual exercising of *chung* in the world is called "harmonizing," and it is what the great Tao does on the cosmic scale.

Second, the Confucians were conscious from very early on of the fact that the structures of the self have the character of signs. They are habits (mainly socially constructed) of physical, cognitive, and emotional behavior that are learned like language. Most of the items among the ten thousand things that have elicited Confucian interest have been people and social structures. Physical habits of paying deference with eye contact, body posture, and appropriate performative speeches, as well as learning to ride and shoot the right way, to move efficiently, and to write beautiful characters, are important elements of physical education. Cognitive development is the acquisition of true concepts and effective speech for analysis and expression. The "truth" involved, according to neo-Confucianists such as Chu Hsi, is not so much a matter of description but rather of learning to discern how the Principle in other things expresses itself in the unique situation of the ordinary world of those things. So, Chu Hsi claimed that the investigation of things and the extension of knowledge consists in learning about Principle. Principle itself is the same in all things, but it functions differently in each thing because of that thing's perspective on the world.[9] However, the conceptual apparatus for discernment and expression is a matter of habit, a function of signs. Similarly with emotions: emotions have no reality except in their exercise, and that exercise has the character of habit, of tendency, and is shaped by learned signs. The Confucians called the signs that make up an educated self "propriety" or "ritual" (*li*), focusing on a ceremonial paradigm. The paradigm is a good one, emphasizing as it does that the signs have to be learned and also that their essence lies in performance, not merely (or even) in symbolizing something else. Even explicitly cognitive signs such as those in economic theory have their truth in performance; performance, for such cognitive signs, consists in actually expressing the economic realities—a sign from an alien language does not communicate and thus cannot perform so as to express a fact. The Confucians knew that signs or ritual propriety are conventional but are to be judged by their performance. Cultures do things differently. But those cultures with no signs allowing for the exercise of friendship, filial affection, good care and nurture of the young, or promotion of the arts are culturally deficient. A given person who has not learned the signs for performing the deeply human things is uneducated, deficient in the Way. Moral reform is less a change of people's intentions than a change of the signs by means of which they perform their lives together.

The self, for the Confucian tradition, is the complex of sign-structured physical, cognitive, and emotional practices that relate the *chung* in a person to that person's world. *The Doctrine of the Mean* calls the excellence or virtue of that relation "sincerity." The chief meaning of sincerity is a kind of clarity, or translucence, such that the true complicated nature and value of the ten thousand things are mediated to the *chung* or heart, and the heart's aesthetically and morally right incipient response is unfolded in action to the things.

Confucians have by no means all developed these motifs of the self in the same way. Mencius, for instance, focused on the innate excellence of the heart and emphasized the negative side of unlearning bad ways of life more than the positive learning of higher structures. Confucius and Hsün Tzu emphasized the importance of inventing and practicing the signs constituting ritual propriety. Neo-Confucianists rethought the motifs from a more speculative standpoint than characterized the ancient thinking. Chou Tun-i, for instance, speculated that sincerity, the expression of *chung* in action, is a function of material force. Chang Tsai interpreted sincerity in terms of the ordering of the different steps toward virtue in the classical *Great Learning*. Ch'eng Hao and Ch'eng I developed the theory of Heaven and Earth, Principle and Material Force, as means to provide an intellectual context for the attainment of sincerity. Chu Hsi reinterpreted sincerity in terms of humanity (*jen*) to which he gave a metaphysical account that represents sincerity or humanity as a kind of cosmic generative principle that unfolds the self with "origination, flourish, advantages, and firmness."[10] Wang Yang-ming deepened Mencius's emphasis with his theory of the heart-mind, and he focused more on the emotional and valuative elements of the self than on the cognitive to which he thought Chu Hsi was biased. Contemporary Confucianism can take great advantage of the pragmatic theories of habit and semiotics to develop a cross-cultural conception of ritual propriety.[11]

Nevertheless, despite all these variations with contrary schools, the basic motifs for a Confucian conception of self are present throughout. None of them involves the doubling back of self-reference so as to mean the containment within the self of the contradictions of intent and performance, of self and other. Where contradictions arise, for the Confucian tradition, they should simply be educated out.

SELF-DECEPTION

Self-deception as understood in the West is deeply affected by the preoccupation with self-reflection and the containment of contradiction. The West has three main species of self-deception, or perhaps there are three main approaches to conceptualizing it.

The first is inner psychological self-deception of the sort thematized by dynamic psychoanalytic theory. Freud's version of this is that much of behavior is directed by the unconscious, which is structured by a kind of primitive and selfish "primary process." The motivations of primary process are not entirely acceptable to the socially constructed "superego" that embodies norms of behavior thought to be essential to civilized social intercourse. The psyche has a censoring mechanism that renders the ideation of primary process unconscious, and its behaviors are hidden or deviously symbolized by the thought processes of the conscious ego. That the pretended conscious ideation of the ego is not the true ideation motivating and shaping behavior is revealed in dreams, slips of the tongue, and other imperfectly censored behaviors. The conscious content of mind is sometimes genuinely deceived about the real motivations behind behavior. For instance, when one acts so as to exercise control over another person, it might seem consciously that the motivation is to help the other person when in fact the primary process motive is anger or a competitive fear. Or one may consciously believe that the remarks and actions of a particular person are hostile and dangerous, when in fact the person is helpful or oblivious and one is unconsciously looking for signs that can be interpreted as hostile, as in paranoia.

In a more pervasive sense, most people have unconscious, or even conscious, needs to see the world in a certain way, and thus see selectively and with distortion. Almost all of us believe that others think about us more than they do and that they act to put us in a place advantageous to them. In fact, we generally overinterpret signs that might have a bearing upon our personal needs, especially psychological needs, and we generally underinterpret very important happenings that do not have much personal bearing upon us. Many self-deceptions are of this sort.

The second species of self-deception consists in the systematic distortions of the meanings and effects of social structures of the sort analyzed by Marxists and others concerned with ideology. According to Marx, people belong to social classes, as defined economically, and the competitive interests of their class color the way they see everything. For instance, members of the capitalist class see the market of free price determination as an expression of human freedom and are deceived about the fact that people who receive wages, or even worse those who simply have no connection with capital production, are not free at all to enter the market. Or a person raised in a particular religious tradition is deceived by the religion's ideology about what people in other traditions are experiencing. Self-deception in this second sense consists in being determined by the interests or prejudices of one's group, on the one hand, in contradiction to what one "ought" to believe, on the other hand; because the person identifies with the group, perhaps unconsciously, as defining identity, this is truly the deception of the self by the self.

The third sense of self-deception in the West comes from an ignorance of the world combined with an ignorance of limits. Here is the heart of the tradition of tragedy. Oedipus was ignorant of his true parentage. He was ignorant of how his status as king was limited by not being of a certain birth, and he deceived himself about his real status. Lear was ignorant of the powers of sin in his own kin. He was ignorant of his capacity to command respect when he abandoned the responsibilities of rule, and he deceived himself about his life's possibilities and about his true friends.

More generally, we construct our world view on the basis of a very limited vision of what is what, and the far deeper underlying forces sometimes break out of our domesticated expectations. We plan a life we think is possible, but it is ruined by war, famine, or plague. We think that steady, well-intentioned behavior will be rewarded, but we discover belatedly that nature's rewards are distributed blindly. We think we are secure in certain people's affections, or to the contrary are locked in bitter struggle, only to find that the forces that govern affection and contention shift the field in meaningless ways. Because the universe is infinitely complex in its causality, and our visions are only finite takes, our ignorance and self-sense are always somewhat self-deceiving.

Most forms of self-deception thematized in the West fall under one or a combination of these three. Each involves the self-reflexive embrace of some kind of contradiction in what constitutes the self's identity. The situation is different for the self as conceived within Confucianism.

Three forms of self-deception stand out as themes arising from the Confucian motifs. First is the form that arises from selfishness; second that arising from inadequate habits, signs, and ritual propriety; and third that arising from misplacing socially defined identity because of lack of humanity (*jen*). These will be sketched in turn.

Selfishness is the core of human evil, on the Confucian account. Wang Yang-ming summed up a long tradition when he expressed the sincerity connecting one's heart-mind with the objective ordinary world as "manifesting the clear character" in "being one body with the world." He

Self and Deception

noted that Mencius's example of the child at the well might be criticized because a child is the same species as the adult, and seeing its danger could be an extended kind of selfishness. But we cringe from the suffering of animals about to be slaughtered, said Wang, and we have at least momentary pity at trees about to be felled; we even feel regret when we see tiles or stones shattered. Therefore, even if we were the butcher, the woodsman, or the demolition expert, we would feel momentary upset at destruction or pain.

> This means that even the mind of the small man necessarily has the humanity that forms one body with all. Such a mind is rooted in his Heaven-endowed nature, and is naturally intelligent, clear, and not beclouded. For this reason it is called the "clear character." Although the mind of the small man is divided and narrow, yet his humanity that forms one body can remain free from darkness to this degree. This is due to the fact that his mind has not yet been aroused by desires and obscured by selfishness. When it is aroused by desires and obscured by selfishness, compelled by greed for gain and fear of harm, and stirred by anger, he will destroy things, kill members of his own species, and will do everything. . . . As soon as it is obscured by selfish desires, even the mind of the great man will be divided and narrow like that of the small man. Thus the learning of the great man consists entirely in getting rid of the obscuration of selfish desires in order by his own efforts to make manifest his clear character, so as to restore the condition of forming one body with Heaven, Earth, and the myriad things, a condition that is originally so, that is all.[12]

Confucians have differed in their opinions of what causes selfishness in the first place if everyone is initially endowed with the Way. Some, following Hsün Tzu, have attributed it to lack of effort in developing good habits; others, following Mencius, have attributed it to having learned bad habits that should be unlearned. Some of the neo-Confucians attributed it to the influence of Material Force through which Heaven-endowed nature must work.[13] For all of them, selfishness constructs or distorts the emotional and cognitive structures of the self, perhaps even the physical structures as in gluttony, so as to "obscure" what things really are and give too selfishly personal an orientation to desires. Wang's attack on desire as such illustrates some of the Buddhist influence on his thinking. But the point is one to which most others would subscribe: selfishness blocks responding to things because of the worth of dealing with them appropriately and instead gives people motives that subordinate that worth to personal benefit.

Yet because selfishness is the great evil in Confucian culture, there is a great motive, stemming from selfishness itself, to rationalize selfish behavior as altruistic. Although contemporary Confucians can learn psychodynamic theory and use it to explain rationalization, there is nothing in Confucian culture itself that would seek out models of inner self-reflexive contradiction, such as primary process opposing the superego, with mechanisms of censorship and repression. Rather, Confucians would note that people tell themselves they are doing good, and redescribe their actions to make that convincing, when they really are acting selfishly. How easy it is to believe a weak or incomplete analysis when it makes us look good! The deep Confucian commitment to self-criticism reflects the tradition's recognition of this kind of self-deception. The long discipline of seriousness in watching and amending one's motives reflects the tradition's recognition of the power of selfish self-deception. The quotation from *The Doctrine of the Mean* quoted above in note 8 continues:

> What can be separated from us is not the Way. Therefore the superior man is cautious over what he does not see and apprehensive over what he does not hear. There is nothing more visible than what is hidden and nothing more manifest than what is subtle. Therefore the superior man is watchful over himself when he is alone.[14]

The self-deception arising from inadequate signs and habits, from what Confucius would have called a "breakdown in ritual propriety," is more complex than selfishness, and it was Confucius's own preoccupation. Herbert Fingarette called attention to the importance of *li* as ritual propriety, employing the contemporary notion of the 'performative elements of symbolism' to make the case.[15] Contemporary pragmatism's semiotic theory is also helpful to understand the Confucian point.

The human realities of life, those over and above the realities to be understood in scientific or naturalistic terms, are those that consist in the exercise of habits structured by socially meaningful signs. To be a friend, for instance, is not to have a particular attitude about someone but to engage in activities with and for that person that constitute friendship, for instance talking, sharing experiences, rendering support, exposing one's vulnerability, and taking care of the person's welfare as equals might. Each of these activities is a tendency or habitual behavior shaped by its own signs. But together they add up to friendship because the abstract signs defining friendly

Self and Deception

behavior as such give each of the components a place and due proportion. A good culture has all the signs needed, signs that can be learned through ordinary experiences, for the prevalent practice of friendship, and of the other human institutions that make for civilized living. A deficient barbarian culture is one that lacks the signs that can shape habits constituting the higher levels of civilized life. It does not matter what the signs are that can shape the habits, or what cultural semiotic system they belong to, so long as they make for the actual existence of civilization. Confucius's project from the beginning was to rediscover, revivify, or in desperation to invent, signs that could reverse the slide of his society into barbarism.

The possibility of self-deception deriving from inadequate signs and habits arises from the relation between relatively more and less vague levels of signs internal to some human excellence, such as friendship. A vague sign, and thus a vague habit, is one that allows several less vague instantiations to be mutually exclusive, or at least alternative to one another, and yet each is equally good. For instance, the vague habit of friendship requires some less vague habits having to do with greeting a friend; the greeting habits might consist in a bow, a handshake, a kiss on both cheeks, or a hug. A greeting habit that is entirely appropriate in one culture might have just the opposite meaning in another culture; a bow is an appropriate greeting in old-fashioned Chinese culture but would be interpreted as a distancing gesture in American culture. There are many other subhabits that go into friendship, having to do with how to talk, how to relate the friend to one's family, how to handle money, and so forth, in which alternative culture forms might serve equally well in different cultures, but are mutually exclusive or counterproductive if combined in one culture. The institutions of friendship, family life, education, political life, cultural life, and many other dimensions of civilization are hierarchies of habits on habits, each level of which tolerates ambiguity below in a vague sense. But in any specific social situation, there must be a definite hierarchy of habits, with only certain ones tolerated by the higher levels of vague habits.

Self-deception arises when a higher level habit is operative but lacks a necessary subhabit. Thus people can believe they have friends and make a show of doing certain things with their friends, identifying themselves as a friend, but might lack crucial subhabits. They may have no way of greeting the friend that is not off-putting; they may have no way of relating the friend to their family, leaving things in confusion and divided affection; they may have no way of handling money with their friend. And so they are self-deceived about their friendship.

The kind of self-deception resulting from faulty signs and habits is learned when one learns one's society's semiotic. It may interact with the self-

A Confucian Construction of a Self-Deceivable Self

deception deriving from selfishness, of course, so that one's preoccupation with oneself affects the ability to relate to another as an equal. But the essential fact is that the signs are at fault. American society places great emphasis on the care of children, but lacks crucial habits for the details of love, nurture, and education; American society is self-deceived about parenting, and so are many individual Americans. Western societies generally place great stock in democratic government, but are inattentive to the educational and economic conditions necessary for persons to participate in a large democratic system. Therefore, democracies are often self-deceived about how democratic they really are when certain groups, by their history, possess the subhabits necessary for democracy and others do not, thereby being disenfranchised. Examples of this sort can be multiplied like Jeremiads.

In certain respects, the self-deceptions arising from faulty signs and habits parallel the self-deceptions arising from ideologies to which Marxists have given attention. But the Marxist analysis emphasizes a contradiction within the deceived self between underlying interests shaped by economic class membership and the ideological understanding of the situation that expresses acceptable values. The Confucian analysis lacks that preoccupation with contradiction. The problem for Confucians is not contradiction within the self but the absence or disfunction of signs and habits that are supposed to be exercised for the higher level excellences to exist. The Confucian remedy is not the overcoming of contradiction in some kind of class struggle, but rather the reshaping of the signs structuring the self in society. Among the signs that might need to be reshaped are those expressing differences in social class; Confucius, for instance, was an egalitarian educator in a time of aristocratic privilege. The Confucian emphasis is on the deconstruction of counterproductive habits and signs and the recovery or invention of servicable habits and signs. Social criticism is the means to identify the problem areas.

The third form of self-deception, the misplacing of social identity because of a failure of humanity, has been the favorite target of Taoists within the Chinese tradition. Precisely because Confucians pay close attention to signs and exercise habits that are socially defined to establish status and relationships, they can deceive themselves about what really is going on and what values are at stake. Dressing according to one's station, greeting people with the style appropriate to the relation between one's own station and theirs, expecting recognition of one's authority and place, and other signs lend themselves to insufferable pomposity and abusive treatment of people who do not know or who disagree about the signs of status.

Within the Confucian tradition, the emphasis on ritual *li*, on exercising the socially meaningful habits, has been tempered with a balancing emphasis on humanity (*jen*).[16] Humanity is the immediate giving of one's heart to others that adjusts the exercising of the socially significant habits into a due proportion. One need not always insist on wearing one's finery, or in being greeted properly, or in being recognized. The first stanza of Confucius' *Analects* includes the following: "Is one not a superior man if he does not feel hurt even though he is not recognized?"

Jen, not *li* as ritual propriety, became the central organizing category for the great neo-Confucians such as the Ch'eng brothers and Chu Hsi. As mentioned earlier, Chu Hsi provided a cosmological interpretation of humanity as the principle according to which things arise and flourish. In our own time, Confucians such as Cheng Chung-ying, Antonio Cua, and Tu Wei-ming have elaborated both historical interpretations of *jen* and contemporary developments of it as a philosophical category.[17] In one way or another, the contemporary accounts employ *jen* as humanity to shape and set the contours of Confucian social policy and the goals of personal education and cultivation. In Tu's theory, humanity is the norm by which to judge both social and personal structures; he interprets family relations as the core from which both personal structures and social structures develop, an ancient theme.

When humanity is missing, or misunderstood, the development and exercise of civilizing signs and habits has no due proportion. Then the hierarchies of signs and symbols can become disfunctional even when they are operative. You slap your friend on the back in greeting, you remember to send his kid a birthday card, and you do not complain when he breaks your lawnmower, and still he makes you feel guilty as if you had not done something for him: he may be missing the openness and attentiveness of your heart that should shine in your eyes and temper your backslap, your avuncular role, and your neighborly forebearance. Even though all the behaviors of friendship seem to be operative, the heart is not in it. The heart can be absent from family duties, from community activities, and from services to high culture. In these cases those civilized activities are hollow and not genuine. But because we understand those high human things from the signs and habits that constitute the exercising of them, we deceive ourselves. It seems we are doing the right thing, but affairs do not originate without compromise, they do not flourish with zest, the advantages that were supposed to accrue do not follow, and the definiteness of their actual practice dissolves into ambiguities. Origination, flourish, advantage, and definiteness are Chu Hsi's marks of *jen*. Sensing the problem, we deceive ourselves into redoubling the effort with better signs and habits, and that merely makes us pompous. The need is for humanity in the signs and habits.

A Confucian Construction of a Self-Deceivable Self

Some rough parallel holds between the Confucian understanding of the self-deception that comes from a misplacing of status from want of humanity and the Western tragic sense of self-deception as in Oedipus and Lear. But in the latter, the self-deception involves an inner contradiction in how one relates to oneself as defined by situation and accomplishment. The contradiction is located in how one relates to oneself in peculiar ignorance. In the Confucian case there may be a misperception of self, such that one is subjected to comic ridicule or social criticism; but the problem is a lack of humanity that would put the signs and habits defining one's place in perspective. Failing that perspective, one can be both pompously ridiculous and morally abusive all the while thinking only of doing good.

In the comparisons here of Western and Confucian understandings of self-deception, nothing new has been said about the Western sense of self as being constituted by self-reflexity containing contradiction. The point of this chapter has been to draw out a Confucian sense of self, a Confucian analogue for the Western notion that does not depend on intensity of self-reflexivity or on the overcoming and containment of contradictions. Rather, Confucian motifs have been developed concerning the self as a structured continuum of signs and habits of physical, cognitive, and emotional behavior uniting the morally incipient heart, *chung,* with the ordinary world of the ten thousand things, *yung.* This distinction between senses of selfhood has been used to explore differences between three senses of self-deception, concerning psychological, social, and status matters. Whereas the West approaches psychological self-deception through the psychodynamic theory of contradictory drives, the Confucian tradition sees it as a problem of selfishness. Whereas the West approaches social self-deception through ideology theory of internalized class conflict, the Confucian tradition sees it as a problem of attaining adequate civilizing signs and habits. Whereas the West approaches self-deceptions of status with the understanding of tragic contradiction, the Confucian tradition understands it as a want of humanity.

In the contemporary world, both of these traditions have something to contribute. Situations of self-deception can be understood in terms of elements of both. No intellectual is only a Westerner, or only a Confucian, except through culpable ignorance.

NOTES

1. Surely this is an initially dubious claim in light of the title of such distinguished works as Wm. Theodore de Bary's *Self and Society in Ming Thought* (New York: Columbia University Press, 1970), a volume to which de Bary contributed as well as edited. Yet in the writings of the various authors of that volume, the term

self is nearly always used simply in its reflexive form, as in self-cultivation, self-criticism, and so forth, not as a noun substantive. One of the main themes of that book, and also of *The Unfolding of Neo-Confucianism* (New York: Columbia University Press, 1975), again edited by and with a contribution from de Bary, is the development of individualism and heightening of subjectivity in Confucianism after Wang Yang-ming. But the noun substantive for that topic generally is *human nature* or *character,* not *self.* The only systematic use of the word *self* as a noun substantive is in Araki Kengo's essay in the latter volume on "Confucianism and Buddhism in the Late Ming" where it is attributed (45, 59–60) to Buddhist thought (now *there's* an oxymoron!). The Neo-Confucians did develop a Confucian analogue to the Western conception of self; they did so out of ancient Confucian ideas, such as those contained in *The Doctrine of the Mean* and in *The Great Learning;* and their conception emphasized the self-cultivated responsibility of selfhood. Yet neither the early nor the late Confucian conceptions of what I call "self" set self-reference at the defining center.

Tu Wei-ming's titles are more complex. One of his books, *Humanity and Self-Cultivation* (Berkeley: Austin Humanities Press, 1979) makes exactly the above point: *humanity* is the noun substantive and *self* is used in expressing the reflexive activity of perfecting it. His *Confucian Thought: Selfhood as Creative Transformation* (Albany: State University of New York Press, 1985) makes the noun *self* a super-substantive (with the *hood*), and the book is written with a clear eye to the Western conception of the self. But his point is that the Confucian conception is different from the Western; for Tu, selfhood arises out of filial (or unfilial) relations with parents, *not* out of themes of *self*-relation (see chapter 7). David Hall and Roger Ames, in *Thinking Through Confucius* (Albany: State University of New York Press, 1987), treat Tu's problematic of selfhood through creative self-transformation as a matter of what they call "person making," neatly avoiding the notion of self in its self-reflexive preoccupation (110–25).

2. See Altizer, *History as Apocalypse* (Albany: State University of New York Press, 1985); *Total Presence* (New York: The Seabury Press, 1980).

3. See Augustine, *Confessions,* bk. 10.

4. Søren Kierkegaard, *The Sickness unto Death,* trans. Walter Lowrie, with *Fear and Trembling* (Garden City, NY: Doubleday Anchor, 1955), 146.

5. Altizer, in *Total Presence,* accounts for the collapse of the large bourgeois ego as part of the death of God, the dialectical abandonment of the plausibility of the claim that God is a self-related, infinitely deep, process of overcoming negations. The endpoint, Altizer says, is a kind of return to Buddhist silence regarding both divinity, which is now emptiness, and humanity, which is a historical surface on which the depths of human emotion are popularized by the universally accessible blues.

6. *The Doctrine of the Mean,* ch. 1, as translated by Wing-tsit Chan in *A Source Book in Chinese Philosophy* (Princeton: Princeton University Press, 1963), 98.

7. *The Book of Mencius,* bk. 2A:6, in Chan, 65.

8. *The Doctrine of the Mean,* opening lines; Chan, 98.

9. See Chan, 610ff.

10. Chu Hsi, *Treatise on Jen,* in Chan, 594.

11. Pragmatism's semiotic was developed by Charles Peirce. I have analyzed this in connection with his theory of habit in *The Highroad around Modernism* (Albany: State University of New York Press, 1992), ch. 1. I have applied it to Confucianism in "The Short Happy Life of Boston Confucianism," forthcoming.

12. Wang, "Inquiry on the Great Learning," in *Instructions for Practical Living and Other Neo-Confucian Writings by Wang Yang-Ming,* trans. Wing-tsit Chan (New York: Columbia University Press, 1963), 272–73; Chan *Source Book,* 659–60.

13. See Chu, "Treatise on Ch'eng Ming-tao's Discourse on the Nature," in Chan, *Source Book,* 598–99.

14. Chan, *Source Book,* 98.

15. See Fingarette, *Confucius: The Secular as Sacred* (New York: Harper & Row, 1972), especially 11ff.

16. This is Fingarette's main point; see above.

17. See Cheng, *Tai Chen's Inquiry into Goodness* (Honolulu: East-West Center Press, 1971), 4ff.; Cheng, *New Dimensions of Confucian and Neo-Confucian Philosophy* (Albany: State University of New York Press, 1991). See also Tu, *Humanity and Self-Cultivation;* Tu, *Confucian Thought: Selfhood as Creative Transformation;* Tu, *Way, Learning, and Politics: Essays on the Confucian Intellectual* (Singapore: Institute of East Asian Philosophies, 1989). See Cua's chapter in this volume, as well as his *The Unity of Knowledge and Action: A Study of Wang Yang-ming's Moral Psychology* (Honolulu: The University Press of Hawaii, 1982).

TEN

THE CLASSICAL CHINESE SELF AND HYPOCRISY

Roger T. Ames

THE PROBLEM

One and many, free will and determinism, reality and appearance, mind and body, knowledge and opinion, good and evil—fundamental metaphysical problems, themselves all variations on the one-many problematic—were not interesting or important in shaping the classical Chinese philosophic tradition. Self-deception becomes a philosophical problem in the Western tradition to the extent that a dualistic world view is assumed, and a unitary and superordinated self is constructed. As Amélie Rorty argues, I think persuasively, self-deception is only coherent as a problem if one can find it as a tension between privileged unitary conception of self articulated in the vocabulary of independence, autonomy, integrity, and so on, and multiple self comprised of semi-autonomous subsystems.[1] This argument is reinforced by the disturbing conclusion reached in David Hall's exploration of what he calls "the ambiguated self"; within the academy, it is the most rational and ostensibly clear-minded colleagues—those who would uncritically consider themselves to be unitary selves—who are in fact the most susceptible to self-deception.

As another version of the one-many problem, then, self-deception is a sometimes Western concern which has little relevance for Chinese philosophy. In the absence of the unitary conception of self necessary to make the problem coherent, I doubt whether anything that we would recognize as self-deception has been part of the Chinese experience. I want to explore the intuition that what we might be inclined on our terms to interpret as self-deception might from a Chinese perspective in fact be shown to be a rather different order of duplicity.

FOCAL SELF: A POLITICAL ANALOGY

Any exploration of classical Chinese thought in search of self-deception must begin from a definition of terms. We must ask how "self" is con-

Self and Deception

structed within the Chinese tradition, and how Chinese assumptions about 'self' differ from our own. In an earlier essay, I attempted to develop what I have called a "focus-field" conception of self in explanation of some fundamental Confucian presuppositions about what it means to be a person.[2] In outlining this model, I followed Plato in using the analogy of political order to describe the articulation of the self. The similarity between Plato's construction of the tripartite psyche and the classical Chinese conception of person is that both Plato and the dominant classical Chinese thinkers begin from the conviction that personal, societal, political, and cosmic order are consistent enough to justify the analogy. The significant differences between the metaphysician Plato (to the extent that we want to continue this unfortunate caricature of a more complex philosopher) and the Chinese model are many, the most obvious being that the senses of order to which they subscribe—Plato beginning from first principles and classical Chinese thinkers from particular details—are irreconcilable. Plato appeals to a theoretical and metaphysically fortified regime to frame his analogy for constructing a self, and on this basis can make universal claims. In the predominantly "anarchic" tradition[3] of classical China which invested little interest in metaphysical questions, the appeal can only be to a historical and cultural analogy, and as such, any claims based upon it are necessarily site specific and provisional. Where Plato in pressing his analogy seeks to discover the conditions which define humanity universally, an exploration of the classical Chinese model will at best uncover some insights about the culturally Chinese construction of person from particular historical data.

The classical Chinese assumption is that personal, societal, political, and even cosmic orders are immanental, coterminous, and mutually entailing.[4] Thus, to the extent we understand order in any one aspect of the human experience, we have a direct insight into other areas of experience as well. In describing the self as "focal," I am invoking a focus-field notion of 'order,' where a focal self inheres in the natural world as its field, and where it shapes and is shaped by the field in which it resides. The focus-field language is useful in underscoring certain of the basic features of this sense of order. First, it suggests a "part-part" rather than a "One-many" or "part-whole" model, where, in the absence of any metaphysical assumptions about the One behind the many or Being behind beings, order emerges from the coordination of so many "this-es" and "thats"—the harmonious correlation of the myriad unique details (*wan wu* 萬物 or *wan yu* 萬有) which make up the world. The dynamic structure and regularity of the focal self is immanental, inhering within it, and making it ever continuous with its context. As such, it is constitutive in its relationship to its world. The focal self is not in any sense discrete or independent, but is rather

The Classical Chinese Self and Hypocrisy

intrinsically related to and interdependent with its field. Similarly, given that the field is always entertained from some particular perspective or other, it is thus interpreted from and implicated within the particular that interprets it. Further, the field of the focal self is not circumscribed or holistic, but is open: an unbounded and inexhaustible reservoir of particular detail which, in graduated degree, has relevance for the focal self. These conditions of the focal self it is hoped will be made clearer by pursuing the sense of order made explicit in the political analogy below.

The concrete historical example used to illustrate the articulation of order in the Chinese world is the formation of the Han dynasty (206 BCE to 220 ACE). The first volume of the *Cambridge History of China* describes the career of the Han empire from its emergence under Liu Pang to its gradual disintegration three and a half centuries later.[5] In this volume, Yü Ying-shih uses the "five zones" (*wu-fu* 五服) of submission as a device for describing the dynamics of the Han world order:

> According to this theory, China since the Hsia dynasty had been divided into five concentric and hierarchical zones or areas. The central zone (*tien-fu* 甸服) was the royal domain, under the direct rule of the king. The royal domain was immediately surrounded by the Chinese states established by the king, known collectively as the lords' zone (*hou-fu* 侯服). Beyond the *hou-fu* were Chinese states conquered by the reigning dynasty, which constituted the so-called pacified zone (*sui-fu* 綏服 or *pin-fu* 儐服, guest zone). The last two zones were reserved for the barbarians. The Man and I barbarians lived outside the *sui-fu* or *pin-fu* in the controlled zone (*yao-fu* 要服), which was so called because the Man and I were supposedly subject to Chinese control, albeit of a rather loose kind. Finally, beyond the controlled zone lay the Jung and Ti barbarians, who were basically their own masters in the wild zone (*huang-fu* 荒服) where the sinocentric world order reached its natural end.[6]

This hierarchical scheme also described the descending degree of tribute—local products and services—that was provided to the court at the center. Although this five-zone theory seems more complex, it is really a focus-field distinction that defines the relative focus of "inner-outer (*nei-wai* 內外)" circles: "China was the inner region relative to the outer region of the barbarians, just as the royal domain was, relative to the outer lords' zone, an inner zone, and the controlled zone became the inner area relative to the wild zone on the periphery of Chinese civilization."[7]

Self and Deception

This "radial" solar system, defined in terms of concentric circles, seems pervasive in, if not a signature of, the Chinese world order. It is a centripetal order articulated outward from a central axis through patterns of deference and importance. These concrete, functioning patterns of deference contribute in varying degrees, and are constitutive of the authority at the center, articulating and bringing into focus the character of the social and political entity, its standards and values. Whatever constitutes the authority at the center—in this political example, the ruler—derives its authority from having implicate within it the order of its field of influence. The ruler does not stand above or outside of the empire; he is the empire.

The Chinese sense of order is generally organized in the language of mutually defining and thus complementary opposites such as "inner-outer" where history is construed as correlated events that move the process along this continuum.[8] Such oppositions are always relative—more or less "inner," more or less "outer," more or less "Chinese," more or less "barbarian." When the center is strong, tribute moves in to reinforce it, with the greatest degree of influence on the center being exerted from elements close to the center itself: the court officials, the aristocracy, the wealthy merchants, the military leaders, the population of the capital. As the center weakens, incidental elements which were on the periphery have the potential to exert an increasing amount of influence in the gradual process of reshaping, and in some instances subverting, the center. To the extent they do so, they move inward and cease to be marginal.

This determinate, detailed, "center-seeking" focus fades into an increasingly indeterminate and untextured field. The magnetic attraction of the center is such that, with varying degrees of intensity and success, it draws into its field, suspends, and harmonizes the disparate, diverse, and often mutually inconsistent centers that constitute its world.

Rudolf Arnheim in his reflections on the visual arts provides us with a useful vocabulary for exploring this classical Chinese conception of order. Arnheim is persuaded that the nature of composition in the visual arts reflects an underlying cosmological tendency: "Cosmically, we find that matter organizes around centers, which are often marked by a dominant mass. Such systems come about whenever their neighbors allow them sufficient freedom."[9] This phenomenon, observes Arnheim, is true both of the vast astronomical space and of the micrcoscopic realm. The center that is so constituted is "the center of a field of forces, a focus from which forces issue and towards which forces converge."[10] These centers, then, relate to each other as a calculus of centers which, from their interplay, produce a balancing centripetal center which tends to distribute the forces of its field symmetrically around its own center:

> Overcoming the egocentric view amounts to realizing that a center is not always in the middle. . . . More often, the environment is dominated by other centers, which force the self into a subordinate position. . . . Speaking generally, one can assert that every visual field comprises a number of centers, each of which attempts to draw the others into subservience. The self as viewer is just one of these centers. . . . The overall balance of all these competing aspirations determines the structure of the whole, and that total structure is organized around what I will call the balancing center.[11]

The notion of composition that Arnheim is elaborating here can be readily appropriated to describe the construction of the Confucian self and the various foci that define its world.

Returning to the concrete historical example of the Han dynasty, within the subcontinent that was Warring States China, the full spectrum of peoples—some paying their allegiance to traditional hereditary houses, some ruled by locally powerful warlords, others organized around religious doctrines, and yet others governed by clan or tribal regulation—were suspended in the Han harmony with each contributing in greater or lesser degree to the definition of Han culture. It was the effective correlation of these constitutive centers which determined the quality of the harmony of the field called "Han."

This sense of order in which all of the diversity and difference characteristic of the multiple, competing political centers of the Warring States period are lifted into the deeply etched and powerful harmony of the Han dynasty has a ready extension in explaining its intellectual world. The intellectual geography of the Hundred Schools in the pre-Ch'in period gives way to a syncretic Confucian-centered doctrine which absorbs into itself and to some degree conceals the richness of what were competing elements, to articulate the philosophical and religious character of the period. Even where absorption has not been total, the lingering shadows of what were competing positions are themselves defined in terms of opposition to this Confucian center. This movement from disunity to unity is better expressed in the language of incorporation and accommodation than in terms of suppression and exclusion.

This correlative order is centripetal. The center sought is defined by and is definitive of that ethnicity from which most later Chinese will come to characterize themselves as "people of the Han."

As the centripetal core of the Han court weakens in the second century ACE and as the political order gradually dissolves into a period of disunity,

Self and Deception

the disparate centers precipitate out of the harmony to reassert themselves, and what had been their contribution to the harmonious diversity becomes the energy of contest among them. What was a tightening spire in the early Han becomes a gyre, disgorging itself of its disassociated contents. In the same period, there is a resurgence of competing philosophical schools and religious movements that reflect a disintegration of the centrally driven intellectual harmony.

FOCAL SELF: ALTERNATIVE ANALOGIES

I have suggested that this centripetal, radial sense of order is pervasive in Chinese culture. The political example of the composition and disintegration of the Han dynasty is only one illustration of this notion of achieved and resolved harmony. We could equally appeal to the systematic cosmology which dawns in China during this transitional period. In late Chou, the Yin-Yang School, promoted by Tsou Yen and other members of the Chi Hsia Academy, becomes a major force. In John Major's work on early Chinese cosmology, he reports on the gradual integration and coordination of previously disparate precosmological fragments into coherent systems.[12]

We could also appeal to Chinese historiography as a way of illustrating this sense of order. Maureen Robertson makes this point. Interestingly, and perhaps not unexpectedly, the directional and conceptual periodizations familiar in the West by and large "have had a teleological character; movement is toward an anticipated end—the perfection of human reason, the Last Judgment, utopian social order, or the triumph of technology."[13] By contrast, the model of irregular periodization that one would associate with the Chinese tradition "claims strict dependence upon the configurations of the data studied, and does not, in its structure at least, display a belief that change obeys laws of regularity or directionality." Instead, "the historian is likely to discover patterns he is culturally predisposed to see."[14] That is, each heir to the tradition is responsible for ordering history's welter of "this's" and "that's" according to some site-specific and particular framework of correlations.

Given the claims made in *Thinking Through Confucius* concerning the fundamentally "aesthetic" nature of the classical Chinese conception of order, one possible way to think about how this culture has traditionally organized its experience would be to compare it with how we are inclined to periodize art.[15] Our own conceptions of art history do not usually entail the theoretical assumptions which dominate other historical generalizations. Instead, a period or movement tends to be "radial." It collects around and is defined by leading exemplars, their product, and their lineages and schools. There is often only the most tentative sense of logical or causal or even conceptual relationship assumed in the movement from one period to the next, and only a temporal rather than a qualitative sense of progress. The assumption is that some periods stand out as having been richer and more compelling than others, and as such, allow for qualitative rather than specific points of comparison.

Another example of "radial" order defining Chinese culture would be the internal structure of Chinese canonical texts and the commentarial tradition that evolves around them. Often a treatise will unfold an image around a particular character or expression. Either this character or expression is returned to for further (not necessarily consistent) elaboration, or alternatively, some loosely related image which is suggested in the elaboration itself is pursued. Sometimes the style of a particular passage will evoke correlations available in the repository of the tradition. Sometimes structure will call to mind associations from other available resources. Often material is carried over from earlier works, or from memory of earlier works, and is reshaped to be meaningful for the new context. As such, the pattern of the text is a pastiche—a concatenation of diverse images and allusions, all made important by the reflections of the author. For the reader, mapping out the geography of the text, separating rhymed passages from parallel text, prose from anecdote, is the first step in understanding it.

A further illustration of the Chinese "radial order" is found in the way in which it organizes knowledge. There is an immediate contrast between an Aristotelian model of classification and the one characteristically found in the traditional encyclopedic or classificatory works (*lei-shu* 類書) of China.[16] The Chinese model is resolutely hierarchical, with the human being *self-consciously* in the center. This "human being" is not acultural, ahistorical "humanity," defined by some abstraction of a common essential quality or nature, but rather the imperial Chinese person embedded within a specific historical, social, cultural, and physical order. The world is not described objectively through an articulation of exclusive categories and subcategories, but is divided up prescriptively into natural and cultural elements which have an increasing influence on the experience of the Chinese court as they move in toward the center. The Chinese cultural experience is embodied in the ruler at the center, and the *lei-shu* not only organizes his world in this particular way but, further, recommends it. When the court is strong, the centripetal harmony is maintained and everything is kept in its proper place; as the center inevitably weakens, elements which were on the periphery come to exert increasing influence. Seemingly insignificant abnormalities in the natural world, for example, reflect disorder at the court, and if not

Self and Deception

responded to in a timely way, can exert a dramatic, even transformative influence on the reigning center. The dynamics of this centripetal center has explanatory force in anticipating the changing configuration of order in the various dimensions of the Chinese world.

FAMILY AND THE FOCAL SELF

The Han court analogy is a heuristic for articulating the classical Chinese self as a more or less focused field of experiences. Primary in this social model, self is a field of selves, constituted through a world of roles and ritually defined relationships which locate one within a given social nexus. But then the court analogy is itself derived from the more fundamental and all-pervasive family model. This focus-field notion of order is precisely that order captured in the Confucian notion of ritually constituted family and community. Constitutive rituals (*li* 禮) and roles (*lun* 倫), defined at the center by the authority of the tradition, not only demand personalization and participation, but further, are always reflective of the quality and the uniqueness of their participants. The family, as the correlation of relationships, is a basic variation on this notion of a graduated, centripetal harmony. In fact, the sociologist Ambrose King (Chin Yao-chi 金耀基) argues persuasively that in the Confucian world, all relationships are ultimately familial:

> Among the five cardinal relations, three belong to the kinship realm. The remaining two, though not family relationships, are conceived in terms of the family. The relationship between the ruler and the ruled is conceived of in terms of father (*chün-fu* 君父) and son (*tzu-min* 子民), and the relationship between friend and friend is stated in terms of elder brother (*wu-hsiung* 吾兄) and younger brother (*wu-ti* 吾弟).[17]

The family as the "in-group," is determinate and focused at the center, but becomes increasingly vague as it stretches out both diachronically in the direction of one's lineage, and synchronically as a society full of "uncles" and "aunties." It is articulated in terms of a network of relationships (*lun* 倫), a ritual "wheel (*lun* 輪)" of social bonds that "ripple out (*lun* 淪)" in fields of discourse (*lun* 論) to define the person as an intersection of roles.

As observed above, the Confucian assumption traditionally has been that personal, familial, societal, political, and ultimately cosmic order are coterminous and mutually entailing, and further, from the personal perspective, is emergent in the process of one's own self-cultivation and articulation. From the perspective of any person, order begins here and extends there. In the immediately human world of the Confucian tradition, these compositions are reflected in an irreducibly social conception of person, families, and communities, where the social grammar is necessarily participatory ritual practices and social roles. It is because of the immanence and hence uniqueness of an order so defined that Confucius, rather than appealing to transcendent beings or principles, can describe the process of personal cultivation in terms of "starting from what is most basic and immediate, and penetrating through to what it most elevated."[18]

IMMANENTAL ORDER AND THE FOCAL SELF

The classical Chinese conception of self does not entail superordination, where superordination is the assumption of some formal and unifying identity or agency that entertains experience, and that is able to objectify both its experiences and itself. Herbert Fingarette, in his *Confucius: The Secular as Sacred,* brings to our attention the seeming absence of an "inner psychic life" in the Confucian model of self:

> Confucius' usage reveals no explicit doctrines of a metaphysical or psychological kind about the details of structure of will, or the processes internal to the individuals' control of the will. There is, for example, no reification of a Faculty of Will, . . . no theatre in which an inner drama takes place, no inner community with ruler and ruled.[19]

Fingarette's explanation for the absence of personal interiority is that the exemplary person (*chün tzu* 君子) does not express his own egoistic will, but wills the noncontingent, nonpersonal *tao*. In Fingarette's own words:

> If one seeks to understand deeply the content of an egoistic will, one must necessarily understand that particular person, the motives, anxieties, hopes, and other personal data that go to make intelligible the conduct of that person. But the more deeply one explores the *chün tzu*'s will, the more the personal dimensions are revealed as purely formal—the individual is the unique space-time bodily locus of that will; it is *that which* controls, but it is nonsignificant regarding why, specifically, or in what specific direction, the control shall be exercised. To understand the content of the *chün tzu*'s will is to understand the *tao*, not the

chün tzu as a particular person. The ego is present in the egoist's will. The *tao* is present in the *chün tzu*'s will.[20]

Fingarette's conclusion, then, is that the self of the exemplary person, insofar as we may call it a "self," is an empty room, a transparent medium through which the order of the world (*tao* 道) is expressed. The self, for Fingarette, achieves a state of "selflessness."

I must confess that in my earlier readings of Fingarette, I was troubled by his use of "selfless" because it seemed to me to imply that Confucius was self-abnegating, while I wanted to suggest precisely the opposite. I was worried that in including Confucian self in a pan-Asian "selflessness," Fingarette was emphasizing some notion of collective harmony at the expense of the particular focus through which the harmony is constituted, and thus collapsing Confucianism into an entirely uncomfortable Brahmanic or Vedāntic monism. I made these criticisms explicit in an essay for a Festschrift for Fingarette, and in his response to my expressed reservations, he made it clear to me at least that we are substantively in agreement on our interpretations of the Confucian self. In Fingarette's own language:

> The point is: Why should we reify "self" by giving it the independent noun form in English, and thus impute to Confucius the notion of some inner entity, some core of one's being—whether egoistic or ideal? If Ames and I are right in our basic view of Confucius's ideas in this area, we ought to make it a point to avoid speaking of "the self" in Confucius. We ought to speak of a person as acting, but not suggesting by "person" this notion of an Actor who somehow embraces inwardly a moral or psychic core which is then expressed in action. On the contrary, the fundamental moral-human reality is (as Ames and I agree) the social nexus, and persons along with many other things receive their specific, humanly relevant nature, as well as their humanly relevant location, by reference to and as a result of the communal life-forms.[21]

For the Confucian, there is no self independent of the communal and natural environments that constitute it.

The French sinologist Jacques Gernet makes the distinction between the traditional Chinese notion of 'person' and its Western counterpart in similar terms, focusing his comments on the inseparability of what we think and how we think about it. Specifically, he discounts any assumption that "rationality" can be taken as a defining human faculty independent of our sensible experience in the world:

> Not only was the substantial opposition between the soul and the body something quite unknown to the Chinese, all souls being, in their view, destined to be dissipated sooner or later, but so was the distinction, originally inseparable from it, between the sensible and the rational. The Chinese had never believed in the existence of a sovereign and independent faculty of reason. The concept of a soul endowed with reason and capable of acting freely for good or for evil, which is so fundamental to Christianity, was alien to them.[22]

What is said here in respect to rationality holds true for the other essential categories or faculties that might be posited as the defining and unifying "deep structure" of Chinese person—a given nature or soul. To enlist such an abstraction only distorts the tradition.

FOCAL SELF AND LOCAL DISPOSITION

In the absence of superordinate and individuated faculties proffered as defining of self, self is always a local, embodied, and site-specific correlation of details: a repertory of experiences, desires, and beliefs, which, in combination, constitute one's person. It is a locus, shaped by an enacted pattern of social roles and relationships. Because this emergent pattern invariably arises from within the process itself, the tension that establishes the line between one's own focus and one's relevant field gives one a physical, psychological, social, and cosmological "skin," a shape, a continuing, insistently particular identity. This dynamic pattern is reflexive in the sense that one's own dispositions are implicate in and affect the shaping of one's environment. One's own "shape" is constantly being reconstrued in tension with what is most immediately pressing in upon one, and vice versa.

These roles and relationships are dynamic, constantly being enacted, reinforced, and ideally deepened through the multiple levels of communal discourse: embodying (*t'i* 體), ritualizing (*li* 禮), speaking (*yen* 言), playing music (*yüeh* 樂), and so on. Each of these levels of discourse is implicit in every other, so there is a sense in which a person can be fairly described as a calculus of specific patterns of discourse. By virtue of these specific roles and relationships, a person comes to occupy a place and posture in the context of family and community. The human being is not shaped by some

Self and Deception

given design which underlies natural and moral order in the cosmos, and which stands as the ultimate objective of human growth and experience. Rather, the "purpose" of the human experience, if it can be so described, is more immediate—to coordinate the various ingredients which constitute one's particular world here and now, and to negotiate the most productive harmony out of them. Simply put, it is to get the most out of what you've got here and now.

The *Chuang Tzu,* one of the classical Taoist texts, contains a passage in which this notion of 'locus' or 'place' is seen as integral to what it means to know:

> Chuang Tzu and Hui Shih were strolling across the bridge over the Hao river. Chuang Tzu observed, "The minnows swim out and about as they please—this is the way they enjoy themselves."
>
> Hui Tzu replied, "You are not a fish—how do you know what they enjoy?"
>
> Chuang Tzu returned, "You are not me—how do you know that I don't know what is enjoyable for the fish?"
>
> Hui Tzu said, "I am not you, so I certainly don't know what you know; but it follows that, since you are certainly not the fish, you don't know what is enjoyment for the fish either."
>
> Chuang Tzu said, "Let's get back to your basic question. When you asked '*From where* do you know what the fish enjoy?' you already knew that I know what the fish enjoy, or you wouldn't have asked me. I know it from here above the Hao river."[23]

Angus Graham in interpreting this passage observes that the expression *an chih* 案知 can mean both "how do you know" and "from whence do you know." But Chuang Tzu is not just depending upon this linguistic ambiguity in order to win a sophistical argument. He has a more philosophic point to make. In a world where knowledge is performative and a function of fruitful correlation—a "realizing" of something in the sense of "making it real"—the knower and the known are inseparable aspects of the same event and knowledge is doing. Agent cannot be isolated from action. As Chuang Tzu says elsewhere, "There must be the genuine person before there is genuine knowledge."[24] One and one's posture or perspective are integral to what is known. Where you are and how you know are one and the same. Knowledge is proximity. Chuang Tzu's experience with the fish makes his world continuous with the world of the fish, and such being the case, his claim to knowledge is a claim to having been there.

The Classical Chinese Self and Hypocrisy

The vocabulary of the classical tradition is an illustration of this site specificity. "Correlative thinking" is basic to "the art of contextualizing," which constitutes a self. *Yin* 陰 and *yang* 陽 are familiar metaphors used in the classical tradition to express contrast and difference. *Yin* and *yang* are elements of a correlative pairing which are pragmatically useful in sorting out "this" and "that." They are not, as often claimed, dualistic principles of light and dark, male and female, action and passivity, and so on, where light and dark exclude each other, logically entail each other, and in their contrast with one another, constitute a totality. Rather *yin* and *yang* are, first and foremost, a vocabulary of qualitative contrast which have application to specific situations and enable us to make specific distinctions. It is this *yin* and *yang* contrast that articulates the focal self.

Yin and *yang* always describe the relationships which constitute unique particulars. Originally, they designated the shady side and the sunny side of a hill. They gradually came to suggest the way in which one thing "overshadows" another in some particular aspect of their relationship. The nature of the opposition captured in this pairing expresses the mutuality, interdependence, diversity, and creative efficacy of the dynamic relationships that are deemed immanent in and valorize the world. The full range of difference in the world is deemed explicable through this pairing. *Yin* and *yang* are ad hoc explanatory categories that report on interactions among immediate concrete things of the world.

Important here is the primacy of particular difference and the absence of any assumed sameness or identity. Things purported to be "the same" are not thought to be "natural kinds" but are deemed to have "family resemblances." The unique one evokes many. Hence, describing any particular phenomenon involves an unraveling of the relationships and conditions of the phenomenon's context and its multiple correlations. Each phenomenon in suggesting other similar phenomena has the multivalence of a poetic image.

THE UNDERDETERMINACY OF THE FOCAL SELF

When we move from these various analogous constructions of order to a consideration of the classical Chinese construction of self, there are several features of this notion of self that must be underscored. We must acknowledge the importance both of the articulated and of the unarticulated aspects of this continuing process of self-construction. Implicit ambiguity or personal "disorder" does not necessarily inhibit or subvert the self-ordering, self-organizing process; on the contrary, it can and often does stimulate it.

Self and Deception

Changes in determinate orders are often irregular and unpredictable because seemingly minute fluctuations on the periphery can have dramatic effects. Returning to our political analogy, the Han syncretism suspends within it a world of conflicted and divided ways of living and thinking. In this dynastic spiral, the achieved harmony, itself lined with positive chaos, is invariably followed by a period of social turmoil and disunity. These recurrent political and cultural interregna, while often taking a toll in life and property, have a very real positive side. These interludes have been a source of revitalization, of creative transformation, of enrichment from what was the margins. The relaxing of the strength which enforces a particular world order allows for the absorption of new and competing cultural and social forces, ideologies, and customs.

Analogously, the regularity and coherence of the focal self does not preclude a world of disassociated and often contradictory beliefs and practices. On the contrary, in the absence of notions of 'unity' and 'autonomy,' the self is constantly refocusing and being refocused to accommodate different situations and demands. The regularity and coherence which, at any particular point, define the character of the self are laced with the undetermined, which, rather than subverting one's dispositions, can provide an opportunity for ongoing personal renewal.

There is a wonderful anecdote in the *Chuang Tzu* which describes the positive contribution of this "chaotic element":

> The ruler of the North Sea was "Swift," the ruler of the South Sea was "Sudden," and the ruler of the Central Sea was "Chaos." Swift and Sudden had on several occasions encountered each other in the territory of Chaos, and Chaos had treated them with great hospitality. Swift and Sudden, devising a way to repay Chaos' generosity, said: "Human beings all have seven orifices through which they see, hear, eat and breathe. Chaos alone is without them." They then attempted to bore holes in Chaos, each day boring one hole. On the seventh day, Chaos died.[25]

This Taoist anecdote describes the interdependent relationship between regularity and irregularity. Order does not overcome chaos; it depends upon it. This Taoist vision eschews presumptions about the absolute value of order to affirm the complementary relationship between chaos and regularity. It is a vision in which "harmony" has a special kind of meaning which is inclusive of the breechless, faceless, orifice-free, Lord Huntun.

In this parable, the domain of Chaos is to be understood relationally, residing within the boundaries of north and south. Prior to the Huntun's demise in the act of having order imposed upon him by his well-meaning neighbors, he makes his contribution by being hospitable to regularity and determinacy, while himself remaining amorphous and uncommitted. It is the absence of formal definition and his insistent particularity which enables him to constantly renew order from within the order itself. The implication is that with the death of vagueness comes the death of life and creativity.[26]

Translating this Taoist affirmation of chaos into a Confucian vocabulary, underdeterminacy distinguishes ritual from rule, enabling the ritual actor to tailor the formal aspects to his own needs and to make the role or the institution his own. The underdeterminacy of culture and tradition enables the contemporary person to carry some of its inventory of values and institutions into the present historical moment and to reshape them to accommodate the uniqueness of one's specific time and place.

FOCAL SELF AND SELF-SUFFICIENCY

We begin from the classical and enduring Chinese assumption that China occupies the center and focuses within itself a self-sufficient human culture. It is important to observe that the term *chung-kuo* 中國, a self-designation for China that is generally translated as "the Middle Kingdom," originates in preimperial times, referring to the collection of disparate polities that made up the "central states." It refers not to one state, but to an interrelated plurality of states. These, although distinct, were conjoined by standing in closer proximity to the shifting cultural center than the *wai-kuo* 外國, also a term of classical vintage referring to the relatively more foreign states. Across the two-thousand-year tenure of imperial China, the world (not the state) was ruled over by the Son of Heaven who would regularly perform ritual sacrifices, insuring an appropriate relationship between Heaven and earth, and the human world between them. Human civilization was thus ordered through a pattern of tributary relationships which drew the plethora of outlying political spheres into the centripetal center at the Chinese court—a peculiarly Chinese kind of ritually constituted political and cultural harmony. As late as the Ch'ing dynasty, over five hundred tribute missions visited the Chinese capital from "foreign" regions. These outlying spheres "belonged" to the Chinese world in varying degrees at various times in its history as China itself moved through cycles of strong dynastic rule to interregnum and disunity.[27] This ritual observance of tribute, managed traditionally within the Chinese government by the Board of Rites, allowed for the uniqueness of the particular performer, and at the same time, translated contribution into social, political, and economic forms understandable and acceptable to the Chinese center.

It is important to observe that China was traditionally a "stay-at-home" culture in which its control over its extended regions derived from its wealth and culture. The goal was always one of self-sufficiency, making the most of what it had rather than harboring expansionist designs prosecuted through trade initiatives and military conquest.[28] Pliny the Elder in his *Natural History* describes the Chinese as "inoffensive in their manners indeed; . . . though ready to engage in trade, [they] wait for it to come to them instead of seeking it."[29]

This notion of achieved self-sufficiency is a defining criterion for the classical Chinese conception of harmony, personal as well as political. In constructing a self, the practical goal is to suspend within one's personal domain sufficient resources to handle effectively all contingencies. More than simply a capacity to handle practical exigencies, however, self-sufficiency is a qualitative assertion. In authoring oneself through personalizing the authority of the tradition, one has become an authoritative person to whom others willingly defer. This process of becoming a working cultural model is captured in Confucius's description of his own growth as it is preserved in the *Analects:* "At fifteen my heart-and-mind was set upon learning; at thirty I took my stance; at forty I was no longer of two minds; at fifty I realized the order prevailing in the world; at sixty my ear was attuned; at seventy I could give my heart-and-mind free rein without overstepping the mark."[30]

The kind of attunement described here in the personal cultivation of Confucius has two aspects: a formal appropriation of the defining cultural order, and the capacity to act in a creative manner and do as one pleases with it. Enjoyment as the goal of communal living emerges at the intersection between determinate cultural behaviors and improvisation.

FOCAL SELF AND SELF-DECEPTION

One immediate reason why our prevailing notion of self-deception cannot find application in the classical Chinese world is because of the irreducibly social nature of self and self-consciousness. Self is contextual; it is a shared consciousness of one's roles and relationships. The "inner" and "outer" (*nei/wai* 內/外) aspects of oneself are continuous and inseparable. One is "self-conscious," not in the sense of being able to isolate and objectify one's essential self, but in the sense of being aware of oneself as a locus of observation and deference by others. It is face, as the skin which differentiates and distinguishes one, and at the same time, conjoins one to the social world. It is a sense of shame, an image of self that is determined by the esteem in which one is held by one's community.

Where self is defined in terms of the consciousness of an autonomous will or reason, as in the contemporary liberal-democratic model, self-consciousness is individuating. Such a "self" refers to one's individual consciousness in relation to other more passive aspects of oneself, or in distinction to other unitary selves. "Self" as a unifying self-consciousness, is a principle of individuation and of separation. This self-consciousness enables one to objectify one's thoughts, feelings, and so on, in the same way that one can objectify other selves.

Self-deception, at least in the Sartrean sense of *mauvaise foi*, requires that one is able to construe self as an object, and in so doing, to deny one's own freedom and hence one's responsibility for what one is. One deceives oneself by being other than oneself. For Sartre, it is a failure of integrity because one is made two. There is a disjunction between self and self-consciousness, and a failure to conform with one's ontic self.

In the *Analects*, there are passages that might be construed as referring to this kind of self-deception. For example: "To realize that you know something when you do, and to realize that you do not when you do not—this then is knowing."[31]

Now, this can have at least two meanings: (1) to deceive yourself into thinking you know something that you do not know, and (2) to act as if you have realized something in your person which in fact you have not. The first of these meanings is familiar to us as what is usually entailed by individualistic conceptions of self-deception: it is a belief. Interpreting it into a classical Chinese world view, however, in the absence of Chinese individuals, it does not make much sense. It is the second meaning that is of real concern to Confucius. He not only condemns dissemblance in others, but is clear as to what he himself has realized in his person and what he has not.[32]

There is a significant equivocation which can slip in with our use of "know" and "don't know" in reference to Confucian philosophy. I have argued elsewhere at some length that for Confucius, knowing is resolutely performative—it is "realizing" in the sense of "making real."[33] Knowing is not a state of mind, but having the wherewithal to accomplish a given action, and actually doing it. Without the separation of theory and praxis, to know how to be a filial son means you are one.

Deception in this tradition as a communal rather than an individual affair is a kind of dissemblance. And dissemblance—someone occupying the wrong place and performing rituals inappropriate to one's status—is a major theme in classical Confucianism.³⁴ The Taoist counterpart to Confucian dissemblance would seem to be coercive activity (*yu wei*), where one forces a situation because of an inconsistency between what one is and what needs to be done. It is acting as if one is something one is not, thus failing to make good on something.

Where self is contextually defined, self-deception would involve a counterfeiting of interpersonal transactions, thereby corrupting and demeaning the character of the community. The classical Chinese conception of self-deception, given the social and performative demands described above, seems to be hypocrisy.

FOCAL "SELVES" AND HYPOCRISY

Hypocrisy is acting where there is a discovered discrepancy between what one asserts and what one really is. It is the uncovering of a front, a façade, a mask. It is a failure to give face and to save face. In Chinese, it is translated as a declarative, *fei chün tzu* 非君子: "this is not an exemplary person." The discovery of the incongruency between assertion and character is not necessarily made by the hypocrite herself; in fact, I suspect most hypocrites enact their roles, fully believing that they satisfy the conditions of them. With hypocrisy, the community and the hypocrite are acting in complicity, and are both culpable.

The *locus classicus* for this kind of hypocrisy is when Confucius declares: "The village worthy is the thief of virtue."³⁵

In explanation of this laconic observation, the *Mencius* fills out the conversation somewhat: "Confucius said, 'The only person who gives me no regret in passing by my gate without coming in, is the village worthy. The village worthy is the thief of virtue.' "³⁶

Mencius then adds his own commentary:

> If you want to condemn the village worthy, you have nothing on him; if you want to criticize him, there is nothing to criticize. He chimes in with the practices of the day and blends in with the common world. Where he lives he seems to be conscientious and seems to live up to his word, and in what he does, he seems to have integrity. His community all like him, and he sees himself as being right. Yet one cannot pursue the way of Yao or Shun with such a person.³⁷

Such a village worthy is overdetermined in the sense of form and regularity so that he is plausible to those who would look to him as a model, yet the creative element necessary for his personalization and renewal of the exemplary role is absent. He has no blood. He is a hypocrite because he has nothing of quality to contribute on his own; there is a failure of self-sufficiency.

Confucius is given the last word in this passage, summing up his concerns about the corrosive influence such a model can have on the quality of the culture:

> Confucius said, "As for my dislike and condemnation of what is specious: I dislike weeds lest they be confused with grain; I dislike flattery lest it be confused with what is proper for one to say; I dislike a glib tongue lest it be confused with integrity; I dislike the tunes of Cheng lest they be confused with music; I dislike purple lest it be confused with vermillion; I dislike the village worthy lest he be confused with the virtuous. The exemplary person simply reverts to the standard. Where the standard is upheld, the common people will flourish, and where they flourish, there will be no perversity or aberration."[37]

FOCAL SELF, FORGING, AND FORGERY

As a footnote, hypocrisy must be carefully distinguished from forgery, which has a positive value in the classical Chinese tradition. In a world where creativity is genealogical rather than individual—most scholarly works, for example, are corporate—tradition moves ahead by a constant revisioning of the past. In art and calligraphy, this means that a particular composition will be copied and recopied over time, until a masterpiece emerges to become the standard. Such "forging," in the sense both of fabricating and of moving ahead, is what invests quality in the tradition. It is how culture is wrought.

NOTES

1. Amélie O. Rorty, "The Deceptive Self: Liars, Layers, and Lairs," in *Perspectives on Self-Deception*, ed. B. McLaughlin and A. Rorty (Berkeley: University of California Press, 1988).

2. David Hall and I first used this focus-field language with reference to the Chinese tradition in trying to find a vocabulary for Confucian cosmology in *Thinking Through Confucius* (Albany: State University of New York Press, 1987). I then used it to discuss the Confucian self in "The Focus-Field Self in Classical Confucianism" in *Self as Person in Asian Theory and Practice*, ed. Roger T. Ames, Thomas P. Kasulis, and Wimal Dissanayake (Albany: State University of New York Press, 1994).

Self and Deception

3. I am using the term *anarchic*—without principles—to suggest the absence of underlying metaphysical assumptions.

4. The *locus classicus* that expresses this interdependence among dimensions of order is the opening passage of the *Great Learning* (*ta hsüeh*).

5. Denis Twitchett and Michael Loewe, eds., *The Cambridge History of China Volume 1: The Ch'in and Han Empires 221 B.C.–A.D. 220* (Cambridge: Cambridge University Press, 1986).

6. Yü Ying-shih, "Han Foreign Relations," in *The Cambridge History of China Volume 1: The Ch'in and Han Empires 221 B.C.–A.D. 220* (Cambridge: Cambridge University Press, 1986), 379–80.

7. Ibid., 382.

8. The fact that this sense of history continues even today can be illustrated by examining contemporary Chinese thinkers. When Mao Tse-tung, for example, defines the relationship between any single event and the course of history in his 1937 essay, "On Contradictions," he is articulating a classic principle of Chinese historiography rather than translating Marxist-Leninist dialectics into Chinese. See "On Contradictions," *Selected Works*, vol. 2, 1937–1938 (New York: International Publishers, 1954), 13–53.

9. Rudolf Arnheim, *The Power of the Center: A Study in the Visual Arts* (Berkeley: University of California Press, 1982), vii.

10. Ibid., 2.

11. Ibid., 5.

12. John S. Major, "The Five Phases, Magic Squares, and Schematic Cosmography," in *Explorations in Early Chinese Cosmology*, ed. Henry Rosemont, Jr. (Chico, CA: Scholars Press, 1984).

13. Maureen Robertson, "Periodization in the Arts and Patterns of Change in Traditional Chinese Literary History," in *Theories of the Arts in China*, ed. Susan Bush and Christian Murck (Princeton: Princeton University Press, 1983).

14. Robertson, 3–4.

15. Hall and Ames, *Thinking Through Confucius*.

16. See Liang Tsung-chieh (Liang Congjie), "Non-Congruent Circles: The Organization of Encyclopedic Knowledge in Chinese and Western Cultures," originally published in Chinese in *Towards the Future* no. 2, 1986, and translated for *Philosophy East and West* (forthcoming). The limitations on this comparison between Western encyclopedias and Chinese *lei-shu* arise when we consider the function of these compilations in each of the traditions. The fact that the *lei-shu* were generally commissioned by the throne as a resource for indoctrinating an emerging bureaucracy has to be taken into account.

17. Ambrose King, "The Individual and Group in Confucianism: A Relational Perspective," in *Individualism and Holism: Studies in Confucian and Taoist Values*, ed. Donald Munro (Ann Arbor: University of Michigan Press, 1985), 58.

18. *Analects* 14:35.

19. Herbert Fingarette, *Confucius: The Secular as Sacred* (New York: Harper, 1972), 133.

20. Ibid., 135.

21. Roger T. Ames, "Reflections on the Confucian Self: A Response to Fingarette," in *Rules, Rituals, and Responsibility: Essays Dedicated to Herbert Fingarette*, ed. Mary I. Bockover (La Salle: Open Court, 1991), 103–14; Herbert Fingarette, "Comment and Response: Roger T. Ames," 194–200.

22. Jacques Gernet, *China and the Christian Impact: A Conflict of Cultures*, trans. Janet Lloyd (Cambridge: Cambridge University Press, 1985), 147.

23. *Chuang Tzu* 17.

24. Ibid., 6.

25. This is the last passage in *Chuang Tzu* 7. Compare A. C. Graham, trans., *Chuang-Tzu: The Inner Chapters* (London: George Allen & Unwin, 1981), 98.

26. The expression *hun-tun* 渾沌 (or *hun-t'un*), here translated "Chaos," requires comment. Angus Graham in rendering this anecdote into English refuses to translate *hun-tun* at all, insisting it must not be confused with what we generally mean by "chaos":

> Hun-t'un is the primal blob which first divided into heaven and earth and then differentiated as the myriad things. In Chinese cosmology the primordial is not a chaos reduced to order by imposed law, it is a blend of everything rolled up together; the word is a reduplicative of the type of English "hotchpotch" and "rolypoly," and diners in Chinese restaurants will have met it in the form "wuntun" as a kind of dumpling.

See A. C. Graham, trans. *Chuang-tzu*, 98–99. Dollops of minced meat are enfolded into amorphous "skin" wrappers which are then immersed to cook in rapidly boiling water. This pot full of tasty "wuntuns" flapping about wildly in the roiling water, then, is the Chinese image of chaos.

27. Vietnam, like Korea and Ryuku, for example, was historically defined so comprehensively by Chinese culture and institutions that even in our contemporary world there are some real questions as to its membership in Southeast Asia as opposed to East Asia.

28. This notion of parochial self-sufficiency seems to be the pattern at the local level as well as on a national scale. A town qualifies as a "city" (*shih*) on the basis of its complete complement of industries and services.

29. See Yü Ying-shih, *Trade and Expansion in Han China* (Berkeley: University of California Press, 160–61.

30. *Analects* 2:4.

31. Ibid., 2:17.

32. See *Analects* 3:11, 5:8, 7:28, 9:8, and 13:3.

33. See "Prolegomena to a Confucian Epistemology," in *Culture and Modernity: East-West Philosophical Perspectives*, ed. Eliot Deutsch (Honolulu: University of Hawaii Press, 1991); "Confucius and the Ontology of Knowing," in *Interpreting Across Boundaries*, ed. G. Larson and Eliot Deutsch (Princeton: Princeton University Press, 1988).

Self and Deception

34. See, for example, *Analects* 3:1, 3:2, 3:6, 3:18, 3:22, 5:25, 9:12, 12:20, 14:31, 17:17, 17:18.
35. *Analects* 17:11.
36. *Mencius* 7B:37.
37. Ibid.
38. Ibid.

ELEVEN

OUR NAMES ARE LEGION FOR WE ARE MANY

On the Academics[1] of Deception

David L. Hall

This volume takes as its theme, not "Self-Deception," but "Self *and* Deception." The major thrust of this chapter will concern the subject of "deception" in the more ordinary of its senses, allowing me to skirt along the edges of the truly problematic notion of self-deceptive behavior. I intend, in fact, to avoid too much explicit discussion of deception per se, concentrating on providing a context within which the phenomenon of deceptive behavior might be assayed in a variety of manners.

The title of this chapter is not meant to allude to the notion of self as a repertory of alternative personality constructs, though that is a legitimate implication. The "many" in the title refers primarily to the many meanings of self embedded in our self-descriptive vocabularies and the theories, systematic and informal, which entail and are entailed by these descriptions, along with the various practices which they enjoin or for which they serve explanatory functions. A second important sort of manyness with which this chapter is concerned is the plurality of significances which may be attached to each of the terms (at least the crucial ones) which are employed in significant acts of communication.

The most important relationship between this massive plurality and the phenomenon of deception is this: The various candidates for the meaning of self, and for the meanings of the terminologies used by selves to communicate with other selves, are embedded in our linguistic practices in tightly clustered, intransigently ambiguous, constructs which even the cleverest and sincerest efforts at stipulation cannot clarify or render necessarily consistent with the practices relevant to them. And as "we" are largely constituted by the vocabularies we employ to describe ourselves and to account for our ideas, feelings, and actions, we are all ambiguated selves. The relevance of this phenomenon to the subject of "self and deception" is that the vagueness of our language of self-understanding, as well as the vagueness of the principal terms we employ in our efforts to communicate—

Self and Deception

a vagueness that has accrued through the course of the history of our intellectual culture—requires that our present communicative practices mix ignorance and awareness in such a manner as to raise the question of deception.

However else one might wish to talk about deception of others and of oneself, the seeds of deceptive behavior are present in our frequent and (apparently) unavoidable resort to the plural entendre. Moreover, as the subtitle of this essay suggests, it is among intellectuals (particularly that subclass of intellectuals called "academics") that the greatest potentiality for deceptive behavior exists, since it is the intellectual whose intentions and anticipations are most explicitly shaped by the complex vocabularies of self-articulation.

THE AMBIGUATED SELF

In a previous essay on the subject of the self,[2] I offered a narrative which focused upon certain moments in the development of philosophical concepts of the self. That narrative is rehearsed here in the briefest of manners in order to suggest that in the course of the raising of our selves to the level of consciousness, both we and the vocabularies we employ in our communicative practices have become increasingly "vague."[3]

The historical development of the semantics of selfhood begins with Homer's early employment of *thymos, noos,* and *psyche* as names for the person[4] and Plato's treatment of the soul as a tripartite structure owning the functions of spirit (*thymoiodes*), appetite (*epithymetikon*), and reason (*logistikon*). Plato wrote the soul large, finding analogies between the parts of the psyche and the classes of the state. Aristotle carried this analogy in a slightly different direction by analogizing between the parts of the soul and the theoretical, practical, and productive disciplines defining the complex of cultural interests. Both Plato and Aristotle—the former by appeal to the four levels of the clarity of knowledge, the latter by recourse to his taxonomy of the four causes—further ramified these analogical operations by adumbrating four sorts of theoretical perspective which eventually would take on names like *materialism, idealism, volitionalism,* and *organic naturalism.*

The elements of reason, appetite, and will or thought, action, and passion grew to be so much a part of the problematic of self that some characterization of these elements appears in almost any full-scale treatment of personality, ancient and modern. We find more than echoes of this psychic structure in Augustine's treatment of the *imago dei,* in Kant's critiques of the value spheres (the aesthetic, moral, and scientific), in Hegel's dialectical analysis of consciousness, as well as in Freud's psychoanalytic categories of ego, superego, and id.

Modern conceptions of the self are dependent upon the modalities of knowing, acting, feeling associated with a variety of models of personality developed in conjunction with the Platonic and Aristotelian taxonomies associated with the divided line and the four causes. The ages-long transmogrifications of the notion of self from Homer to the present can be told as the self's journey from the Many to the One, from the disparate and unfocused actions, dispositions, and understandings which variously expressed the human mode of being in its world to the unity of the individual human being. Unfortunately, at least for the aims of the rationalist, this press toward unity created a new plurality, a plurality of ways of characterizing the unity of the person.

The human adventure seems now to have turned about and has begun to retrace its path, moving from One to Many. The "postmodern" self well might be the original disparate self, but with a remarkable difference. What is left over from the failed project of the Enlightenment, which sought in the unity of rational selfconsciousness the highest expression of human sensibility, is not, of course, the unity of the self but the consciousness of self as a candidate for a variety of distinctive interpretations. This consciousness is, among intellectuals, a kind of "metamentality"—a consciousness of the options for shaping one's conscious (and unconscious) lives.

There are a number of possible responses to this situation. We may take a dogmatic stance which opts for some particular version of the self-descriptive categories, attempting either to ignore or to refute our rivals. Alternatively, we can take the position that none of the alternatives is viable and seek a new, more adequate vocabulary, thus adding to the inventory of theories which articulate the self. Or we can take the stance of the pluralists—those taxonomists who classify or organize the various theoretical visions without seeking to argue for the superiority of any view or views. I am concerned with this latter response.

The pluralist movement is associated with the systematic and interpretative pluralisms of thinkers such as Richard McKeon and Stephen Pepper.[5] Stephen Pepper's *World Hypotheses*[6] provided a taxonomy of ways of thinking in terms of a selection of hypothetical constructs, each of which is thought to ground a coherent characterization of the world. These hypotheses—formism, mechanism, contextualism, organicism—are grounded in "root metaphors" (similarity, machines, historic events, organism). These hypotheses, together with their root metaphors, characterize general directions in thinking, as well as more formal systems of thought.

Each of these visions was derived, according to Pepper, by assessing actual ways of thinking. Each serves as a relatively complete means of operating with, and interpreting, the data of intellectual culture. Any attempt to organize two or more of them into a more general theory would be doomed due to the fact that they function as closed systems, autonomous languages.

A second major twentieth-century metatheorist is Richard McKeon, who developed a semantics of philosophic views by appeal to logical and rhetorical categories.[7] Through the analysis of the categories of things, thoughts, words, and terms, or selections, methods, principles, and interpretations (notions analogized from the Aristotelian doctrine of the four causes), McKeon was able to formulate what he held to be exhaustive categories permitting him to classify systematic philosophers and to assay the lineaments of potential controversies engendered by the co-presence of mutually incompatible forms of thinking. Pluralists of this systematic variety ground their taxonomic interests upon the irreducible diversity of ways of thinking.

The aim of the metatheoretical pluralist is not dialectical refutation nor the resort to dismissive reductionism; his purpose is rather to account for the variety and diversity of viewpoints. Such thinking remains legitimately pluralistic only if it discovers some means other than logical or rational organization to realize the appropriate ordering of the insistent particulars which comprise our psychological, social, and natural environs[8]—for the aim of rationality is clear consensus consciously entertained, a consensus which guarantees that stipulated ideas lead to practices consistent with them.

What Pepper and McKeon have done is to provide tools for the consideration of types of thinking which had been accepted under more informal classifications, such as Platonism, naturalism, idealism, pragmatism, and so on. The effect of raising to the level of consciousness the variety of ways of thinking, and then of demonstrating not only the relative adequacy of schemes of thought, but their closed status as semantic systems invulnerable to the dialectical arguments emergent from alternative points of view, is to cancel a principal motive for intertheoretical engagement. For the more aware we become of the variety of autonomous visions, the greater is our indifference to the questions of adequacy or inadequacy of the selected alternatives comprising the elements of their taxonomic schemes. Moreover, the proponents of single theories become increasingly aloof and unresponsive to any engagement with alternative views.

The physiologists's characterization of human behavior in terms of neuronal firings, Freud's reduction of human experience and expression to libido, and of human culture to sublimated products of libidinal sexuality, along with B. F. Skinner's reckoning of human individuality by appeal to contingencies of reinforcement in local environments, establish a materialist axis in Western culture which goes back through Thomas Hobbes, who conceived individuals as matter swirling in social space, to Democritus, who believed that men were mere collocations of atoms who "emerged from the ground like worms, without a maker and for no reason."[9]

At the opposite extreme from this materialist interpretation lies the characterization of personality by appeal to mind, consciousness, or reason. Plato's characterization of psyche in terms of the guidance of the rational element, Hegel's claim that "the real is the rational," and Husserl's delineation of the transcendental ego, are points on a line constituting the rational axis of interpretation.

In addition to these interpretations that emphasize the solitariness of the self, there are two others that stress the self as a function of social and or political contextualization. Aristotle's naturalism, which conceived the human being as a language-bearing organism whose experience is constituted by social interactions, received elaboration and nuance in George Herbert Mead's and John Dewey's visions of the mutually constitutive relationships of self and social ambiance. This social view persists in a variety of forms in sociology, social psychology, and political science.

The volitional tradition persists in the twentieth century both as a poetic vision and as a political vision which characterizes personality as a function of persuasive power. This view is political insofar as it promotes power relationships as the contexts within which meaningful human existence is to be found. This vision may be construed poetically insofar as the position enjoins self-creativity by appeal to new metaphors of the self. The powerful and/or creative person is the most authentic by virtue of the fact that she establishes the context of meaning within which others articulate themselves. Michel Foucault's critique of the conspiracy of knowledge and power in the formation of social institutions, and Derrida's virtuosic deconstruction of the coherence of the texts of our tradition instance this volitional turn in contemporary philosophy.

What does it mean to be an individual? A physiological mechanism swirling in social space? A mind or consciousness detachable from its bodily housing? An acting, willing, deciding creature whose meaning is determined by persuasive efficacy? A socially interactive, goal achieving organism? The usual response to these questions when posed by systematic or interpretative pluralists is either flailing hostility or the smuggest of indifference. This would suggest that the pluralist movement has hardly been seriously engaged by other than its own practitioners. However, I would claim that the movement not only is an attempt to classify abstract theoretical

Self and Deception

schemes, but is associated as well with the rationalization of practices constituting the sphere of public praxis. Typologies do not simply chart once and future *philosophical views,* they can as easily be seen as organizing principles deemed relevant to the variety of intellectual disciplines (physics, sociology, history, literary criticism), as well as the plurality of public practices—educational, political, economic, eleemosynary. Said another way, materialisms, idealisms, and so on, may name not only types of worldview, but types of institutionalized practice, as well.[10] If this is the case, then what otherwise might seem a rather silly supposition—namely, that the alternative vocabularies of self-description and communicative interaction ambiguate the selves contextualized by them—becomes, if not plausible, at least credible. For each of us, particularly the academic intellectual, is immersed in the morass of alternative vocabularies of self-description and the practices which are both occasions for and consequences of those vocabularies.

But quite apart from the more general sense of pluralism, there is real evidence that pluralistic philosophy has directly influenced our intellectual culture. For example, one may note the influence of Richard McKeon upon generations of philosophers, social scientists, and literary critics. I grant that many of McKeon's students found his taxonomic approach to the history of philosophy, while providing a powerful set of tools for textual analysis, somewhat stultifying. McKeon students have often found it difficult to escape the typological mentality and have become bedazzled curators of others' thoughts rather than original thinkers in their own right. But McKeon has influenced individuals of a more creative bent as well. Richard Rorty may be a case in point.[11]

Rorty's approach to the problems of relativism and intertheoretical communication may be seen as his particular means of escaping from the taxonomists' net. His first effort is evident as early as 1961[12] when, after distinguishing approaches to metaphilosophy into three principal types, with a variety of subcategories, Rorty endorses metaphilosophical pragmatism as a view which sees "philosophy as the greatest game of all precisely because it is the game of 'changing the rules' "[13]

Pragmatic metaphilosophers are *meta*-metaphilosophers. "Metametaphilosophy makes possible communication among metaphilosophers [and] since communication is the goal, rather than truth (or even agreement), the prospective infinite series is a progress rather than a regress: it becomes a moral duty to keep the series going, lest communication cease."[14]

If one treats "truth" pragmatically in terms of the "satisfaction of needs" and if one claims that the need philosophy best satisfies is that of communication, then, in our age of hyperconsciousness, the pragmatist trained in the arcane arts of philosophy has no moral choice other than to be a metaphilosopher. This outlook, Rorty contends, "is fairly close to the attitude Dewey adopted toward the history of philosophy."[15] In his metaphilosophical pragmatism Rorty differs very little from the thinking of Pepper and McKeon.

Rorty's second response to the metaphilosophical character of our contemporary period involves his treatment of philosophical relativism. Rorty believes relativism to be the reddest of herrings. Sophomoric formulations of relativist positions such as "Everybody has a right to his opinion" and "Any belief is as a good as any another" are too crude to count for very much. No one, upon interrogation, would hold to such a view. However, nuanced formulations of relativism in terms of the incommensurability of semantic contexts leading to the irrefutability of one theory by another err in the other direction. Such convictions are sound enough but irrelevant to the actual circumstances which define the sphere of praxis to which theories are meant to be applicable.

Rorty distinguishes between *philosophical* theories and *real* theories—the former constituting schemes which serve to ground special theories; the latter constituting detailed and specific formulations pertinent to concrete issues in physics or politics.[16] Relativism with respect to philosophical theories does not entail relativism of real theories. We might easily accede to the relativity of Pepper's world hypotheses or McKeon's types of semantic systems, but that is a rather empty and unproductive assent. When it comes to the specific ways in which Platonic, Aristotelian, Kantian, or Heideggerian language is employed to address issues of technical or practical concern, we are no longer relativists—we reflect upon, discuss, and debate the alternatives with the realization of specific desires in mind.

I believe Rorty is a very good illustration of a thinker who has taken seriously a very serious problem. Theoretical pluralism (if not the relativism that threatens to come along with it) is a fundamental, intransigent aspect of our intellectual culture. Most philosophers (along with other assorted academics and intellectuals) attempt to ignore the phenomenon, maintaining a rather closed-minded preference for their own particular theories, believing (it seems) that wan hope coupled with bold rhetoric can eventually carry the day.

I do agree with Rorty (among many others) that philosophy is pretty much done for if we continue to expend the major portion of our energies pumping out newer, subtler versions of the same old same-old. As one of the few outside the ranks of the pluralist movement to engage the issues of theoretical pluralism at a sophisticated level, Rorty well understands that the metatheorist's views are relevant both to the theoretical and to the practical spheres. There are serious problems attending the acts of defining one's terms at the request of another, or the rationalizing of a practice, or the employment of an action to demonstrate the meaning of an idea or belief. The clarity and articulation often required in order to respond to questions such as, What do you mean by that? or Why did you do that? or Would you show me what you mean? are more than likely to mitigate than to promote the aims of communication.

Consider the question of the relationship between political principles and practices. Rorty argues that pragmatic liberalism can get along quite well without articulating a theory of human nature. The communitarians' claim that political institutions are no better than the philosophical principles that ground them may be reshaped into the pragmatic claim that the philosophical ideas used to articulate liberal institutions are constructed by reflections upon those institutions. It is the institutions that "justify" such reflections, not the reverse.

Far from merely inverting the relationship between principles and their practical implementation, Rorty treats principles as "reminders of practices, not supports for them."[17] In this way he is permitted to avoid articulating the relationship between his actions and his reasons for acting. In a liberal democratic society, such articulation can lead to conflict due to the fact that alternative justifications for a practice are possible. What was relatively harmonious at the level of action can lead to real ideological conflict.

Rorty's defense of the refusal to clarify overmuch the relations of principles and practice is valuable. I confess that I am not as optimistic as Rorty seems to be about our ability to avoid the relativizing effects of pluralism by distinguishing *merely philosophical* theories from real ones. The philosopher (or any other theory monger), having raised to the level of consciousness the plurality of systems and narratives within which important terminologies are developed, is hard pressed to background at will all but the single one relevant to his particular concerns.

What is perhaps most novel among the defining characteristics of late modern intellectual culture is the degree of our theoretical awareness. This awareness forces intellectuals into a mode of hyperconsciousness in which, if they are to engage the history of ideas, they must try to encompass a variety of diverse, mutually incompatible, ways of thinking. Responsible intellectuals then become, at the very least (if only tacitly), pluralists who formally or informally employ conceptual and metaphorical classifications to sort and organize their interlocutors prior to assessing their views. The purpose of such activity cannot be the search for truth or the realization of consensus, only the promotion of a context within which communication is made possible. The effect of such bloated consciousness is that stipulations which aim at selecting a single, univocal meaning for a concept from among a variety of possible meanings are often simply unsuccessful. When they are successful, they lead to the alienation and idiosyncrasy of the closed-shop mentality, which leads to the abdication of the intellectual's duty to engage his peers.

On the face of it, the claims I am making might appear absurd. Why should I believe that the character of the selves inhabiting a society of pluralistic beliefs and institutions would be ambiguated? This certainly seems to place too much weight on the potential consequences of "mere" vocabularies. The best explanation I can give for the apparent extremity of my views is that I am unable to believe that any of us is detachable from the full range of ideas and affects deposited in the intellectual culture in which we participate. This is to say that one is more determinate with respect to the cultural milieu in which one exists than our liberal rhetoric of autonomy would suggest.[18]

A part of my argument involves the claim that we should take Plato seriously but invert his analogical model by writing small the culture of late modernity. By modeling the soul after the plurality of visions and values characteristic of our late modern cultural sensibility, we can see contemporary selves as avatars of a fractured Absolute. The absence of a social, political, or cultural consensus entails the denial of the consensual self. This denial doesn't lead to an easygoing relativism in which everybody gets to be the sort of being he or she wishes. As vague, ambiguated selves, we are all things to all men for the sake of the gospel of (post)modernity.

CLARITY, VAGUENESS, AND THE FUTILITY OF STIPULATION

Attainment of the absolutest clarity is a romantic ideal of the reasoning creature. Clarity of the logical and semantic sort is associated with univocal definition which guarantees unambiguous usage. Normally, clarity may be contrasted with confusion—a state of unarticulated ideas or feelings. But, if we are to make sense of our hyperconscious era, it is important to contrast "clarity" not only with "confused" or "muddled" ideas but with "vague" notions or feelings, as well.

Muddled ideas are essentially unarticulatable because potential senses of the notion cannot, for whatever reason, be sorted into meaningful units. However, vague ideas are richly determinable in the sense that a variety of meanings are associated with them. Leaving muddled thinking aside, we may distinguish two primary senses of vagueness—semantic and pragmatic.[19]

A concept is semantically vague by virtue of its possession of a number of actual or potential interpretations. Both concepts and actions may be

Self and Deception

pragmatically vague. A concept is said to be pragmatically vague when a number of discrete actions are occasioned by it. The vagueness of an action is a function of the number of ways it might be rationalized.

Semantic vagueness may be either "literal" or "metaphorical." Literal vagueness is the consequence of our contemporary metamentality. Notions such as 'freedom' and 'love' are literally vague in the sense that a number of stipulatable senses, derived from a variety of theoretical contexts, may be unpacked from the locution. Metaphorical vagueness is the sort of richness associated with the new uses of words. It is from metaphors that new meanings emerge.[20]

Both clarity and vagueness might be contextualized in yet another manner. We might distinguish between intratheoretical and intertheoretical forms of vagueness and clarity. In the first instance, terms are either stipulated or not within the context of a single theoretical context. In the second instance, the putatively same locution is provided alternative stipulations by appeal to two or more theories.[21] For the sophisticated intellectual in late modern culture, terms are almost always both semantically and pragmatically vague. Further, this clarity is, largely, of the literal sort. That is, both with respect to the meanings of one's ideas, and the practices associated with them, vagueness reigns. There are "one to many" relations among ideas and their definitions, and "many to one" relations among practices and the ideas that are presumed to initiate or to interpret them.

It is useful to consider pragmatic and semantic versions of vagueness in terms of historical and intertheoretical varieties:[22] Historical vagueness is a complex form of pragmatic vagueness resulting from the co-presence of alternative narratives accounting for the relation of the present to the past. With regard to the subject of intellectual culture, these narratives may begin with Plato or with Kant; with respect to our political culture, they may begin with Plato or with the French Revolution. Historians of modern scientific culture might wish to begin with Kepler, Newton, or Bacon.

There is a relation between Nietzsche's idea of active forgetting and my use of the term *vagueness*. There are at least two viable senses of active forgetting: One sense would require either a suppression or a strong misreading of any narrative which would threaten one's own creative agency. A second sense involves the foregrounding of all perspectives upon an object which establishes the truth about the object as the total of interpretations. In the latter sense, the burden of the past is not felt since there is no single best manner of interpreting. Thus by denying the exclusivity of a particular meaning or meanings, maintaining the sum of interpretations as a vague cluster, we can achieve the ends of active forgetting.

Intertheoretical vagueness is a type of semantic vagueness occasioned by the refusal or inability to employ a term in a single stipulated sense. Gregory Bateson discusses intertheoretical vagueness under the rubric of "Learning III,"[23] which involves an awareness of the context of theoretical contexts leading to an experience of the parity of theories. The self as "a habit of acting in contexts and of shaping and perceiving the contexts in which [it] act[s]" is radically redefined by such experience. Ch'an or Zen Buddhism seeks the dissolution, or decentering, of the self by the employment of the *kung-an* or *koan*—a conceptual puzzle that requires the compresent entertainment of inconsistent meanings.

To the reasonably aware, reasonably well-trained, philosopher, intertheoretical vagueness is a species of literal vagueness in which ambiguated concepts have a variety of stipulated senses attached to them, much as barnacles to the hull of a ship. To the squinting eye of reason, these are nothing more than mutated grotesques, but to a more open gaze they are seen to be perhaps the most representative artifacts of our hyperconscious age. They are "cluster concepts."

Now, if we ask about the consequences to the acts of communication of the loss of the metaphysical comfort of a final essence and the historical comfort of a single narrative thread, the simplest response is that, under the conditions of having to operate in a context in which the principal self-descriptive and communicative vocabularies are vague, the self is *permanently ambiguated* or (in more fashionable language) *decentered*. The entertainment of a vague notion involves self-ambiguation—the decentering of ideational, practical, or affective modalities of the personality. We are all little Hamlets, urged from within to substitute "and" for "or" at the crucial moment in our soliloquies.

This is not to suggest that this is what most of us who call ourselves "intellectuals" believe we are doing. It is rather what we perforce must do, whether we recognize it or not. To state the case as baldly as possible: When we assert, we often do so oxymoronically. When we *mean*, we often mean *inconsistently*. We cannot avoid asserting or meaning more than we consciously intend.

Odd as this claim may seem, there is substantial evidence for it. This and the following sections will instance the following: (1) the difficulty of achieving clarity by stipulation or definition and (2) the inability to establish any unproblematic connection between principles and practice. The thesis which these evidences defend is that both semantic and pragmatic vagueness are, generally speaking, unavoidable. An equally problematic claim, one which I shall not defend in this context,[24] is that such vagueness is a causal determinant of the character of selves and their communicative acts.

Self and Deception

We have all caused our students not a little suffering by mimicking Socrates's carping insistence upon definitions rather than instances or examples. Were we to take Confucius as our pedagogical model, we would insist that our students come up with an example, a model. Thus Confucius wouldn't ask after the definition of "virtue"; he would call for an example of a virtuous person. This virtuous person—one of the sage kings (Yao or Shun)—is one about whom stories would have been told, one to whom one would be *disposed*.

For such a pathos-based appeal to be effective, meanings would have to be somewhat fixed by appeal to communally entertained emotional associations. That is, meanings would not be fixed by objective reference since the crucial terms of the language would not be left to chance variations among forms of emotional associations. The consistency of emotional response and dispositional activity can be depended upon to insure that words are communicable in an efficacious and harmonious manner.

In the extreme, a community grounded in this manner would have to be reasonably uniform as regards ethnicity and language, as was, of course, classical Chinese society. It could not afford to have significant contacts with alternative communities whose members would have a different inventory of emotional responses, or contrasting semantic systems of meaning, or who would demand objective reference as a condition of meaning.

Something of the pathos-based interest is retained in rhetorical theory in the West. A survey of rhetoric texts would yield the following meanings of connotation and denotation with respect to exercise of definition: Denotation is simply the dictionary definition of a term, while connotation is the emotional baggage carried by a word or term. At the level of connotation, one may be disposed toward (or away from) a word.

However, any good logic text would use the following language: Denotation refers to all of the items serving as members of the class named by the word. Connotation indicates all of the common properties owned by the members of the named class. Occasionally, but not always, a logic text will divide connotation into objective and subjective senses, allowing in the latter case for the rhetorical use of terms. The message of such texts is that if we define our terms precisely enough and construct propositions with sufficient care, we can employ arguments in a manner so as to express our thoughts with clarity and cogency. Rhetoric texts speak another language. By omitting consideration of objective connotation, language is treated as a strictly persuasive medium in which the "emotional baggage" is paramount.

No one consults a dictionary any longer to discover *the* meaning of a word. Dictionaries provide us a plethora of meanings of any given word. Moreover, the academic intellectual has usually encountered the alternative

On the Academics of Deception

theoretical contexts within which a given locution takes on its various meanings. Therefore, the demand that one stipulate or define a concept advertises both the narrowness of any particular univocal sense and the plurality of alternative significances available.

Lately, another serious blow has been dealt to the concern for univocity. The belief in subjective connotation as constitutive of the meaning of a word or term is creeping back into our professional philosophic discourse. One of the distinctive aspects of the pun-ishing idiosyncratics of the later Derrida[25] is the manner in which he manipulates the emotional baggage of words. Likewise, Richard Rorty's praise for Harold Bloom's strong poet as the creator of new metaphors and his urging that we should "let a thousand vocabularies blossom" press philosophic thinking away from the scientific and toward the literary mode of reflection.

There is a real question as to the degree to which stipulations aiming at either intra- or intertheoretical clarity serve the ends of communication. Often the greater the clarity of opposing views, the greater is our assurance that we have not communicated anything other than the extent of our disagreements. Even if we find that we agree by virtue of sharing the same theory, a next level of clarification may lead to a further theoretical split.

The first consequence of clarification is either to set up opposing semantic contexts or to create a context in which agreement is (temporarily) achieved. If the former is the result, our ships either will pass in the night, or will collide in a storm. Neither alternative leads to effective communication. If the latter is the consequence, increased levels of clarification lead to differences in understanding the meaning and the import of the explicated notions or propositions and we find ourselves back to indifference or unproductive conflict.

In any given intellectual discipline, sophisticated theoretical activity could lead to the generation of a large number of closed systems. In principle, we could strive for a situation in intellectual culture in which no unambiguous uses of language remain. Vagueness would be lost. If there is no viable realm of unprofessionalized or demotic discourse, intertheoretical engagement is impossible since the constitutive rules of alternative discourses frustrate communication across ruled-defined boundaries. We see this phenomenon with the contrast of alternative axiomatic systems within a given scientific discipline. Such systems have as their aim the exclusion of anything like intertheoretical vagueness. The extremes of clarity would lead to a situation in which there are as many languages as language users. A promoter of such an "idiolect" view gets as close to solipsism as possible without the stars (in all but her sky) beginning to blink out.

Self and Deception

Axiomatized language may be the paradigm of clarity, but communication succeeds at this level of clarity only if, *per impossibile*, the communicants employing the language agree on the stipulations. This agreement is harder to realize than one might think. One may instance the creation and subsequent interpretation of Whitehead and Russell's *Principia Mathematicia*. The general philosophical dispositions of the two men were, of course, vastly distinct. Their interpretations of the axioms housing their views on the relations of mathematics to logic were subsequently just as diverse.

The consequence of clarification is the generation of opposition and closed systems. The final result is a move toward opposing idiolects with increasingly fewer communicants employing the same language. The ignominious end is the fall into a "solipsism by default."[26]

If we try to stipulate in too refined a manner, we risk the creation of alternative semantic contexts which are not productively related one to the other. The standard way of saying this is to claim that if language S_1 relativizes concepts $t_{1...n}$ and language S_2 relativizes concepts $r_{1...n}$, then the immediately preceding English sentence entails the consequence that (assuming s_1 is the English language) S_1 relativizes both $t_{1...n}$ and $r_{1...n}$. Thus, the intent of the English sentence, *"Knowledge" and the Chinese word, chih 知, have quite distinctive conceptual contents* is compromised by the fact that the norms of the English language determine the meanings of the sentence, including of course, the English meaning of the Chinese word, *chih*.

Perhaps each of us owns his or her own language. These private languages then beg for translations each into the others. But, of course, no transformational rules or translation equivalents could be possible under such circumstances. This solipsism results from Cartesianism gone bad. The recognition that such a consequence is inevitable on the Cartesian model leads to behaviorist and instrumental models of language which presumably do not require that one look inside one's own or another's "mind" or "experience" for "meanings." Such causal theories of communication claim that it is not the logic and semantics of the language, but the causal efficacy, the rhetorical force, of locutions that permits communication.

A typical response to this overly sophisticated production of theories is to make the quasi-Wittgensteinian claim that intellectual culture ought be constituted by "language communities" within or among social or cultural contexts which are constituted by alternative rules. In the model Wittgenstein proposes, although there is never any final assurance that two people are playing precisely the same game, this must be the presumption in many cases. What makes two games similar is that they both have rules. However, the specificity of the rules of different games militates against participation in both games at once. But this is just another argument for intertheoretical vagueness.

VAGUENESS AND DECEPTION

The vagueness of our language guarantees that we say more than we can coherently mean. Thus, academics, college professors, high-brow intellectuals—those who read lots and lots of books and are involved in a reasonably active life and who talk to many sorts of individuals (including, occasionally, some nonintellectuals)—ought not be altogether too optimistic about their ability to communicate. For they know very well that words have histories of accrued meanings; they are aware of the evidences of the systematic and interpretative pluralists to the effect that there are a number of incompatible semantic contexts from which meanings are drawn for our vocabularies.

Academic intellectuals, the decentered selves of (late-?) (post-?) modern society, know that "freedom" can mean free choice amidst limiting circumstances, or a kind of knowledge, or the realization of determination, or the power of the willing, deciding creature. Love can mean sexual passion, a meeting of minds, feelings and actions associated with procreation, or conquest and seduction. When we say the word *freedom*, can we successfully stipulate in such a manner as to *effectively* exclude other semantic associations than the one we announce? Given the association of love with lust (in addition to its finer meanings) and of freedom with license (as well as its nobler meanings), can we really avoid the consciously unintended connotations of the terms when we use the words *love* and *freedom*?

The important terms in our conversations are all richly vague semantic clusters, which are formed by combining different senses of the term. Every stipulative act threatens to raise alternative meanings to the level of consciousness. Stipulations tend to take the form of expressions such as *I come to bury Caesar, not to praise him*, or *I will not speak of my opponent's prison record* or *I shall by no means mention the name of that foul offal excreted by the bowels of animals and human beings—including, of course, the modest Celia*.

Among the really high-brows, at least, communication is a parapraxial exercise in which, except now and again, usually by accident, and only with respect to our most formalized discourse, we speak or write as clustered selves expressing clustered meanings. In the attempt to master the texts of her culture, the intellectual is fragmented, decentered, destabilized through a continued encounter with intentionally vague, or unsuccessfully stipulated, cluster concepts.

Self and Deception

Terms characterized by recourse to a cluster indifferent to the question of logical coordination are, nonetheless, contextually defined. Such "definitions" must result from aesthetic juxtapositions which highlight the tensions of contrasting and conflicting referential associations against the background of an aesthetically complex, if logically inconsistent, context. Our understanding of such terms would have to be closer to the experience of "enjoyment" and "appreciation" than to that of an act of grasping cognizable import. The only hope of accommodating the incoherences, incongruences, and inconsistencies embedded in cluster concepts is that the self appropriating these notions must be of the same flexible form as the notions themselves. In this case, a mind becoming like that which it knows leads to a seriously ambiguated self.

What meaning can a cluster have if the semantic elements are mutually inconsistent and yet in some complicated manner may be shown to possess their meaning by virtue of the clustering process? Meaning is a funny thing, as we all know. We might consider the meaning of x as the possible senses associated with x. Or we might insist upon dealing with the subject of meaning solely within the context of a communicative act, in which case we would need to concern ourselves both with the "intended" and with the "anticipated" meanings of x. It is this latter sense with which we must be concerned.

We presume that communication requires that the intentions of the addressor match the anticipations of her addressee. Under what conditions is such a presumption realistic? I would argue that there may be no empirical situations which would assure either party to a conversation that a harmony of intention and anticipation has been realized.

But the likelihood of such harmony must be presumed in advance if we are going make the effort to communicate. One person cannot presume to communicate with another unless there is an expectation that his intended meaning will match her range of anticipations. Thus when the line *Never pain to tell thy love* is expressed, the speaker or writer (William Blake in the first instance) must tacitly or explicitly believe that the range of anticipated meanings for "pain" in the minds of his readers or listeners would include (if only after seeing the locution in its context) "attempt," "exert oneself." If he could not, for whatever reason, believe this, he could not attempt in good faith to communicate.

Now, if both anticipated and intended meanings are vague in the sense employed in this essay, at least the intention of the speaker or writer is problematic. A vague intention may be no intention at all. There is a paradox afoot here. For if one stipulates sufficiently to focus one's intentions, he will fall heir to all of the problems of the pursuit of clarity rehearsed above. If he leaves his intentions vague and anticipates vagueness in the anticipated meanings of his communicant, then the sense in which he could be said to be intending truth or falsity is in question. And if *that* is in question, then we are hard put to say how the individual would be capable of deception in any form.

I recall the complaint of an older student in one of my philosophy classes to the effect that, after learning of the various meanings of the term *love* in the Western philosophic tradition, he had a serious argument with his wife of thirty-plus years when each learned that the other had "totally different meanings of love." His experience was much like that of the materialist disheartened to learn that when he touches the cheek of his lover, it is his own fingers that he feels. In this instance, when over the period of his marriage he heard the words *I love you* it was his own meaning he enjoyed.

I tried to persuade this fellow that the devotion he and his wife felt for one another should not be undermined by the idea that incommensurable meanings of 'love' at the level of theory must lead to incommensurable practices. Alternatively, their (presumed) mutual devotion over many years attested to a commonality of practice which argued against the importance of the conceptual conflict. Shared beliefs do not guarantee shared action any more than shared practices argue for shared concepts, though the latter is more likely to be the case. What was troubling to me was that the gentleman was not really satisfied by my reply. He seemed genuinely convinced that the meaning of 'love' was in the meaning of the word rather than of the associated actions.

The settled practices of the married couple in my example did not require justification. Moreover, their vague senses of 'love' did not require stipulation. Perhaps we are wise to avoid being drawn into discussions of the theoretical implications of our unannounced beliefs and our unarticulated practices as a means of maintaining the tolerant, pluralistic, and harmony-producing character of our thinking.

Communication takes place, if at all, among ambiguated selves employing vague locutions. The consequence of stipulation, or clarification is usually a frustration of communication. Most communication in a pluralistic society follows patterns not unlike that of my married couple before receiving semantic enlightenment. Demotic communication of that sort is characterized by a desirable semantic and pragmatic vagueness.

In an academic environment in which professionals are called upon to communicate from their explicit disciplinary commitments, communication is *intra-* or *inter*theoretical. Here discursive interactions may be characterized either by relative clarity or by vagueness. Too much clarity will lead to the development of closed-shop ideologies of the sort met in almost any university discipline. Instancing philosophy, for example: analysts, phenomenologists, deconstructionists tend to speak professionally to those of their own persuasion. However, vagueness will be difficult to achieve at the professional level since specialists are usually quite aware of the differences that obtain between their views and those of another school and will be rather quick to move to the let's define our terms stage of interaction.

Vagueness among professionals is considered desirable only with respect to those subjects that either approach the level of demotic discourse or are issues drawn from professional languages of neither party to the conversation. Two philosophers, one an analyst, the other a new Rortyan pragmatist, will likely prefer a conversation about baseball or genetic engineering. Seldom, in their more reasonable moments, will they attempt to talk about issues central to either party's philosophical positions.

There are a variety of mutually incoherent vocabularies of self-description and communication. Attempts to stipulate meanings as a means of clarifying one's concerns lead, ultimately, to a default solipsism. Communication involves the recognition that principal terms are objectively vague. However, the maintenance of vagueness runs contrary to the academic's disposition and training. The academic is caught in a situation in which she knows that (a) vagueness is essential to communication but (b) that clarity is essential to the responsible performance of her profession. Thus academics are often forced, by their professional oaths, into idiosyncrasy and default solipsism. The tension between the demands for clarity and precision, on the one hand, and the recognition of the need for vagueness, on the other hand, creates the context in which the academic is tempted into a life of deception—first of herself, then of others.

Among intellectuals, academics, the theoretically conditioned self-deception begins at the metalevel with the notion that such a thing as an unambiguous, ego-centered self exists. Most of us really know better. This self-deception entails the deception of others when, as ambiguated selves, we confidently present univocal ideas as our beliefs or rationalize our actions by appeal to clear principles. There is, of course, little choice but to act in this manner. If we are ever to finish answering a question or bring a conversation to an end, or account in any way for our actions, we have to present a disambiguated façade.

Given our vague awareness of the manyness that we are, holding the self to be in any real sense integral, persistent, coherent is the beginning of self-deception. For the real conditions for deceptive behavior are the senses of clarity, autonomy, individuality, and integrity. Honesty and candor require the admission of the vagueness that we are.

NOTES

1. I am here using the term *academics* in something like the sense of *aesthetics* or *ethics*.

2. "To Be or Not to Be: The Postmodern Self and the Wu-Forms of Taoism," in *The Self as Person in Asian Theory and Practice*, ed. R. Ames, T. Kasulis, and W. Dissanayake (Albany: State University of New York Press, 1994).

3. I am using this term in something like the Peirceian sense. A concept is richly vague when it may be articulated and/or applied in a variety of distinct and important manners.

4. See A. W. H. Adkins, *From the Many to the One* (Ithaca, NY: Cornell University Press, 1970).

5. Systematic pluralism is concerned with the development of taxonomic schemes which exhaustively classify ways of thinking. Interpretative pluralism is less concerned with achieving a complete taxonomy of philosophic visions and more with celebrating the diversity of ways of thinking as a means of promoting the heuristic function of philosophical vocabularies. McKeon is a systematic pluralist, and Pepper is an interpretative one.

6. Pepper, *World Hypotheses* (Berkeley: The University of California Press, 1942). This taxonomy was worked out over many years, concluding with his *Concept and Quality: A World Hypothesis* (La Salle, IL: The Open Court Press, 1967).

7. See McKeon, "Philosophic Semantics and Philosophic Inquiry," in *Freedom and History and Other Essays: An Introduction to the Thought of Richard McKeon* (Chicago: The University of Chicago Press, 1990), 242–56. Indeed, Robert Brumbaugh, a student of McKeon, translated his teacher's pluralistic insights along more constructive, Platonic lines. See Robert Brumbaugh, "Preface to Cosmography," "Cosmography," and "Cosmography: The Problem of Modern Systems," *The Review of Metaphysics* 7 (no. 1): 53–63, 25 (no. 2): 337–47, 26 (no. 3): 511–21, respectively. See also Robert Brumbaugh and Newton Stallknecht, *The Compass of Philosophy* (New York: Longmans, Green and Co., 1954).

8. This is the basis of the aesthetic orientation of American philosophy expressed in the thinking of Edwards, Emerson, James, Peirce, Whitehead, and the new pragmatists.

9. Lactantius *Inst. div.* vii. 7. 9 (DK 68 A 139).

10. Certainly this is the opinion of the practicing pluralist. See James Edwards, "Systematic Pluralism: Introduction to an Issue," *The Monist* 73 (no. 3) (July 1990).

11. Rorty was an undergraduate at the University of Chicago when McKeon was at the peak of his influence. Though Rorty himself might wish to dismiss the pervasiveness of the early influence of McKeon, I am unable to avoid the suspicion that his views have been profoundly shaped by his reaction to that early training. Thus I disagree with C. G. Prado when he remarks in *The Limits of Pragmatism* (Atlantic Highlands, NJ: Humanities Press, 1987), 41, that the views of McKeon (and Brumbaugh) were "inspirational for Rorty, rather than methodologically influential."

12. See "Recent Metaphilosophy," *Review of Metaphysics* 15 (Dec. 1961): 299–318. This article, written more than thirty years ago, sounds very like the contemporary Rorty. So much for those who believe in a Rortyan *Kehre*.

13. Ibid., 301.

14. Ibid., 301–02.

15. Ibid., 302.

16. Rorty, "Pragmatism, Relativism, Irrationalism," in *Consequences of Pragmatism* (Minneapolis: The University of Minnesota Press, 1982), 167–69.

17. Quoted in Milton Fisk, "The Instability of Pragmatism," *New Literary History* 17 (1985): 23 NN30.

18. In our *Anticipating China: Thinking Through the Narratives of Chinese and Western Culture* (Albany: State University of New York Press, 1995), Roger Ames and I have illustrated the manner in which, in classical Chinese culture, the relative homogeneity of ethnicity, language, education, politics, and art insured a community of common dispositions which precluded substantial resorts to rationalization. The consequence was a permeable boundary between the self and its cultural ambiance in which what was present in the tradition was accessible to the self in a manner not unlike one is able to access one's own memories. I believe that such interconnectedness of self and environs is a characteristic of our own culture as well. I would, of course, grant that the difference of degree might be significant.

19. In accordance with the thesis of this essay, any attempt at stipulation is potentially duplicitous. These distinctions are made in a tentative and heuristic manner.

20. Often a term may be vague in both senses. Thomas Kuhn's notion of 'paradigm' has been rendered in numerous ways both by Kuhn and by his discussants. Most of the meanings were a part of the traditional cultural inventory, but others were apparently new uses of the term.

21. Questions of synonymy do not begin with the query whether different verbal locutions have the same meaning. The more primitive question is whether two utterances of the putatively same locution carry the same sense. As the mainstream analysts would have it, two individuals do not mean the same thing by x ostensively recognized if they say quite different things about x.

22. For discussion of these types of vagueness see Hall, "Reason and its Rhyme," *Journal of the Indian Council of Philosophical Research* 9 (no. 2) (January-April, 1992): 25–46.

23. See Bateson, *Steps Toward and Ecology of Mind* (New York: Ballentine Books, 1972), 279–303.

24. See Hall and Ames, *Anticipating China*, ch. 2, "The Contingency of Culture" for a defense of this claim.

25. See Derrida, *The Postcard from Socrates to Freud and Beyond*, trans. Alan Bass (Chicago: University of Chicago Press, 1987).

26. Recall Bertrand Russell's account of how he was saved from solipsism by reading his erstwhile collaborator's *Process and Reality*. Solipsism, he realized, was fallacious since he reckoned he could certainly not have written that work! I myself

On the Academics of Deception

have been saved from solipsism in much the same manner. Faced with the theories that confidently urge the possibility of real communication, I am quite certain that I could not have produced them! Perhaps the deeper, though equally ironic, concern is with the academic who fails to recognize the viability of any but his own views. It is perfectly possible to see in that thinker's desire to gather others under the protective cover of his own particular theory something of the skewed poignancy of the new convert to solipsism setting out to organize a club.

TWELVE

A HALF-DRESSED EMPEROR
*Societal Self-Deception and
Recent "Japanokritik" in America*

William R. LaFleur

SELF-DECEPTION AND A NATIONAL PATHOLOGY?

The abundant literature on the phenomenon of self-deception shows that it has provided twentieth-century philosophers and students of psychology with an intriguing and important problem.[1] In almost every case, however, the locus of inquiry has been the individual—whether or not self-deception is an epistemological possibility and, if it is, the reasons for its appearance and persistence within the mind and life of a given person.

However, is it possible for an *entire society* to be in a state of self-deception? And, if so, might such a condition persist over a protracted length of time? How and from what perspective might such a condition be detected? And is it not possible that, at least in some cases, such a "detection" might, in fact, itself be a cultural and/or intellectual construction?

The purpose of this chapter is to examine and offer criticisms of a specific research tradition within Western scholarship on Japan—a mode of research based on the assumption that the object of study is in fact a society in such a protracted self-deceptive state. One objective here will be to show that during the 1980s much of American scholarship on Japan in the mode of *Ideologiekritik* was predicated on a notion that Japan has been and remains a society onto which the patterns of self-deception have been institutionally inscribed. Along the way it is important also to examine how that notion has been constructed and why the entire construction is seriously flawed.

Before proceeding into such an analysis, however, it is worth noting that the idea that Japan might be a place where one could detect an exceptional level of societal self-deception was one which, at least for Americans, was based on the assumption that a society capable of extraordinary deceptiveness would likely also be one in which self-deception was off the charts of the ordinary. The link here was between, on one hand, the interpretations of the December 7, 1941, attack on Pearl Harbor as the "day that will live in infamy" because of the depth of Japanese deceptiveness and, on the

Self and Deception

other, discussions in the immediate postwar period of what then was taken to have been an extraordinary level of *self*-deception on the part of the Japanese people as a whole during the final two years of that war.

Specifically, at that point in time it seemed important to persons in the West and to Americans in particular to uncover what structure within the social-psychology of the Japanese had driven a nation of 100 million people to believe in military victory when for at least the final two years of that war all the evidence available to them showed the absolute certainty of defeat. Postwar analyses took it as proven that what had happened internally during the war years had been more than merely a top-down manipulation of the populace through deception and disinformation. It was, rather, that there was also something in the societal structure or in the national psychology of the Japanese that had induced them—and still could lead them—to repress and deny facts before their eyes. That is, the pattern of deception from above seemed to be complemented by a "national personality" given to collective self-deception.

In the period immediately after World War II, a consensus formed among intellectuals, at that point in time not only outside of Japan but also within it, that this trait of the national character was due to the fact that there had been something incomplete about Japan's "modernization"—that, in fact, there existed a serious gap between, on one hand, the advanced state of Japan's military and technological capabilities and, on the other, the retarded condition of its social and political institutions.[2] This was a disparity which some critics were quite ready to refer to as something constituting a "national pathology."[3]

However, this consensus broke down with the passage of time. By the mid-1950s and especially by the 1960s the mainstream within American scholarship on Japan tended to see Japan as having made—with the exception of the fifteen-year fascist period prior to 1945—an exemplary degree of progress in modernization, at least for an Asian society, and a society which, by being progressively democratized,[4] was a model for other nations in the so-called developing world.

Within this form of American Japanologie the problem of whether or not Japan was a society with deeply inscribed patterns of deception and self-deception gradually disappeared. In the view of these scholars, there could be no serious doubt that Japan was a modern nation and that the problem raised by the period of fascism had been largely corrected by the reforms instituted during the American occupation of Japan from 1945 through 1952. The goal was in sight, and there was little doubt that at some point in the future there would be a "convergence" between the modernization level of Japan and that of the West. The scholars holding this view, referred to largely by their opponents as the advocates of "modernization theory" or "convergence theory," had a sanguine assessment of Japan's future potential to become a fully open and liberal society, one in which the proclivity for collective self-deception would be erased.

It is important that absent from the statements of these optimistic theorists of modernization was any suggestion that an ancient and quasireligious institution such as Japan's hereditary emperor system *(tennōsei)* would have to be jettisoned in order to attain full modernization. Their position clearly envisioned no need either for any deep, revolutionary upheaval or for the destruction of the institution of royalty in Japan. In fact, after approximately 1960, the scholars of modernization theory tended to say nothing about any lingering proclivity for collective self-deception on the part of the Japanese as a people. This was no doubt due to their belief that such, if it existed at all, would be progressively dispelled by a growth in the power and role of a free press, the practices of academic freedom, political parties, the enjoyment of liberal capitalism's benefits, and Japan's growing solidarity and treaty links with the democratic societies of the West.

IDEOLOGIEKRITIC AND SOCIETAL SELF-DECEPTION

In this essay, however, the focus of exploration as well as of criticisms will be on a form of scholarship which, first, explicitly rejects the assumption of those who see Japan as a normal society that is progressively modernized and, second, reverts back, at least implicitly, to the judgment that a proclivity for collective self-deception still runs deeply, even somewhat pathologically, in Japan. This alternative mode of questioning, one which made a very strong showing within American scholarship on Japan during the 1980s and early 1990s, accepts many of the basic tenets of neo-Marxism and has concentrated on the study of modern Japanese intellectual life as almost solely constituted by a corpus of ideological production.

Why it happens that those who do *Ideologiekritik* have little difficulty envisioning collective self-deception enveloping a complete society is itself an interesting question. It is a question to which Robert Solomon has given a succinct answer. He writes: "The neo-Marxist notion of 'false consciousness' and one common use of the word 'myth' have reinforced the idea that a whole society could be in self-deception."[5]

Solomon here signals the need to be alert to the ways in which a word such as *myth* will tend to be used by practitioners of *Ideologiekritik* when such a critique is directed against an entire society deemed caught in a state of self-deception.

Self and Deception

The word *myth* when dropped at strategic points into statements claiming to expose ideology and/or collective false consciousness is relied upon to do much of the rhetorical work in the kind of statement I wish to review. Assumed within such statements to be a term synonymous with falsehood or untruth—only *one* of its common uses—myth, when claimed to be publically operative within a given society's political and social life, is also taken to demonstrate that that society remains stuck at some developmental stage in which rationality and the rational ordering of things are still seriously underdeveloped. That is, many of the practitioners of *Ideologiekritic* go on using 'myth' in a way that most philosophers have long since abandoned—that is, as a necessarily odious and irrational something that hangs on in the individual mind or in peoples at an earlier, still relatively unenlightened, stage of development.[6]

It is a premise of such an interpretation that for a person or society to embrace myth at this point in human history is to transgress doubly— *epistemically* by mistaking a proven fabrication for the truth and *developmentally* by casting one's lot with an anachronistic idea or institution at a time in history when rationally realized individuals and/or societies have gone beyond the need for such things. My point here is that what is seen as an epistemic error and what is taken to be a developmental one become, at least within some forms of neo-Marxism, intertwined and conflated. When this occurs, "false consciousness" comes to be viewed not only as something that regularly opts for the lie-that-is-myth but also for self-entrapment within a stage of mental and societal development that is chronologically anterior to—and "lower" than—the stage within which the practitioners of *Ideologiekritik* locate themselves.

I find that this is exactly what is taking place in the following, a quotation from a 1991 essay by Masao Miyoshi and H. D. Harootunian entitled "Japan in the World":

> The [postwar] effort to retain an archaic imperial institution by removing its original source of divine legitimation created still another ambiguity in Japan's national consciousness. Nobody foresaw in 1946 what now appears as an inherent disposition to continue the myth of prewar Japanese order. As Japanese prosperity began to invite closer attention from the world, it became evident that one of the enabling factors of this economic order has been the recycling of the older elements in the national myth of racial homogeneity and familial consensuality that were capable of eliminating opposition and criticism and allowing claims to national uniqueness. These ideologies have combined

to establish a social imaginary marked by a network of tight social relationships modeled after the patriarchal household. ... Again, the reification of this model of social relationship was fundamentally legitimated by the machinery of emperorism.[7]

The word *myth* does most of the rhetorical trapeze work here. It allows for the swift swing from the category of epistemology to that of history and back again.

But the linkage is also unfurled in a way to suggest that, if things will be understood at a really deep level, the epistemic and the evolutionary *converge*. Rationality is not only the condition of statements that are free of falsehood but also a condition of historical moments or stages that are free of anachronism.

And what is the most obvious anachronism in Japanese society? That which Miyoshi and Harootunian call "the machinery of emperorism" fills that role. But this is the common view. In virtually every analysis of Japan as ideology, that nation's monarchy becomes an indispensible part of the argument being made—something which is more fully examined later. Here, however, I wish to establish the point that those who do a neo-Marxist type of analysis seem to have considerable difficulty wriggling free of Marx's pronounced belief in a nineteenth-century notion of inexorable, stage-by-stage historical progress.[8] And since it is supposed that such movement through historical stages represents a rational unfolding, to resist such progress is to run counter to reason.

This means that an individual or a society opting to hold onto an idea or an institution whose time has putatively "passed" is defying not only the march of time but also the canons of rationality. Thus, in spite of some changes in terminology and approach, this form of neo-Marxism retains classical Marxism's supposition that societies will or ought to move through a sequence of stages that is *logico*-historical. When a given society fails to be consistent in all its parts and all the way down, it will be, by definition, a society in "contradiction."

The fact that *Ideologiekritik* retains, although in semi-concealment, this notion of whole societies as falling into illogicality when they embrace anachronism is, I suggest, also the reason why the neo-Marxist critics of Japan write about that society as one in which collective self-deception has been institutionally inscribed. Just as some philosophers have described self-deception in an individual as an attempt at a *simultaneous* holding both of *A* and of non-*A* as truths, the critics of ideology seem to believe that instances of collective or societal self-deception are constituted by the attempt within such societies at a simultaneous holding

Self and Deception

of the institutions of the present with those of the past. They are, then, not just individuals holding onto irreconcilable tenets, but whole societies in a state of contradiction.

MARRYING THE FEUDAL AND THE POSTMODERN

American scholars doing analyses of ideology in Japan have been preoccupied with what they see as the ongoing significance of E. Herbert Norman (1909–1957), a Canadian scholar-diplomat whose writings analyzed Japan's "modernization" as superficial and Japanese society as at bottom still set squarely in the historical stage called "feudalism." Norman held that talk about Japanese modernization could not conceal the fact that Japan as a society remained locked in feudalistic socio-psychological patterns—patterns given support by the antiquated religious philosophies of Buddhism and Confucianism.

Norman wrote his analyses of Japanese history during and immediately after World War II. In order to understand what he meant by the term *feudalism* and Japan's embeddedness in its structure, it is instructive to recall that the notion that Japan was still feudalistic rather than advanced (at least to the stage of modernity represented by bourgeois capitalism) was something that had its origin in prewar Marxists' attempts to ascertain exactly where Japan lay within the various historical schemata offered by Marx and Marxist theorists.

At times the prewar Comintern and Japanese Marxists as well had been happy to define Japan as still "Asiatically backward" and locked in what Marx had called "Oriental despotism."[9] On this analysis Japan was like all the other ancient societies of Asia in being still two historical stages away from bourgeois capitalism's break with feudalism. Others, picking up on hints within Marx's own writings,[10] saw Japan as having gone beyond other Asian societies in having developed at least to the stage of feudalism.

Either way, of course, Japan was being described as a society not having yet demonstrated the characteristics of those societies—all "Western" in both versions of what Marx had meant to say[11]—which had progressed to the stage of bourgeois capitalism and, what is important, to the condition of *modernity* that was part and parcel of that stage.

To return to the significance of E. Herbert Norman to neo-Marxists, it is important to recognize that Norman's analysis was designed to show that Japan had been and remained basically feudalistic in the Marxist sense of that term. Central to his analysis was the person of Andō Shōeki

(1703–1762), celebrated by Norman as "a lonely figure in the intellectual landscape of his age."[12] Andō was portrayed as the sole person perspicacious enough to see both through the oppression of peasants during the feudalistic era in which he lived and through the ways in which Buddhism and Confucianism provided the ideological support for that oppression. Andō was an Enlightenment-type writer in Japan's eighteenth century but, unfortunately, one who had no appreciable impact in terms of moving his society into a more rational and modern stage of development. His was a light that went unnoticed.[13]

The value of Andō's writings to Norman lay in how they served to show, through contrast, the entrenched feudalism of Japanese society. And that fundamental feudalism was one which, at least in Norman's view, had not been undercut by the government-sponsored modernizing and Westernizing programs of Japan's Meiji and Taishō periods (1868–1926). Nor had it, if we can judge from the fact that Norman's most important work on Andō was written as late as 1949, been undercut in any fundamental way by the reforms, including massive redistributions of land, instituted by the American occupation of Japan.

The core claim here was that supposedly "modern" Japan was, once you strip off the technology, really still locked within the feudalistic stage of history. No informed historian of Japan—at least to my knowledge—would overtly use the word *feudalistic* to describe Japanese society today. Norman's terminology has dropped away. Nevertheless, the notion that Japanese society remains one with its various parts severely *out of joint* hangs on strongly. And it does so most conspicuously in the writings, many by Americans, which during the past decade have focused on providing a critique of Japan's so-called postmodernity.

This critique would not have come into being if it had not been for the fact that during the late 1970s and the 1980s many Japanese artists, architects, and intellectuals not only stood in the forefront in the use of expressive modes internationally recognized as postmodern but went on to write and speak about Japanese society as unusually receptive to postmodernism. The possible link between the emergence of the style dubbed "postmodernist" and the newly confident form of capitalism expressed during the 1980s is a phenomenon that neo-Marxists and what the practitioners of "cultural criticism" have focused on with a vengence during the past decade.[14]

As a consequence, the eagerness with which certain Japanese seemed to embrace postmodernity, especially when viewed in the context of Japanese politicians' and economists' claims of being in a society which had gone *beyond* the industrial phase, struck neo-Marxists not only as an instance of the essential correctness of their position but also as perhaps the paradigmatic case of a society caught in an especially flagrant form of historical disjunction.

The opening salvo in this twist of American scholarship on Japan into a development which might properly be called "Japanokritiek," was the summer 1988 issue—entitled "Postmodernism and Japan"—of the *South Atlantic Quarterly*. With only sporadic hints of a more nuanced approach, the essays there tended to indict Japan as a society which, although on the ideological surface now talking about its own postmodernity, is one which can—with the tools of neo-Marxist criticism—be shown to be, in fact, intransigently *pre*modern at its most fundamental levels.

Thus in the *South Atlantic Quarterly*'s issue on Japan's postmodernity, J. Victor Koschmann wrote an essay entitled "Maruyama Masao and the Incomplete Project of Modernity," in which he presents a sympathetic account of the longstanding contention by Maruyama, whom Koschmann rightly calls Japan's "leading theorist and advocate of modernity,"[15] to the effect that, due to the under-development of the political dimension, Japan even today is a society that is not yet sufficiently modern.

Of crucial importance to a number of the essays in the volume on Japan's postmodernity is the fact that, beginning in the late 1930s and most famously in a series of midwar round-table talks appearing in *Chūō kōron* in 1942, some Japanese intellectuals, especially younger members of the so-called Kyoto School of Philosophy, had already used phrases such as *overcoming modernity* in what clearly seem to have been statements engineered to mesh with the political and military objectives of the Greater East Asia Co-Prosperity Sphere.

Essays by H. D. Harootunian and Naoki Sakai offer sophisticated analyses of the round-table talks by Japanese philosophers in 1942, but there is something of a bottom-line theme woven into almost all the references to the Kyoto school philosophers of the 1930s and early 1940s. Simply put, their references to "overcoming the modern" are of a piece, at least politically, with positive references to Japan's postmodernity in the 1980s and 1990s. Asada Akira has no trouble making the equation and even reads the terms in reverse. He refers to the philosopher Nishida Kitarō—someone who, in fact, never seems to have used a phrase such as *overcoming the modern*—as having provided the "foundation for the *postmodernism of the 1930s*."[16]

Never explicitly stated, the implicit assumption is that Japan is a society in which a "resistance" to real modernity remains entrenched. If it were the case that the first references to overcoming the modern appeared in an epoch which was blatantly fascist, similarities in the locutions as well as in how they are being used give us sufficient reason, it is implied, to be on the alert for

A Half-Dressed Emperor

at least a latent fascism in the current Japanese fascination with postmodernity.[17] In any case, discourse about postmodernity is all ruse, something intended to disguise the fact that Japan remains stubbornly *pre*modern on some basic levels. In their introduction to the volume, Miyoshi and Harootunian say as much: "[Japan's] discourse on the postmodern can never hope to be anything more than an inexpertly concealed attempt to cover up the aporias that dogged an earlier modernist discourse, even as it seeks to fulfill the role of a simulacrum."[18] The reason for skepticism about Japan's postmodernity, ultimately, is that in the view of this volume's editors, such discourse conceals "an unfinished agenda which still demands completion."[19]

What is the point of my review of these arguments? Basically, it is that we need to see that the crux of the neo-Marxist charge against Japanese postmodernity really is that the postmodern posture only exacerbates the fundamental *contradictions* in what Miyoshi calls the "chronopolitical" situation. My claim is that the old Marxist view of history as a lock-step movement through stages lives on in reincarnated form in the language of the neo-Marxist critique of Japan's postmodernity. So too does E. H. Norman's criticism of Japan as still too feudal to deserve being called really "modern."

Norman's terminology, very much embedded in the rigid historical theories of classical Marxism, will not be accepted at face value or employed as such by today's neo-Marxist students of Japan. Yet the notion that Japanese society remains one with its various parts severely *out of joint* hangs on. To be a society which is postmodern in some areas, modern in others, and premodern someplace else is, on this kind of analysis, to be a society in a condition of dislocation, one in "chronopolitical" contradiction. It is one which is either failing or refusing to be what it should be *all the way down.*

This model is ruled by the notion that a society ought to have all its parts, like vertebrae along the spine, in a straight line. It is at bottom a notion of *logical* consistency, but one that becomes pernicious and distortive when set alongside real societies as the model to which they in turn *ought* to be conforming. It is, as suggested earlier, also a model of history that shows—perhaps due to its genesis within the Enlightenment—a striking similarity to the older, now generally discredited, definition of self-deception—namely, as the mind's *simultaneous* holding both of *A* and of non-*A* as truths.

WRESTLED INTO TRUTH

One line of clear continuity between old-style Marxist and neo-Marxist analyses of Japanese society is their focus upon the *tennō* system, Japan's royal institution, as the most concrete embodiment of what is wrong with that society.[20] Both within and outside of Japan the Marxist position has been that if the Japanese monarchy were to be abolished, many positive developments would automatically result. In the neo-Marxist perspective, the institution of emperorship is ideologically engineered to function like the plug holding in place a bathtub full of dirty, visually impenetrable water. It renders opaque the process of actual political decision and interestedness in Japan and, therefore, leads to injustice on a grand scale. The continued existence of the emperor system is, furthermore, linked directly to what is claimed to be the perpetuated absence of real "subjectivity" in the Japanese people.[21]

Principally, however, this institution becomes in their eyes an empirical proof that on a level deeper than the superficial, Japan remains "stuck" in some stage of socio-historical consciousness that is not fully modern. Its very existence proves the justice of writing about Japan as a society that remains, if not feudal, at least premodern in crucial ways. That which, in a quotation above, Miyoshi and Harootunian referred to as the "machinery of emperorism" is what is assumed to be facilitating the Japanese public's tolerance of its own unchanged, basically immature national psyche, one in which collective self-deception can flourish. And this is *the* Japan problem, a situation which, once recognized, is profoundly pathological.

In Japan itself language about this abolition of the *tennō* system and the benefits that would accrue from such a motive has in no way been limited to the conversations of intellectuals and theorists. There it has been translated most conspicuously during the 1960s and the 1970s, both into political slogans and into forms of politicized social drama.

This, its "trickle down" impact, was dramatically carried forward in a very prominent way by Kenzo Okuzaki, a radicalized ex–realtor, a man whose personal crusade to achieve these ends became the subject of a documentary film that has received much praise and international attention.[22] It is a remarkable film, one deserving some close attention here. My purpose in analyzing this film will be to see it as a text which highlights some of the most crucial problems—both social and philosophical—implicit in the view that Japan still desperately needs a radical upheaval in its political and social structure in order to qualify as a truly "modern" nation and in order to defuse what is seen as its people's ongoing proclivity for collective self-deception.

In 1986, *Yukiyuki to Shingun,* a film directed by Kazuo Hara, was released outside Japan under the English title *The Emperor's Naked Army Marches On.* Hara had agreed to the proposal of its principal subject, Okuzaki, that he film the latter's personal struggle both against the *tennō* system and to expose an egregious pattern of self-deception on the part of a select group of Okuzaki's contemporaries. Hara planned the film as an utterly realistic and uncompromising account of the public activities of Okuzaki over a fourteen-month period during 1982 and 1983. As a director, Hara succeeded brilliantly in this, although things did not work out at all as Okuzaki had planned.

Okuzaki, a seventy-year-old, strong-minded, conscience-stricken veteran of Japan's Pacific War, wished to force a group of his contemporaries, all of them participants in a military atrocity in 1945, to acknowledge what they had done. Nearly forty years earlier in a jungle in New Guinea, these men, officers in the Japanese army, had deliberately and without provocation killed some of their juniors, with the intention of cannibalizing them. This act had occurred twenty-three days after Japan's capitulation, at a time when the officers, fully aware of the war's end, were progressing toward the place designated for their unit's surrender. The film records Okuzaki's attempts to force these men into a confession of their terrible deed.

However, Okuzaki had already long had his sights on a person of even higher rank. Numbered among those Japanese totally convinced that Hirohito, Japan's emperor between 1926 and 1989, deserved designation as "the top war criminal," Okuzaki turned himself and a few associates into a small paramilitary group intent on dismantling the entire *tennō* system.

Already in 1969 he had gained headline attention by a quixotic and wholly symbolic effort to do this by slinging a few (*pachinko*) pinballs at Hirohito in a public place. Okuzaki, who seems at that point to have literalized the notion of the emperor as "king-pin," was jailed. At the outset of Hara's documentary, Okuzaki has been released from prison and is driving through Tokyo in a vehicle which declares, by its written slogans and loudspeakers, messages such as the following:

> "To kill [Prime Minister] Kakuei Tanaka would be the way to bring enlightenment to all mankind!"

His rhetoric is strong and his campaign is unrelenting.

The film then follows Okuzaki as he, entirely on his own initiative and bankroll, seeks out one by one the officers who had cannibalized their juniors in the New Guinea jungle. He wants to elicit from them confessions about their horrible deeds and forces his way into their homes, insisting that they "remember" the jungle incident—often while they are surrounded by family members, persons who until that point had been completely ignorant of what had happened decades earlier in New Guinea. In one case, Okuzaki contends that the illnesses of his interrogee are caused by the latter's willed refusal to admit the truth of what he had done in 1945. Okuzaki in the most literal sense tries to wring confessions from these men. He sometimes wrestles them to the ground to force an avowal—on occasion with success. Police are called to witness the violence of his tactics, although they do not arrest him. In defense of these methods, he claims: "After all, violence is my forté," and "As long as I live I will use violence if it brings good to mankind."

This may also lie at the base of why Okuzaki has no compunction about wresting the film itself away from its documentary objective and turning it into a dramatization when that seems justified by the objective of his crusade. This change, perhaps unique in the history of film, occurs when some of Okuzaki's real-life assistants dissociate themselves from his project and he feels the need to replace them with "actors." Well into the film, two persons, living relatives of soldiers murdered in the jungle and in that sense authentic witnesses, resign from the crusade when they begin to have qualms about Okuzaki's strong-arm tactics; they are offended by his lack of concern for how disruptive his forced avowals will be to the unsuspecting family and friends of the men charged with the murders. But when they withdraw, Okuzaki blithely plugs in others—his own wife for instance—who then not only "act" the part of aggrieved relatives but also conceal the fact that they are playing roles. Okuzaki trains the actors himself in the methods of dissembling.

This sudden plunge into total simulation is, of course, both highly irregular and ironic in the very midst of a project whose whole premise is that truth, uncompromised and unsullied, alone will make for freedom. However, Okuzaki's obsession seems to make him oblivious to the contradiction. Utterly determined to carry out his sequence of exposés to the end, he becomes, in effect, the "director" of a fictive modality which is created within Hara's documentary. Hara, to his credit, records this deeply ironic turn and simply lets it stand as it is.

The emotional climax of the film, however, is reached when Okuzaki, in trying to force one of the soldiers, Koshimizu, into an avowal of the latter's own part in the jungle murders, finds his efforts thwarted. At that point Okuzaki's zeal to force this issue goes far beyond wrestling his antagonist to the ground. Totally frustrated, on the property of the resistant interrogee, Okuzaki focuses on a surrogate for the man he seeks. Stating that "[Koshimizu's] son will do," Okuzaki then shoots and kills this totally innocent man. The film ends with scenes of Okuzaki in prison, sentenced to twelve years of hard labor.

CRUSADES AND CRUELTY

In her *Secrets: On the Ethics of Concealment and Revelation* Sissela Bok writes perceptively about the proclivity for what she calls "zealotry" in persons deeply committed to the exposure of self-deception in others:

> To attribute self-deception to people is to regard them as less than rational concerning the danger one takes them to be in, and makes intervention, by contrast, seem more legitimate. But this is itself dangerous because of the difficulties of establishing that there is self-deception in the first place.... Aiding the victims of such imputed self-deception can be hard to resist for true believers and enthusiasts of every persuasion.[23]

One might even go further, since the danger here may be even greater than Bok suggests. The supposedly altruistic impulse to "aid" the self-deceived can all too easily turn into a self-appointed program to *force enlightenment* on the other through acts of exposure. And the compulsion to carry this forward can easily become an obsession, a state of mind in which the person carrying out the exposé becomes oblivious to new, subtle, self-deceptions which are his or her own.

In many ways *The Emperor's Naked Army Marches On* becomes a paradigmatic instance of this inversion. The ironies are patent. Just as the man self-appointed to bring old murderers to justice himself becomes a murderer in the process, so too his whole campaign to unmask the self-deception of others turns into a protracted exercise in self-deception. His crusade to bring "enlightenment" to Japanese society ends in him being cast out of society and into prison—not due to some institutional injustice, but because his own criminal acts make this necessary. Okuzaki's intention of revealing a "pathology" endemic to Japanese society unravels in a sequence of actions that move from being quixotic to ones that smack strongly of lost sanity in the man who has become obsessed with exposing what is supposedly pathological in his own society.

However, even to point this out is to invite the criticism of being deeply engaged in an exposé of the folly of *all* deeply committed exposés—that is, in a self-contradictory enterprise. In other words, I run the risk of being confronted with what is called the "self-refutation charge." Therefore, I will take refuge in what elsewhere in this volume is Barbara Herrnstein Smith's deft demonstration that this charge, when examined in terms of its "rhetorical, psychological," and "institutional operations," turns out to be much less potent than has often been assumed by professionalized philosophers.[24]

In addition, however, there is something else which can defuse the self-refutation charge here. It is simply that what I have taken from the Okuzaki episode is surely not a claim that *all* attempts at unmasking are bound to end in folly and an unraveling. My hypothesis is merely that what is wrong with a crusade such as Okuzaki's is that it has *privileged the exposure*

Self and Deception

of truth to such an extent that all other ethical concerns have been pushed out of sight and made irrelevant. That is, the goal has eclipsed all concern for how the methods to expose that truth might, in fact, have become vicious, cruel, and, at least in this instance, downright homicidal.

My perspective on this owes much to the change in our thinking brought about by the work of Judith N. Shklar and to things written by Richard Rorty in pursuit of the implications of her suggestions. And since my reason for discussing Okuzaki's crusade lies in my belief that it graphically illustrates a serious flaw in the work of many—not all—scholars who apply *Ideologiekritik* to the study of Japan, these connections now need to be made clear.

My claim would be that the fundamental reason that much of the neo-Marxist critique of Japanese society is fraught with contradictions, remains relatively ineffective, and in recent years has become increasingly strident in its rhetoric is that the ethical base of such a critique is too narrow, too much designed to privilege only one value, namely the exposure of truth. That is, such *Ideologiekritik* seems unable to grasp the import of Shklar's recommendation that intellectuals generally should no longer go on prioritizing hypocrisy and lying as the worst of vices but should, instead, "put cruelty first."[25] This seemingly slight suggestion is one which can, in fact, make for a sea change in intellectual life.

Shklar's attempt to reorder what we should favor as *the* vice most strenuously to be condemned has enormous potential for assisting people in general but intellectuals most especially to change their idea of what they can and should do to fulfill their ethical and political duties within society. My suggestion is that one of the more concrete benefits derivable from Shklar's insight is to show why the carrying on of *Ideologiekritik,* especially when in the crusade mode, may not in fact be the most honest or even the most effective way to contribute to real societal justice and liberty.

By calling our attention to the fact that "ideological discourse puts hypocrisy into the forefront of political sins,"[26] Shklar suggests that this easily becomes a move through which attention is turned away from *actual cruelty* within society and toward *theoretical acounts* of supposed socioeconomic structures and toward how these have gotten to be ideologically configured. This unfortunately distorted prioritization is one into which intellectuals, given their interests, can almost be expected to fall. Robert Solomon reminds us that "Immanuel Kant took the prohibition against lying as his paradigm of a 'categorical imperative,' the unconditioned moral law."[27] What we all know already about the sociology of knowledge will suggest why this was so.

Neo-Marxists follow this intellectualist trend, assuming that by engaging in ideological unmasking they are doing *the most basic work* to ensure the creation of a more just and free society. Marx himself may have set this in motion when in *Das Kapital,* the late writing which he designed as his *magnum opus* and regarded as "his most important scientific and scholarly edifice,"²⁸ he moved in the direction of a theorizing and schematizing increasingly distant from the particulars of society and injustices therein.

However, even much more problematic for Marxist and neo-Marxist intellectuals has been what so many of them seem to have shared with Okazaki—namely, a stubborn refusal to see and acknowledge the horrendous social cruelties that seem in multiple contexts to result directly from the programs intended to implement their own ideological ideals—everything from Stalin's systematic slaughters, to the Gulag, to the horrors of the Cultural Revolution in China.²⁹ In things such as these the fault of the intellectual in general and of the neo-Marxist intellectual most especially has been that of commitment to a theory, perhaps cherished for what is taken to be its logical tidiness or its "chronopolitical" descriptive power, to the exclusion of facts that not only countervene that theory but also cry out for attention because of the human pain they exhibit.

In the important final section of his *Contingency, Irony, and Solidarity,* Richard Rorty demonstrates that for philosophers to see cruelty as what they should recognize as the most vicious of vices would be, at least for them, merely to be catching up with something that had already been fairly well established in the praxis of writers of fiction. Rorty discusses Nabokov and Orwell as twentieth-century writers who had powerfully described the dynamics and viciousness of cruelty even though "there was an antitheoretical streak in Orwell, which he shared with Nabokov and which made them both unable to take Marxist theory seriously."³⁰

JUNGLES, THICKETS, AND WAYS OUT

There can be detected more than a hint of frustration and anger in the more recent writings about Japan by neo-Marxist Japan scholars such as Miyoshi and Harootunian.³¹ It is not difficult to see that they believe the factually correct account of Japanese society—namely, the state of affairs revealed by the kind of ideological unmasking they themselves provide—has failed only because it has been subverted by rightist politicians in Japan who manufacture ideological illusions and by American scholars who have muddied matters with the pernicious idea that in Japan, modernization can and has taken place without need for a proletarian revolution or the abolition of Japan's monarchy.

When the critique of ideology enters the crusade mode, sensitivity to irony finds an exit door and departs. One of the striking facts about what

Self and Deception

I suggest might be called the "recent spate" of neo-Marxist *Japanokritik* is that its authors seem unable to acknowledge that one of the reasons their analyses have had next to no social impact within Japan might be due, in fact, to problems inherent in that critique itself. A case could be made that much of the radicalized criticism which actually had a fairly large place in Japanese intellectual life for the first four postwar decades, proved to be notoriously ineffective. In the realm of theoretical discourse, it turned out to be the precise counterpart to the ineffective and abortive leftist political actions of the period.

While I would not go so far as to draw a parallel between these "accomplishments" within the realm of theory and those of the "Japanese Red Army" in the realm of praxis, it is at least instructive to note that neo-Marxists who write about Japan have to date, at least to my knowledge, been loath to condemn the Japanese Red Army's sporadic but utterly murderous terrorist activities not only within Japan but also in places as far away as Israel, Naples, and New Jersey.[32] Is this a matter of too deep an investment of belief in a tottering theory, an investment serving to prevent the seeing and censuring of actual acts of patently public cruelty?

Also absent from the neo-Marxist analysis of what derailed the prospects for a proletarian revolution in Japan is any reference to what the Japanese as a people could and, in fact, did learn about how revolutions had fared in neighboring states such as the People's Republic of China and the Democratic People's Republic of Korea. News of disastrous economic policies such as that of Mao's Great Leap Forward, of a totalitarian hold on all aspects of life, and of gruesome reigns of terrors such as that during the Cultural Revolution of 1967 through 1968 did not, when these things were recognized for what they were, help much to convince the Japanese as a people that the Marxist or Maoist revolutionary route was worth pursuing. Neo-Marxist critiques of American influence on Japan have characteristically been written as if, during the period between 1945 and 1990, the Japanese people either had no geographical neighbors or did not register a message about something wrong with Marxist revolutions and societies.

My hypothesis is that during this period, the Japanese were not so ideologically duped and could, in fact, differentiate between governments, both Marxist and neo-Fascist, which regularly beat and killed their citizens for political deviation and those—perhaps their own—which limited their activities to the channeling of minds. That is, their own kind of on-the-ground "materialism" meant that they could differentiate between screws applied to the body and those applied to the mind. The difference was considerable. That which deserves to be called "cruelty," they judged, shows itself more in the former than in the latter, type.

Inasmuch as they ingored what *actual* Marxist praxis did to undercut the humane goals of the revolution they themselves had dearly wanted, neo-Marxists critics engaged in some self-blinding. In order to trace the reasons why, especially in 1960, Japan's prospects for a revolution came to nothing, these analysts have focused exclusively on what they construed as the powerful ploys of crypto-fascism in Japan and American cold-war policy. Miyoshi's *Off Center* and the *Japan and the World* issue of *Boundary 2* tend to construe everything in such terms. Yet in all of this there is a note of desperation, a sense that even though now all hopes for radical social upheaval have been dispelled, the politically sensitized intellectual can *at least* still expose ideology—that is, he or she can shine the flashlight of cultural criticism into an actual fascist abyss.

A revolution which has run aground, perhaps because of its own faulty assumptions, can at least escape into the medium of theater. The objective, now limited to the provision of a quick epiphany of *the truth*—without any expectation that that revelation will refashion society—can at least have a moment on stage. A frustrated but still hopeful Okuzaki at that point hurls pinballs at a monarch from a distance from which they could never possibly reach him. Quixotic it may be, but at least it provides a momentary epiphany of the way things really are. In fact, as has been already suggested, it is the unmasker's quasi–religious,[33] single-minded dedication to disclosing the truth as defined by the unmasker that renders him or her unaware of the self-deception and dangers involved. Monomania and obsession disallow that level of reflexivity. Okuzaki focused so exclusively on the events in the jungle almost forty years earlier that he made himself unaware of the cruelties of his own current behavior. His total "investment" of himself in his crusade blocked awareness of the inconsistencies, savagery, and personal peril involved.

Merely to be able to offer this kind of critique of *Ideologiekritik* is also, perhaps implicitly, to note how far we have moved away from Sartre's notion of self-deception as merely "bad faith," something which can be identified as such by the rational mind and then rejected. In commenting on what he calls the "cold-bloodedness" of Sartre's model of self-deception, Robert Solomon notes: "Our consciousness is not the 'translucent' pool [Sartre] suggests but a thicket of investments and value structures which can be sorted out and recognized only with considerable difficulty and great courage."[34] This is, of course, not only to recognize that our metaphors of the mind have greatly changed but also that they *had* to change when it became clear that those metaphors handed down to us from the Enlightenment—mirror, translucent pool, and the lot—had themselves been put in place because, at least in part, they effectively *denied* or sought to hide the facts of the existing "investment" of our consciousness.[35]

Self and Deception

To move from an image of consciousness as translucent pool to one as a thicket of investments can facilitate our grasp of how patterns of self-deceptions occur and why it so often is the case that, when these occur, events seem to fall out in unintended, ironic patterns. Such a move also helps explain why so much of *Ideologiekritik,* dependent as it is on the older, Enlightenment-based metaphor of the mind, has turned out to be far less effective than its practitioners have claimed in terms of changing actual societies for the better. It has been dogged by its shunned ironies.

DRESSING DOWN THE EMPEROR

It would be a mistake to go only halfway with Shkar's proposal for a reordering of priorities in the intellectual's registry of vices. If there is to be value in our recognition that the Enlightenment-enshrined task of unmasking logical inconsistencies and self-deceptions may, in fact, not automatically do as much good for society as intellectuals formerly thought, it then becomes all the more important that we follow through on Shkar's suggestion and not neglect to put "cruelty first."

The requirement that we be sensitive to demonstrable instances and patterns of cruelty would require that, when useful to help put an end to such things, acts of unmasking too should be pressed into service. I suspect this is the reason Richard Rorty states that even an anti-essentialist such as himself can and should recognize the usefulness of *Ideologiekritik* when appropriate. "We pragmatists," he writes, "view the 'critique of ideology' as an occasionally useful tactical weapon in social struggles, but as one among many others."[36]

The qualification that such will be only "occasionally useful" and as a "tactical weapon" derives, I infer, from Rorty's concern to follow Shklar's demand that attention to actual cruelty not be subverted by the intellectual's penchant for falling into an intellectualist interest in *Ideologiekritik* as if it had autotelic value.

Therefore, what makes Norma Field's *In the Realm of a Dying Emperor: A Portrait of Japan at Century's End* a compelling book is that when all is said and done, its sustained focus on *concrete instances* where the Japanese emperor system has, in fact, been used in recent years by ultra-rightists to bring real cruelty into the lives of Japanese citizens. Field's narrative concerning the abuse of a Christian woman's right to bury her husband according to her beliefs, of an Okinawan maltreated by an ultra-nationalist program, and of the harassment and attempted assassination of the Nagasaki mayor who called attention to Hirohito's war guilt is a narrative full of rich, concrete data.[37] The abuse of fellow humans in such contexts was patent, and the current Japanese emperor's refusal to address and condemn such things when supposedly done "for his sake" might suggest that he, at least through omission, might become culpable of a charge of silent complicity.

The contrast between the victimized persons described by Field and the crusade of Okuzaki in *The Emperor's Naked Army Marches On,* however, is clear. What happened to the persons depicted by Field continues to stand as evidence of a pattern of cruelty. It shows up as a serious problem which the Japanese public, and especially those who think of themselves as "royalists," need to address so as to take corrective measures.

Being neither Japanese nor someone who knows—or wants to experience—the emotions of the Tory or royalist, I have some difficulty generating empathy for the person who cherishes the *tennō*. If I were Japanese I suspect I would be one of the multitude which, in fact, took the days of Hirohito's death-rites as an opportunity for a personal holiday. In doing so I would be joining a large portion of a population which has, by its actual behavior, already adopted a de-sacralized view of the *tennō*. This suggests that Japan's "king" is increasingly perceived, even by many Japanese, as basically a "bourgeois monarch."[38]

My point is that the problem posed by the Japanese emperor system is not one of "chronopolitics" but an assessment of costs and benefits to Japanese society. It is not that monarchy represents prima facie evidence that the society giving it a role is less than modern. The charge that Asian societies might be inferior to European ones simply by virtue of their monarchies is as old as the Hippocratic writings of ancient Greece[39] and is deeply inscribed into the European construction of Asian "otherness."

The question is not whether or not the Japanese royal institution is an anachronism and simply too "archaic" to be allowed to continue. The world is full of archaic institutions for which new functions have been either discovered or made. It is, rather, whether or not the societal benefits might not in fact be outweighed by the societal costs.

However, once we are released from any notion of historical evolution as propelled by Reason and an ethically charged chronopolitics, that question might be asked of any society at any time.

NOTES

1. See works such as Raphael Demos, "Lying to Oneself," *Journal to Philosophy* 57 (1960): 588–95; Herbert Fingarette, *Self-Deception* (New York: Humanities Press, 1969); Brian McLaughlin and Amélie Rorty, eds., *Perspectives on Self-Deception* (Berkeley and Los Angeles: University of California Press, 1988).

Self and Deception

2. Respected as a historian in midcentury much more than today, Arnold Toynbee, who was widely read in Japan, articulated this view in the chapter on Japan in his *The World and the West* (Oxford University Press, 1953).

3. The philosopher Watsuji Tetsurō (1889–1960) was not so convinced a national pathology existed. In his 1950 study entitled *Sakoku* he offered an alternative explanation. See my "Haikyo ni tatsu Risei: Sengo Gōrisei ronsō ni okeru Watsuji Tetsurō no Iso," in *Sengo Nihon no Seishinshi: Sono Saikentō*, ed. Tetsuo Najita, Maeda Ai, and Kamishima Jirō (Tokyo: Iwanami shoten, 1988), 112–44.

4. This position, consciously designed as an alternative to Marxist views widely held within Japan at the time, was articulated by most of the American scholars at a conference in Hakone, Japan, in 1960. Essays by John Whitney Hall and Marius B. Jansen in *Changing Japanese Attitudes toward Modernization* (Princeton: Princeton University Press, 1965) were the noteworthy examples. Sheldon Garon provides an incisive overview and analysis of all these trends in his "Rethinking Modernization and Modernity in Japan: A Focus on State-Society Relations," *Journal of Asian Studies* 53:2 (May 1994): 346–66.

5. Robert C. Solomon, "Self, Deception, and Self-Deception in Philosophy," in this volume.

6. Even as fine a book as *Japan's Modern Myths: Ideology in the Late Meiji Period* by Carol Gluck (Princeton: Princeton University Press, 1985) derives at least part of its rhetorical punch, as the title itself shows, from the kind of linguistic operation noted by Solomon.

7. Miyoshi Masao and H. D. Harootunian, "Japan in the World," in *Japan in the World* (special issue of *Boundary 2* 18:3 [Fall 1991]: 2.

8. Robert Nisbet, *History of the Idea of Progress* (New York: Basic Books, 1980), 258ff.

9. In his 1853 essay, "British Rule in India," Marx used this term, characterized Asian societies as "undignified, stagnatory, and vegetative," and viewed British colonial rule in India as "sickening," but at the same time as what was historically needed to being about "a fundamental revolution in the state of Asia." See Eugene Kamenka, ed., *The Portable Karl Marx* (New York: Penguin, 1983), 329–36.

10. Debates on this had been intense and caused in part by the fact that in *Das Kapital* Marx had referred to Japan as having gotten to a stage comparable to that of feudal Europe and to that extent in advance of those still locked in what he called "the Asiatic mode of production." An excellent study of this is Germaine A. Hoston, *Marxism and the Crisis of Development in Prewar Japan* (Princeton: Princeton University Press, 1986), espec. 131 and 327, n. 15.

11. Edward W. Said recognizes that if one of the tell-tale marks of "Orientalism" is a Western writer's assumption that Asian societies need to be saved from themselves by contact with the West, Marx was surely in the Orientalist tradition. See Said, *Orientalism* (New York: Vintage, 1979), espec. 153ff. Neo-Marxist analyses of Japan customarily show the same tendencies.

12. E. Herbert Norman, *Andō Shoeki and the Anatomy of Japanese Feudalism* (Tokyo: The Asiatic Society of Japan, 1949); rep. University Publication of America, 1979), 248.

13. Not all scholars share that view of Andō. Jeffrey Hunter, the translator of one of Andō Shōeki's core works, notes that "the premises of Shōeki's philosophy are rife with contradiction" and that he articulated a philosophy "more unwieldly than most," one which "for all its claims to be based on empirical observations, is very hard to see in the life around us." See Jeffrey Hunter, "Introduction," in his translation, *The Animal Court: A Political Fable from Old Japan* (New York: Weatherhill, 1992), x and xi. The view of Andō Shōeki as a uniquely progressive figure has periodic revivals—as, for instance in Tetsuo Najita's presidential address to the Association for Asian Studies (published as "Reflections on Modernity and Modernization," *Journal of Asian Studies* 52:4 [Nov 1993]: 845–53). Najita recasts Andō as an ahead-of-his-time ecologist and feminist.

14. The most prominent works are perhaps Christopher Norris, *What's Wrong with Postmodernism: Critical Theory and the Ends of Philosophy* (Baltimore: Johns Hopkins University Press, 1990); Fredric Jameson, *Postmodernism, or, The Cultural Logic of Late Capitalism* (Durham: Duke University Press, 1991).

15. J. Victor Koschmann, "Maruyama Masao and the Incomplete Project of Modernity," in *Postmodernism and Japan* (*The South Atlantic Quarterly* 87:3), ed. Masao Miyoshi and H. D. Harootunian), 507.

16. Asada Akira, "Infantile Capitalism and Japan's Postmodernism: A Fairy Tale," in ibid., 632. Emphasis mine.

17. In a patent overstatement but one which, nevertheless, throws out an insidious hint about *fascism in the present*, the volume's editors write of Japan's postmodernity as something which today succeeds in "silencing all the . . . dissenters" (Ibid., 391).

18. Ibid., 396.

19. Ibid., 397.

20. An important exception to this within Japanese Marxism was the faction known as *Rōnō-ha;* its adherents regarded the emperor as a "bourgeois monarch," much like the occupants of the British throne. See Hoston, 183.

21. Although he criticizes Maruyama for not going as far as Mao Tse-tung and Frantz Fanon in these matters, Miyoshi writes: "Maruyama's analysis of the emperor system and its effects on Japan's intellectual and political history is astute, and his observation of the general absence of *shutaisei* [usually translated as "subjectivity"] in Japanese thought and action can be ignored only at a serious risk" (Masao Miyoshi, *Off Center: Power and Culture Relations between Japan and the United States* [Cambridge: Harvard University Press, 1991], 108). For Maruyama to have refrained from going as far as Mao and Fanon would in the view of other interpreters be cause for praise.

22. Among important reviews are those by François Niney in *Cahiers du Cinema* 406 (April 1988): 41; Jill Forbes, *Sight and Sound* 59:1 (winter 1989/90): 2; Carol Lutfy, *Far Eastern Economic Review* (Dec. 17, 1987): 56; and Akira Iriye, *American Historical Review* 94:4 (Oct. 1989): 1036–37.

23. Sissela Bok, *Secrets: On the Ethics of Concealment and Revelation* (New York: Vintage Books, 1983), 65.

24. See Smith, "Unloading the Self-Refutation Charge," in this volume.

25. Judith N. Shklar, *Ordinary Vices* (Cambridge, MA: The Belnap Press of Harvard University Press, 1984), 1–86.

26. Ibid., 48.

27. Robert Solomon, "Self, Deception, and Self-Deception in Philosophy," in this volume. Coming at the question from a different angle, Megumi Sakabe, perhaps currently Japan's preeminent philosopher, arrives at a comparable position in his *Risei no fuan: Kanto tetsugaku no seichō to kōzō* (The Uneasiness of Reason: The Growth and Structure of Kantian Philosophy) (Tokyo: Keisō shobō, 1976). This is related to Sakabe's argument in *Kamen no kaishakugaku* (The Hermeneutics of Masking) (Tokyo: Tōkyō daigaku shuppankai, 1976), that it is especially *modern* to think of the mask as merely an instrument of deceit and that truth lies only in the mask-free face.

28. Eugene Kamenka, *The Portable Karl Marx* (New York: Penguin Books, 1983), 373. Kamenka notes there that later Marxists have felt compelled to distance themselves from the later Marx of *Das Kapital*.

29. Two outstanding eyewitness accounts of the Cultural Revolution in China are Liang Heng and Judith Shapiro, *Son of Revolution* (New York: Viking, 1983) and Jung Chang, *Wild Swans: Three Daughters of China* (New York: Anchor Books, 1991).

30. Richard Rorty, "The Last Intellectual in Europe: Orwell on Cruelty," in *Contingency, Irony, and Solidarity* (Cambridge: Cambridge University Press, 1989), 184.

31. Both scholars at an earlier stage in their respective careers published solid, widely respected works.

32. The nihilistic aspect of these activities, the last of which took place as recently as 1988, is patent. An excellent study of the *sekigun* is Patricia G. Steinhoff's "Highjackers, Bombers, and Bank Robbers: Managerial Style in the Japanese Red Army," *Journal of Asian Studies* 48 (Nov. 1989): 724–40.

33. Shklar, 48.

34. Robert C. Solomon, *The Passions: The Myth and Nature of Human Emotion* (New York: Anchor Press, 1976), 405.

35. This, of course, is one of the central points of Richard Rorty's *Philosophy and the Mirror of Nature* (Princeton: Princeton University Press, 1979).

36. Richard Rorty, "De Man and the American Cultural Left," in *Essays on Heidegger and Others: Philosophical Papers Volume 2* (Cambridge: Cambridge University Press, 1991), 135. I have attempted to explore the utility of such a balanced approach in my "Poetry and Risk: Ideology's Edge in Dōgen and Tamekane," *Eastern Buddhist* n.s., 24:2 (Autumn 1991): 123–40.

37. Norma Field, *In the Realm of a Dying Emperor: A Portrait of Japan at Century's End* (New York: Pantheon Books, 1991).

38. The Rōnō faction within Japanese Marxism, as noted above in note 20, took the position that the *tennō* was such a monarch.

39. After a lengthy account of why it is that "Asia differs from Europe in the nature of everything that grows there, vegetable or human," the unknown author of the Hippocratic text *Airs, Water, Places* puts the finishing touch on his case by charging that a "lack of courage" and desirable bellicosity in Asians is due to the fact that they are still "subjects of a monarchy." See G. E. R. Lloyd, ed., *Hippocratic Writings* (New York: Penguin, 1978), 167. "Orientalism," Marx's notion of "Oriental despotism," and neo-Marxist criticisms of Japan's monarchy would all seem to have roots reaching back as far as texts such as this.

THIRTEEN

FACING THE SELF WITH MASKS

*Perspectives on the Personal from
Nietzsche and the Japanese*

Graham Parkes

To speak of the self's being faced by masks suggests that masks front or confront some thing called the "self," something that maintains its personal identity behind the procession of different personae one adopts in the course of a day or a life. There is the impression, reflecting on the experience of masking one's feelings or speaking from behind a mask, that how one appears or what one says is other than what one is or believes, that one's "true" self remains veiled. And that if one would, one could choose to abandon the deception, drop the pretense, face up to reality and simply be oneself, one self, one's real self. But what would such a self be like? Would it be like—or even be—anything? Or is there perhaps nothing behind the masks, a void beneath the surface, an abyss of emptiness—that might yet turn out, after all, to be some kind of source?

The roles played by masks in the process of deception are complex and multifarious. Just as the literal mask may function to disguise or protect the wearer's face, so a person may engage in metaphorical masking for the purpose of self-protection or deception. The use of a mask is not necessarily to deceive, even though it conceals the face; and indeed the beauty of masks as disguise lies in their duplex function of presenting and withholding, revealing and concealing, at the same time. The opaque surface may in this sense serve as a sign for what lies behind it.

The mask is duplex in another sense, in that it may also be turned toward the inside, as it were. We may deceive ourselves either by masking aspects of the external world we are unwilling to acknowledge ("putting a good face on things"), or by "internal" masking, whereby we conceal from ourselves parts of our selves we would rather not face. At the same time, we seldom present ourselves to the outer world fully, but mostly through the medium of masks that conceal some part or parts of our person. Such masking is not necessarily deceptive for the sake of self-interest, as exemplified by "putting up a good front." Its external effect may in turn affect

Self and Deception

what lies within, insofar as the choice of a particular mask signifies a part of the person and may eventually bring out a side of the personality that would otherwise remain hidden.

The various dualities of the mask as bidirectional mediator between self and other, inside and outside, may be traced back (in the Western tradition) to a figure whose duplex being governs them all: the Greek god Dionysus, who, in addition to being a distinguished progenitor of ancient Green drama, is a power that annuls personal identity through his roles as god of wine and intoxication, of madness and the dance.[1] The mask, like its patron deity, effaces individuation. It is in principle usable by anyone, insofar as a young boy can play the part of an old man with the help of a good mask and appropriate posture. A mask that transforms one's appearance radically can be passed to another, and it will alter the appearance of the other person in a quite different way; and yet it will annul both respective individualities equally. The production of a plurality of effects by one and the same mask bears testimony to the remarkable multiplying power of masking as a manifestation of Dionysus—*polueidēs and polumorphos*—god of many forms.

The best known disciple of Dionysus in the modern age is Friedrich Nietzsche, in whose work we find an especially comprehensive and subtle treatment of the phenomenon of masking.[2] This treatment can be lent greater depth when highlighted or shadowed by perspectives from the Japanese tradition, where masking plays an even more important role than in the West. In view of the association of masks with something other than the self, Western cultures have tended to perceive the otherness of the Asian—and especially the East Asian—as in some sense masked. The inscrutable Chinese and the extreme reserve of the Japanese are both associated with a higher power of masking, a heavier harboring of hiddenness, a more intense degree of concealment. In those worlds the worst imaginable fate is "loss of face." To be seen for what one is is, as long as one has not intended to be so seen, intolerable to the East Asian sensibility. A good amount of self-effacement is considered only civilized—indeed, an indispensable element in the cultivation of oneself into a fully human being.

Japan is distinguished as a culture in which the use of masks to conceal true feelings and impulses for the sake of harmonious interaction with one's fellow human beings is more highly developed than in any other. But the art of masking is ubiquitous also in the West—as evidenced by the fact that the words for mask both in Greek and in Latin soon came to mean "person." It is significant that at the beginning of this tradition the person—in the strict legal sense of the agent responsible for actions and so to be rewarded or punished for them—was seen in the image of the mask rather than the head or body behind it. Consider, too, that in the course of a day a person in society is called upon to act a number of parts; and to help play different roles, we use various kinds of masks, which reveal even as they conceal. Metaphorically speaking, the face becomes a mask or series of masks.

After some preliminary reflections on the relevant words for mask, let us compare the role and function of masks in the classical drama of the two traditions, in ancient Greek tragedy and in the Noh theater of Japan. This will serve as a background for presenting Nietzsche's ideas on masking, interwoven with considerations of comparable views drawn from the novel *Confessions of a Mask* (*Kamen no kokuhaku*) by Mishima Yukio. The discussion will then be rounded out by a brief consideration of the phenomenon of masking as it appears in the work of two contemporary Japanese philosophers, Nishitani Keiji and Sakabe Megumi (both of whom are, like Mishima, acquainted with Nietzsche's works).[3]

I

The literal mask is first and foremost a surface, mediating between outside and inside. *Larvatus prodeo:* masked I go forth, presenting myself *as* such-and-such a person. As it reveals, the mask also conceals: while it protects the most vulnerable part of the body (the death mask and the surgical mask are special and interesting cases), it also conceals that aspect of our exterior which most betrays the inner life. The skin of the face is a fine medium of revelation: through facial expressions—the blush, the twitch, the sudden pallor—we may look shocked, guilty, or shamefaced. Hence the attraction of a mask, behind which the eyes—"windows of the soul"—can see without being easily looked into. Yet these functions of the mask depend on its not being whole: there must be gaps in it—for without holes for the eyes and mouth it resists being seen and spoken through. A literal mask thus allows selective expression—through dynamics of speech and gestures of the head—of the wearer's feelings, intentions, and desires.

The roots both of the Japanese and of the European words for masks lead us back to the face. The origins of our word *mask* are, appropriately, veiled in obscurity; several dictionary entries report: "derivation disputed." A relatively young word (not appearing in French and English until the sixteenth century), it is presumed to come from the Latin *massa* meaning "paste"—whence "mascara"—and *masca* meaning "demon," or "sorcerer." (With the face apparently transformed and transfixed by a mask, the gestures of the rest of the body can become daemonically expressive.) The word's Latin and Greek equivalents connect immediately with the idea of the person. In Latin the image is acoustical, insofar as the components of the word *persōna*, meaning "mask," "character," "person," mean literally "through sound." The Greek *prosōpon* means "front," "façade," or "face"; whence "mask," "character" (in a drama), and "person"—in the original, legal sense. The image is optical, *prosōpon* meaning "at the eyes": as front or façade, that which the eyes meet; as mask that too, but also something held at or worn in front of the eyes.

The masks referred to by *prosōpon* and *persōna* were those worn by actors in Greek and Roman drama and had a transformative and revelatory function. They served both to identify the character—often a divine personage—and to raise the actor to the plane of the paradigmatic or the realm of the archetypal by concealing his particular, all-too-human traits and imperfections. Being larger than the face, the mask formed a sounding board (whence the name *per-sōna*) to allow the actor to project his voice up to the far back of the open-air amphitheater while at the same time concealing facial expressions that might detract attention from the eloquence of the speeches.[4]

The Japanese word for mask, *kamen*, is composed of two characters; *ka*, meaning "temporary," or "provisional," and *men* meaning "surface," "front," or "face." It thus signifies the provisional front one presents to the world, the face one puts on, and on things. As with *prosōpon*, to introduce an optical element by adding the graph for eye, *moku*, produces *menmoku*, meaning "face" in the sense of honor, dignity, reputation. That most horrendous of catastrophes for the Japanese, losing face, is *menmoku o ushinau*: to lose the mask that fronts and confronts the eyes.

An alternative reading for the character *men* is *omote*, meaning "outside" and again "face" in the sense of honor or reputation. This is the usual reading for referring to the masks used in Noh drama.[5] The functions of the Noh mask have much in common with those of its Greek counterpart, though the former is generally smaller than the face. Its purpose is again to identify the character and to eliminate facial expressions—but in order to draw attention to the carefully understated movements of the actor's body (more than to the speech issuing from behind the mask). Something about the size and fit of the Noh mask tends to diffuse rather than concentrate the voice, making it appear to issue from no particular location. But the same uncanny phenomenon occurs when viewing both Noh and Greek tragedy: the mask conduces to the impression of a more-than-human being and provides a screen for a range of projections from the audience's imagination elicited by factors such as speech, posture, and movements of the mask.

II

The themes of masks and masking are central in Nietzsche's work, both in his looking at life through metaphors of the mask and other aspects of the dramatic arts, and in his literary styles, which mask his meanings with layers of irony, parody, and other tropes.[6] They are also central to his life: at the personal level, he often felt use of masks an absolute necessity if he was to be able to go on living.[7]

In Nietzsche's first book, *The Birth of Tragedy* (1872), there is a central figure, a major presence that never appears again in any of his subsequent works—at least not under the name of "the mysterious primordial One" (*BT*, 1—the language is distinctly Schopenhauer-Wagnerian). Insofar as the Apollonian and the Dionysian, as "art-drives of nature," also play through the human being, the primordial One assumes a quasi personal aspect: the Dionysian artist who has lost his individuality in song and dance is said to become, in turn, an artwork in the hands of "the Dionysian artist of worlds." Nietzsche suggests in retrospect that the One is the god Dionysus, through whom an aesthetic meaning for the world can be created in the wake of the death of the metaphysical God of the Platonic-Christian tradition.

> In fact the whole book knows only an artistic meaning as a deeper meaning behind all occurring—a "god," if you will, but certainly only a completely reckless and immoral artist-god, who wants to experience in building as in destroying... his own pleasure and autarchy, and who in creating worlds redeems himself from the *distress* of fullness and *overfullness,* from the *suffering* of the conflicting forces compressed within him.[8]

The human counterpart to this figure would be the person of the lyric poet, who, as a precursor of the Attic tragedian and prototype of the human being in general, is a mask of the primordial One. When the lyrist says (or sings) "I," the word actually issues from a deeper source: "The 'I' of the lyrist resounds out of the abyss of Being."[9] Whereas the epic poet (and the plastic artist, who is related to him) is able to contemplate his images as something separate from his self, the lyric poet is one with his—as projections from the primordial One. The self of the lyrist is then itself an artistic composition of images projected from a deeper self, and his identity as an I dependent on the primordial One, who is the only true "I-ness." The person of the lyrist is, as it were, a mask of a deeper personality, something that both conceals and reveals the real I behind or beneath it.

Self and Deception

Nietzsche goes on to argue that a work that is merely subjective is no work of art and a subject in the sense of the egoistic individual can be no artist: "Insofar as the subject is an artist, it has already been released from its individual will and become as it were a medium, through which the one truly existing subject celebrates its redemption in appearance.... We are simply images and artistic projections for the true creator and have our highest dignity in our significance as works of art."

The drama of life, then, is a "comedy of art" created by the primordial One (also known as the World-Genius, the True Subject, the Genuine Creator—all Dionysian personifications of Schopenhauerian Will) for its own eternal entertainment, of which it is simultaneously "creator and spectator." The dignity of the lyric genius—and by extension, though to a lesser extent, of the rest of us—lies in his ability to merge with the primordial world artist in the act of artistic creation, and thereby become at once "poet, actor, and spectator."

In his discussion of the role of the satyr chorus in Greek tragedy, Nietzsche argues that its members were consummate artists insofar as they were able not only to project a vision of hosts of spirits onto the scene behind them, but also to induce the audience to identify with them and thus participate in the projection. In the collective Dionysian experience in the Greek theater, "we have a surrender of individuality through entering into an other nature." It is this surrendering of individuality, together with the dramatic effect of the mask, that gives Greek tragedy its enormous power.

> The dithyrambic chorus has the task of exciting the mood of the audience to such a Dionysian degree that, when the tragic hero appears on the stage, they see not the awkwardly masked human being but rather a visionary figure born as it were from their own rapture.... Involuntarily [the spectator] transferred the image of the god [Dionysus] which magically trembles before his eyes to that masked figure and, as it were, resolved its reality into a spirit-like nonactuality.[10]

The tragic mask, through concealing the all-too-human face behind it, induces the collective projection of a superhuman image onto the figure of the actor.[11] One can imagine that the mask also helps the actor lose his sense of individuality and allow the image of his role—which the truly gifted actor will see "hover perceptibly before his eyes"—to play itself out through him. Something comparable happens in Noh drama: the mask effaces the actor's awareness of himself, allowing him to *become* the mask and the person it represents; and the accompanying music of flute and drum—at times totally Dionysian—works on the spectator in such a way that the appropriately clothed and masked actor appears a superhuman presence. In both contexts the mask's concealing serves its revelatory purpose both for actor and for audience.

A similar phenomenon occurs in interactions between persons outside the theater, in the everyday world. Naturally masking, a person puts up a front, a screen that in certain situations invites the projection of an image of divine power. It is in fact precisely there, where strong emotions and passions hold sway, that the personal is infused with a transpersonal power, that thanks to the mask the personal relationship is enhanced by a superhuman presence. Just as Nietzsche's remarks about tragedy are to be taken to refer to the larger human drama as well, so his talk about masks and projections are susceptible of psychological generalization. But let us defer discussion of the role of masks in Nietzsche's subsequent work until after the introduction of some ideas from the Japanese side.

III

Nietzsche's ideas had a considerable impact when they reached Japan at the beginning of this century, influencing a number of leading novelists as well as philosophers.[12] *The Birth of Tragedy* was an especially influential text, and especially on one of Japan's most prolific writers, Mishima Yukio.[13] Mishima's first full-length novel, which he wrote at the age of twenty-five, was *Confessions of a Mask* (1949). This work is a masterpiece of quasi autobiography that belongs to that "in-between" genre of confessional novel and prose poem.[14] The title *Kamen no kokuhaku* (Confession[s] of a mask or masks) suggests not that someone is confessing about using a mask but that a mask is itself doing the confessing, and not necessarily about its being a mask. Mishima's choice of the first-person narrative style is significant in the light of the prevailing popularity of the *shishōsetsu*, the confessional "I-novel" in which the author puts himself into the work with minimal disguise. But while many details of the protagonist's life are congruent with the author's own, Mishima was an inveterate player with masks both in his writing and in his life, and his vehement insistence on art as an absolutely autonomous realm suggests an ironist's playing with the form of the I-novel. An acute psychologist, Mishima wants to inquire into the status of the I in the traditional I-novel. His inquiry prompts the questions: Just *who* is speaking the I of the first-person narrative? and Is the first person really singular here?

In its inquiry into the relationship between masks and the self, *Confessions of a Mask* dwells at length on the narrator's childhood and youth.

Self and Deception

Mishima apparently shares the belief (held by Nietzsche and depth psychologists such as Freud and Jung) that one can fully become oneself only through retrieving or redeeming one's childhood, on the grounds that early formative experiences continue to inform our being here now.[15] The emphasis on childhood also prompts the consideration that we are not born wearing masks: masks are given or shaped later, with the ability to use them depending on the development of a vocabulary of facial expression and the acquisition of spoken language.

Mishima's narrative lives up to its title insofar as it presents, with apparently remarkable candor, a number of archetypal fantasies of obsessive sensuality and cruelty, most of them homoerotic. However, the orientation of the sexuality the narrator has to mask is not the important feature, but serves primarily to intensify the problems faced by every person growing up in society. (While Japanese culture has usually been far more accepting of male homosexuality than most Western societies, it also places far greater demands on the emergent person in general.) The issue is the presentation of desire simpliciter and the conforming of its expressions to socially acceptable modes. While Mishima's understanding of the self and masks derives in part from a thorough grounding in classical Chinese and Japanese literature, it is important to know that during the decade before writing *Confessions of a Mask* he also had read intensely a wide range of European authors, including Nietzsche.

The drama of *Confessions of a Mask* is set on what the narrator calls the "stage of childhood and youth," "a stage on which time and space become chaotically interfused" (*CM*, 15). The book opens with a series of childhood recollections (Freud would say fantasies of childhood memories) from the first few years of life. The earliest image, which the narrator says is a source of constant torment to him, is of a fateful encounter at the age of four with a supremely "tragic" figure. Climbing a slope near his home, the boy encounters coming down a youth

> with handsome, ruddy cheeks and shining eyes, wearing a dirty roll of cloth around his head for a sweatband. He came down the slope carrying a yoke of night-soil buckets over one shoulder, balancing their heaviness expertly with his footsteps. He was a night-soil man, a ladler of excrement. He was dressed as a laborer, wearing split-toed shoes with rubber soles and black canvas tops, and dark-blue cotton trousers of the close-fitting kind called "thigh-pullers." (*CM*, 8)

This figure represents for the four-year-old boy his "first revelation of a certain power, [his] first summons by a certain strange and secret voice," and occasions "a presentiment that there is in this world a kind of desire like stinging pain."

> Looking up at that dirty youth, I was choked by desire, thinking, "I want to change into him," thinking, "I want to *be* him." . . . toward his occupation I felt something like a yearning for a piercing sorrow, a body-wrenching sorrow. His occupation gave me the feeling of "tragedy" in the most sensuous meaning of the word. . . . a certain feeling of intimacy with danger, a feeling like a remarkable mixture of nothingness and vital power. (*CM*, 9)

His mentioning the word *tragedy* suggests that the precocious protagonist is being driven by the Dionysian desire to "transform himself and speak out of other bodies and souls," and that the tragic figure of the young night-soil man affords him a premonition of "the primordial One, its suffering and contradiction." The "mixture of nothingness and vital power" is especially characteristic of the Dionysian experience as described in *The Birth of Tragedy*. The suspicion that the night-soil man is a mask or a screen for some kind of projection is confirmed by the protagonist's saying that his ambition to become a night-soil man was later "transferred with those same emotions" to other figures, such as the operators of festival streetcars and ticket-punchers in the subway (*CM*, 10).

The clothes worn by these figures, especially the "thigh-pullers" of the night-soil man, stimulate a desire in the protagonist that he will later understand as sexual. The Dionysian drive is associated with this kind of energy (though perhaps more bisexual than homosexual), insofar as the satyr of Greek tragedy is "a symbol of the sexual omnipotence of nature" (*BT*, 8). Nietzsche remarks that sexual licentiousness was a central feature of the barbarian Dionysian festivals that were the forerunners of the Greek festivals, in which "the wildest beasts of nature were unleashed, including even that horrifying mixture of sensuality and cruelty that has always seemed to me the real 'witches brew' " (*BT*, 2). Such a horrifying mixture is precisely what informs most of the fantasies that mark the subsequent development of the Mishima boy's psyche.

The scene that most fully embodies "childhood itself" for the narrator concerns a summer festival procession that passes in front of his home. He eagerly awaits the arrival of the principal shrine, which is carried by a group of half-naked youths:

> And within the thick scarlet–and–white ropes, within the guard-rails of black lacquer and gold, behind those fast-shut doors of gold leaf, was sixty-four cubic feet of pitch-blackness.

Self and Deception

> This perfect cube of empty night, ceaselessly swaying and leaping, to and fro, up and down, reigned boldly over the cloudless noonday of early summer. (*CM*, 31)

Suddenly the bearers of the shrine begin to lurch through the gate of the protagonist's house. Someone whisks him upstairs to a balcony on the second floor, from where he watches in fascination the youths rampaging around the garden carrying the shrine.

> It was difficult for me to tell what was happening. The noises were neutralizing each other, then it seemed exactly as though my ears were being assaulted by alternating barrages of frozen silence and meaningless rumbling din.... Through it all there was only one thing that was vividly clear, something that both horrified and lacerated me, filling my heart with unaccountable agony. This was the expression on the faces of the young men carrying the shrine—an expression of the most obscene and unrestrained drunken ecstasy in the world. (*CM*, 33)

Not only is this account forcefully reminiscent of the experience of Dionysian intoxication in which one "has identified with the primordial One, its suffering and contradiction" (*BT*, 5), but the conjunction of overwhelming din and sudden silence is also paradigmatic of the Dionysiac experience—"deathly silent noise," Nietzsche calls it in one of the *Dionysus Dithyrambs*.[16]

The Mishima boy's first experience of masks, which he dates to his fifth year, is a traumatic one with a decisive impact on his sense of gender. Among the pictures in the books in his possession at that time, one in particular exerted a powerful fascination, a picture of "a knight mounted on a white horse, holding a sword aloft" (*CM*, 11). The boy imagined that the knight was "confronting either death or, at the very least, some hurtling object full of evil power." If he turned the page quickly enough, the boy fancied he could see the knight being killed. It thus came as a devastating revelation to learn that the figure whose face was masked by armor was actually Jeanne d'Arc: "The person I had thought a *he* was a *she*" (*CM*, 12). As a result of this bitter experience of unmasking, this "revenge by reality," the boy abandons the treacherous picture book forever.

Shortly thereafter, on being taken to the theater to see Tenkatsu, an exotic woman magician, the boy is seized by the desire to "become her." This manifestation of the Dionysian drive to "enter into an other nature" may at the same time be a reaction to the betrayal by the image of Jeanne d'Arc and an attempt to identify psychologically with the antagonist. To help the process of identification along, the boy resorts to a masquerade in which he dresses up as Tenkatsu, wearing the most exotic women's clothes he can find in the house. But when he presents his impersonation to the other members of his family, the reaction to his extravagant costume and make-up is one of horror, and his mother immediately has him "stripped of [his] outrageous masquerade" (*CM,* 19). After being taken to see a film about Queen Cleopatra, he is gripped by a similar desire to play the part of his new idol, but this time he prudently keeps the masquerade a secret.

Shortly after this episode, the boy is able to gain some respite from the oppressive atmosphere of his immediate family by spending time at the home of two girl cousins. But he finds that in this household he is all the more under the burdensome obligation to "act like a boy," so that out of a "sense of social duty" he finds himself proposing games of war and battle to his two playmates. The only consolation is that such games provide the opportunity to play at being killed on the battlefield: "The reluctant masquerade began. . . . I was beginning to understand vaguely . . . that what appeared to other people to be play-acting on my part was actually the expression of a need to return to my essential nature, and that precisely what appeared to be the natural me was a masquerade" (*CM,* 27–28).

As the narrator grows up and enters adolescence, his desire begins more and more to project itself in vivid images of sadistic homosexual fantasy. On realizing his difference from his peers, whose sexual fantasies are directed toward girls, he denigrates his penchant as merely a disgusting childish habit—while at the same time seeing through this piece of self-deception. The first half of the book ends with a resolution to "begin living": "It was as though I had not yet realized that what I was now disgusted with was my true self, was clearly a part of my true life; it was as though I believed instead that these had been years of dreaming, from which I would now turn to 'real life,' " (*CM,* 100). But before engaging the second half of Mishima's novel, let us go back to Nietzsche in order to see how his ideas on the mask develop after *The Birth of Tragedy.*

IV

When Nietzsche's interest shifts to the metaphorical mask, he tends at first to see psychological masking as something inauthentic. In the *Untimely Meditation* on history, the mask is a mere front set up to conceal the "weakened personality" characteristic of the modern human being (*HL,* 5). Since we have lost the innocent insight of the child and our instincts have been extinguished by a surfeit of history, "no one any longer dares to show his person, but masks himself as a cultured man, a scholar, a poet, a politician." Such a weak personality, lacking an inner drive by which to orient itself, timidly consults history in order to learn how to react: "He thus gradually becomes an actor and plays a role—indeed many roles usually, which is why he plays each one so badly and flatly." Here masks are understood as a compensation for a lack of life-force flowing through the individual, a failure of the instincts to guide the person's life.

In *Schopenhauer as Educator,* Nietzsche elaborates the theme of the man who is "totally exterior surface with no kernel, a tattered, daubed, puffed up bag of clothes." Out of laziness and fear we cover our individuality with veils that conform to conventional appearances: "But how can we find ourselves again? How can the human being know itself? It is a thing dark and veiled; and if the hare has seven skins, the human can slough off seventy times seven and still not be able to say, 'Now that is what you really are, that is no longer outer shell,' " (*SE,* 1).

Nietzsche is not so much condemning surface appearances as bemoaning the fact that human beings are reluctant to engage in the difficult work of penetrating these layers of masks for the sake of self-understanding. He goes on to talk of how people "reach passionately for the fantastic events portrayed in the theater of politics, or else themselves proudly parade about in a hundred masks . . . industriously mindful of their common comedy and not at all of themselves" (*SE,* 4). Here the metaphor of the theatrical play illuminates an inauthentic way of being, in which one simply plays a role and loses oneself in it—remaining empty of the life-force.

In *Human, All Too Human,* however, Nietzsche intimates a realization that the difference between authentic being and masked seeming may not be so great after all. In an aphorism entitled "How Seeming [*Schein*] Becomes Being [*Sein*]," he writes about how the person easily becomes the role that is at first only played:

> The actor is ultimately unable, even in the deepest pain, to cease thinking of the impression his person and the whole scenic effect is making, at the funeral of his child for example: he will weep over his own pain and its expressions as his own spectator. The hypocrite who always plays the same role ends up no longer being a hypocrite. . . . When someone fervently wants for a very long time to *seem* something, it will eventually be difficult for that person to *be* anything else. The profession of almost everyone, even of the artist, begins with hypocrisy, with an imitating from outside and a mimicking of what works effectively. One who always wears the mask of friendly expressions must even-

tually gain power over benevolent moods, without which the expression of friendliness cannot be effected—and finally these moods gain power over him, and he *is* benevolent.[17]

To the extent that the player becomes the role and the face the mask, the difference between authentic and inauthentic would seem to dissolve. Does it make sense to say that the true self is left behind, behind the mask, when the person has become the *persōna* and the individual has identified with the role? In the presence of Dionysus, god of the mask, the self itself becomes problematic—and all the more so as Nietzsche pursues his reflections on the multiplicity of the personality.

The idea of masking parts of ourselves from ourselves is expressed in an especially pithy aphorism from *Dawn of Morning,* which alludes to the way the sense of self is formed by the opinions of others as well as to the theme of making oneself a work of art: "We are like shop windows in which we ourselves are constantly arranging, concealing, or illuminating our supposed qualities, which others ascribe to us—all in order to deceive *ourselves*" (*DM,* 385). Life as drama is, for Nietzsche, a special case of life as artwork—and can be realized simply by looking in the right way, using what he calls "the third eye":

> What! You still need the theater! Are you still so young? Be clever and look for tragedy and comedy where it is better played! Where things are more interesting and interested! It is not that easy, admittedly, to remain a spectator in such cases—but learn to be one! And then in almost all difficult and painful situations that befall you will have an escape hatch to joy and a refuge, even when your passions assail you. Open your theater-eye, the great third eye that looks into the world through the other two! (*DM,* 509)

The injunction to learn to be a spectator is less an encouragement to detachment than an invitation to double vision and bipresence: to open the theater eye is to supplement the perspective of the actor with that of the spectator rather than to substitute the latter for the former.

By now Nietzsche has become reconciled to masking as a basic trait of life. In *The Gay Science,* he writes of "the pleasure in masks, the good conscience of everything masked" as something inherent in the beginnings of Western culture, as "the bath and recreation of the ancient spirit" (*GS,* 77). Past masters of the mask are, of course, actors: "Only artists, and especially those of the theater, have given men eyes and ears to see and hear with some pleasure what each man himself is, . . . only they have taught us . . . the art of putting ourselves 'into a scene' for ourselves" (*GS*, 78). Nietzsche appears to be more charitable toward the histrionic art because he is now beginning to understand falseness as the manifestation of a fundamental human drive to falsify and simplify the world for the sake of control (*GS*, 110–12). This is a form of the archaic fantasy that conditions all our experience.[18] Not to take responsibility for participating in the constitution of the world, actively to forget that the ancestors and we ourselves have been making most of it up as we go along, to take facts as simply given, and to play our parts with undiluted seriousness, is to be cowardly, naive, and comical. It is not the fantasizing per se that he objects to—it belongs to our nature—but our pretending that we had no part in it, playing the role of the dispassionate spectator viewing with the innocent I.

Nietzsche writes enthusiastically of the possibility of participating in the workings of archaic fantasy with reflective awareness, playing them out fully, living the myth further, dreaming the dream onward. As a counterpart to the masking of aspects of the self involved in "giving style to one's character" (*GS*, 290), we can "learn from artists" how to mask aspects of the rest of the world through a variety of aesthetic strategies, and thereby become "poets of our own lives" (*GS*, 299). Nietzsche clearly wants to retain from the *Untimely Meditations* the view that most people are simply self-deceiving in their refusal to face up to the grim facts of life. But there is another kind of masking that could be called, on account of its self-awareness, "authentic." Indeed, at its most authentic, this play of masking reaches the level of poetry, where the actor becomes the author. Nietzsche argues that "the higher human beings" who are capable of "seeing and hearing thoughtfully" are no longer simply "*spectators* and *listeners* before the great play of sights and sounds that is life," nor are they simply "*actors* in this drama." They are actually "the true poets and continuous creators of life," by virtue of their creating, as artistic philosophers, "the whole eternally growing world of valuations, colors, weights, perspectives, scales, affirmations and negations," making of this world a *Dichtung,* a poetic play and literary work (*GS*, 301). Not that they compose this poem *ex nihilo* or arbitrarily make it up—any more than a literal poet creates out of nothing or anarchically. As with the rest of us, their fantasy constitutes in concert with other projections a common reality.

Just as the image of the mask in Nietzsche is ambiguous, his remarks in the last book of *The Gay Science* on actors and role playing remain somewhat ambivalent.[19] On the one hand, European society forces people into a particular role, determined largely by their occupation; one becomes identified with the role, which then constricts development of character along other dimensions: "Almost all Europeans confuse themselves with their role . . . they forget . . . how many other roles they *could have played*" (*GS,* 356). The mask is seen here as something constricting, something that inhibits—as the literal mask does—the range of expression of the fully human being. The pressures of life can form the face into a mask, which then *becomes* the person so well that the self fuses with, comes to be, its mask. However, it is possible to go to the other extreme—Nietzsche gives "the Americans today" as an example (one just as valid *today*)—of assuming that a person can play absolutely any part whatsoever. This leads to one's becoming a total actor and forgetting altogether that one is playing roles.

Nietzsche also pursues the analogy between masks and clothing: "It seems that we Europeans absolutely cannot do without that masquerade which one calls clothes" (*GS,* 352). While clothes conceal, they also share the expressive function of masks insofar as they present aspects of our selves and project the appropriate "image." (Again the effect is bidirectional: much of the impression a well-tailored three-piece suit makes on the viewer comes from the effect it has on the wearer, from the way it draws her out—and into the part.) As for concealment, Nietzsche claims that it is not even "the wild beast of prey" in us that we wish to cover up, but rather "the shameful sight of the tame animal" that morality has made us become. (One thinks, for example, of the modern leather jacket.)

While Nietzsche is now able to recommend histrionics in the nonpejorative sense, he remains deeply ambivalent about "the problem of the actor," which arises precisely from the histrionic art. He puts it here in quite Dionysian terms that are applicable to life in general:

> Falseness with a good conscience; the pleasure in dissimulation bursting forth as a power that pushes aside the so-called "character," flooding and sometimes extinguishing it; the inner demand for a role and mask, to enter the mode of *seeming* [*Schein*]; an abundance of all kinds of adaptability that can no longer be satisfied in the service of the most immediate and narrow utility. All this is perhaps true not *only* of the actor? (*GS,* 361)

The talk of *Schein* recalls the theme of the Apollonian from *The Birth of Tragedy*. There Nietzsche speculated that the ancient Greeks were forced, in order to be able to live at all, to mask the terror of the Dionysian abyss by projecting a veil of "beautiful sheen" over it (*BT,* 1–2). Since the Apollonian is, like the Dionysian, an "art-drive of nature," the projection of a world of images in dream or in fantasy is not simply an avoidance strategy on the part of a people who finds the real world a vale of tears, nor an arbitrary piece of self-indulgent whimsy on the part of an individual wishing to escape the constraints of reality: it is rather, Nietzsche claims, a process inherent in the nature of things and informing the structure of all life.[20] The process of masking is thus of considerable ontological significance, insofar as it is not something contingently practiced by human beings but is rather woven into the very fabric of existence. Thus, when Nietzsche wonders whether "all this is perhaps true not *only* of the actor," he is suggesting that it *is* true not only of artists but of the actor and artist in himself and in every person. "Falseness with a good conscience" is possible because falseness is impossible to avoid: but a good conscience can be enjoyed as long as one faces up to that upon which one is putting a better face, as long as one becomes conscious of playing a part.

Nietzsche's understanding of the necessity and desirability of masks finds its consummate expression in *Beyond Good and Evil*, which is his first major exercise in literary masking—aside from *Zarathustra*—and a masterpiece of esoteric writing.[21] Early on the author announces, self-referentially, that "everything that is profound loves masks" (*BGE*, 40). A note from the period points up the pathos behind this utterance, remarking the necessity—for some—of *"taking refuge"* in happiness:

> We sit ourselves down on the street where life rolls by in a drunken procession of masks ... doesn't it seem as if we know something that makes us *afraid*? With which we don't want to be alone. A knowledge of something that makes us tremble, whose whispering makes us pale? This stubborn aversion from mournful dramas ... this arbitrary Epicureanism of the heart, which worships the mask as its ultimate deity and savior.... It seems as if we know ourselves to be all too fragile, perhaps shattered already and unhealable; it seems as if we fear the hand of life, and that it must shatter us, and we take refuge in life's sheen.... We are serious, we know the abyss: *that's* why we are defensive with respect to everything serious.[22]

Numerous themes come together here, from the necessity for a veil of Apollonian *Schein* to mask the abyss, to the idea that all life is a play, drama, intoxicating and devastating tragedy—and that the sense of theater must be maintained if one is not to go under.

The aphorism from *Beyond Good and Evil* emphasizes again the extent to which the mask, the surface of one who is profound, is formed also by external forces, projections from outside. Everyone who knows his depths well enough will want a mask, "and supposing he does not want it, he would still some day realize that there is nevertheless a mask of himself there—and that that is good. Every profound spirit needs a mask: moreover, around every profound spirit a mask is continually growing, thanks to the constantly false, namely *shallow* interpretation of every word, every step, every sign of life he gives." In fact one need not even be so profound to have experienced incongruous reactions from other people based on their projections of inappropriate features onto one's expression. The drive to dissimulate recurs in this text, in the form of "that not unproblematic readiness of the spirit to deceive other spirits and to dissimulate before them, that constant pressure and compulsion of a creative, image-forming, changeable force: in this the spirit enjoys the multiplicity and craftiness of its masks, and also enjoys the feeling of security in this—it is precisely through its protean arts that it is best defended and concealed!" (*BGE*, 230).

Again this creative force is understood as a natural drive, and as such is neither to be lauded nor deplored: our responsibility is to be aware of how it works through us, and our prerogative to let it play. But the "creative, image-forming, changeable force" mentioned here is always in tension with another drive of "the spirit": "*Counter to* this will to sheen [*Wille zum Schein*], to simplification, to the mask and cloak, to the surface in short—since every surface is a cloak—there works that sublime inclination of the one who would know, who takes and *wants* to take things profoundly, multiply, thoroughly: as a kind of cruelty of the intellectual conscience and taste." This passage makes clear Nietzsche's view that there is in the human spirit a fundamental tension generated by the opposing drives to mask and to unmask. Nietzsche the genealogist, the great unmasker, is at the same time a past master of masking and a consummate respecter of veils.[23] The mask is behind one of the last questions of the book, in which the author asks "Whether behind every one of [the philosopher's] caves there is not, must not be, another deeper cave ... an abyss behind every ground, beneath every 'grounding?' " prompting the further question: "Behind every mask, another mask?" Perhaps there is no firm face as foundation for the makeup, no substantial self. Or is Nietzsche not to be trusted in this matter, with these confessions of a mask? He ends the aphorism after all with the enigmatic caution: "Every philosopher also *conceals* a philosophy; every opinion is also a hiding-place; every word also a mask" (*BGE*, 289).

Let us now pursue the theme of acting and masks further with reference to *Confessions of a Mask*. The scene for the second half of the book is set by the opening sentence: "Everyone says that life is a stage." The narrator continues: "By the end of childhood I was already firmly convinced that it was so and that I was to play my part on the stage without ever

Self and Deception

revealing my true self. . . . I believed optimistically that once the performance was finished the curtain would fall and the audience would never see the actor without his make-up" (*CM*, 101).

The boy understands his part as consisting in "the role by means of which one attempts to conceal, often even from himself, the true nature of his sexual desires" (*CM*, 102). An account follows, one of the psychologically most penetrating in any literature, of the gamut of roles, masks, disguises, and other forms of "autohypnosis" by which the young adolescent dissimulates his desire in order to conform to the expectations of the social group. The masquerade proceeds smoothly at first, as when in the presence of his rather prudish school friends he affects the jaded air of a man of the world. But the sustained pretense of being in love (undeclared) with the sister of a classmate turns out to be exhausting: "In the intervals between these artificial mental efforts I would sometimes be overwhelmed by a sense of their hollowness, and, in order to escape, would shamelessly go on to a different kind of fantasy. Then immediately I would come alive, would become myself, and would blaze toward strange images" (*CM*, 121). With consummate artistry the player would abstract the feeling from the (homosexual) image that fired it and transfer it to the figure of the girl as the "natural" stimulus for sexual passion—"and again I deceived myself." The mask that was at first turned toward others now faces inward as well.

After a period of recuperation, Mishima's adolescent eventually embarks upon another feigned love affair, this time with somewhat more enthusiasm, with the young and beautiful Sonoko, the sister of one of his friends. He is to meet her and other members of her family at a train station near their house, to go together to visit her brother at his army barracks some distance away (*CM*, 140–41). The narrator's reaction to his first sight of Sonoko at the station is startling for the reader—an effect he anticipates and immediately responds to:

> In all my life my heart had never before been so touched by the sight of beauty in a woman. My breast throbbed; I felt purified.
> The reader who has followed me this far will probably refuse to believe anything I am saying. . . . If the reader persists in such doubts, then the act of writing has become a useless thing from the beginning: he will think that I say a thing simply because I want to say it so, without any regard for truth. (*CM*, 142–43)

The reader naturally wonders whether the mask here protests too much—especially in accordance with Nietzsche's dictum (with which Mishima was surely familiar): "Does one not write books precisely to conceal what one harbors?" And yet it seems after all as if the narrator's archetypal fantasies, hitherto engendered only by males, might also be promptable by this eighteen-year-old girl—even though the experience is followed by a quite different emotion:

> She came running down the platform toward me with a graceful motion like the trembling of light.
> What I saw come running toward me was not a girl, not that personification of flesh which I had been forcibly picturing to myself since boyhood, but something like the herald of the morning tidings.... Yet each second while I watched Sonoko approach, I was attacked by unendurable grief... [which] seemed to undermine and set tottering the foundations of my existence... but a grief that was no part of my masquerade. (*CM*, 143–44)

Any relief at the fact that the narrator finally feels genuine emotion is dispelled when, late that night, the grief returns and the narrator proclaims "Every word I had spoken and every act I had performed that day [with Sonoko] had been false" (*CM*, 152). And yet, as he continues to be led around "in endless circles of introspection," he begins to wonder—with good reason, in view of Nietzsche's idea that the impersonator tends to become the person and the wearer's face the mask—whether some kind of reversal may not have taken place.

> My act has become an integral part of my system. It's no longer an act. The consciousness that I am pretending to be a normal person has corroded my inherent normality, so that finally I had to tell myself every time that that too was nothing but a pretense at normality.... My feeling of wanting to regard Sonoko's attraction for me as sheer counterfeit might be nothing but a mask to hide my true desire of believing myself genuinely in love with her. (*CM*, 153)

These musings capture perfectly the way reflections on masks and roles can dissolve into dizzying multiplicities as the sense of one solid person behind the masks and separate from the roles begins to fade.

The young man's supposition that his lack of erotic interest in Sonoko may be a mask for his true desire for her is exploded by an overwhelming masturbatory fantasy of ritual murder (modeled on his favorite image of the martyrdom of Saint Sebastian) in an atmosphere of pagan ceremony:

> Your heart quivers with an overflow of primitive sensual feeling. The deep joy of the savage is reborn in your heart. Your eyes shine, the blood flares up through your entire body, and you overflow with the manifestation of forms of life embraced by savage tribes. After ejaculation . . . you float for a while in the memory of a huge, ancient river. Perhaps by some chance the memory of the deepest emotion in the life force of your savage ancestors has taken utter possession of your sexual functions and pleasures. (*CM*, 176)

One is indeed a mask of the primordial One. For Mishima, retrieving or redeeming images from childhood seems to be in the service of getting behind the masks, insofar as early childhood is a period that antedates the acquisition of masks in any form. But with this fantasy, the regression goes farther back, beyond birth, and encounters a primordial manifestation of the life force—which is at the same time a force of death and destruction.

From this point in the narrative, the life force of the protagonist seems gradually to ebb, as he agonizes long and miserably over his relationship with Sonoko until finally finding the occasion to break it off. Sonoko gets married not long thereafter to someone else, but the narrator, having convinced himself that he loves her for her soul, initiates a series of secret rendezvous. In the final scene of the book, they go to a low-class dance hall, where the sight of a young hoodlum bare to the waist with a wonderfully muscled upper body inflames once again the narrator's desire. The realization of the antithesis between his intellect and his sexual feelings appears unlikely to resolve anything, though the ending is left open, with the masks still in place.

V

A turn here to the work of Nishitani Keiji may afford a helpful perspective on this question. Nishitani quotes with approval two of those passages on masks in *Beyond Good and Evil*, in the course of an inquiry into the relationship between the personal and the impersonal.[24] Nishitani argues, from the standpoint of Zen, against the narrowness of what he calls the "person-centered view of person." He encourages an existential conversion away from this view to one of person as *phenomenon:* "When I say that a person is a phenomenon I do not wish to imply that there is some other 'thing' behind personal being, like an actor behind a mask. Person is an appearance with nothing at all behind it to make an appearance. That is to say, 'nothing at all' is what is behind person; complete nothingness, not one single thing, occupies the positions behind person" (RN, 70). Remember the Mishima boy's experience of the tragedy of a life as "a mixture of nothingness and vital power" and at the Dionysian rout the "perfect cube of empty night" accompanied by the "frozen silence and meaningless rumbling din." But Nishitani would call this kind of nothingness or emptiness "nihility," a condition that must be passed through in order to attain the standpoint of absolute nothingness.[25] Through Zen practice the conceptions, prejudices, and presuppositions that help constitute the personality are emptied out, as it were, and the disposition of the body honed with disciplined practice so that one can respond naturally and spontaneously to every changing situation. But because of the unique disposition of each body, these responses and activities are also unique in a way that makes them, once again, personal.

In the kind of existential conversion that produces living nothingness, for Nishitani,

> the self does not cease being a personal being. Person is constituted at one with absolute nothingness as that in which absolute nothingness becomes manifest.
>
> In this sense we can understand person as *persona*—the "face" that an actor puts on to indicate the role he is to play on stage—but only as the *persona* of absolute nothingness. We can even call it a "mask" in the ordinary sense of a face that has been taken on temporarily, provided that we do not imply that there is some other "true" or "real" thing that it cloaks. (RN, 71)

Insofar as the person is realized as a mask of absolute nothingness, "every bodily, mental, and spiritual activity that belongs to person displays itself as a play of shadows moving across the stage of nothingness" (RN, 73). On the one hand, then, the person is a mask or a phenomenon since it is "constituted at one with absolute nothingness," while, on the other, it is absolutely real, since nothingness can become manifest only in some mask or phenomenon.

It is in this context that Nishitani quotes Nietzsche on masks from *Beyond Good and Evil*, saying that they "have something in common" with his own idea of the person as a mask of absolute nothingness, "yet they are not the same" (RN, 72). There are two ways of understanding the difference. First one could say that, for the Nietzsche of *The Birth of Tragedy*, what is behind the person as phenomenon, "the Apollonian of the mask," is "the abyss of Being," "the primordial One, with its suffering and contradiction," or the Dionysian life forces of eternal creation and destruction. For Nishitani, this would be the equivalent of nihility, or relative nothingnes, and not of absolute nothingness.

One could also point to another way in which Nietzsche understands the Dionysian dissolution of the person—namely, into a multiplicity of persons or subjects within the particular individual. On this view, behind the multiplicity or masks one dons in the course of a day, or the range of roles one plays in the course of a life, is a plurality of persons to play them. This idea of psychical multiplicity runs throughout Nietzsche's thinking.[26] Especially in the final decade of his writing, working increasingly under the crazed eye of his patron Dionysus, Nietzsche performs the painstaking alchemical opus of dissolving the unitary I behind the masks into a series of multiplicities—first into a community of persons, then into a plurality of drives (*Triebe*—the "instincts" of psychoanalysis), and finally into a polycentric force field of interpretive energies.

While the ultimate answer to the question of "Who speaks?" behind the masks is: "the interpretive energies of will to power," Nietzsche's intermediate answers are psychologically more thought provoking: "This particular perspective, such-and-such a drive, the person who is so-and-so." There is thus no one person behind the masks: the stage of the world play provides no firm ground on which a unitary ego could take a stand; there is no independent actor, director, or producer behind the various dramatis personae. To suppose that there is is to succumb to the tendency (which Nietzsche shows to be unnecessary) to posit a speaker behind every speech, a doer behind every doing, an actor behind every action. *Au fond*, the abyss alone speaks. The drama is all, and it is no more possible to separate the faces from the masks than the dancer from the dance or the players from the play.

What appears to constitute the difference between this view and the Zen understanding proposed by Nishitani is the consideration that the play of interpretive energies that is will to power, while in no sense a "thing," is nevertheless not absolutely nothing either. And yet it is not clear that Nishitani's reading of Nietzsche on this topic is radical enough, insofar as he tends to understand will to power as "a metaphysical principle" (*RN*, 158). Indeed, Nishitani's own description of what he calls "the field of emptiness" (equivalent to absolute nothingness) is strongly reminiscent of Nietzsche's view of the self and world as a play of will to power. On the field of emptiness (or *śūnyatā*), it is not as if all things collapse into an undifferentiated unity: the field is rather "an absolute unity on the field where multiplicity and differentiation are absolutely radicalized."[27]

In conclusion, let us turn briefly to a recent discussion of the phenomenon of masking by the contemporary Japanese philosopher Sakabe Megumi, whose hermeneutics of the mask is a profound enterprise to which only scant justice can be done in the space remaining here.[28] Sakabe approaches the issue from several perspectives: on the one hand, he adduces the number of considerations from the realm of Noh drama, and especially from the works of Zeami (1363–1443), the great Noh dramatist and theoretician; while, on the other, he draws insightfully from poststructuralist anthropology, deconstructionist philosophy, and recent philosophically relevant work in linguistics.

Sakabe begins by considering the modern (post-Cartesian) philosophical understanding of masks as façades for a "true face," in the sense that behind the temporary fronts, or the roles that one might play, is an "ego-subject" that maintains its identity throughout the changes on the surface (*KK*, 4). Corresponding to this is a conception of the phenomenal world, the world revealed by the senses, as a mask or front for some "true" world lying behind it. (He mentions in this context the intelligible realm of Plato and Nietzsche's calling this a *"Hinterwelt."*) And just as the world of the eternally self-identical Ideas lends to the world of experience whatever identity and continuity it may possess, so the idea of an eternally self-identical God is the guarantor of the identity of the human ego.

But after "the death of God" and the collapse of what Derrida has called the "metaphysics of presence," human beings and the world of experience become masks without real faces behind them—or else, in an interesting turnabout—faces without masks (*KK*, 6). Sakabe wants to inquire into the status of the person, or *persōna*, in the face of the untenability of the traditional metaphysical dualisms. Taking his cue from the phenomenon of the voice, which has traditionally been held to signify the living presence of the subject, Sakabe echoes Derrida in calling the self-evidence of this conception into question.[29] The source of the voice when someone speaks—and especially through a mask—is indeterminate and cannot be identified and specified as something in visual space (*KK*, 17). (This is surely the motivation behind Nietzsche's persistent question: Who speaks?)

The question of the source of the voice can be pursued by inquiring into the referents of the personal pronouns when pronounced by a particular voice. Who says *I*? And to what do *you* or *she* ultimately refer when I say them? Sakabe notes a difference among the personal pronouns: between *I* and *you* which are dependent on a living context, and *he, she,* and *it* which are not. The third-person pronouns would appear to be less personal than the first and second, insofar as they are independent of a living, speaking

Self and Deception

subject. Insofar as they figure in third-person narratives, the question arises concerning the source of the voice that narrates the narrative. Looking again to Noh drama as an image of the human condition, Sakabe notes that the chorus in Noh sings for any one of the masked figures on the stage. Indeed, the situation of each of the main characters is established by the song and music of the chorus. This consideration leads him to posit the existence of some kind of impersonal "arche-person" (*genninshō*) as the source of the voice that comes through the various masks that signify individuals. This arche-person is comparable both to Nietzsche's primordial One in *The Birth of Tragedy* and to Nishitani's absolute nothingness that is inseparable from its personal manifestations.

Let us sum up the points on which there seems to be substantial agreement between the Nietzschean and the Japanese perspectives we have considered. The received view is discredited which sees masks as mere fronts for some kind of true face and real person behind them. While it is agreed that masks can serve to dissimulate "something," this is regarded as a superficial or inauthentic function. While, on the one hand, an inability to play with masks leads to monotony and impoverishment of the personality, on the other, an unreflective identification with the masks is no less stultifying. Because masks are formed as much by projections from outside as by desires from within, it is easy to become nothing but a blank screen for the projections of others—all husk and no kernel—or else to lose oneself in a play or mirrors looking for the actor who is not a reflected image.

The narrator of Mishima's novel appears to oscillate between such extremes—perhaps as a result of identifying with the creative-destructive forces of archaic life while failing to achieve a break with them that would afford space for reflection. In the regression back beyond his birth, he fails to see—as one of Zen's more silently striking images puts it—"one's face before one's parents were born."

If, however, one can harmonize one's playing with the cosmic play of will to power as understood by Nietzsche, or can realize it as a manifestation of absolute nothingness in Nishitani's sense, one will be able to play one's parts with authentic abandon, following effortlessly the script of the world drama because one is identified with the poet and author of that play. The aim would be to fulfill one's role with flair—while realizing that it is only a role, and yet that the player has no identity beyond the totality of parts played and is no more than a succession of roles, part after part, different faces every time.

NOTES

1. For an account of Dionysus's association with masks, see W. F. Otto, *Dionysus: Myth and Cult* (Bloomington: Indiana University Press, 1965), especially the chapter entitled "The Symbol of the Mask." The references will make use of the following abbreviations:

    CM —Mishima Yukio, *Confessions of a Mask,* trans. Meredith Weatherby (New York: New Directions, 1958)
    KK —Sakabe Magumi, *Kamen no kaishakugaku* (Hermeneutics of the mask) (Tokyo: Chikuma, 1976)
    RN —Nishitani Keiji, *Religion and Nothingness* (Berkeley: University of California Press, 1985)

Nietzsche's works:

    BGE—*Beyond Good and Evil*
    BT —*The Birth of Tragedy*
    DM —*Dawn of Morning*
    GS —*The Gay Science*
    HL —*On the Use and Disadvantage of History for Life (Untimely Meditation 2)*
    SE —*Schopenhauer as Educator (Untimely Meditation 3)*

In the case of Nietzsche's aphoristic works the numbers refer to the aphorism, and of the other works to the page numbers. Translations of passages from Nietzsche's texts are my own, and I have on occasion modified the English translation of passages from Mishima's novel in the light of the Japanese original.

2. Nietzsche often refers to himself as a "disciple of Dionysus." The last section of *Twilight of the Idols,* "What I Owe to the Ancients," ends with the words: "I, the last disciple of the philosopher Dionysus—I, the teacher of eternal recurrence."

3. Two other Japanese novels available in English translation which deal with the topic are *Masks (Onna men)* by Enchi Fumiko, and *The Face of Another (Tanin no kao)* by Abe Kōbō. Of the two treatments, both of which are instructive, Abe's is philosophically the more interesting and engages several of the themes of the present essay.

4. Nietzsche maintains that the Greeks "made facial expressions and easy movements impossible for the actor and transformed him into a solemn, stiff, masked dummy," because they wanted to dictate to the passions "a law of beautiful speeches" (GS, 80).

5. A good account of the mask in Noh drama is to be found in Kunio Komparu, *The Noh Theater, Principles and Perspectives* (New York and Tokyo: Weatherhill, 1983), 224–39.

6. Some of the discussion of Nietzsche that follows is drawn from ch. 9 of Graham Parkes, *Composing the Soul* (Chicago: University of Chicago Press, 1994).

7. See, for example, the letters to Erwin Rohde of late February 1870 and to Franz Overbeck of 10 February 1883, where Nietzsche bemoans the fact that he is forced by circumstances to lead a life that is masked and veiled.

8. *BT,* 5, "Attempt at a Self-Criticism." It is clear, especially from the mention of autarchy, that the figure of Dionysus is here emblematic of the great human being who is capable of sustaining the tensions produced by powerfully conflicting drives.

9. *BT,* 5. Kaufmann mistranslates *aus dem Abgrund des Seins* as "from the depth of his being": Nietzsche's whole point is to deny that the "I" issues from the lyrists's being and to emphasize its transpersonal origin.

10. *BT,* 8. Sakabe Megumi mentions with approval Nietzsche's idea that the persons of Greek tragedy have their origin in the satyr chorus, but he notes that the principles of Noh drama dictate that "the dance should arise from the voice and settle into sound" (*KK,* 16). This grants a priority to the voice that is not emphasized in Nietzsche's account of Greek tragedy, in which the chorus generates the vision of the action "with the whole symbolism of the dance, tones, and words" (*BT,* 8).

11. For a fine account of the mask of Greek tragedy, see John Jones, *On Aristotle and Greek Tragedy* (London, 1962), especially the chapter entitled "Human Beings." While Jones makes only one, rather slighting, reference to Nietzsche, what he says about the mask seems quite consonant with Nietzsche's later ideas on the topic. For instance: "By the erosive flow of action the individual features are carved out, no potent shaping spirit lodges aboriginally behind the face; and thus the Aristotelian stage-figure receives his distinctive qualities" (38). "At the living heart of the tradition the actor is the mask and the mask is an artifact-face with nothing to offer but itself. It has—more important, it is known to have—no inside. Its being is exhausted in its features" (45).

12. For a brief account see my essay "The Early Reception of Nietzsche's Philosophy in Japan," in Graham Parkes, ed., *Nietzsche and Asian Thought* (Chicago: University of Chicago Press, 1991), 177–99.

13. Mishima read *The Birth of Tragedy* with great enthusiasm towards the end of the war, and subsequently wrote an essay on it, under the title "Higeki no tanjō ni tsuite" (*Mishima Yukio zenshū*).

14. *Confessions of a Mask* has a great deal in common with Rilke's *Notebooks of Malte Laurids Brigge* (1910), which surely influenced its composition. For some aspects of a comparison, see Graham Parkes, "Facing the Masks: Persona and Self in Nietzsche, Rilke and Mishima," *MOSAIC: a Journal for the Interdisciplinary Study of Literature* 20:3 (1987): 65–79.

15. The necessity for Nietzsche of a "redemption" of images from childhood is most clearly expressed in *Thus Spoke Zarathustra,* especially in the first half of the book.

16. *Dionysus Dithyrambs,* "Fame and Eternity," sec. 3. See also Otto, *Dionysus,* ch. 7.

17. *Human, All Too Human,* 51. See also the next aphorism, in which the process by which seeming becomes being is further elucidated: deception is more effective if one pretends to believe in it oneself; and eventually through repeated

professions and expressions of belief it becomes incorporated, such that one actually comes to have faith and belief in one's own deception—which thereby ceases to *be* a deception.

18. See, especially, *DM,* 119; *GS,* 54, 57; *BGE,* 138, 192, 224, 264. For an account of Nietzsche's conception of this kind of fantasy activity, see *Composing the Soul,* chs. 3, 8.

19. Chronological sequence would demand a consideration of *Thus Spoke Zarathustra* at this point, since book 5 of *The Gay Science* was added later, in 1886. The justification for forgoing this is that the text contains hardly any explicit mention of masks—though the figure of Zarathustra is naturally a mask for the book's author (as, one could argue, are all the other characters in the book).

20. A note from 1888 reads: "In the inorganic world, dissimulation [*Verstellung*] appears to be lacking; in the organic, cunning begins; plants are already masters in that" (*KSA,* 12:10[159]).

21. The theme of esoteric writing is first sounded at *BGE,* 30; see, on this topic, Laurence Lampert, *Nietzsche and Modern Times,* esp. 306–10. See also the discussion of Nietzsche's self-maskings in terms of irony in Ernst Behler, *Irony and the Discourse of Modernity* (Seattle: University of Washington Press, 1990), ch. 3, "Irony in the Ancient and the Modern World."

22. *KSA,* 12:3[33]; 1885–1886.

23. See, on respect for veils, *GS,* preface, sec. 4.

24. "This is typical Nietzsche, deep in insight and full of subtlety" (*Religion and Nothingness,* 72).

25. Nishitani discusses in detail the relation between nihility and true nothingness in *The Self-Overcoming of Nihilism,* trans. Graham Parkes with Setsuko Aihara (Albany: State University of New York Press, 1990).

26. For a full account of the theme of psychical multiplicity in Nietzsche, see *Composing the Soul,* chs. 3, 8, 9.

27. *RN,* 164; ch. 4, "The Standpoint of Śūnyatā," develops this important but difficult point.

28. Sakabe Megumi, *Kamen no kaishakugaku* (Hermeneutics of the mask). (Tokyo: Tokyo University Press, 1976).

29. Jacques Derrida, *La voix et le phénomène* (Paris: 1967); English trans. David Allison, *Speech and Phenomena* (Evanston: North Western University Press, 1973).

FOURTEEN
SELF-DECEPTION
A Comparative Study

Eliot Deutsch

> Self-deception is a form of self-compromise that systematically sows confusion and disorder within the self.
> —Herbert Fingarette, *Self-Deception*

The phenomenon of self-deception is exceedingly complex. Recent studies in philosophy and psychology in particular have brought forth a rich variety of descriptions and explanations—some of which, because of the alleged hopelessly paradoxical nature of the phenomenon, have even been bent on denying its very existence. Then how much more complex and confusing the issue becomes when we introduce Asian thought and experience into the picture! This study will be exploratory in nature. It is less concerned with proffering another theory of the phenomenon—albeit I will refer briefly to some of my own ideas on the matter—than with looking at various ways in which the phenomenon itself may be reconceptualized in the light of certain aspects of Asian thought and experience. I will concentrate on an Indian perspective.

A basic problematic which underlies this inquiry, however, is this: Do we have the same phenomenon of self-deception in different cultures, the differences residing only in the ways in which it is conceptualized? or, Is the phenomenon itself different in virtue of varied social practices as these are themselves informed by different social values and ways of interpretation? For example, in a society, say, where "lying" is often an accepted social practice, justified as good manners and the like, does self-deceit—which in the West has been modeled so strongly on the analogy with deceiving another person—mean behaviorally the same thing as it would for someone in a society in which "honesty" at all costs is a central value?

In any event, as I have indicated, a comparative approach to self-deception, from the standpoint of a Westerner, looks for ways in which the problem as we have tended to formulate it might be altered and enriched in the light of Asian thought and experience. A comparative approach in

Self and Deception

philosophy, both for a Westerner and for a non-Westerner is not so much a matter of juxtaposing—literally comparing and contrasting—different views, looking, where appropriate, for sameness and difference for its own sake, as it is a creative undertaking which compels one simply to think in a more global manner.

I

Let us turn first to the West. One point is immediately evident, and that is that differing accounts of self-deception rest very clearly on different fundamental views regarding the nature of the self. For those of a more psychoanalytic persuasion, the picture of the self in general is one grounded in *conflict*—in some fundamental division or other within the self (e.g., between ego and id) so that one domain of selfhood is able to keep—and quite purposively—something of threatening importance from another domain of that very same self. Philosophers such as Robert Audi are thus able to argue that self-deception can be understood rationally only as a conflict of unconscious and conscious experience as this is supported by a particular "want."[1] Others with a more epistemological-analytic approach, which seem to presume some form of what might be called a "rational view of the self," tend to see self-deception as a matter of someone's holding what appears to be irreconcilable beliefs—that *A* believes both *P* and not-*P* at the same time—a gross affront to our notion of 'rationality.'

Herbert Fingarette, in his seminal work on self-deception, argued, to the contrary, that self-deception is not necessarily connected at all with one's holding irreconcilable beliefs, but rather is to be understood within the framework of personal identity—as the refusal of someone to avow or to acknowledge some aspect of one's self and one's activity in the world because such an acknowledgement would be, so the deceiver believes, unbearable in virtue of its being disruptive to one's established habits and values. Self-deception, then, becomes a systematic and persistent refusal to "spell-out" one's situation and to take responsibility for it.

However, social psychological interpretations that rest on the premise that "self-conceptions are largely shaped by how we interpret other people's interpretations of us"[2] seem to build into their understanding of self-deception the very paradox they want so strongly to avoid. If my own self-conception rests on my interpreting others' interpretations of me and those "others' interpretations" being possible only on yet others' interpretations of them (which would seem necessarily to follow) then we quickly have a circle that is clearly nonhermeneutical in character.

Still others (perhaps Richard Rorty, Parfit), with their variants of a "postmodern" view, deny in the first place the reality of a unified self in favor of a multiplicity of temporary selves, not all of which, or even any of them, necessarily communicating or contending with each other, self-deception then being essentially nonexistent.

My own analysis of self-deception, as cast in Western terms, is more closely akin to Fingarette's approach. One is in self-deception[3] whenever there is a fundamental discrepancy between what one (believingly) avows to be the case about oneself and one's action, and what is patently the case. Self-deception is a refusal to acknowledge who I am and what I am doing, not out of simple ignorance, but from what appears to be a kind of unselfconscious willful perversity. I am in self-deception whenever, while having the opportunity for self-knowledge and person development (and especially when confronted with that opportunity), I refuse to acquire the knowledge and undertake the development.

Resting explicitly on my own view as to what it means to be a person, I distinguish several domains of self-deception. One of the most prominent is the situation where one refuses to affirm (to acknowledge or accept as a condition for altering) various specific qualities of one's personality that are quite apparent to others. One either (believingly) affirms what is not the case about oneself (I am generous) or (believingly) denies what is patently the case (I am not envious of you); that is, one either claims to be what one is not, or refuses to acknowledge what one evidently is.

Self-deception here is not simply a matter of one's wanting to be other than one is; on the contrary, it is the expression of one's desire to be precisely what one already is. The conflict arises because one recognizes that the appropriate social value runs directly counter to that wished-for acceptance.

When John, say, who is extremely self-centered, says, "I am generous," he is fact expressing the desire to be self-centered and ungenerous. However, he knows that generosity and not self-centeredness is the prevailing social value and will control the judgment of his character. He is claiming (and believing) to be what he evidently is not, while all the time wanting to be what he is. If he did not want to be what he is, he would acknowledge what he is in the hope that others might excuse him or affirm him, in spite of this quality, or he would acknowledge what he is as the first step in a process of seeking to change himself.

Self-deception as involving a "wanting to be what one is" implies, then, that one does not truly own "what one is" so long as, in the absence of other overriding values, others withhold their assent from it. Now one

317

Self and Deception

cannot deny that there often exists a tension between the claims of person development and societal values. Often indeed the "herd values" of mediocrity, mere conformism, and so on, as Nietzsche so clearly saw, become serious obstacles to the creative becoming of a person; but usually there is no problem of self-deception here, as the tension is very much engaged in and recognized for what it is. Also, frequently a person may reject a particular social value (e.g., patriotism) and want nothing less than the approval of others with regard to it. For this reason we have the qualification *in the absence of other overriding values*. When overriding values are present, we do not have a self-deceptive situation; we have simply an acknowledged conflict of values.

This account of a common variety of self-deception still leaves unanswered questions concerning the actual psychological mechanisms of self-deception and fails also to resolve the paradox of self-deception, which here takes the form that the deceiver must somehow not desire what one does desire. Like the Freudian censor, the deceiver must again, in some way, be on both sides of the deception. But whereas the paradox, when it is located in the domain of knowledge, appears to be self-contradictory, rendering the phenomenon unintelligible, it can, when it is placed in the domain of desire, more readily be tolerated (and ameliorated considerably); for as is so often the case with desire, ambivalence already reigns. Incompatible urgings do seem to coexist in our emotional life (love/hate dualities and the like) and provide many of the interesting complexities of that life. We do desire and not desire something simultaneously, and not just with regard to different qualities of the thing; we want and do not want something of ourselves. A paradox remains but becomes more acceptable.

One other domain of self-deception—the most fundamental one—has close kinship with Indian thought. It is a "root" form of self-deception. It revolves around the refusal of someone to allow the spontaneity of the self to be a creative force in his or her life. To "disallow" spontaneity means to occupy oneself completely with a certain particularized world. It means to fill oneself up, as it were, with the nonself. Submitting to the distractions (and what at times seems to be the compelling necessities) of the world, one no longer becomes available—one is no longer poised—to realize the self. This making oneself unavailable is, in the last analysis, due to the preoccupation of an individual with his or her own ego. One makes of the little "me" the center and way of being of his or her world. One seeks every opportunity to avoid having to be, in the fullest sense, who one is. And one does this, it seems, out of fear, fear of losing oneself, fear of ego annihilation, fear of encountering an abyss and nothingness. *We hesitate to awaken out of fear of losing our dream.*

A Comparative Study

II

This brings us quite naturally to Asian thought and experience. As I mentioned before, I will concentrate on India—and within that venerable and rich tradition I will concentrate further on Vedāntic thought in its nondualistic (Advaita) form, the mainline philosophical system most often associated with Brahmanic or Hindu thought in general. The Buddhists, with their *anātman* or "no-self" teaching, have little to say on the subject of self-deception other than to give a possible reading of what has just been referred to as "root" self-deception which, like Vedānta, they ground in a special kind of "ignorance" (*avidyā*). If there is no substantial, empirical self or I then, in the spirit of postmodernism, there cannot be an I in deception. Self-deception would itself be, for the Buddhist, a kind of philosophical illusion or, unlike the postmodernist, a kind of literal madness, a *derangement* of the *skandhas,* the "elements" or "aggregates" (such as consciousness, feeling, perception) that constitute empirically what we take to be the individual self.

Let us turn, then, to Advaita Vedānta. To begin with, and going back to my original problematic, it should be noted that, at least to my knowledge, there is no explicit philosophical treatment of the problem of self-deception as this is formulated typically in the West.[4] Vedānta, like Buddhism, tends to concentrate on root self-deception, but, unlike Buddhism, it would then go on to deal with various empirical forms of self-deceit in terms of its doctrine of levels of consciousness and the accepted notions of *karman* and *dharma.*

According to Śaṁkara (ca. 830), the leading exponent of the Advaita Vedāntic tradition, our root self-deception is a basic and pervasive self-confounding of our own making. We incessantly and quite naturally misidentify ourselves and wrongly attribute to our true selves characteristics which properly belong only to our empirical individuality; we "superimpose" (*adhyāsa*) attributes of the nonself onto the self and of the self onto the nonself. In our ordinary consciousness of ourselves we are thus subject to a profound ignorance (*avidyā; ajñāna*). In his oft-quoted introduction to his commentary on the *Brahma-Sūtras,* Śaṁkara writes:

> It is matter not requiring any proof that the object and the subject, whose respective spheres are the notion of the 'Thou' (the Non-Ego) and the Ego, and which are opposed to each other as much as darkness and light are, cannot be identified. All the less can their respective attributes be identified. Hence it follows that it is wrong to superimpose upon the subject—whose Self is intelligence, and which has for its sphere the Ego—the

object whose sphere is the notion of the non-Ego, and the attributes of the object; and vice versa to superimpose the subject and the attributes of the subject on the object. In spite of this it is on the part of man a natural procedure.[5]

For example: "Attributes of the body are superimposed on the Self, if a man thinks of himself [his essential, spiritual self] as stout, lean, fair, as standing, walking or jumping."[6]

In other words, we quite naturally misidentify ourselves by attributing to our real self, which is, in essence, identical to Reality itself, qualities and characteristics that belong only to our empirical individuality. When I conceive of myself as—when I believe that I really, as distinct from only empirically, am—of a certain height and weight, with such and such an IQ, possessing this or that thing, I am subject to *avidyā*, to ignorance, and am engaged in *adhyāsa*, superimposition. Self-deception, as usually understood in Western terms, would thus be a kind of secondary phenomenon—a (purposive) mistaken notion about those empirical qualities (that, say, I allow that I am smart when in fact I am stupid). For Vedānta, then, self-deception, in its most fundamental form, is more of a (universal) metaphysical affliction than, as for the West, a (personal) epistemological or psychological state or condition. For Vedānta, self-deception at its root involves not so much a division within oneself as a break between that self and reality. When a person comes to realize her true identity with a nondifferentiated reality, when, that is to say, self-understanding and freedom (*mokṣa*) are obtained at the essential level of spirituality, the very possibility of empirical self-deception is eliminated.

Turning to the empirical forms of self-deception, which those of us who have failed to achieve self-understanding are prone to be victims of, Indian thought in general, as disclosed in its rich mythology, often depicts cases of these deceptions as a kind of self-forgetfulness (as one comes under the power of *māyā*) losing one's memory, as it were, of who one once was and empirically more truly is—say, one is in fact a noble prince, while one forgetfully plays the role of a dissolute wanderer. For Indian thought, it is not so much that there is a double self (a self-deceiving and a self-deceived) or a split personality of some sort, but a self who is asleep, as it were, and the (same) self who is awake. To awaken metaphysically, as we have noted, means to condemn one's dream—and within its strictly phenomenal or empirical forms this awakening is also always extremely difficult, for it means to reject oneself as one has become.

For Vedānta, this is expressed philosophically in terms of its doctrine of levels of consciousness. Four such states are identified: waking, dream, deep sleep and a transcendental condition. Self-deception of at least one empirical form would be interpreted empirically as a confounding of the dream state (with its desire-driven modalities) and the waking state; which is to say that a person in self-deception would be one who, while awake empirically, functions as though he or she were in "dream" as far as being clouded by involuntary desire, while all the time claiming and believing that he or she was acting quite "rationally." This is perhaps the closest Vedānta would come to a Western-like analysis which would understand self-deception as a conflict within consciousness as based on desire.

For the most part, though, Vedānta would appeal to two of the most axiomatic (and interrelated) notions in Indian culture to account for empirical forms of self-deception, namely *karman* and *dharma*. For Indian thought generally, in the domain of human social life each person is said to have his or her *dharma* or "law" or "duty" to oneself and to others, and this is determined by one's station in life (one's *varṇa* or "class," one's *aśrama* or "stage of life," and one's *puruṣārtha* or "aim of life"), which is itself the result of one's past action; one's law or duty is thus self-made.

Karl Potter has shown, quite convincingly, that the best way to understand *karman* in traditional Indian thought is in terms more of "making" than of "action," as we understand these terms in contemporary Western thought. Words based on the Sanskrit root *kṛ*, Potter argues, call up expectations in Sanskrit users

> that it will be possible to identify a maker (*kartṛ*), some materials out of which the making is intended, a purpose or purposes (*puruṣārtha*) being served by the making, an operation (*vyāpāra*) by which the making is carried out, and of course a resulting thing made (*karman*), which will serve the purpose or at least perform a function conducive to the eventual satisfaction ultimately sought.... So, for example, when in Indian thought we hear of something *kṛta*, we should understand the reference is not only to some deed, something done, completed, but further that it refers to something made, produced from some material by someone for somebody's purpose.[7]

Purposive making, Potter goes on to note, always yields results that are frustrating or satisfying in varying degrees. We make ourselves purposively, then, with varied degrees of success. In fact, most of us make ourselves rather poorly. Lacking sufficient imagination, insight, and freedom, we allow

Self and Deception

ourselves to be more "products" than "artifacts," more the sum total of the conditions of our individuality as given to us biologically and socially than that unique particularity which exhibits a full integrity or wholeness of one's being. Self-making, to *sva-kṛ,* as it were, within the traditional Indian conceptual scheme also requires indefinite time spans, with one's present "making" (*karman*) only affecting incrementally what one may become. It is also very much a part of that conceptual scheme as well that *karman* is a source, indeed the principal source, of our human bondage. Freedom (*mokṣa*) is precisely the overcoming of, the release from, *karman.*

Self-deception, then, for Indian thought generally, would involve some kind of fundamental confusion about one's karmic-based *dharma,* a confusion regarding the kind of person one has made oneself to be. In self-deception one might thus attribute to one's empirical self various roles (that of an intellectual or a worker) for which one is totally ill-equipped to perform. Self-deception here is a kind of (deluded) *performance,* an enactment of a role (for others) for which one is mis-suited. In the West we often see this as a comic situation (à la Moliere); for India it would be somewhat more tragic.

Further, in this context, self-deception might also be said to consist in one's believing that one can alter fundamentally one's *karman,* perhaps in order to make it more socially acceptable, while lacking the means or even the will to do so, and/or announcing that one's *karman* determines, rather than only conditions, one so as to render one helpless to do anything whatsoever about one's self-making. According to Indian teaching, *karman* does condition, but it does not determine. I am conditioned by the accidents of my birth to speak English: this does not mean I am determined as such to say whatever I do say. I am, to be sure, predisposed, by the acquisition of various habits (*saṁskāras*) to say certain things, and especially in certain ways, but this does not preclude my altering my habits and developing new ones. In any event, in these cases one is confused about one's *dharma* while refusing to recognize, to avow, to spell-out, that very confusion.

In short, for Vedānta, the opposite of self-deception is, from the absolute standpoint, *mokṣa* and, from the relative standpoint, self-consciously accepting and fulfilling one's karmic-based *dharma.* In the *Bhagavadgītā,* Arjuna, the *kṣatrīya* or "warrior" is initially under the delusion that he can forego his appropriate responsibilities in the world; it takes Kṛṣṇa, his divine mentor, the entire text to disabuse Arjuna of his deception; in the course of which, he must explain to him—and show experientially—the entire nature of the cosmos, his own divine nature, and the right way for society to be organized. Needless to say, we cannot go into all of that here.

One thing, though, that is evident from this text, and is made explicit throughout discussions about the self and *karman/dharma* in Vedānta, is that every person is held completely responsible for his or her actions (and state of being) and hence a self-deceiver can never rightfully look elsewhere to excuse or justify that deceit. I suspect that Indians more than Westerners would tolerate self-deceiving persons but would never condone their condition or look for ways to justify (or even celebrate) it as a way, say, of providing a basis for self-esteem that would in turn enable one to cope effectively in the social world.

Let us turn now to the creative "comparative" part of our inquiry.

III

I stated at the beginning that a comparative philosophical approach to the phenomenon of self-deception would look for ways in which the problem as we might define it in contemporary Western thought might be reformulated in other more fruitful ways in the light of the thought and experience of other non-Western cultures. Our brief discussion of Indian, namely Vedāntic, thought suggests three closely interrelated aspects that might happily be pursued in such a reformulation. These are (1) the ontological dimension of self-deception; (2) its social grounding; and (3) the responsibility one bears for one's deception.

A great deal of effort has been made in many areas of contemporary Western culture to rethink the notion of the self from that of an atomic-like individual set over against other individuals and over against an independent natural order to that of a person intimately bound-up with others in various communities and traditions (e.g., Alasdair MacIntyre and Charles Taylor) and inextricably connected ecologically, as it were, to its environment (e.g., Arne Naess). Self-deception, however, for the most part, in contemporary philosophy is still dependent on a picture of the self as essentially atomic or as essentially nonsocial. Indian thought may indeed help us move further in the other direction as it takes that direction surely as far as it can go.

Self-deception needs to be redefined so that its full ontological character is disclosed. One is in self-deception to the degree to which one believingly becomes just that atomic-like individual referred to; one is in self-deception to the degree to which one denies one's most essential relation with reality by living opposed to that relation while all the time believing and proclaiming that one is in fact affirming one's essential spirituality. Self-deception needs, then, to be recognized as a kind of ontological illness and thus as something that might be overcome only with the utmost arduous effort and disciplined attention. We delude ourselves in believing that only a few other persons are in self-deception, namely those who bear a kind of shadow psychological madness, and hence that it takes no (or very little) effort on our part to retain our essential integrity and freedom. When understood in broader ontological terms, however, self-deception is clearly a pervasive phenomenon. We do indeed need to awaken from our dream if we are to realize the potentialities of what it means to be a human being.

On the social side as well, Indian thought can enrich our idea of self-deception. With few exceptions, contemporary social philosophers thought of self-deception as a kind of (sometimes justified) manipulation of self and others. Daniel T. Gilbert and Joel Cooper, for example, in their "Social Psychological Strategies of Self-Deception," go so far as to allow that they "assume that all of the self-deceptive procedures that we shall describe can be effected without benefit of consciousness."[8] They say, then, that "we shall describe self-deceptive strategies as though the person were indeed behaving with calculated insincerity, but this narrative convenience should not obscure our conviction that self-deceptive strategies are complex but overlearned behavioral procedures that are conditioned and maintained by the contingencies of the social world and the needs of the individual."[9]

Béla Szabados draws from all of this that, socially, self-deception is only a kind of fictitious game that we play with each other. He asks: "If self-deception could not possibly exist [because of its logical paradoxical nature], then why did we nevertheless have to invent it? ... Why do we deceive ourselves into believing in 'self-deception?'"[10] He answers:

> The answer given is that self-deception is really [only] a game we play with and for other people. We all partake in a conspiracy by having made an unspoken treaty with each other to play this game. The aim of the game is to confuse people so as to make them unsure how to judge us. To deceive oneself is really to pretend that one is self-deceived in order to confuse others so that one gets away scot-free or with little blame for what is a blatant lie or pretense.[11]

But how much more fruitful it might be to understand self-deception in its social dimension in the more Indian-like terms of role models and their fulfillments and failures. Now the social structures of traditional societies, such as the classical Indian (and Chinese), set forth a far more rigid and clearly defined set of social roles to be performed by persons than is to be found in the so-called modern (and postmodern) world; nevertheless, it seems to be the case that every society demands the performing of certain roles by its members however flexible and changeable these might be. Self-deception, when understood in role terms, does indeed become a kind of game, not in the rather superficial sense described by Szabados, but in that self-forgetful way alluded to in Indian thought.

Self-deception can be interestingly reformulated in terms of a person either (a) so becoming his or her social role(s), fulfilling in an obsessive way, if you will, his or her *dharma,* that everything else gets squeezed out and one simply becomes what society demands without remainder, while all the time allowing that one is really fulfilling the potentialities of one's true nature;[12] or (b) failing rather badly in fulfilling a social role and then dismissing the failure by asserting that the role was not worth pursuing in the first place.

To be active socially and not to be in self-deception would mean that one does perform various roles but with the understanding that the performance is a kind of *play,* a creative underatking to which one is not obsessively attached.

The *Bhagavadgītā,* in its teaching on *karmayoga,* urges us to act with nonattachment to the fruits of our actions, but with devotion (*bhakti*) and knowledge (*jñāna*) and thus to fulfill our *dharma* while retaining our freedom. This is what it means to be without self-deception while functioning fully within the social order. One acts with a reverential spirit in the knowledge that one is intimately bound up with nature and yet, at the same time, is identical to an essential freedom which allows for—indeed calls for—a creative person making.

And for all of this the individual is fully responsible insofar as to be in self-deception does not mean an inability not to be so. As with the root ontological condition, it might very well be that one can overcome the self-deceptive situation only with the utmost effort and discipline; nevertheless, the notion of 'responsibility' is built in to the very description of the phenomenon. One's own dispositions and habits, one's fixations and obsessions, one's anxieties and insecurities—whatever they might be—are precisely one's own and of one's own making (*karman*) and hence are, in principle and in fact, if one is so dedicated, subject to one's own power to deal with. In short, the very meaning of "self-deception" is that one can, through creative play, be undeceived and can act freely. This is one of the prime lessons we might learn from Indian thought.

NOTES

1. See Robert Audi, "Self-Deception and Rationality," in *Self-Deception and Self-Understanding: New Essays in Philosophy and Psychology*, ed. Mike W. Martin (Lawrence, Kansas: University Press of Kansas, 1985), 169ff.

2. Mike W. Martin, in *Self-Deception and Self-Understanding*, 70.

3. The following account of self-deception is taken, often by direct quotation, from my *Creative Being: The Crafting of Person and World* (Honolulu: University of Hawaii Press, 1992), ch. 2.

4. In Karl H. Potter's extensive *Bibliography of Indian Philosophies* (Delhi: Motilal Banarsidass, 1970), there is not a single entry under any recognizable category of "self-deception."

5. Śaṁkara, *Brahmasūtrabhāṣya*, trans. George Thibaut, *The Vedānta-sūtras with the Commentary of Śaṅkarāchārya*, in vol. 35, *Sacred Books of the East*, ed. Max Muller (Oxford: Clarendon Press, 1890), 3.

6. Ibid., 8–9.

7. Karl H. Potter, "Metaphor as Key to Understanding the Thought of Other Speech Communities," in *Interpreting Across Boundaries: New Essays in Comparative Philosophy*, ed. Gerald James Larson and Eliot Deutsch (Princeton: Princeton University Press, 1988), 26.

8. *Self-Deception and Self-Understanding*, 76.

9. Ibid., 77.

10. Ibid., 144.

11. Ibid.

12. This might be seen as a subtle variant of Sartre's *mauvaise foi;* a "subtle variant" because Sartre, in his analysis of bad faith or self-deception, is concerned primarily with the freedom of the person to have chosen his role and with his acknowledgment of responsibility for the choice, and not with an avowal concerning "fulfilling the potentialities of one's true nature."

FIFTEEN

SELF-DECEPTION AND CULTURAL CONTEXTUALIZATION
Reflections on Two Indian Novels

Wimal Dissanayake

Self-deception is a topic that has attracted the attention of philosophers for a considerable period of time. How a person can believe both *p* and not *p* at the same time is a question that has elicited many and contradictory answers. Self-deception is indeed a multifaceted phenomenon, and hence it is hardly surprising that it has given rise to variety of approaches and optics calculated to clarifying its bewildering appearance. Philosophical disagreements about the nature of self-deception are complex and varied, and they enter into the discursive domains of consciousness, intentionality, rationality, belief, cognition, and so on, thereby generating a many-sided inquiry. The paradox which seems to lie at the heart of self-deception as well as its psychological and moral dimensions have received much valuable scholarly attention. However, an issue that has as yet not received sufficient attention of scholars is the role of culture in our understanding of the phenomenon of self-deception. This chapter focuses on this relatively neglected aspect of the problematic of self-deception by examining two highly acclaimed works of fiction from South Asia: *The Serpent and the Rope,* by Raja Rao,[1] and *The English Teacher,* by R. K. Narayan.[2] Two topics that are vitally related to self-deception are those of self and rationality. It is my conviction that in order to comprehend these two concepts at their full complexity, we need to pay attention to the ways in which they are embedded in and constituted by culture.

Both of these novels have been widely discussed in India and have been the focus of attention outside India as well. At one level, which is a highly decontextualized one in terms of culture, it can be said that both these works thematize the problem of self-deception. However, in order to understand the true complexity of the problematic that is being textualized in these novels, we need to relate them to the wider cultural discourse from which they derive meaning and significance.

The explication in this chapter proceeds in three stages. First, I point out that by using exogenous criteria, that is, criteria external to the cultures

Self and Deception

with which the novelists are concerned, we can maintain that the protagonists of the two novels are guilty of self-deception. Second, by analyzing the experiences textualized in the novels more closely and the motivations of the leading characters more carefully, I show that the whole question of self-deception is largely located in culture. Richard Rorty says that "the important thing about novelists as compared to theorists is that they are good at details."[3] I have chosen to use two novels for illustrative purposes because the details characteristic of a novel enable us to ground our discussions in cultural determinations more productively. Third, on the basis of the analysis of the novels, I underline the need for using endogenous and culturally determined criteria for understanding the problematic of self-deception.

A bald summary of *The Serpent and the Rope* follows. Ramaswamy is an Indian student who goes to France for his higher education. There he happens to meet Madeleine, a lecturer in history. He falls in love with her, and they get married. Ramaswamy's intention was to complete his doctorate and then return to India with Madeleine, but this never happens. Ramaswamy hears that his father is dying and returns to India. This return has the effect of generating in him a deeper awareness of India and his heritage. Transformed by this experience he goes back to France only to realize that there are clear incompatibilities between him and Madeleine, and they begin to grow apart. On his visit to India he met Savithri, a girl who is researching in England, and they become lovers. Their affair does not lead to marriage. Ramaswamy obtains a divorce from Madeleine, and becomes a recluse resolving to sever connections with the world. Savithri marries someone else. Ramaswamy is filled with a sense of mystical yearning, and we are made to understand that he is now engaged in a quest for a higher reality.

A summary of the novel may lead one to conclude that the protagonist of *The Serpent and the Rope* is a victim of self-deception. He is seeking to convince himself that he is no longer interested in mundane reality and that his goal is a far nobler one, namely, seeking to comprehend higher reality. One can argue—and indeed some have done precisely that—that Ramaswamy is trying to conceal his failures and inadequacies by presenting himself as a person who has moved on to a higher reality. In short, he is prey to self-deception.

The second novel, *The English Teacher,* by R. K. Narayan, thematizes a related issue. This novel can be summarized as follows. Krishna, a teacher of English, is married and has a daughter. He lives in the school hostel, leading a typical teacher's life. His parents encourage him to leave the hostel and find a house so that he can live with his wife and daughter. He acts accordingly. Three years later, Krishna and his wife, Susila, look for a newer house. She catches thyphoid and succumbs to it. Krishna is shattered by this unexpected turn of events. He now lives alone with his daughter. A series of events strengthen his belief in communicating through the help of supernatural powers. Krishna believes that he can communicate with his wife through a medium and actually has a vision of her. It can be argued that Krishna is only deceiving himself, or that he is making use of self-deception as a means of overcoming his loss and sorrow.

Both of these novels, then, appear to textualize the problem of self-deception. However, when we begin to contextualize the respective experiences culturally, we realize that there are alternate readings that suggest themselves. Self-deception is imbricated with self-justification, self-legitimization, self-knowledge, self-doubt, self-invention, self-image, and a whole host of kindred discourses. These are all indissolubly linked with questions of culture. Hence a decontextualized and mentalistic summary of the novels does not enable us to get at the culturally embedded meanings contained in the two novels. Moreover, it can be fairly said that our current investigations into the phenomenon of self-deception are excessively intrapersonal and that issues pertaining to cultural dimensions of self-deception need to receive greater attention. The complex and intriguing ways in which people make sense of their behavior and construct systems of meaning and strategies of intelpretation are grounded in the terrain of culture. Hence any discussion of the phenomenon of self-deception must take into account the determining power of the cultural discourse with which it is vitally connected. With this imperative in mind, let us examine the two novels more closely.

The protagonist of *The Serpent and the Rope*, Ramaswamy, is a Brahmin. He grew up in a Brahminic household and imbibed the Brahminic culture. His attitude to society and interpersonal relationships is clearly guided by this cultural conditioning. The opening passage of the novel draws attention to this vital aspect of his subjectivity:

> I was born a Brahmin—that is, devoted to Truth and all that. "Brahmin is he who knows Brahman" etc. etc. ... but how many of my ancestors since the excellent Yajnyavalkya, my legendery and Upanishadic ancestor, have really known the Truth accepting the Sage Madhava, who founded an empire, or, rather, helped to build an empire, and wrote some of the most profound of Vedantic texts since Sri Sankara? There were others, so I am told, who left hearth and riverside fields, and wandered to mountains distant and hermitages "to see God face to face." And

Self and Deception

some of them did see God face to face and built temples. But when they died—for indeed they did die—they too must have been burnt by tank or grove or meeting of two rivers, and they too must have known that they did not die. I can feel them in me, and know they knew they did not die. Who is it that tells me they did not die? Who but me.

This opening passage of the novel establishes very clearly how being a Brahmin is crucial to his self-constitution and self-understanding.

Brahmins are famous for their learning and in many ways represent the elitism of Indian culture along with its attendant exclusivities. When Ramaswamy goes to France, he is attracted by the high culture and the dynamism of the country, and Madeleine comes to incarnate those attributes in his eyes:

Madeleine was so lovely—with golden hair—on her mother's side she came from Savoy—and her limbs had such pure unreality. Madeleine was altogether unreal. That is why, I think, she had never married anyone—in fact she had never touched anyone. She said that during the Nazi occupation, towards the end of 1943, a German officer had tried to touch her hair; it looked so magical, and it looked the perfect Nordic hair.

Ramaswamy is attracted by her beauty, her individuality, and her quickness of mind; he is attracted by her individuality as much as by her symbolicity. When he is called back to India to see his dying father, he feels a sense of belonging, a feeling of cultural closeness he had not experienced before. The topography, the distinctiveness of the land, the natural beauty, the power of myths, the strength of tradition and history all acquire a renewed meaning for him. His Indianness foregrounds itself with reinvigorated force. Transformed by this experience, he returns to France only to realize that he and Madeleine are drifting apart as their incompatibilities surface with undiminishing clarity.

It is not as if Madeleine were totally imprisoned in her own culture and that she did not make an attempt to reach out toward Indian culture. As a matter of fact, one reason why she found Ramaswamy attractive was because she found Indian culture so fascinating. She immersed herself in Buddhism. That she was attracted to Buddhism—a religion which is seen as a heresy by Brahmins—certainly added to the tension between them. Moreover, Ramaswamy thought that the kind of Buddhism adhered to by Madeleine was a corrupt one. For a traditional Brahmin, the life of a woman is defined by the way she ministers to his worldly requirements, as the provider of a son who is expected to light the funeral pyre in order to release his father's soul and carry on the family line. However, Madeleine fails to produce a son. Consequently, in Ramaswamy's eyes, she fails to fulfill obligations traditionally expected of a wife.

Similarly, we can understand better his relationship with Savithri if we bear in mind the fact that his mind set is decisively influenced by his Brahminic outlook. She is an undergraduate at Cambridge. She is enamored of Ramaswamy's intellect and originality of mind. Savithri was "made of such stuff that for her the real had to be clothed in terms of the illusory to make it concrete; truth was to be made the revelation of a puzzle, a riddle, a mathematic of wisom." Ramaswamy for his part constructs a fantasized image of Savithri. He feels that in her company, he is capable of realizing the essence of femininity, the nondual status as that of Shiva and Shakti, or Radha and Krishna. This indeed is a mental condition he could never attain in his relationship with Madeleine. Ramaswamy says of Savithri, "She is whole and simple wherever she is; for her there is only on world, one spot one person even—and that is he who is before her. No one can be near her—except perhaps me, I told myself—for she is everywhere, and you had to be her to be her." Descriptions of Savithri such as the following which are found frequently in the novel serve to reinforce this point: "Savithri proved that I could be I." "When Savithri touched my arm the whole world rose into my awareness." "Savithri was there not in me but as me."

Ramaswamy sees his relationship with Savithri operating at a highly abstract level, which some readers may find incomprehensible. When Savithri asks, "If you stood by me there is a grave question I would ask you: if I asked you, would you marry me, will you? Ramaswamy's reply, couched in Upanishadic language may appear to be puzzling at one level. He says, "You can marry when you are One. That is, you can marry when there is no one to marry another."

The narrative strategies that produce Savithri are closely interrelated to Hindu religious intertextualities. As the novel progresses, we see how Savithri becomes the means for him to realize a state in which the ego is extinguished and the dualities that characterize life sublated. The discursive production of Savithri is imbricated with the religious and semiotic space occupied by Advaita Vedānta.

This discussion about his failed marriage to Madeleine and his emotional attachment to Savithri underline the fact that when related to the wider cultural discourse from which the novel draws emotional and intellectual power, what at first appeared to be human weaknesses on Ramaswamy's part, which by an act of self-deception he tries to cover up, turn out to be facets of his religious outlook. He is a seeker after the higher truth, and all his actions are but reflections of that questing voyage. Many literary critics who have commented on the novel have adopted this viewpoint. For example Kathleen Raine says that *The Serpent and the Rope* is a "most profound demonstration of Indian metaphysics."[4] The well-known scholars, C. D. Narasimhaiah[5] and William Walsh[6] subscribe to the same view. When we examine the problems and privations of Ramaswamy in relation to the wider culture in which they are situated, we are in a better position to understand the human meaning of his experiences. What could have been construed as a simple act of self-deception, when culturally contextualized, takes on the complexity of a multivalent textualization of human attachments and detachments; the way they are defined and valorized in the Hindu cultural tradition adds a greater depth of significance to them.

One way in which numerous philosophers have sought to resolve the seeming paradox of self-deception is by positing a plurality of subselves. On this view, human beings are constituted by subsystems with their own special goals, strategies, and plans of action, and self-deception takes place when one subsystem willfully deceives another. As Amélie Rorty points out, if the self is conceived of as rationally integrated, automatically monitoring and rectifying its beliefs, self-deception appears to be incoherent. However, a self that is taken to be a loosely organized system consisting of relatively independent subsystems seems amenable to the feasibility of self-deception. As she remarks, "Self-deception is demystified and naturalized, and even to some extent explained, if the self is a complexly divided entity for whom rational integration is a task and an ideal rather than a starting point."[7] A cultural contextualization of the experience of Ramaswamy in *The Serpent and the Rope* will enable us to understand better the concept of self that is crucial to the phenomenon of self-deception as a complexly divided entity.

The Serpent and the Rope can best be characterized as a metaphysical novel. As the novel closes, we see that Ramaswamy has succeeded in severing most of his worldly links. He has obtained a divorce from his wife, who has chosen to lead a life of renunciation. Savithri has settled down to married life; Ramaswamy in his quest for the deeper meanings of life is seeking the guidance of a guru:

> I knew His face, as one knows one's face in deep sleep. He called me, and said, "It is so long, so long, my son. I have awaited you. Come, we go." I went.... I will not return. I have gone whence there is no returning.... Do you ... need a candle to show the light of the sun? Such a Sun I have seen; it is more splendid than a million suns. It sits on a riverbank, it sits as the

formless form of Truth; it walks without walking, speaks without talking, moves without gesticulating, shows without naming, reveals what is Known. To such a Truth was I taken, and I became its servant, I kissed the perfume of its Holy Feet, and called myself a disciple.... It is the gift that Yajnyavalkya made to Maitreyi, it is the gift Govinda made to Sri Sankara. It is the gift he made to me. My Lord. May I be worthy of the Lord. Lord, my Master! O thou abode of Truth.

The novel concludes by pointing out the value of pure love, uncontaminated by worldly desire. As Rao himself has remarked, the novel thematizes the search for the Ultimate. According to him, the goal of human beings should be to find the Absolute. The classical Indian tradition valorizes the guru as incarnating the absolute. The phraseology as well as the logic of the arguments here derive their meaning from Advaita Vedānta, which is central to the meaning of this novel. When placed against this backdrop of thought, the idea of self-deception which a decontextualized summary of the novel might foreground takes on a complex configuration of meaning.

The theme of true love paves the way to the illumination of the wider quest inscribed in the novel, namely, the search for self-knowledge. The essence of the novel is vividly placed before us with all the resonances of Advaita Vedāntic writings when Ramaswamy says to Madeleine that the world is either unreal or real—the serpent or the rope. There is no in-between. The essence of the Advaita Vedānta philosophy can be captured in three brief statements: Brahman is nondual and immutable reality; the world is illusion; man's eternal self (Ātman) is no different from the ultimate reality (Brahman). In discussing the question of the relationship between Brahman and the world, Advaitins introduce the concept of *māyā*. *Māyā* is believed to be the power by which Brahman is concealed, and the apparent world, which in point of fact is a distortion, comes into being. The concept of 'knowledge' upheld by the Advaita Vedāntins is also significant in this regard. According to the Advaitins, higher knowledge is not a form of subjective knowledge with reality as object. Instead we are urged to understand it as the awareness of the identity of the knowing subject with reality itself. To phrase it differently, in higher knowledge, the essence of the knowing subject is realized to be identical with the essence of the objective world. What we see here is the merging of knowledge and reality, epistemology and ontology, in nonduality. Therefore, it can be said that when the essence of the knowing subject is known, all reality is known. As the Chāndogya Upanishad says, "That which is the first essence—this whole world has that as its soul. That is Reality. That is Ātman. Thou art that."

Self and Deception

This background of thought is vital to an understanding of the discursive horizon within which the quest of the protagonist of *The Serpent and the Rope* takes place. It is indeed interesting to observe that Ramaswamy does not search for the Ultimate Reality by traversing the path adopted by ancient ascetics; instead, he seeks to enter this reality by exploring the meaning and significance of womanhood. He sees the notions of 'illusion' and 'reality' in terms of the two women—Madeleine and Savithri—who enter his life. Hence what at first appear to be somewhat egotistical emotional encounters on the part of Ramaswamy, thereby thematizing the problem of self-deception, has an alternative reading. This alternative reading is a highly culturally contextualized one, situated as it is within the discourse of Advaita Vedānta.

The Serpent and the Rope ultimately deals with the question of the metaphysical self and its attendant problematics. As Raja Rao has remarked, everything one writes is autobiographical. But *The Serpent and the Rope* is a metaphysical novel. However, in order to textualize this metaphysical self in his novel, the author has to bring into a fruitful dialogue two warring cultural selves: one is a Western-oriented scholar who is enamored of Western culture; the other is a man who has been influenced by the imperatives of Brahminic culture. How these two cultural selves are juxtaposed has much to do with our understanding of the notion of self-deception. In a sense, the novel, much more so than poetry, serves to semioticize the intersection of the trajectories of such warring selves. As Mikhail Bakhtin, who has written so perceptively on the poetics of the novel, has pointed out, the very medium of language deployed by the novelist makes such a venture essential. As Bakhtin remarks,

> The novelist does not acknowledge any unitary, singular, naively (or conditionally) indisputable or sacrosanct language. Language is presented to the novelist only as something stratified and heteroglot. Therefore, even when heteroglossia remains outside the novel, when the novelist comes forward with his own unitary and fully affirming language (without any distancing, refraction or qualifications) he knows that such language is not self-evident and is not itself incontestable, that is uttered in a heteroglot environment, that such a language must be championed, purified, defended, motivated. In a novel even such unitary and direct language is polemical and apologetic, that is, it interrelates dialogically with heteroglossia. It is precisely this that defines the utterly distinctive orientation of discourse in the novel . . . this discourse cannot forget, or ignore, either through naivete or by design, the heteroglossia that surrounds it.[8]

The heteroglossic imperative is central to the discourse of the novel.

In *The Serpent and the Rope* there are two warring cultural selves which serve to foreground the thematics of self-deception. On the one hand, we have Ramaswamy, the Westernized academic and connoisseur of European culture, who initiates one dominant trajectory of the narrative. The various descriptions of Paris and London, the references to Rilke and Baudelaire, Valery, Mann, and European culture and intellectual traditions act as signifiers in delineating this self:

> Paris somehow is not a city; it is an area in oneself, a Concorde in one's being, where the river flows by you with an intimacy that seems to say the divine is not in the visible architecture of the Orangerie or the presence of the Pont des Arts, but where the trees would end; and even when the lorries have trundled over the cobbled streets—with potato and onion, geese, lard, margarine and cow's flesh; oranges, birds, Roquerfort; petits pois de Clamart, bottes de persil, romarin d'Antibes; sugar, mint and pepper—there opposite, begirtin his isle of existence, is the Mother of God, to whom man has built a sanctuary, a convocation of stone, uttered truly as never before.

Here we find the narrator firmly and happily situated in the spatiality of Paris. Ramaswamy sees Paris as the center of intellectual, political, and religious activity, and his narrative is studded with references to French history, geography, and tradition. France in a sense takes on the aura of an intellectual imaginary.

However, we find Ramaswamy culturally a deeply rooted Indian and Brahmin. The representational space opened up by the narrative bristles with semiotic markers of Indian grandeur and majesty: "India is not a country like France is, or like England; India is an idea, a metaphysic. Why go there anyhow, I thought. I was born an exile, and I could continue to be one. My India I carried her wheresoever I went. But not to see the Ganges, not to dip in her again and again.... No, the Ganges was an inner truth to me, an assurance, the origin and end of my Brahmanic tradition." Passages such as these represent the other self—a self overdetermined by Indian culture. If seen from the point of view of the first self, what Ramaswamy does can be construed as self-deception. If seen from the vantage point of the second self, Ramaswamy's behavior as textualized in the novel cannot be interpreted as an act of self-deception. However, for self-deception to appear as a troublesome phenomenon, each of the two contending selves has to in some way recognize the existence of the other. Moreover, the two contending viewpoints have to be juxtaposed, balanced, evaluated in some fashion, without which the full force of self-deception cannot be appreciated. As Amélie Rorty remarks, an interesting irony related to self-deception is that "it is only when an agent takes the unification of his traits, his thoughts and actions, as a central project that he is capable of self-deception and *akrasia*"[9] What happens in *The Serpent and the Rope* is that the narrator seeks to combine these two culturally variable selves as a means of transcending them both. Interestingly, this effort has the effect of focusing attention on the self-deception practiced by Ramaswamy as well as sublating it. Jon Elster observes, "Barring pathological cases . . . we ought not to take the notion of 'several selves' very literally. In general, we are dealing with exactly one person—neither more nor less. That person may have some cognitive coordination problems, and some motivational conflicts, but it is his job to sort them out."[10] This observation by Elster has a pointed relevance to the character of the protagonist in *The Serpent and the Rope*.

I hope the discussion thus far has established the importance of situating self-deception in a wider discursive space inflected by culture. The decontextualized summary of *The Serpent and the Rope* that we began with left the impression that this is a novel that thematizes self-deception. However, when we locate the narrative in the representational space of culture, the once seemingly simple issue of self-deception takes on a far more complicated appearance. It is interesting that while on the one hand a culturally situated reading of the novel serves to complexify the theme of self-deception by bringing into view a plurality of relevant and interlocking discourses and diverting the attention elsewhere, on the other hand, it introduces a newer modality of self-deception. The protagonist of this novel is in search of true self-knowledge, and he has resolved to sever the links with the phenomenal world in the pursuit of that quest. However, as Nietzsche has forcefully reminded us, self-knowledge and self-invention are inextricably linked. Ramaswamy can attain self-knowledge by an act of self-fashioning, and this is what the writing of the novel entails. The irony here is that even as he is seeking to disaffiliate himself from the phenomenal world in his quest for the higher and transcendental truth, his very act of textuality, involving as it does the use of language which is the primary medium of social communication, mires him deeper and deeper in the phenomenal world. Writing a novel is a representational practice. It is a performance, an act of make-believe. Hence the very act of narrativization undercuts the narrator's quest for a transcendental truth, thereby introducing a newer form of self-deception.

Is self-deception a vital component of all acts of literary creativity? Let us now consider the second novel, *The English Teacher*. Its author, R. K. Narayan, is regarded by many as the leading novelist in India. His novels are set in the imaginary south Indian town of Malgudi, with its odd but charming mixture of Hindu and British cultural legacies. He writes mainly about the problems and privations of middle-class people, journalists, teachers, moneylenders, candy sellers, sign painters, and so on. These types of characters predate the British Raj, but in Narayan's historical frame, their unique problems are significantly conditioned and complicate by the impact of the British on traditional Indian society. *The English Teacher* is Narayan's fourth novel and in many ways his most autobiographical work. The protagonist of this novel, Krishna, is an English teacher. He lives in the precincts of the college where he teaches. He gets up "at eight every day," reads "for the fifth time Milton, Carlyle, and Shakespeare," and "looks over the compositions, eats a quick breakfast and rushes out of the hostel just when the second bell sounded at college."

His parents as well as his in-laws feel that Krishna should move out of the hostel and live with his wife and daughter. Accordingly, he moves out of the hostel into a new house and starts a new life with his wife and daughter. Everything seems to be in place, and Krishna and his wife, Susila, appear to be leading a very harmonious life:

> She gave me coffee. We left the kitchen, and sat down in the hall. The child went over to her box in a corner and rummaged through its contents and threw them about and became quite absorbed in this activity. My wife sat at the doorway leaning against the door and watching the street. We spent an hour or more, sitting there and gossiping. She listened eagerly to all the things that I told her about my college, and work and life. Though she hadn't met a single person who belonged to that world, she knew the names of most of my colleagues and the boys and all about them.

Three years later, Krishna and Susila decide to move to a newer and better house. They find an attractive house. However, while house hunting, Susila catches typhoid, which eventually leads to her death. Krishna is devastated by this unexpected turn of events. He continues to live in the old house with his daughter. One day he receives a message from a man who reportedly has been in communication with the deceased Susila. Krishna begins to receive messages from his wife through this medium, and he seeks to communicate with her. The novel ends with Krishna returning home from his last day in college (he decides to become the headmaster of the nursery school that his daughter had attended), and having a distinct vision of his wife:

Self and Deception

> My mind trembled with the rhythm. I forgot myself and my existence. I fell into a drowse whispering, "My wife, wife." How long? How could I say? When I opened my eyes again she was sitting on my bed looking at me with an extraordinary smile in her eyes. "Susila! Susila" I cried. "You are here!" "Yes, I'm here, have always been here." I sat up leaning on my pillow. "Why do you disturb your self?" she asked.
>
> "I am making a place for you." I said, edging away a little. I looked her up and down and said: "How well you look!" Her complexion had a golden glow, her eyes sparkled with a new light, her saree shimmered with blue interwoven with light as she had termed it. "How beautiful!" I said looking at it. "Yes I always wear this when I come to you. I know you like it very much" she said. I gazed on her face. There was an overwhelming fragrance of jasmine surrounding her. Still jasmine-scented I commented.
>
> Oh wait, I said and got up. I picked up the garland from the nail and returned to bed. I held it to her. For you as ever. I somehow felt that you wouldn't take it. . . . She received it with a smile, cut off a piece and stuck it in a curve on the back of her head. She turned her head and asked: Is this all right? Wonderful I said smelling it. A cock crew. The first purple of the dawn came through the window, and faintly touched the walls of our room. Dawn she whispered and rose to her feet. We stood at the window, gazing on a slender, red streak over the eastern rim of the earth. A cool breeze lapped our faces. The boundaries of our personalities suddenly dissolved. It was a moment of rare, immutable joy—a moment for which one feels grateful to Life and Death.

Many have found the ending of the novel to be sentimental and claim that it represents a case of self-deception. Here again, we need to understand the frame of mind of the protagonist from within his own specific cultural universe. As in the case of Ramaswamy in *The Serpent and the Rope*, in Krishna we see the interaction of two contending cultural selves. On the one hand, we see the Krishna who is Westernized, interested in English literature, highly observant and satirical; on the other, we have the brooding, introspective man who believes in the efficacy of supernatural powers. He grew up in two interlocking cultural universes, and the contending selves are a reflection of that. In the end, the sheer pressure of his own personal tragedy makes him even more accommodating of the power of supernatural forces. Hence it is possible to argue that what some would perceive as a self-deception on Krishna's part is really one belief system gaining the upper hand over the other.

In his autobiography, *My Days,* Narayan comments on this novel:

> More than any other book, *The English Teacher* is autobiographical in content, very little part of it being fiction. The English Teacher of the novel, Krishna, is a fictional character in the fictional city of Malgudi; but he goes through the same experience I had gone through and he calls his wife Susila, and the child is Leela instead of Hema. The toll that typhoid took and all the desolation that followed, with a child to look after, and the psychic adjustments are, based on my own experience. The book falls into two parts—one is domestic life and the other half is spiritual. Many readers have gone through the first half with interest and the second half with bewilderment and even resentment, perhaps feeling that they have been baited with the domestic picture into tragedy, death, and nebulous, impossible speculations. The dedication of the book to the memory of my wife should to some extent give the reader a clue that the book may not be all fiction; still, most readers resist, naturally, as one always does, the transition from life to death and beyond.

Later on Narayan makes the observation that out of all the tragic and abnormal experiences he has had, there developed within him a newer conception of self that has remained with him since. He says that our normal view is confined to a physical perception in a condition of restricted time like "the flashing of a torchlight on a spot, the rest of the are being in darkness." He goes on to observe, "If one could have a total view of oneself and others, one would see all in their full stature, through all the stages of evolution and growth ranging from childhood to old age, in this life, the next one, and the previous ones." To Narayan, his communication with his dead wife is a real one. We need not always consult the author for the meaning of a work of fiction. However, in this case, it is not out of place to relate the author's personal views to understand better the behavior of his protagonist, who is in point of fact no more than a thinly disguised version of the author. Hence to dismiss Krishna's communication with his deceased wife as an act of self-deception is to ignore the experiential world from within which he makes that reality.

This discussion of the question of self-deception as it manifests itself in *The English Teacher* alerts us to the interrelationship among self, meaning, and social order, and its relevance to an understanding of self-deception.

Self and Deception

The protagonist of the novel inhabits a space in which supernatural powers, transmigration of souls, and worlds beyond are very real. For him there is more to social order than meets the eye; there is indeed a metaphysical dimension. We may not believe what he believes. However, his convictions and behavior grow out of that distinct world and its processes of meaning. Hence we need, in seeking to understand the nature of his self-deception, to look at it from within his world view.

A social order is based on shared meaning. It is indeed true that one can establish social order through force and coercion, but such attempts are at best of short duration. Real social order is founded on shared meanings, and this entails the adjustment of individuals to collective orientations. A social order encompasses a collectivity of people interacting with each other in a shared representational space. This order needs to be understood as a constructed social reality, and this constructedness implies an interesting interplay among self, social order, and meaning. The social order comes into being and functions as a unity as a consequence of the actions of collective individual selves, while the individual selves are largely governed by the compulsions of the social order that they inhabit. All this takes place within a shared economy of meaning. In the case of *The English Teacher,* we see that the protagonist's view of social order is deeply colored by metaphysical concerns and symbolic interests. Human beings are symbol creators and symbol sharers; the social existence of human beings is firmly anchored in symbolic universe. As is made very clear to us in the novel, human interaction and organization are inconceivable without a shared symbolic universe. The metaphysical dimension, in *The English Teacher* is closely linked to the symbolic. The author seems to be saying that we can understand fully the complexity of any given social order only by investigating its metaphysical foundations. The order of mundane reality is inadequate to represent or totally embody the order of human existence because human beings participate in the order of being which transcends the mundane. We may or may not agree with Narayan's projected vision of social order; however, when we seek to examine the self-deception that the protagonist is said to be guilty of, we need to situate his experience in the wider vision of the author. To Krishna, as well as to the author, communication with the dead through the agency of supernatural forces is very real, and this conviction is intimately related to the cultural world which they inhabit. Hence any estimation of self-deception has to take into consideration this important fact. Krishna's interpretive framework is constructed on the basis of these metaphysical and symbolic imperatives.

Reflection on the question of self-deception in relation to *The Serpent and the Rope* focuses attention on three important topics: self and culture, rationality and culture, and the nature of meaning production. Let us consider each of them. In order to understand the true complexity of the phenomenon of self-deception, we need to understand the nature of self. The dualities pertaining to the concept of self—such as self as fact versus construct, self as subject versus object, self as structure versus process, self as unitary versus fragmented, self as consistent versus inconsistent—have received some scholarly attention. Likewise the relationships between self and society, self and psyche, self and language, self and ideology have been the focus of much informed and stimulating discussion. An equally important area that merits closer attention is the interplay between self and culture. This is indeed a topic, as evidenced by our discussion so far, that is crucially linked to a proper understanding of self-deception.

In examining the interrelationship between self and culture, the work of cultural anthropologists can prove to be extremely illuminating. Of the many scholars who have pointed out the vital role played by culture, A. Irving Hallowell invites closer attention. He underlines the importance of what he terms the "behavioral environment" on the formation of the self. This behavioral environment, as he sees it, is essentially culturally constituted. While agreeing with the notion that self-awareness is a generic human trait, Hallowell makes the observation that the nature of the self, when examined in its conceptual context, has to be seen as a culturally identifiable variable. Just as diverse peoples harbor diverse notions about the nature of the universe, likewise, diverse people entertain diverse notions about the self. He feels that an individual's self-image and his or her interpretation of his or her own experiences cannot be divorced from the concept of self that is characteristic of his or her society. According to Hallowell,

> such concepts are the primary means through which different cultures promote self-orientation in the kind of meaningful terms that serve to make self-awareness of functional in the maintenance of a social order. To the extent that the objectives of the individual are at the level of self-awareness, they are structured with reference to a self-image that is congruent with other fundamental orientations that prepare the self to act in a culturally constructed world.[11]

Hallowell emphatically makes the point that the self is a product of culture and that culture constitutes the behavioral environment in which human beings function. Culture provides them with the basic orientations that enable them to act intelligently and functionally in a world so constituted. This line of thinking has important implications for the understanding of self-deception.

Self and Deception

Clifford Geertz who does not totally endorse the views of Hallowell on the concept of self, nevertheless makes the point that becoming human is becoming individual, and we become individual under the guidance of cultural patterns, historically created systems of meaning in terms of which human beings impart form, order, point, and direction to their lives.[12] Hence the role of culture and inherited history is crucial to Geertz. He then remarks that just as culture has shaped us as a single species, it has also shaped us as separate individuals. What we have in common is neither an unchanging subcultural self nor an established cross-cultural consciousness. For example, in his analysis of the Balinese person, he shows very clearly how cultural codings and presuppositions are vital to a proper understanding of the notion of self found in that culture. In his exegesis of Balinese self, the thematizations that come to the fore are not those such as motivation, will, and individuation, which would figure prominently in Western discourses, but an entirely different set of themes intimately linked to Balinese culture. Commenting on the concept of self, Geertz says, "The Western concept of the person as a bounded, unique, more or less integrated motivational and cognitive universe, a dynamic center of awareness, emotion, judgment, and action organized into a distinctive whole and against its social and natural background, is, however incorrigible as it may seem to us, a rather peculiar idea within the context of the world's cultures."[13] If this is true, in seeking to understand the multifaceted nature of self-deception it seems especially important to culturally contextualize it.

Some of the concerns of Hallowell and Geertz have been fruitfully expanded by modern ethnopsychologists who are interested in the cultural understanding and cultural formulation of the self and the processes and dynamics of interplay by means of which these enunciations find articulation in quotidian life. These ethnopsychologists are trying to rectify some of the deficiencies associated with the earlier culture and personality studies in which the emphasis was clearly on the motivational constructs of individual, and their centrality in inflecting human, behavior. In these earlier studies very little attention was paid to the modalities of interpretation of the people regarding questions of self and how they have a direct bearing on the wider cultural discourse of a given society. In this regard, the work of some of the new ethnopsychologists serves to open up a new and interesting discursive space in understanding self. If, in order to understand self-deception, we need to understand the nature of self and its formation, and if culture is so central to the construction of the self, then it stands to reason that we need to pay much greater attention to the question of self-deception and cultural contextualization. Our reading of *The Serpent and the Rope* certainly points in this direction.

Next we need to consider the relationship between rationality and culture that is also crucial to a proper understanding of the dynamics of self-deception. It is patent that questions of rationality and belief are at the center of current excursions into self-deception. This of course means that the nature of rationality, bounded rationality, pseudorationality, irrationality, belief, desire, and so on, are vital to the discussion. On the one hand, there are those scholars who would assert that self-deception represents the potency and the pervasiveness of irrationality in human behavior; others would argue that it does not constitute a form of irrationality based on incoherence of belief, but rather an incongruity between the self-conception of a person and his or her actions. Fingarette espouses the latter view.[14] Jon Elster would argue against the assumption that the function of rationality is to indicate to the agents what to do, so that if they behave in a way that is antithetical, they are irrational; instead, he would maintain that all that rationality can do is to exclude certain alternatives while providing no direction regarding the choice among the remaining.[15] While these and other related discussions of rationality and belief have largely been conducted within the discursive horizons of Western culture, it is important to enlarge the discursive boundaries by bringing non-Western cultures into the discussion. It is indeed here that the role of culture becomes supremely important.

As we delve into the terrain of culture and rationality, we need to pay ever closer attention to questions of culturally grounded styles of reasoning and the understanding of rationality from within the discursive spaces of given cultures. Rationality can be broadly defined as logical consistency. However, this definition does not focus on a number of important areas that are related to culture. Are there alternate ways of conceptualizing rationality that challenge in some way the Enlightenment view with its valorization of universal laws of human nature, objectivity, and scientific method for arriving at Truth quickly. Nietzsche remarked,

> What then is truth? A mobile army of metaphors, metonyms, and anthromorphisms—in short a sum of human relations, which have been enhanced, transposed and embellished poetically and rhetorically, and which after long use seem firm, canonical and obligatory to a people: truths are illusions about which one has forgotten that this is what they are; metaphors which are worn out and without sensuous power; coins which have lost their pictures and now matter only as metal, no longer coins.[16]

Hollis and Lukes observes that this mobile army is more like a gang of local militias, each keeping order in its own province.[17] Peter Winch observes,

"The criteria of logic are not a direct gift from God but arise out of and are intelligible only in the context of ways of living and modes of social life."[18] Now these observations of Nietzsche and Winch are certainly not accepted universally; what they suggest, though, is that we take the cultural dimension of rationality far more seriously than we are in the habit of doing.

Let us for example consider the question of common sense. It is closely bound up with rationality, and the immediate response is to see it as universal. However, as the anthropologist Clifford Geertz has pointed out, it is important that we see common sense as a cultural system.[19] He believes that common sense is as much an interpretation of the immediacies of experience, a gloss on them, as are poetry, painting, myth, epistemology, and so on, and like them, historically constituted and subject to historically formulated norms of judgment. He goes on to argue that common sense is not what the mind freed of cant spontaneously apprehends, but what the mind filled with presuppositions and prejudgments concludes. The implications of this line of reasoning is that we need to pay much closer and sustained attention to the ways in which cultural traditions, social practices, and inherited axiologies articulate, regulate, and transform notions of rationality. This is of course not to suggest that transcultural judgments of rationality and irrationality cannot be made. They certainly can; however, before we venture to make them, we have to examine the cultural embeddedness of rationality and its implications for transcultural judgments. In the case of self-deception, which is indissolubly linked to rationality, it is of the utmost importance that we focus on this cultural dimension. In our reading of *The Serpent and the Rope,* we saw how important it is to pay close attention to culturally grounded styles of reasoning.

Closely related to these two topics is the whole question of meaning production. Many of the writers who have sought to examine self-deception have done so with a specific model of self and meaning production in mind. This is basically a mentalistic model in which the individual is solely responsible for the production of meaning. It presupposes an objective space where the individual is not subject to the pressures of culture, tradition, history, ideology, and the like, in the generation of meaning. This model implies that human beings as producers of meaning operate within an economy of meaning that is self-created and over which they have control. Moreover, this model also implies that the social order in which the individual functions is seen as a series of isolated and purposive behaviors on the part of other social factors. That this social order is also a meaning-generating process is ignored. What the study of the two novels, *The Serpent and the Rope* and *The English Teacher* underlines, is that we need to go beyond this mentalized world of intentionalities and bring into the discussion of meaning production questions of culture, history, tradition, and so on. Self-deception is inextricably linked to meaning production, and in order to understand the full complexity of this phenomenon, we need to situate it in a discursive space traversed by forces of culture.

Jon Elster, while recognizing the importance of the work of Freud, Sartre, Fingarette, and Schafer in explaining self-deception, finds their work unconvincing because they tend to reproduce the primary paradox of self-deception in more subtle forms.[20] He suggests a diversified strategy, explaining different cases of what is termed "self-deception" along different lines. First, some cases may be interpreted as unsuccessful attempts at self-deception, and therefore no more paradoxical than any other attempt to achieve contradictory objectives. Second, some cases can best be understood in relation to higher-level and lower-level beliefs, so that a person can willfully choose not to acquire the lower-level beliefs that would give substance to one's higher-level beliefs. Third, some cases may be interpreted as failed attempts at character modification. Fourth, a person can cause him- or herself to believe something at a later time. Fifth, some cases can be understood as wish fulfillment. The kind of self-deception found in the two novels can best be examined in accordance with Elster's second characterization, namely, the conflict between higher-level and lower-level beliefs. However, in order to understand the full implications of this it is absolutely necessary to locate the act of self-deception in the larger cultural discourse from which it derives its meaning. Hence the importance of culturally contextualizing self-deception.

In this chapter, as a way of coming to grips with the tangled question of self-deception, I have chosen to focus on two novels primarily for two reasons. First, the rich details of life worlds and thought worlds provided by fiction enable us to delve deeper into the issues of self-deception in terms of lived reality. Second, novels focus on the question of selfhood and individualism in complex and productive ways. Milan Kundera once remarked that the novel is the imaginary paradise of the individual. In societies in which the voice of the group still takes precedence over the needs of the individual, the novelization of experience presents in a rather vivid form the antagonisms and affiliations between individuals and society. This is indeed important in understanding the nature of self-deception in such societies in that it serves to focus attention on the individual and his or her behavior and motivations in a clearly demarcated social space.

One of the main points I have sought to establish in this chapter is that in our attempt to decode self-deception, we need to pay greater attention to endogenous criteria of evaluation based on the specificities of cultural experiences. All cultures function in accordance with explicitly articulated or implicitly suggested models of self. What endogenous criteria of evaluation aim to do is to uncover these culturally sanctioned models of self so that we could better understand the phenomenon of self-deception in terms of cultural discursivities. The chapter points out that it is generally believed that self-deception constitutes an inconsistency in thinking. Richard Rorty has said that an increased inability to treat apparent inconsistency should be regarded not as something to be repudiated but as a sign of the inadequacy of the vocabularies of explanation and adjudication currently in use.[21] In order to understand the true dimensions and dynamics of self-deception, it is important to widen the discursive boundaries within which self-deception is examined and fashion newer vocabularies of explication. The cultural contextualization of self-deception will enable us to move forward in that preferred direction.

NOTES

1. Raja Rao, *The Serpent and the Rope* (New York: Overlook, 1986).
2. R. K. Narayan, *The English Teacher* (Mysore: Indian Thought Publications, 1955).
3. Richard Rorty, *Essays on Heidegger and Others* (New York: Cambridge University Press, 1991), 81.
4. Kathleen Raine, "On *The Serpent and the Rope*," *World Literature Today* (autumn 1988), p. 61.
5. C. D. Narasimhaiah, *Rajo Rao* (New Delhi: Arnold Heinemann, 1973), p. 93.
6. William Walsh, *Commonwealth Literature* (Oxford: Clarendon, 1973), p. 54.
7. Amélie Oksenberg Rorty, "The Deceptive Self: Liars, Layers, and Lairs" in *Perspectives on Self-Deception,* ed. Brian P. McLaughlin and Amélie Oksenberg Rorty (Berkeley: University of California Press, 1988), 12.
8. M. M. Bakhtin, *The Dialogue Imagination* (Austin: University of Texas Press, 1981), 332.
9. Amélie Oksenberg Rorty, "Self-Deception, *Akrasia* and Irrationality," in *The Multiple Self,* ed. Jon Elster (Cambridge: Cambridge University Press, 1988), 131.
10. Jon Elster, *The Multiple Self,* 30.
11. A. Irving Hollowell, *Culture and Experience* (Philadelphia: University of Pennsylvania Press, 1955), p. 76.
12. Clifford Geertz, *The Interpretation of Cultures* (New York: Basic Books, 1973), p. 89.
13. Clifford Geertz, *Local Knowledge* (New York: Basic Books, 1983), p. 59.
14. Herbert Fingarette, *Self-Deception* (London: Routledge and Kegan Paul, 1969), p. 42.

15. Jon Elster, *Sour Grapes* (Cambridge: Cambridge University Press, 1985), p. 112.

16. Friedrich Nietzsche, in *The Portable Nietzsche,* in ed. W. Kaufman (New York: Viking Press 1954), p. 108.

17. Martin Hollis and Steven Lukes, *Rationality and Relativism* (Oxford: Basil Blackwell, 1990), p. 63.

18. Peter Winch, *The Idea of a Social Science and Its Relation to Philosophy* (London: Routledge and Kegan Paul, 1958), 100.

19. Clifford Geertz, *Local Knowledge,* p. 73.

20. Jon Elster, *Sour Grapes,* 149.

21. Richard Rorty, *Contingency, Irony, and Solidarity* (Cambridge: Cambridge University Press, 1989), p. 80.

SIXTEEN

RITUAL, SELF-DECEPTION, AND MAKE-BELIEVE
A Classical Buddhist Perspective

Richard P. Hayes

INTRODUCTION

Everyone, with the possible exception of those who are really good at it, is personally familiar with the phenomenon of self-deception. Anyone who has been conscious of struggling with a temptation to do what goes against her own better judgment and has then found justification for yielding to temptation is familiar with self-deception. So if I may be allowed to begin with the assumption that most of us have experienced a phenomenon that we would identify as some form of self-deception, what I shall try to do in this chapter is to examine how one particular theory of personal identity can account for the phenomenon. Having done that, this chapter looks into the question of one of the mechanisms of self-deception and then into the question of whether there are occasions in which the mechanisms of self-deception may be regarded as producing more positive results.

THE BUDDHIST VIEW OF A MODULAR SELF

The theory of personal identity from which this whole issue is is examined is the one provided within classical Indian Buddhism, which is referred to simply as "Buddhism" throughout this chapter.[1] In contrast to most of the other philosophical systems in classical India, the Buddhists argued for a modular view of personal identity. According to this view, there is no characteristic or set of characteristics that remains constant throughout the life of a complex organism. This being the case, a complex organism does not really have an identity, at least in the etymological sense of the word *identitas*, which literally means "sameness": a complex being, at the end of its existence, need not have any parts that were present at the beginning of its existence. Insofar as an organism has any identity, it consists of no more than an agreement within society to regard a cluster of properties or an assembly of events as a single being—as in the apocryphal story of the museum that proudly displayed a hatchet that once belonged to George Washington, although the blade had been replaced twice and the handle three times since it had left Washington's hands. The Buddhist theory also does not regard an organism as an individual, at least in the etymological sense of the word, which indicates the fact of being indivisible. Rather, an organism is seen as an aggregation of distinct parts that may cooperate with one another and to some extent depend upon one another in order to function, but which are, nevertheless, in principle at least, quite separable from one another. It might be more accurate, according to Buddhist anthropology, to call a person a "party," that is, a group of individuals—in this case, individual simple properties—assembled for a particular purpose. In fact, for the rest of this chapter, the legal term *party* shall be used to refer to what we intuitively take to be a single person; using this temporary convention will help serve as a reminder that in the theory under discussion, no person is really an individual.

Not only is the physical body modular, according to Buddhist theory, but so is the mind. Rather than speaking of a single principle of integrated awareness. Buddhist literature describes separate actions of awareness, such as an awareness of the color yellow, an awareness of the color red, or an awareness of differences in shade and other chromatic properties. Each of the five physical senses provides an entirely discrete channel of information, such that no two faculties of sense are capable of experiencing the same type of sensible property: the eye senses only colors, the ear only sounds, and so on. Not only is all consciousness modular, say the Buddhists, but so is a party's character or personality. A party's character is the product of a great diversity of types of instruction and indoctrination, all of which leave at least some impression. Since these external influences come from a number of sources, it is to be expected that they should often be incompatible with one another. And as a result, the character or personality of a complex organism such as a human being is naturally full of contradictory opinions, incongruous desires, and incompatible aspirations. Even the human memory is fragmented, for memories are usually triggered by sensations, so that one's sense of the past is constantly shifting. Not only do we have varying perceptions of who we are, but we also have continually changing perceptions of who we have been and who we hope to become.

In all this instability and internal inconsistency, the human being mirrors the world as a whole. The totality of events is not, in Buddhist theory, a cosmos, for $\kappa o \sigma \mu o \varsigma$ means order. Nor is it a universe, for it does not move as a single whole. Rather, the totality of events is an unsupervised chaos that has no beginning and no single purpose. It is a noisy and random jumble of events caused by innumerable different and often irreconcilable volitions, over which there never has been and never could be a single-minded, intelligent superintendent.[2] This being the nature of the world as a whole, the only workable strategy for attaining contentment, according to Buddhism, is to relinquish all hope for the impossible and to learn to accept reality as it is and as it always must be. Among the impossible dreams to be abandoned by the wise are those for such things as personal and collective security, predictability, uniformity, and harmony, for reality is characterized by constant and dangerously chaotic change.

This view of the human being and its place in the world is not the view of any one Buddhist thinker. Rather, it is a mosaic put together over the course of some fifteen centuries by scores of Buddhist philosophers from south and central Asia. These philosophers differed from one another in many respects, but they shared a preoccupation with the problem of change and transformation, and they agreed on the principle that modularity is the only way to account for such change. Like Charles Darwin and other nineteenth-century biologists of Europe, who built their theory of evolution upon the ideas of modularity and dissociability and in so doing argued against the essentialism of anti-evolutionists such as the paleontologist Georges Cuvier, the Buddhists of India developed the idea that change is possible only in modular beings who are capable of replacing their various components at differing rates of change.[3] If there were such a thing as a being whose consciousness was simple rather than modular, such a being could neither learn nor think nor perform any kind of mental activity. And so any being who is capable of thinking about anything at all must be modular. And of course the more complex a modular being is, the greater the likelihood of internal inconsistency and other forms of physical and psychological chaos.

The Buddhist thinkers themselves explicitly made the point that the concept of a path or method of improving one's own character made sense only in the context of a doctrine of a modular and therefore inherently unstable self. In the second century C.E., for example, the philosopher Nāgārjuna argued that no changes of character would be possible if the self were of a fixed nature. Buddhist tradition already had a special term for the idea that a party has no fixed nature of its own: they called this condition "emptiness." Nāgārjuna argued that empty beings are the only beings subject to change.[4] The aspect of emptiness that is unwelcome to most people is that change is not only possible but inevitable, and that one of the many types of change to which every being is subject is the one known as death. The tenacious presence of premonitions of one's own death often has the effect of spoiling experiences that might otherwise be enjoyable. Sentient

Self and Deception

beings suffer because of their emptiness. But emptiness also has a more welcome consequence, which is that it is not necessary to suffer anxiety about one's own death and therefore not necessary to have one's pleasures spoiled by the lingering promise of the unavoidable dissolution of one's own body and mind. Death may be inevitable for empty beings, but uneasiness about death is a psychological state; like all psychological states, it has antecedent causes and conditions, and once those conditions are eliminated, then so is the dread of dying. Therefore, concludes Nāgārjuna, it is only a philosophy based on the doctrine of emptiness that is capable of accounting for the fact that people can achieve the great result of being liberated from the fear of death by making a number of small, incremental changes in their beliefs and attitudes.

Neither Nāgārjuna nor any other Buddhist philosopher that I am aware of made any explicit comments about self-deception. However, it can be argued that the doctrine of emptiness, being merely another way of expressing the modular view of the human being, has the potential to provide a reasonable account of the phenomenon. What follows is an attempt at a brief sketch of how a Buddhist theory of self-deception might look.

A Possible Buddhist Account of Self-Deception

First, it will be recalled that the human character is regarded in Buddhist psychology as the product of innumerable impressions that have been experienced virtually at random. A number of attitudes that one forms early in life are the result of the kind of training that one receives as a child from parents and other family members. Given that mothers and fathers are only rarely in perfect harmony with one another, a child usually acquires and cultivates traits that are at least slightly different and perhaps even incompatible. As the child grows older and comes into contact with an ever greater circle of influential friends and mentors, it becomes ever more likely to acquire conflicting patterns of thinking and behavior. By the time one is a young adult, the odds are probably in favor of one's having at least mildly conflicting sets of desires, aspirations, attitudes, and beliefs.

At this stage of the description, two further suppositions of Buddhist psychology come into play. The first is that basic attitudes can be classified into two categories: those that are competent and those that are incompetent at producing a feeling of well-being.[5] According to most systems of classification, for example, hostility and mental rigidity are among the basic emotional and mental traits that impede contentment in the world, whereas sympathy and mental flexibility are among the traits that generate feelings of happiness or enhance already existing pleasure. The second supposition is that at any given moment, all one's basic attitudes are either competent or incompetent; hostility and mental flexibility cannot occur in the same mentality at the same time. At any given moment, then, a party's mind is supposed to be driven by attitudes that are propelling it either toward or away from satisfaction, but never toward both satisfaction and dissatisfaction at the same time. However, there can be oscillation between these two polarities, and the mental continuum in which this oscillation occurs normally regards itself, and is regarded by society at large, as a single being, even though it is in fact not.

Among the mental traits that can be classified either as competent or as incompetent, according to Buddhists, there are various kinds of belief. Believing in one's own individuality and believing that one's own needs and desires are any more urgent or important than the needs and desires of other sentient beings are two stock examples of incompetent mental states. Given the modular nature of the human character, and given that beliefs are acquired from a variety of sources, it is possible for a human being to hold different beliefs at different times. It is possible, for example, to believe in some situations that when one's desires conflict with the desires of others, that it is preferable to satisfy one's own desires even though this may entail making others unhappy; and in some other situations, one may believe just the opposite, namely, that satisfying one's own desires at the expense of causing another being's displeasure is less likely to make one truly happy than modifying one's desires. There may very well be situations in which a party's mind oscillates quickly between these two beliefs, until one of them finally becomes strong enough to overpower the other. If it should turn out that the incompetent set of beliefs overpowered the competent set of beliefs, then the Buddhist would say that the party had become a victim of self-deception. It would be a deception in the sense that the party had become convinced to act in a way that did not conduce to its optimum well-being, and it would be *self*-deception in the sense that the victorious set of false beliefs and the defeated set of true beliefs both belonged to the same party, that is, to what is conventionally considered to be the same person.

It should be apparent from all that has been said up to this point that a Buddhist account of self-deception is a species of a genus of accounts in which the principal strategy is to see the deceiving agent and the deceived patient as two different and relatively independent subsystems of a single system. Presumably, the Buddhist account is liable to all the criticisms of the whole genus.[6] Rather than trying to answer those criticisms, let me now move on to the issue of one of the mechanisms for self-deception that seems to have been recognized by the Buddhists.

Self and Deception

RITUAL AS A MECHANISM OF SELF-DECEPTION

What is being presented here is not a recapitulation of explicitly stated Buddhist doctrines. Rather, this section offers some speculations on the kind of thinking that may have been behind Buddhist doctrines that were explicitly stated. Le us begin from the safety of a brief recapitulation of those doctrines before venturing onto the more hazardous ground of speculation.

The Stages of Progress Toward Competence

As has already been pointed out, Buddhist theory portrays the human mentality as an unfortunate aggregation of conflicting desires, beliefs, and attitudes in which competent mental states contend with incompetent mental states: the result is inconsistent behavior and frustration. A very important factor in determining which kind of mentality prevails, according to Buddhist theory, is the company that one keeps. Comrades tend to exert a strong influence on how one behaves, and their influence extends to such forms of behavior as what one believes and which values one gives top priority. Therefore, it is important to make company with salutary friends, people who encourage one always to cultivate competent mental habits and attitudes.[7] If one is fortunate enough to have such friends, then the odds are much more in favor of gradually developing good habits and eliminating bad ones. The ultimate goal, of course, is to eliminate the bad habits altogether, to eradicate them so thoroughly that they can never again arise. Only at this final stage of progress can one be said to be fully integrated, thus a person of integrity (wholeness, unity). A person who reaches this final stage is an *arhant* in Buddhist literature, a person worthy of respect.[8] Now on the way to becoming an arhant, it is said that a person passes through several stages of development. It is not necessary for our purposes here to examine these stages in detail. Suffice it to say that at each stage of development a person is said to eliminate a certain set of psychological traits that act as obstacles to complete and imperturbable happiness, and that the closer one gets to being an *arhant,* the more subtle and difficult these obstacles are to eradicate. Rather than focusing on the subtle end of the scale, this chapter focuses on just the first two obstacles, elimination of which marks the first stage of progress toward health and respectability.

The first of the two obstacles that Buddhist literature says must be removed before any further progress is possible is *sat-kāya-dṛṣṭi* in Sanskrit. This term literally means the "belief that collections are real." Generally speaking, this term refers to any belief that a collection or set or group of things has any reality over and above the members of the group. More particularly, the term refers to the belief that a party, who is a complex of dissociable physical and psychological characteristics, has an existence of its own, apart from its components. Given that the belief in the separate existence of the complex wholes is one that should be discarded, according to early Buddhism, we can say that early Buddhism is antiholistic (as well as anti-individualistic, atheistic, and acosmic); holistic thinking is seen as standing in the way of genuine happiness. The second of the two obstacles that must be removed if one is to make any further advancement toward being an arhant is *śīla-vrata-parāmarśa* in Sanskrit. This term literally means "addiction to customs and rituals," especially devotional (or what we might today call "religious") rituals. As Buddhism grew as an institutionalized religion, this term naturally came to be interpreted as addiction to customs and rituals of any religion other than Buddhism, but there is evidence to suggest that in its earliest usage it referred to the addiction to rituals of any kind.

Why Must Rituals Be Abandoned?

At this point, we leave the safety of description and march into the more perilous terrain of unwarranted speculation. The question here is: Why are these two obstacles always presented together as a pair? Are they simply two separate impediments to be overcome one after another, or is there some organic relationship between them that would enable us to regard each of these obstacles as an aspect of the other, or at least as a reflection of the other, such that overcoming one requires also overcoming the other? I shall argue the latter and more particularly, that the belief in one's own individuality can be seen as the ultimate form of self-deception and that customs and rituals can be seen as one of the most powerful mechanisms by which this deception is sustained.

First, it has already been established that the Buddhist tradition regarded as an error the belief in individuality. A party cannot be an individual in the sense of being an undivided whole, since such an entity would be incapable of action or change. Since a party does act and change, it cannot be an undivided whole. But neither is a party an individual in the sense of having an identity that makes it distinct from other beings in that way that would warrant a preferential treatment of itself over others. Moreover, according to a Buddhist way of looking at things, the erroneous belief in personal identity is not a harmless error. On the contrary, it is believing in oneself as an object of warranted preferential treatment that is said to serve as the cause of modes of behavior that ultimately work to one's own disadvantage. To cite just one obvious example, theft is a form of behavior that is warranted only by the assumption that one's own desire or need for a piece of property is more important than the desire or need of the being who is currently in possession of that property. But acting as a thief to alienate the person from whom the property is taken, and to alienate others is at best to lose their cooperation; at worst it is to provoke them into some form of unpleasant retaliation. There is a Buddhist adage: "Abuse always has two victims: the abusive party and the party abused." Therefore, theft is an incompetent method of taking care of one's own interests. And since theft is motivated by a belief in one's individual identity, it can be said that this belief is also a form of incompetence.[9] As we discussed earlier, in a Buddhist context, when an incompetent set of beliefs and attitudes prevails over a competent set within the same party, the party can be said to be a victim of self-deception. Therefore, the belief in personal identity can be regarded as a form of self-deception.

For the discussion that follows the word *individualism* is used to mean the belief that a party has in its own uniqueness. Let me now make a distinction between degrees of individualism. The limiting case of individualism would be the belief that one is radically isolated from all other parties in such a way that one's own personal needs and desires are justifiably taken into account in preference over the needs and desires of all other parties. Let me take advantage of the fact that the Greek word for private or separate is ιδιος and call this view of oneself as radically separate from all others "idiotic individualism." Distinguished from this is what we could call "semi-idiotic individualism" or "partisanship," namely, the conviction that one belongs to a group of other individuals and that this group as a whole is uniquely privileged over all other living beings in such a way that the needs of this group justifiably take precedence over the needs of all other groups. Common expressions of partisanship would be ethnocentrism, racism, nationalism, sexism, and what biologist David Suzuki calls "speciesism" (the conviction that human needs and wants count for more than the needs of all other forms of life in the biosphere). If individualism as a genus is a form of self-deception, then both idiotic individualism and partisanship are forms of self-deception as well.

Relatively few people, aside perhaps from psychopaths and sociopaths adhere to what I am calling "idiotic individualism." Considerably more people partake, at least occasionally, in partisanship of one kind or another. When people collect themselves into groups which in turn come to regard themselves as somehow distinct from the rest of society (or from the rest of life itself), they must find a way of maintaining a sense of group solidarity. This should involve overcoming the tendency toward idiotic individualism that prevails among the parties in the group so that the members come to regard the common needs of the group on a par with or more important than their own private needs. The group must also find a way of helping its members feel that the group itself is distinguishable from all the parties who do not have membership in the group. One of the most effective ways that human beings have found to maintain cohesion within a group and separation of the group from the outside is ritual action. Some piece of behavior that is performed in exactly (or nearly exactly) the same manner by all members of the group serves to cement them into a whole on the principle that however different the members may be from one another, they have in common at least this set of actions that they all do in the same way. But this piece of behavior is really effective to bond the group together only if it also excludes everyone who does not perform it in the prescribed manner. It is not at all difficult to come up with examples of ritual behavior that bonds those who perform it against the rest of the world. There are patriotic rituals such as singing national anthems and saluting flags; political rituals such as staging massive rallies, chanting slogans in unison, and attaching pithy aphorisms to one's automobile; religious rituals such as reciting creeds, going on pilgrimages, and venerating consecrated objects; military rituals such as saluting, wearing uniforms and insignia, and marching in unison; athletic rituals such as keeping mascots, displaying trophies, and cheerleading; academic rituals such as giving students examinations and then dressing them up in funny hats when they have passed through a requisite number of such ordeals; and family rituals such as the celebration of birthdays and wedding anniversaries. When one begins to think about all the rituals in one's life, the list is seemingly endless.

Given that in the Buddhist view individualism is a form of self-deception, and given that partisanship is a species of individualism, and given that ritual behavior is one of the most effective mechanisms of partisanship, I would argue that it is no accident that individualism and ritualism are always paired together in standard Buddhist lists of obstacles to genuine contentment.

SELF-DECEPTION AND MAKE-BELIEVE

On the basis of what has been said so far, it might be expected that a Buddhist attitude toward ritual would be uniformly negative, since ritual can be seen as an instrument of self-delusion. But if one observes the actual practice of Buddhists throughout history, one finds that there is anything but a disdain for customs and rituals. This discrepancy between what the theory predicts and what one actually observes could be accounted for in one of several ways. It could be the case that Buddhists have historically tended to have a rather poor understanding of the principles that once stood as the foundation of their practices. Or it could be that in this presentation, it is I who have seriously misrepresented the theoretical basis of Buddhist attitudes toward ritual. Let me assume that the latter is the case and try to make suitable adjustments in my presentation of Buddhist theory.

Fortunately, the amount of adjustment necessary in order to salvage this theory is not too extensive. Recall that the point was made earlier that it is considered very important to keep company with people who encourage one to cultivate a competent mentality. Indeed, the ideal situation for a person is to be within a community of people whose sole interest is to cultivate skill in themselves and to help others do the same. Insofar as rituals and customs within such a community help it to stay together as a community, they would not be seen as entirely negative. But this is still far from saying that ritual could be seen as playing a positive role in a party's endeavor to become more virtuous. What remains to be seen now is whether ritual, and the self-deception that accompanies it, can ever been seen as something wholesome, as opposed to being merely not entirely insidious.

Let us begin by considering the case of a party who has just recently embarked on the venture of becoming more virtuous. One in this situation, it will be recalled, is normally still vulnerable to influences that draw one away from a competent mentality. While a party is in a state of indecision about whether or not to yield to those incompetent influences, it is usual to begin to doubt whether it is even possible or indeed desirable to have a skillful mentality. It is at just these moments when rituals can be effectively used to restore a party's belief in the possibility of being skillful. By fingering a string of beads, for example, or by reciting a memorized formula, or by recalling a vow that one has made, the party may overcome the doubt about whether there is really any point in being judicious in one's behavior. In a case such as this, the ritual has been instrumental in doing two things. First, it has reminded the party of his or her membership in the community of wise people; this feeling of membership in a community, it will be recalled, is from a Buddhist point of view a kind of self-deception. Second, the ritual has helped to make the party believe once again in something about which for moment there had been doubt. By being made to believe in skill once again, the party actually acts competently and thus rejoins the community of the wise.

Ritual can be seen as a kind of make-believe in two senses of the word. First, in a literal sense, it can have the effect of making one believe in something that one had momentarily doubted. It is an action of faith rather than an action of knowledge. Second, in the usual idiomatic sense of the term, ritual very often is make-believe in the sense of a kind of pretend-

A Classical Buddhist Perspective

ing or a suspension of reality. In order to illustrate this second point, let me use the concrete examples of two rituals that are in fact commonly performed among Buddhists.

One ritual that exemplifies the element of make-believe in both of the senses described above is one that is virtually universal within Buddhist communities. This is the ritual of bowing respectfully to an image, usually a representation of the Buddha; it is often accompanied by making an offering of incense, flowers, or food. This ritual is obviously an act of pretending in that one is acting *as if* one were in the presence of the living Buddha, even though one is obviously not actually in his presence. One is offering beautiful flowers as if the Buddha could see them, fragrant incense as if the Buddha could smell it, and delicious food as if the Buddha could eat it. These ritual gestures of generosity are also a kind of play acting; since the custom among Buddhists is to eat food after it has been presented to an image of the Buddha, one is not really giving anything away at all in the final analysis, but rather one is enjoying eating the food as if it had never been given to anyone, and smelling the incense as if it had been ignited solely for one's own personal sensual pleasure. To get the full benefit of performing the ritual requires that one suspend one's sense of reality, in about the same way that getting the full benefit of watching a cinema or a dramatic presentation on stage requires that one forget that one is actually the spectator of a portrayal of events rather than the direct spectator of the events themselves.

A second ritual that is very common, but by no means universal, among Buddhists is that of sitting in meditation. When performed with a group, this ritual involves sitting on the ground in a posture approximately like that in which the Buddha is supposed to have sat and staying in that posture for a prescribed period of time. Sitting in this way re-creates a rough resemblance to the Buddha's external appearance when his mind was serene and calm and free of desires, aversions, and delusions. As anyone who has participated in this ritual is aware, adopting this posture is very often a form of play acting, in much the same way that making an offering of food to an image is a kind of play acting. Very often the mind of the meditator is anything but calm and serene, and it is free from desires and aversions only for a few seconds at a time. And yet the meditator struggles to maintain every outward appearance of having the psychological traits of a Buddha. It is a ritual in which one makes believe that one is either a Buddha or someone on the way to becoming either a Buddha or an *arhant.* Like the ritual of making offerings to a representation of the Buddha, the ritual of sitting in meditation also requires that the practitioner be willing to suspend reality and enter into a realm of make-believe.

Self and Deception

In addition to the element of pretense already indicated, both of the two rituals described above have in common that they reinforce the participant's sense of belonging to a community, namely, the community of Buddhists. Bowing and making offerings to an image is something that all Buddhists have in common. Bowing to an image specifically of the Buddha differentiates this community from those who venerate other images and from those who pay homage to no images at all. Moreover, within the Buddhist community there are many different styles of performing devotional rituals. The particular manner in which one bows serves to cement one's relations to a given Buddhist sect and to exclude those who belong to other forms of Buddhism. In other words the ritual has the effect of increasing the participant's feelings of membership in a group. Moreover, this group is seen as a special group, for it is part of the community of the wise, who are elevated above the level of ordinary beings. Believing oneself to be a member of a privileged group, as we saw above, is partisanship, which we argued was a kind of self-deception. Therefore, the rituals that we have been describing can be considered instruments of self-deception.

Rituals That Make Believe; Rituals That Deceive

What is it, then, that distinguishes these rituals from the kinds of rituals that Buddhist theory condemns? Let me suggest something along the following lines as a possible redeeming virtue. Although it can be said that one is only pretending to be generous when one offers food to an image, and pretending to be serene when one sits in a meditation posture, at least one is pretending to do the right sort of thing. That is, one is pretending to do something that would be competent and skillful and conducive to the happiness of oneself and others if one were really doing it. Moreover, going through the motions of doing an action, even if one is not really doing it, is said to reinforce certain habits. Make-believe, in other words, can be seen as a kind of rehearsal, like the preparation that an actor goes through in learning to play a dramatic role convincingly, or the practice that an athlete undergoes in preparation for a real competition. When the well-rehearsed actor steps onto the stage, or the well-trained athlete into the arena, the real performance seems natural, spontaneous, and effortless, because the performer has gone through the motions so many times that the motions require very little conscious effort. Similarly, when disciples perform the ritual of pretending to be generous hundreds or even thousands of times a year for several years, then when they step out of the world of make-believe and begin to act with real sentient beings, their generosity is spontaneous.

A Classical Buddhist Perspective

Given what has been said about Buddhist views on the capacity that repetitious actions have in the formation of competent and incompetent mental attitudes, it should be clear that no ritual is ever purely empty, for it always bears at least the power to reinforce a habit, whether good or bad. Make-believe actions performed countless times become second nature, and because of this, good teachers think carefully about the kinds of rituals they recommend that their disciples perform. Care must be given to consider not only the intended results of the ritual, such as the cultivation of habits of generosity and other competent attitudes, but also the possible secondary results, including negative side effects such as the inadvertent reinforcements of incompetent habits. Given that some attitudes are said to be competent and others incompetent, one can make a similar distinction between kinds of ritual, according to whether they have the effect of reinforcing good habits or bad. A ritual that has the effect of reinforcing competent mental habits such as generosity, for example, would be classified as a healthy ritual, whereas a ritual that merely has the effect of reinforcing a party's tendency to partishanship would be an unhealthy one. Generally speaking, then, a ritual that makes the performer believe in the advantages of being virtuous is a positive ritual, while one that enables the performer to reinforce forms of self-deception such as the belief in individuality and a sense of solidarity with a group is a negative one. Therefore, it is predictable that Buddhist teachers would tend to avoid having disciples perform rituals as a group and would prefer instead to suggest particular ritual practices to particular disciples only after having time to become acquainted with their present mental habits.

CONCLUSION

In this chapter, I have tried to arrive at an approximation of how Indian Buddhist thinkers might have treated the issue of self-deception, given what is known about the psychological categories with which they dealt. The aim was not to try to defend the Buddhist theory as the best available account of the phenomenon, although I hope to have sketched out roughly how a defense of the theory might be conducted by those whose assumptions were similar to those of the classical Indian Buddhists. In general, the theory presented here is a member of the class of theories that attempt to account for self-deception by offering an account of a fragmented self, or what I have called a "modular self." Here the collection of modules is called a "self" only in casual and informal everyday language, but not in any rigorous sense of the term. Deception may be regarded as the act of one

Self and Deception

intentionally causing another to believe what is false or detrimental to the other; under this theory it is one module that persuades another module to act on a false belief; and it is only insofar as both modules in question are intuitively, but mistakenly, regarded as belonging to a single self that the deception can be regarded as self-deception.

After sketching out this Buddhist theory of self-deception. An attempt was made to show that two common forms of deception recognized by early Buddhists were individualism (believing in one's individual uniqueness) and partisanship (belief that one belongs to a social group that is unique). On the basis of the observation that rituals can be a strong mechanism for promoting partisanship, it was argued that a possible reason behind the Buddhist rejection of ritualism was their insight into the potential that rituals have for creating a false sense of group solidarity. It has also been argued that ritual behavior in general is not a kind of action but rather a form of pretending to act. But then, noting that Buddhists in practice do quite frequently resort to rituals, this chapter suggested that some rituals can be seen as promoting, under carefully monitored circumstances, confidence in the advantages of cultivating what are regarded as healthy attitudes. It is only under these special circumstances that ritual behavior can be called something other than a form of self-deception.

NOTES

1. By classical Indian Buddhism, I mean the period of about a millennium, roughly 100 B.C.E. until around 1000 C.E., during which time Buddhist thought became increasingly systematized in India. Most of what is presented here is characteristic of what one finds in Vasubandhu's *Abhidharmakośá*, Buddhaghosa's *Vissuddhimaggo*, Dharmakīrti's *Pramāṇa-vārttika*, Śāntarakṣita's *Tattvasaṅgraha*, Karmalaśīla's *Bhāvanākrama* and numerous other writings in Sanskrit and Pali. Good accounts in English appear in numerous secondary sources; I would recommend both Steven Collins *Selfless persons: Imagery and Thought in Theravāda Buddhism* (Cambridge: Cambridge University Press, 1982), 85–195, and Akira Hirakawa *A History of Indian Buddhism: From Śākyamuni to Early Mahāyāna*, trans. Paul Groner (Honolulu: University of Hawaii Press, 1990) 38–59 and 127–219, for their clarity. Th. Stcherbatsky's *The Central Conception of Buddhism and the Meaning of the Word "Dharma,"* 4th edn. (Delhi: Motilal Benarsidass, 1970), though dated, is one of the most frequently cited accounts in English.

2. An account of the arguments that Indian Buddhists adduced in favor of atheism appears in Richard P. Hayes, "Principled Atheism in the Buddhist Scholastic Tradition," *Journal of Indian Philosophy* 16 (1988): 5–28..

3. For a summary of Cuvier's essentialist definitions of biological species and Darwin's rejection thereof, see Stephen Jay Gould, "Mozart and Modularity," *Natural*

History, February, 1992: 8–16. As for the importance that the early Buddhists placed on the observations that modules undergo substitution at different rates of change, see David Kalupahana, *Causality: The Central Philosophy of Buddhism* (Honolulu: University Prass of Hawaii, 1975), 103–104.

4. Nāgārjuna's arguments that no change is possible except in beings that lack an essence or a permanent structure can be found in, for example, his *Mūlamadhyamikakārikā* 24, 16–20. See translations by Mervyn Sprung *Lucid Exposition of the Middle Way: The Essential Chapters from the Prasannapadā of Cadrakīrti*. (Boulder, Colorado: Prajñā Press), 237–240, and David Kalupahana, *Nāgārjuna: The Philosophy of the Middle Way*, (Albany, N.Y.: State University of New York Press, 1986), 339–342.

5. The Sanskrit terms in question here are *kuśala*, which has connotations of competence, skill, health, wholesomeness, and general goodness, and its negative *akuśala*, which indicates the absence of all those properties. Competence is regarded by Buddhist systematists as a second-order property, that is, a property belonging to primary mental properties such as kindness.

6. Rorty presents a nicely argued defense of another species of this genus of account of self-deception. See "The Deceptive Self: Liars, Layers, and Lairs," in *Perspectives on Self-deception*, ed. Brian P. McLaughlin and Amélie Oksenberg Rorty (Berkeley: University of California Press, 1988), 11–28.

7. The importance of companionship is found, for example, in Dhammapada 328–30: "If on the journey of life a man can find a wise and intelligent friend who is good and self-controlled, let him go with that traveler; and in joy and recollection let them overcome the dangers of the journey. But if on the journey of life a man cannot find a wise and intelligent friend who is good and self-controlled, let him travel alone, like a king who has left his country, or like a great elephant alone in the forest. For it is better to go alone on the path of life rather than to have a fool for a companion. With few wishes and few cares, and leaving all sins behind, let a man travel alone, like a great elephant alone in the forest." *The Dhammapada: The Path of Perfection*, trans. Juan Mascaró (New York: Penguin Books, 1973), 82.

8. Rorty, *op. cit.* 13 states, "If the self is essentially unified or at least strongly integrated, capable of critical, truth-oriented reflection, with its various functions in principle accessible to, and corrigible by, one another, it cannot deceive itself. According to the classical picture, the self is oriented to truth, or at least directed by principles of corrigibility that do not intentionally preserve error." Although the classical picture that Rorty has in mind is no doubt that of classical Greece, what she says applies equally well to the portrayal of the ideal person in classical India; the prototypical arhant in Buddhism is, of course, the Buddha himself who was said to be incapable of uttering a falsehood, even in jest. A rather humorless fellow, perhaps, but wholesome to the very core.

9. Incidentally, this line of argument about theft can also be made mutatis mutandis about ownership of property, but it is considered rude to make this argument outside monastic circles.

CONTRIBUTORS

Roger T. Ames received his Ph.D. in classical Chinese philosophical texts from the University of London. He is Professor of Philosophy at the University of Hawaii and is Director of the Center for Chinese Studies. He is Editor of *Philosophy East & West,* the journal of comparative philosophy, and Executive Editor of *China Review International.* Professor Ames has published many books and articles in Chinese and comparative philosophy, including *The Art of Rulership* (1983), *Thinking Through Confucius* (1987), *Anticipating China: Thinking Through the Narratives of Chinese and Western Culture* (1995) (both with David L. Hall), and a translation of *Sun-tzu: The Art of Warfare* (1993), and *Sun Pin: The Art of Warfare* (1996) (with D. C. Lau).

Annette C. Baier received her B.A. (1951) and M.A. (1952) from Otago University, New Zealand, and her B.Phil. from Oxford University, England, 1954. She has taught at the University of Aberdeen, Scotland; University of Auckland, New Zealand; University of Sydney, Australia; Somerville and Lincoln Colleges, Oxford; Australian National University, Canberra; Carnegie-Mellon University, Pittsburgh; and is currently Distinguished Service Professor at the University of Pittsburgh. She has published many articles in the philosophy of mind, ethics, and the history of philosophy, some of which are collected in *Postures of the Mind* (1985, 1986). More recently she has published *A Progress of Sentiments: Reflections on Hume's Treatise* (1991), and a recent collection of essays on ethics, *Moral Prejudices* (1994).

Antonio S. Cua is Professor of Philosophy at the Catholic University of America. He received a Ph.D. from the University of California at Berkeley in 1958. Among his publications are *Reason and Virtue: A Study in the Ethics of Richard Price; Dimensions of Moral Creativity: Paradigms, Principles, and Ideals; The Unity of Knowledge and Action: A Study in Wang Yang-ming's Moral Psychology;* and *Ethical Argumentation: A Study in Hsun Tzu's Moral Epistemology.* He has served as President of the Society for Asian and Comparative Philosophy and as President of the International Society for Chinese Philosophy.

Eliot Deutsch is Professor of Philosophy and Chair of Graduate Studies in the Department of Philosophy, University of Hawaii. He is past editor (1967–1987) of the international journal *Philosophy East & West*, Director of the Sixth East-West Philosophers' Conference, and a past president of the Society for Asian and Comparative Philosophy. Deutsch received his Ph.D. from Columbia University and has been a visiting professor at the University of Chicago and Harvard. He has been an invited lecturer at numerous universities and colleges in Asia, Europe, the USSR, and the Americas, and is the author of eleven books, including *On Truth: An Ontological Theory; Advaita Vedānta: A Philosophical Reconstruction; Personhood, Creativity and Freedom; Studies in Comparative Aesthetics;* and *Creative Being: The Crafting of Person and World*, and many articles and reviews in professional journals.

Wimal Dissanayake is Senior Fellow at the East-West Center in Honolulu, and in this capacity was responsible for organizing and hosting the conferences which produced the trilogy of State University of New York Press books on "the self": *Self as Body in Asian Theory and Practice* (1993), *Self as Person in Asian Theory and Practice* (1994), and *Self as Image in Asian Theory and Practice* (1996). He is the author of several books on literature, cinema, and communication and six books of poetry and is the Editor of *East-West Film Journal*. His most recent work (with Stephen Alter) is the *Penguin Book of Modern Indian Short Stories*.

David L. Hall is Professor of Philosophy at the University of Texas at El Paso. He received a Bachelor of Divinity degree summa cum laude from the Chicago Theological Seminary and a Ph.D. in philosophy from Yale University. Professor Hall has written several books in the philosophy of culture and culture studies. He is the author (with Roger Ames) of *Thinking Through Confucius* (1987) and *Anticipating China: Thinking Through the Narratives of Chinese and Western Culture* (1995). His most recent publications include *The Arimaspian Eye,* a philosophical novel, and a book on the philosophy of Richard Rorty, *Richard Rorty: Poet and Prophet of the New Pragmatism.*

Richard P. Hayes teaches Indian Buddhism and Sanskrit in the Faculty of Religious Studies at McGill University. His principal research interest is in the epistemological and metaphysical writings of the Buddhist scholastics of classical India. He has been assistant editor of the *Journal of Indian Philosophy* for several years and is currently serving as Subject Editor for the entries on Indian philosophy in *The Routledge Encyclopedia of Philosophy.*

Barbara Herrnstein Smith is Braxton Craven Professor of Comparative Literature and English at Duke University and director of its Center for Interdisciplinary Studies in Science and Cultural Theory. The author of a number of studies in literary, linguistic, and critical theory, including *Poetic Closure: A Study of How Poems End* (1968), *On the Margins of Discourse* (1978), and *Contingencies of Value: Alternative Prospectives for Critical Theory* (1988), she is also co-editor (with Arkady Plotnisky) of a recent issue of *The South Atlantic Quarterly* on *Mathematics, Science, and Postclassical Theory* (May, 1995). Her contribution to this volume is drawn from work in progress titled *Belief and Resistance: Dynamics of Contemporary Theoretical Controversy.*

Kathleen Marie Higgins is Professor of Philosophy at the University of Texas at Austin. She is the author of *Nietzsche's* Zarathustra and *The Music of Our Lives* and co-editor (with Robert C. Solomon) of *Reading Nietzsche, The Philosophy of (Erotic) Love, From Africa to Zen,* and *World Philosophy: A Text with Readings,* among other books and articles.

Joel J. Kupperman is Professor of Philosophy at the University of Connecticut and has been a visiting fellow at colleges in Cambridge, Oxford, and Villa Serbelloni, Bellagio. He is the author of *Character* (1991), *The Foundations of Morality* (1983), and *Ethical Knowledge* (1970), as well as a number of journal articles.

William R. LaFleur is Professor of Japanese Studies and Joseph B. Glossberg Term Professor of Humanities at the University of Pennsylvania. Most of his publications focus either on medieval Japan or on ethical and philosophical problems in modern Japan. His *The Karma of Words: Buddhism and the Literary Arts in Medieval Japan* (California) derives from the first focus, and his *Liquid Life: Abortion and Buddhism in Japan* from the second. He is currently doing a study of body and mind in medieval Japan (Zone Books) and also researching the comparative significance of current Japanese debates about the religious and ethical dimensions of brain death and organ transplants.

Brian P. McLaughlin received his Ph.D. in Philosophy from the University of North Carolina, Chapel Hill. He is a Professor of Philosophy at Rutgers University. He is the co-editor with Amélie Rorty of *Perspectives on Self Deception* (1988), and with Ernest LePore of *Actions and Events* (1985) and the editor of *Dretske and His Critics* (1991). He is also the author of numerous articles in philosophy of mind and metaphysics.

Robert Cummings Neville is a Confucian pragmatist whose recent *Normative Cultures* (State University of New York 1995) develops Confucian themes to interpret theory and practical reason in a cross-cultural context. He teaches philosophy, religion, and theology at Boston University where he is Dean of the School of Theology.

Amélie Oksenberg Rorty is Professor of the Humanities and the History of Ideas, Brandeis University. She is the author of *Mind in Action* (1988) and numerous essays on the history of moral psychology and the philosophy of mind. She also edited *The Identities of Persons* (1976), *Explaining Emotions* (1980), (with Owen Flanagan) *Identity, Character and Morality* (1990), and *Essays on Aristotle's Rhetoric* (1995).

Graham Parkes is Professor of Philosophy at the University of Hawaii. He is the editor of and a major contributor to the anthologies *Heidegger and Asian Thought* (1987) and *Nietzsche and Asian Thought* (1991), and, with Setsuko Aihara, the translator of *The Self-Overcoming Nihilism* by Nishitani Keiji (1990) and co-author of *Strategies for Reading Japanese: A Rational Approach to the Japanese Sentence* (1992). His latest book is *Composing the Soul: Reaches of Nietzsche's Psychology* (1994).

Robert C. Solomon is Quincy Lee Centennial Professor at the University of Texas at Austin. He is the author of *From Rationalism to Existentialism, The Passions, In the Spirit of Hegel, From Hegel to Existentialism, About Love*, and *A Passion for Justice*. He is also editor (with Kathleen M. Higgins) of *From Africa to Zen: An Invitation to World Philosophy* and *Readings in World Philosophy*. His latest book is *Up the University*.

INDEX

A

Advaita Vedānta 4, 26–27, 319–323, 331–336
akrasia (weakness of will) 5, 73, 75
Altizer, Thomas J. J. 202
amaeru 2
Ames, Roger T. 13, 19–21, 111, 112, 113, 173, 188, 189, 190, 191
Arendt, Hannah 169
arhant 354
Aristotle 96, 98, 99, 115, 150, 242–245, 247
Arnheim, Rudolf 222
Asada, Akira 270
ātman 4
Atwood, Margaret 53
Audi, Robert 47, 316
Augustine, Saint 92, 203, 242
avidyā (ignorance) 4, 26, 319, 320

B

bad faith 2, 14–15, 17, 123–131, 133, 136–138, 167, 235, 279, 326
Baier, Annette C. 7–9, 110, 163
Bakhtin, Mikhail 334
Bhagavadgītā 322, 325
bhakti (devotion) 325
Blakney, R. B. 161
Bloom, Harold 253
Bok, Sissela 101, 104, 106, 274–275
Borges, Jorge Luis 55
Brahminism 329–336
Braude, Steve 97
Buddhism 4

C

Camus, Albert 97, 105
canonical texts, Chinese 225
Chang, Tsai 207
chaos 232–233
Ch'en, Ch'un 179, 180
Ch'en, Pai-sha 188
ch'eng (sincerity) 177–179
Cheng, Chung-ying 214
Ch'eng, Hao 188, 207
Ch'eng, I 207
ch'eng-yi (making one's thoughts sincere) 180–184
Chou, Tun-i 207
Chu, Hsi 179, 181, 182, 183, 184, 206–207, 214
Chuang Tzu 185, 230, 232
Chung Yung (*Doctrine of the Mean*) 178, 187, 189, 204–207, 211
classification, Chinese 225–226
Coady, Tony 91–92
Confucianism 4
Confucius 17, 167, 170, 172, 173, 174, 182, 212, 213, 214, 234, 235, 236, 252
conservatism, cognitive 153
contradictory belief condition 6, 7, 32, 33, 35, 40, 47
convergence theory 264–265
Cooper, Joel 324
correlative thinking 231
cosmology, Chinese 224
Cua, Antonio S. 18–19, 214
Cuvier, Georges 351

D

Darwin, Charles 351
Davidson, Donald 5, 44, 58, 143
deception, self-induced 36, 37, 39
Democritus 245
Demos, Raphael 1
Dennett, Daniel 162
Derrida, Jacques 91, 143, 154, 245, 253, 309
Descartes, René 8–9, 13, 59–70, 83, 86, 110, 111
Deutsch, Eliot 2, 26–27, 165
Dewey, John 245, 247
dharma (duty) 26, 319, 321, 322, 323, 325
Diogenes 94
Dionysus 288, 291–292, 295–296, 299, 301, 307–309
Dissanayake, Wimal 23, 27–28
Doctrine of the Mean see *Chung Yung*
Dōgen 93
Dostoevski, Fyodor 97
Dutton, Denis 133

E

Elster, Jon 3, 5, 28, 343, 345, 336
emptiness 29
Enlightenment, the 73–74, 85
excluders 6

F

facticity 124–131
fallacy, the egalitarian 147
family, Chinese conception of 226–227
Faulkner, William 168
feudalism, Japanese 268–270
Feyerabend, P. K. 143
Field, Norma 280–281
Fingarette, Herbert 2, 3, 5, 18, 20, 162, 170, 183, 188, 189, 190, 211, 227–228, 315, 316–317, 343, 345
"five zones" 221–222
focal self: and hypocrisy 236–237; and self-deception 234; and self-sufficiency 233; structure of 219–224; underdeterminacy of 231–233
Foucault, Michel 143, 245
Four Beginnings 205–206
Frankfurt, Harry 67
freedom (*mokṣa*) 320
Freud, Sigmund 19, 112, 162, 208, 243, 244, 294, 318, 345

G

Gateson, Gregory 251
Geertz, Clifford 28, 342, 344
Gernet, Jacques 228
Gilbert, Daniel T. 324
Goffman, Erving 166
Goodman, Nelson 143
Graham, Angus 230
Great Learning 207
Greater East Asia Co-Prosperity Sphere 270
Greek tragedy 289–290, 292, 295

H

Habermas, Jürgen 143, 148
Haight, Mary 2, 5
Hall, David L. 21–22, 24, 219
Hallowell, A. Irving 28, 341–342
Hara, Kazuo 23, 272–274
Harootunian, H. D. 266–268, 270–272, 277
Harries, Karsten 14, 131–134
Hayes, Richard 28–29
Hegel, Georg Wilhelm Friedrich 111, 203–204, 242, 245
Heidegger, Martin 110, 247
Higgins, Kathleen Marie 14–15
Hirohito, Emperor 280–281
historiography, Chinese 224
Hobbes, Thomas 245
Homer 242, 243
homuncular subsystems 7, 17, 40–42, 49–50, 162–164

Hsün Tzu 18, 177–178, 182–187, 189, 207, 210
Hughes, Richard 170
Hume, David 11, 54, 81, 143, 167
Huntun, Lord 232–233
Husserl, Edmund 148, 245
hypocrisy 21, 236–237

I
ideal reflective equilibrium (IRE) 162–164
Ideologiekritik 22–23, 263–281
ignorance (*avidyā*) 319
individualism 356
individualism, Augustinean 203
intentionality 1, 44–46, 106

J
James, William 169
Japanokritik 23–24, 263–281
jñāna (knowledge) 325
Johnson, Samuel 104
Johnston, Mark 17, 36–39, 42–43, 164, 166
Jung, Karl Gustav 105, 294

K
Kant, Immanuel 13, 73, 92, 95–96, 98, 106, 111, 164, 242, 247
karman 26–27, 319, 321–323
Kierkegaard, Søren 168, 204
King, Ambrose 226
Kitayama, Shinobu 110, 112
kitsch 14–15, 123, 131–138
knowing dupe condition 6–7, 33–35, 40, 47
knowledge (*jñāna*) 325
koan 251
Koschmann, J. Victor 270
Kuhn, Thomas 143
Kundera, Milan 14, 131–134, 136–137, 345
Kupperman, Joel 17
Kyoto School 270

L
LaFleur, William R. 15, 22–24
Legge, James 161
Lun Yü 187, 189
Lycan, William 162
lying 12–13, 34, 44, 84, 91–109, 315
Lyotard, Jean-François 143

M
MacIntyre, Alasdair 323
Mair, Victor 161
Major, John 224
Markus, Hazel Rose 110, 112
Marquez, Gabriel Garcia 135
Marx, Karl 19, 208
Marxism 213
masks 24–26, 287–310
Mauss, Marcel 111
māyā 320, 333
McKeon, Richard 243–244, 246–248
McLaughlin, Brian P. 1, 5–7
Mead, George Herbert 190–191, 245
meaning production 344–345
Mencius 173, 183, 187–188, 204, 210, 236
Milgram, Stanley 169
mind, architecture of the 46–47
Mishima, Yukio 25, 289, 293–297, 303–307, 310
Miyoshi, Masao 266–268, 277, 279
Mo Tzu 185
modernization theory 264–265
mokṣa (freedom) 26, 322
myth 265–268 265

N
Naess, Arne 323
Nāgārjuna 91, 351–352
Narasimhaiah, C. D. 332
Narayan, R. K. 27, 327–346
natural kinds 231
neo-Marxism 265–272, 276–279
Neville, Robert Cummings 18–19

Nietzsche, Friedrich Wilhelm 24, 91–93, 95, 99, 105, 138, 143, 167, 250, 288–289, 291–310, 318, 336, 343–344
Nishida, Kitarō 270
Nishitani, Keiji 25–26, 289, 306–310
Noh drama 24–25, 289–290, 292, 309–310
Norman, E. Herbert 23, 268–271

O

objectivity 147–150
obscuration (*pi*) 4, 18
orthodoxy 143–155

P

Parfit, Derek 317
Parkes, Graham 24–26
pathology, Japanese national 263–265
Paul, Saint 202, 205
Pears, David 5, 58, 67
Pepper, Stephen 243–244, 247
pi (obscuration) 184–186
Pincoffs, Edmund 95
Piper, Adrian 56–59, 69
Plato 20, 85–86, 91–92, 96, 170, 220, 242–244, 247, 309
Pliny the Elder 234
Potter, Karl 321–322
Protagoras 15, 143, 145–148
Putnam, Hilary 143, 148

R

Raine, Kathleen 332
Rao, Raja 27, 327–346
rationality 1, 96, 229, 266–268, 316, 343
rationality, and culture 343–344
Rawls, John 54, 110
relativism 147
Robertson, Maureen 224
root metaphors 243
Rorty, Amélie Oksenberg 5, 8, 9–11, 14, 28, 30, 58, 70, 104, 112, 123, 130, 166, 219, 332, 336

Rorty, Richard 21, 24, 91, 143, 246–248, 253, 276–277, 317, 328
Rousseau, Jean Jacques 110
Ruddick, William 44, 66
Russell, Bertrand 254

S

Sakabe, Megumi 25, 289, 309–310
Sakai, Naoki 270
Śaṁkara 26, 319–320
Sartre, Jean-Paul 2–3, 5, 14–15, 17, 95, 100, 103, 110– 111, 113, 123–131, 133–134, 136–138, 164–165, 167–168, 170–171, 173–174, 235, 279, 326, 345
Schopenhauer, Arthur 111
Scott, Sir Walter 105
self: Buddhist conception of modular 28–29, 349–352; Christian conception of the 202–204; Confucian conception of 4, 20–21, 186–191, 219–224; focus-field conception of 20–21; Japanese conception of 4; one-many model 19–20; the ambiguated 22, 242–249; the Chinese "focal" 219–237; Western conception of the 201–204; Western definitions of 21–22
self-contradictory condition 32
self-deception: and Buddhism 349–362; and Confucianism 177–199, 201–217; and kitch 123–141; and other deception 44–45; and personal identity 316; and rationality 54–59, 73–75; and responsibility 27; and ritual 354–362; benefits of 81–85; Buddhist conception of 28; cross-cultural dimension of 2, 4–5; Confucian models of 19; externalist model of 13–14, 112–115; internalist model of 13–14, 112–115; Japanese 263–281; misconceptions about 76–78; ontological dimension of 27, 323; paradox of 1–2; rationality and 1–3, 8–9, 16, 27, 68–70; René

Descartes and 59–70; responsibility for 323–325; selective ignoring as 7–11, 53–72; social dimensions of 3–4, 9–14, 20–21, 27, 76–77, 82–84, 102–105, 109–115, 265–268, 323–325; strategies of 78–81; the beneficiaries of 82–85; unavoidability of 73–89; user-friendly 73–89; the very possibility of 31–52
self-refutation 15–16
self-refutation drama 149–151
self-refutation, the charge of 143–160
selfishness, in Confucianism 209–211, 215
"selves"-deception, Confucian notion of 20–21
Shklar, Judith N. 276–277, 280
Shōeki, Andō 268
Sidgwick, Henry 91–92
skandhas 4
skepticism 143–155
Skinner, B. F. 245
Smith, Barbara Herrnstein 15–17, 30, 275
Socrates 73, 93, 95–96, 145–148, 150–151, 252
Solomon, Robert C. 8, 11–14, 163, 265, 279
Stevenson, Charles 163
Sullivan, Harry Stack 130
Suzuki, David 356
Szabados, Béla 324–325

T

Ta-hsüeh (Great Learning) 18, 177, 180, 184
Tai, Chen 179, 180
Tan, Amy 134–135
Tao Te Ching 17, 161, 163, 165, 167
Taylor, Charles 174, 323
Theaetetus 150
Theaetetus 15–16, 145–155
Toulmin, Stephen 18, 187

truth 11–12, 16, 23–24, 28, 73, 91–109, 126, 135, 145–149, 150, 152, 154–155, 161, 177–179, 246, 271–281, 336, 343
Tsou, Yen 224
Tu, Wei-ming 18, 188–190, 214
Turner, John 190
tzu-ch'i (self-deception) 180–184

U

universalism, as Western ethnocentrism 16

V

vagueness 249–258
vagueness, fruitful 22
van Fraasen, Bas 81, 166
village worthy 236

W

Walsh, William 332
Wang, Yang-ming 178, 186, 188, 207, 209–210
Watson, Burton 185
White, Stephen 17, 40, 162–164
Whitehead, Alfred North 254
Winch, Peter 28, 343–344
Wittgenstein, Ludwig 93–94, 98, 254
Wood, Allen W. 14, 31, 123–124, 130, 139

Y

Yang, Liang 184
yi (one's thoughts) 179–180
yin-yang 231
Yü, Ying-shih 221
Yukiyuki to Shingun 272

Z

Zeami 309

www.ingramcontent.com/pod-product-compliance
Ingram Content Group UK Ltd.
Pitfield, Milton Keynes, MK11 3LW, UK
UKHW021832140426
5217IPUK00021B/1411

9 780791 430323